D1516589

Lives, Events, and Other Players

DOWNSTATE PSYCHOANALYTIC INSTITUTE
TWENTY-FIFTH ANNIVERSARY
SERIES

Mark Kanzer, M.D., General Editor

Volume   I. Mark Kanzer, M.D. and Jules Glenn, M.D., Editors
Volume II. Mark Kanzer, M.D. and Jules Glenn, M.D., Editors
Volume III. Shelley Orgel, M.D. and Bernard D. Fine, M.D., Editors
Volume IV. Joseph T. Coltrera, M.D., Editor

EDITORIAL BOARD

Alan J. Eisnitz, M.D., *Chairman*
Jacob A. Arlow, M.D.
Harold P. Blum, M.D.
Robert Dickes, M.D.
Maurice R. Friend, M.D.
Merl M. Jackel, M.D.
Samuel Lanes, M.D.
Roy K. Lilleskov, M.D.
Sandor Lorand, M.D.
Peter B. Neubauer, M.D.
William G. Niederland, M.D.
Robert A. Savitt, M.D.
Leonard L. Shengold, M.D.
Otto Sperling, M.D.

Lives, Events, and Other Players

Directions in Psychobiography

Volume IV
Downstate Psychoanalytic Institute
Twenty-Fifth Anniversary Series

Joseph T. Coltrera, M.D., Editor

WITHDRAWN

New York • Jason Aronson • London

Copyright © 1981 by Jason Aronson, Inc.

All rights reserved. Printed in the United States of America. No part of this
book may be used or reproduced in any manner whatsoever without written
permission from the publisher except in the case of brief quotations in
reviews for inclusion in a newspaper, magazine, or broadcast.

ISBN: 0-87668-369-3

Library of Congress Catalog Number: 79-51910

Manufactured in the United States of America.

PREFACE TO THE SERIES

Freud's royal road to the unconscious was the dream. However, as the father of psychoanalysis, his legacy to all included a far broader royal road, psychoanalysis itself, which pointed the way to the understanding of the psychology of man. Could even Freud himself have envisioned the complex routes taken by the discipline he fathered, its influences upon the arts and social sciences as well as practically every form of psychotherapy? Could he have foreseen the many tasks required of psychoanalytic institutes and psychoanalytic educators?

Psychoanalytic education with its many demands could well be a full-time job, yet it has so far been able to enjoy the wise luxury of requiring that its educators also have a firm footing in clinical psychoanalysis; that its teachers also be, often full time, clinical practitioners. The benefits of this somewhat anachronistic tradition have been considerable, but the price has been high. Psychoanalytic teachers must attend to their patients and then search for precious hours with which to plan, organize, and accomplish their teaching mission. Is it a mission in the full sense? Perhaps not, but it can be a most compelling and fulfilling aspect of one's career, as it has been for those of us who have been part of the Downstate Psychoanalytic Institute.

The Institute, founded by Drs. Howard Potter and Sandor Lorand, and itself parent to, and later in some respects child of, the Psychoanalytic Association of New York, has been shameless in its demand on the time and energy of its members. And yet it has become a part of us, a structuring part of our professional identity, of our self systems, and, by extension, an important and loved foundation of our professional family ties.

Absorbed in this demanding relationship, we were surprised to discover that this parent-child to us all, so warmly and ambivalently loved, in the sense that all such love is ambivalent, would in 1974 celebrate its twenty-fifth birthday.

We had a new task: to determine how a twenty-fifth anniversary of a psychoanalytic institute should most appropriately be acknowledged. There were to be, of course, the usual celebrations and testimonials. But these excellent occasions, relatively private gatherings, occur and become memories.

Perhaps more important are the desirable group self-observations and developmental evaluations. A psychoanalytic institute should, first and foremost, educate graduates who are able practitioners of psychoanalysis. But while this may be a necessary and wholesome criterion of adequate accomplishment, by itself it scarcely represents excellence. For it is always a hope that among the graduates will be some with the creative spark enabling them to make original scientific contributions. Even this is not enough: a healthy institute must also provide the systems and structures which enable its teachings programs to continue and develop, constantly supplementing courses and faculty with new ideas and new people. Ultimately, older faculty members will retire, and new teachers must be available. Finally, the institute must be able to take its place, as well as should its members individually, within the scientific and professional community.

Evaluating these steps according to a rough timetable, one could say that by age ten a psychoanalytic institute should be able to point to a growing body of graduates beginning to participate scientifically and organizationally on local levels and beyond. From years ten to twenty the institute's own graduates should be able to form the core first of the teaching faculty and then of the training analysts of the institute. Eventually, the administrative positions of the institute should be filled by its own graduates, who by this time have had the chance to gain experience at these tasks. At twenty-five, Downstate has completed these steps, though happily without the parochial rigidity which might otherwise have precluded a welcome to talented and congenial colleagues from other programs who wished to join and enrich us.

We of the Downstate Psychoanalytic Institute are pleased with the quality of our programs and our graduates. We believe that we have accomplished these goals while creating a cohesive psychoanalytic group with a shared commitment to ideals which in no way detracts from the individual styles of its members. We hope that we are not complacent in our judgment that the goals for the first twenty-five years have been achieved well.

After all the anniversary celebrations, there was still the feeling that something more should be done. For this we have turned, through these volumes, to our colleagues, that we might share with them through their work an affirmation of our ideals as analysts—as observers, seekers of knowledge, enlighteners, and helpers. We hope that these four Anniversary Volumes will, through the work of the members of Downstate Psychoanalytic Institute, provide a glimpse of what we all treasure so much about our Institute: an atmosphere where we can work together pursuing our common goals individually and collectively, inspiring one another and enriching the creative capacity of all. The Downstate Institute has offered such an atmosphere. In return we offer these volumes as an expression of our gratitude for its existence and its excellence.

There are many people to whom we are indebted for their work on these volumes; only a few can be singled out for their contributions. Dr. Mark

Kanzer, General Editor, comes first. He has been not only a wise editor but a stimulator of new ideas and contributions. The only problem was to limit his efforts, for his quest for excellence and his productivity know no bounds. Dr. Jules Glenn was his able assistant overall and co-editor with him for Volumes I and II. Drs. Shelley Orgel and Bernard Fine were co-editors for Volume III, Dr. Joseph Coltrera editor for Volume IV. Each of them gave many hours of enlightened editorial advice to authors and fellow editors alike. It was a pleasure to work with all of them.

We are grateful to the Department of Psychiatry of the Downstate Medical Center for providing our Institute its home, and to Drs. Howard Potter and those after him who chaired the Department of Psychiatry during these twenty-five years.

Special thanks are due to Drs. Robert Savitt, Merl Jackel, and Samuel Lanes, Presidents of the Psychoanalytic Association of New York during the years that these volumes were in preparation. It was the understanding sponsorship of the Psychoanalytic Association of New York that allowed this project to get under way. More than special thanks are due also to Drs. Howard Potter and Sandor Lorand for their instrumental role in the formation of the Downstate Institute, and to Drs. Sylvan Keiser, Mark Kanzer, Sidney Tarachow, William Console, Maurice Friend, Leonard Shengold, and Roy Lilleskov, and to Miss Vera Krassin and all those others who have worked so hard to help the Institute grow and prosper. Finally, we are indebted to all of the candidates and to all of the faculty members who, collectively, made the Downstate Institute such a wonderful place to work, to teach, and to learn.

Alan J. Eisnitz, M.D.
Director, Downstate Psychoanalytic Institute 1972–1975
Chairman, Editorial Board, 25th Anniversary Series

Postscript: After these volumes were completed and the above preface written, an important change occurred to our Institute. As conditions in Brooklyn, and more specifically at the Downstate Medical Center, no longer favored the continued development of psychoanalytic education there, it was decided to move.

On July 1, 1979 The Psychoanalytic Institute transferred its affiliation to the New York University Medical Center. This entailed moving the offices and classes to Bellevue Psychiatric Hospital in Manhattan. While we now have a new name — The Psychoanalytic Institute at New York University

Medical Center — and a new home, the candidates, faculty, and administration remain the same. We are still the same psychoanalytic institute.

To extend Dr. Eisnitz's developmental analogy further, we can say that the Institute had achieved the degree of independence and autonomy which permitted it to leave home when that departure was indicated. We now look forward to our new affiliation with New York University in hopeful anticipation that our spirit and our accomplishments will continue as before.

In a sense, therefore, these volumes not only celebrate the anniversary which occasioned their preparation, but are also a tribute to our thirty years at the Downstate Medical Center.

Roy K. Lilleskov, M.D.
Director, Downstate Psychoanalytic Institute 1978–1979
Director, The Psychoanalytic Institute
   at New York University Medical Center

CONTENTS

I. Introduction

II. A Walk in a Darker Wood

III. The Childhood of the Artist

IV. A Holy Sinner

Lives, Events, and Other Players

PART I

Introduction

Chapter 1

LIVES, EVENTS AND OTHER PLAYERS: DIRECTIONS IN PSYCHOBIOGRAPHY

JOSEPH T. COLTRERA, M.D.

Emma Bovary, c'est moi.
— Gustave Flaubert

Each of us is on a mission to
shape the world.
— Novalis

The blood-dimmed tide is loosed,
  and everywhere
The ceremony of innocence is drowned;
The best lack all conviction,
  while the worst
Are full of passionate intensity.

. . . . .

And what rough beast, its hour
  comes round at last,
Slouches toward Bethlehem to be born?
— William Butler Yeats

Psychobiography and its natural child, psychohistory, are born of an old romantic faith that great men radicalize their times, its art and its thought, at the "decisive moment" where the shaping forces of their creative imagination and creative unconscious meet in critical and defining conflict. It is a tragic vision whose literature has dominated applied psychoanalytic studies into our own time (Coltrera 1965). While seemingly an historical method, it really operates in the mythic asides of history, as reprise of the classic oedipal conflict writ large for great men and larger still for the history they make upon the resolution of their necessarily great and decisive conflicts. It is a method whose intrinsic problems and whose methodological critiques have bred a significant literature of its own (Greenacre 1955, 1963, Kohut 1960, Coltrera 1965, Mack 1971, Bergmann 1973).

Psychobiography is interpretation, albeit an interpretation *manqué,* its strengths and weaknesses as applied psychoanalytic method related directly to its participation in the historical development of interpretation as a necessarily joined empirical and intellectual idea. The first studies in the applied psychoanalysis of art, religion, society and of great men begins shortly after and as a result of *The Interpretation of Dreams* (Freud 1900) with its radical commitment to the philological model of *Deutung,* by which an original wish-meaning is adduced from an encoded disparate order of manifest meaning. Freud, unlike Jung, never sought the key to great art, religion, and thought in ur-phenomena, but rather from an analogical interpretation of these works as orders of "waking" dream-work; as analogical forms of condensation, displacement, symbolic function and sublimation. Applied psychoanalysis begins with the device of *Deutung* intrinsic to the general sense of *Die Traumdeutung,* in the dedication of that device to an unmasking of the instinctual vicissitudes of the dream-work and all its "waking" analogues. I feel that psychobiography and psychohistory fail as applied psychoanalytic method whenever they concern themselves less with the vicissitudes of meaning — the proper work of interpretation — and more with generalizing statements about root origins. We can do no less than follow David Hume's admonition that general statements, masked as they often are as tautology and teleology, have no meaning in an empirical science. Even great men live only a single conflicted life in a special conjunction of time and place, a psychohistorical conjunction where commonly experienced conflicts are consensually validated as belief and concerns.

Psychobiography and psychohistory as psychoanalytic interpretations continue the Enlightenment's polemical commitment to reduce illusion and remove mystery wherever it is found. Thus Freud (1939) would see Moses' great gift to the Jews to be a dematerialization of God, while Moses had been nominally committed to the future of that illusion, his denial of God as ikon was essentially dedicated, in Freud's mind, to reducing the illusory premise of that illusion. In this tradition, interpretation was dedicated to the expunging of personal and collective myths in the affairs and ideas of men, especially as they contribute to the "falseness" of consciousness which Freud — as did Nietzsche, Marx, and Heine before him — believed to be the constant flaw in man's existence.

I believe that applied psychoanalysis grew out of a remarkable humanistic dialogue that began in the last half of the nineteenth century and continued almost to the 1930s, reaching its apogee with the work of certain social thinkers during the 1890s. Between the deaths of Nietzsche in 1889 and Charles Péguy during the first battle of the Marne in 1914, a remarkable congruence of radically innovative minds gave both intent to the thought and name to the concerns of the modern predicament. It is fitting that the time be bracketed by the death of two great moralists, for there have been few times so committed to the definition of values and to a concern for both the meaning and intentionality of human acts. What began as a moral inquiry into man's nature ended in a radical questioning of free will and rational choice. Hughes (1958) has pointed out that all the great social thinkers of the generation after Nietzsche and Marx — Freud, Weber, Croce, Durkheim — were in essential agreement that the basic characteristic of human existence was the intrinsic limitation of human choice. While their world still held fast to an old Enlightenment faith in the freedom and responsibility for metaphysical and ethical choice, they declared that man lived an overdetermined existence upon which he exercised but a limited determinancy. It was a generation for whom the discovery of unconscious determinancy represented a last passage from innocence. With the rational goodness of human nature compromised, the acts and rituals of history became a Black Mass for them. Celebrating with the dark saints of this darker faith, Nietzsche and Dostoyevsky, they developed a new aesthetics of the daemonic. This heralded the birth of a new romanticism and a neo-mysticism in which the *geist* of the age was above all dedicated to the right of the one over the many, the single act of reflective awareness defining the limits and integrity of reality as a uniquely psychic event. It was a return to a romanticism which did not reject reason as much as reason's narrow applications, turning to the extralogical as an adaptively alternate way to enlarge conception and perception.

Both psychobiography and its implicit assumption of psychohistory must be viewed as integral participants in this critical inquiry into the nature and limitations of human choice and commitment. It is as if, their time come, ideas drive men before them into history. So it was with these radical minds, all of whom reached the beginnings of their greatness in the 1890s. Between 1856 and 1877 Sigmund Freud, Max Weber, Benedetto Croce, Emile Durkheim, and Henri Bergson were born. In a sense they were the last cast of a long tide's running, preceded as they were by the great figures of Friedrich Nietzsche, Karl Marx, Fyodor Dostoyevsky, Charles Darwin, Ludwig Feuerbach, and Wilhelm Dilthey. These last were the direct participants in the great intellectual and creative century of *Mitteleurope* — between 1760 and 1860 — and as such they and those who followed must be considered heirs of a romantic faith in the shaping force of the creative imagination.

Far from the otherworldly image usually assigned it, romanticism was above all a humanist polemic directed against the dehumanizing intent of the industrial revolution and its reduction of a man to a replaceable object. And despite his mechanist rhetoric, Sigmund Freud was essentially a romantic humanist in both belief and inclination. So much so, that he, with Max Weber, always had to be on guard against romantic assumptions in his scientific beliefs. There can be no true understanding of his applied psychoanalytic method unless we recognize and give full value to the fact that Freud lived and created in the German romantic world of a *Mitteleurope,* believing with that world that great men radicalize their times, along with its thought and notions of beauty, as an adaptive condition of the resolutions of their necessarily great conflicts.

As interpretation, psychobiography and its implicit assumption of psychohistory were not only heir to the Enlightenment's commitment to demythologize man's history and his need for mystery in the explanation of his origins, but also heir to the Enlightenment's antagonism to the past. This antagonism was expounded in evolutionary theory, the special passion of a nineteenth century rationalism and the avowed scientific faith of the young Freud.

As part of the broad idealist stream that coursed through the nineteenth century, of which the psychoanalytic idea was an integral part (Ricoeur 1970, Coltrera 1981), certain neo-idealist reformers of the historical method — Wilhelm Dilthey, Ernst Troeltsch and Friedrich Meinecke — advanced the historicist thesis that men made their history out of their experiences, so that all manifestations of culture must be timebound and relativist (Hughes 1958, Coltrera 1965). In this view, the history of another age is told according to a rhetoric of sensibilities particular to the time that writes that history. Historicism sacked and burned history as a Platonic ideal, and the psychobiographic method lent itself to that pillage which laid waste the Augustinian City of God and the abiding belief in the inherent goodness of the captain-heroes that built its walls.

Central to Freud's psychobiographic method is the historicist assumption of *Kairos,* the "decisive moment," a romantic faith in the one crucial event which determines and explains all subsequent events (Rieff 1963, Coltrera 1965, Lifton 1970). For Freud the lives of great men and the history they made always turned on an occasion of *Kairos,* either a "decisive moment" in the mythic reprises of history or an instance of creative psychopathology.

In the first, the mythic paradigm, Freud saw the *Kairos* representing the mythopoetic function of psychosexual stage epigenesis and its resident conflicts, whereby the history of one man and all men becomes the oedipal conflict writ large and larger still. Lifton (1970) points out that Freud's historical model is not historical at all, referring as it does to a time when myth preceded history, to that time of first mythic encounter between the primal father and his rebellious sons who finally rose and killed the father. In consequence of that first parricide, the sons suffered a primeval guilt, whose expiation demanded the instinctual renunciation upon which all society and civilization then descends.

From its first stating in *Totem and Taboo* (Freud 1912–1913) to its last statement in *Moses and Monotheism* (Freud 1939), Freud held to this model of history. Accordingly, Moses was seen as the "father" who chose the Jews over his own people, the Egyptians, giving to them the crucial gift of monotheism, only to be cast off and murdered in the end by his "chosen people," his "chosen sons."

The inclusion of this ahistorical model within the premises of oedipal myth studies necessarily excludes their use in valid historical commentary. Such studies are essentially methodologically flawed, lending themselves as they do, because of the limited variables of their major and minor criteria, to semantic exposition. They reduce all history to the sameness of psychological recurrence wherein historical events become a reprise of a "return of the repressed" (Coltrera 1965). The major criteria of such oedipal myth studies are those of prophecy, parricide, and incest; its minor criteria the ones of succor from exposure, rearing by another king, and fulfillment of prophecy (Freud 1900, 1913–1914, Rank 1909, Roheim 1950). Most classical myth studies, such as those of Oedipus Rex (Freud 1897–1902, 1900, 1905a, Rank 1909, Kanzer 1948b) and those of Hamlet (Freud 1897–1902, 1900, 1905a, Jones 1949) concern themselves for the most part with the major criteria, with the minor criteria most usually reserved for studies illustrating the "family romance" (Freud 1897–1902, pp. 188–191, 225–227; Freud 1900, Rank 1909, Kris 1935, Greenacre 1957, 1958).

The model for the "family romance" has best served the psychobiographic method in its recent concern for the artist's increasing sense of isolation and exile in a dehumanizing industrial society. In one view, the romantic idea must be viewed as a humanistic rebuttal to the notion of man as an object, especially in its radical insistence that the self bears a uniquely defining role to its experience through granting it representation and meaning. By this measure, the examples of Luther addressing himself directly to his God as part of working through his own self-representation and its attendant autonomous body of moral directives, and that of the Renaissance idea of art as a projection of an inner vision represent disparate though reinforcing psychohistorical sources of a later romanticism. Both are expressions of a rising concern for psychological introspectiveness in Western man, beginning testimonies to the primacy of the self as an exceptional and excepting experience. Commenting on this beginning quest for identity in Western art and thought, Kris (1935) described the classical "family romance" in the Renaissance artist, using the example of Giotto and his master, Cimabue. The shepherd boy, whose talent is developed in solitude, is discovered by an older established artist who then becomes his patron: the younger artist found "again" by his "real" father in genius.

An interesting transposition of the criteria of the "family romance" — succor from exposure, rearing by another kind, and fulfillment of prophecy — has been made within a more sophisticated, developmental psychological framework and related clinical studies of children, and as such applied by Glenn (1974) and Blum (1969) to the many adoption themes that run through the plays of Edward Albee, himself an adopted child. Shengold (1975) has also emphasized the effect of a brutalizing adoption — as "soul murder" — on Rudyard Kipling, tracing its residue to the many "family romance" themes in his writings. In a similar manner, many of the heroes of Joseph Conrad, like himself, lost their parents in childhood and wander the world in spiritual quest for other parents (Meyer 1967). The family romance of the artist as exile, I believe, is expressed in the form as well as the content of Conrad's writings. He was born a Pole, acquired French as a second childhood language, came to England as an orphaned exile, and became one of the great masters of English prose. The family romance reprise of the artist who must live and create in exile has become the special voyage metaphor of the Daedelian exile in the modern novel (Coltrera 1963, 1965) in the *Portrait of the Artist as a Young Man* and *Ulysses* of James Joyce and in the *Kunstlernovellen* of Thomas Mann. Samuel Beckett, secretary for a time to James Joyce, subscribes to this metaphor not only in the many themes of his plays but even in his choice of language, for the Irishman Beckett writes his plays in French, perhaps an ultimate expression of the artist as exile.

The second and perhaps more insidious paradigm intrinsic to Freud's psychobiographic model is one in which the *Kairos* is a "decisive moment" of creative psychopathology. Whereas the first mythic paradigm, especially in its earliest and classic "primal horde" form, is largely avoided in serious psychobiographic studies — save for a few biographers and historians and a thankfully diminishing group of psychoanalysts who continue to use *Totem and Taboo* as their simplistic psychoanalytic hornbook — it is the second paradigm that maintains its pernicious and reductionist hold on many psychobiographers and psychohistorians.

Among modern psychobiographers, Kurt Eissler is the leading proponent of Freud's second paradigm on the determinancy of psychopathology in the creation of art and thought. "The danger of an outbreak of a psychosis in a genius . . . should not be underrated. I believe that every genius is a potential psychotic because the production of great art may involve the transformation of psychotic-like structures by means of mechanisms that resemble sublimation" (Eissler 1963, p. 1097).

I have stated my disagreement with this point of view more fully elsewhere (Coltrera 1965). I believe the nature of creativity can be better conceptualized within the conditions of a general theory of psychoanalytic psychology, reciprocally inclusive of all the metapsychological points in accord with the holistic nature of behavior, than it can by a psychopathological model. A short historical reprise of this oldest of daemonic aesthetic theories may be in order so that we might better understand the origins and descent of not only a major methodological bias assumed in most early psychobiographic studies but also a continuing problem for the method in our own time of ego psychology.

To think of the creative person as inherently flawed and deflected from madness by the creative act itself is among the oldest aesthetic theories. The idea was first advanced by Pindar in the West, but the lines of the issues were most clearly drawn in Plato's attack on Homer's notion of the poet as the sorcerer-entertainer. In Book X of *The Republic,* Plato specifically rejects the Homeric contention that poetry is the magic force used to stir men's passions and so blind them to truth. For Homer, the poet is the singer, *aidos,* and his song an enchantment, *kelethmos,* and not till a later Greek time would the word for poet be replaced by *poietas,* with its less daemonic connotation of a craftsman. In the *Ion,* Plato offers an alternate theory of poetic creation through divine possession and inspiration. Here are the bare bones of a modern commitment to creativity through a dialectical expansion of consciousness. In the Platonic mode the poet does not create by his own powers; instead, deprived of his own senses, he utters the prophecies of the gods. The ecstatic states of early childhood of many creative people cited by Greenacre (1956) and Eissler (1961, 1963) seem to be metapsychological transpositions of sorts of Plato's thesis in the *Ion,* by which poetry and art were considered to be the transcendent devices by which the Godhead entered the differing ontological orders of this world (Coltrera 1965). Plato's idea that the poem is related to the day-dream as a marginal experience of an expanded state of consciousness—a "waking" dream, as it were—is essentially consensual with Freud's (1908) later thesis in "Creative Writers and Day-Dreaming."

Plato's sense that the poet is necessarily apart from all other men, mad because the gods talk through him and kept from going mad by his poetry, descends to us in the image of the artist as the anti-realist of eighteenth century Romanticism. In the more scientific though no less romantic nineteenth century, the notion became Nietzsche's belief in the daemonic wellsprings of creativity. Perhaps more importantly, the idea donned the clock of scientific semblance preferred at this time, becoming the *dégénérés supérieurs* of Morel, Lombroso, and Nordeau, relating creative genius to insanity no less certainly than did Pindar and Plato.

If ideas too can be said to turn on an occasion of *Kairos,* then that of psychobiography, and indeed all of applied psychoanalysis, may have been German Romanticism—and, to a lesser degree, French Romanticism. The romanticist cosmologies of *Mitteleurope* were the psychohistorical contexts in which the great social thinkers of the 1890s—Freud, Weber, Croce, Durkheim—lived and created. It was a world inclined by its romanticist bias to accept the primacy of the creative unconscious and the descent into self as an ontological quest, a world whose neo-romantic and neo-mystical revivals lent rhetoric and imagery to the existential concerns of the modern predicament it first named.

German Romanticism was in part a reaction against the spiritual dryness of the Reformation and its notion of religion bereft of mysticism. As such it had an abiding faith and interest in magic and mystery, conditioning modern man to the notion that the surface of things and events were but the nearer and more suspect aspect of the appearance of things, and the "falseness" of the consciousness that subserves their apprehension. Nietzsche, Marx, and Freud all began their basic derivation of interpretation as *Deutung* from the basic premise of this "falseness" of consciousness (Ricoeur 1970, Coltrera 1981). For German Romanticism, the altered states of consciousness and the prophetic dream were the phenomenological causeways to beauty and truth. Nearly a hundred years before Freud did so, G. H. von Schubert, one of the so-called Romantic physicists, wrote a

Traumdeutung entitled *The Symbolism of the Dream.* These same Romantic physicists imbued the age with the doctrines of a correspondence between natural and spiritual phenomena, animal magnetism, second sight, the concept of the "double," and the prophetic dream. Would such a world reject the basic premise of a dynamic point of view and the notion of a repressive boundary separating inner from outer? A world that had already accepted Swedenborg's doctrine of correspondence and heard Paracelsus say, "As it is in the inner, so it must be in the outer; as it is in the outer, so it must be in the inner." Would a tradition that accepted the notion of Mesmer's animal magnetism be put off by an economic point of view?

The rise of the self in the consciousness of the West is probably the single great heritage of German Romanticism, deriving its impetus as it did from the large body of Eastern mystical works translated in the late eighteenth century. Not only did these present Western man with a system that operated apart from the strictures of Aristotelian logic, but they also reawakened interest in an occult body of Eastern works that had existed in Europe since the Middle Ages. German Romanticism proved to be a second renaissance for Gnostic, Manichaean, and Pythagorean works, and, more importantly, for the Kabbala and the Egyptian *Corpus Hermeticum.* The last two played a critical role in the revival of secret societies — Rosicrucians, Freemasons, Martinists — in Germany during the last half of the eighteenth century. The role of these secret societies cannot be underestimated, since hardly a German of intellectual or political consequence of the time did not belong to one of them. Mozart, for example, openly presented Masonic initiate rites in *The Magic Flute,* using as the source for its libretto a standard Masonic work on the Egyptian Mysteries (Bays 1964).

The rituals of the Rosicrucians and the Freemasons were based on the initiation rites of Osiris, the sun-God and life-giver, and his wife Isis, and were dedicated to bringing an inner illumination, the shining of the sun within the initiate. So when Freud dealt with arcane Egyptian mysteries and beliefs in his psychobiographic studies of Leonardo and Moses, he was addressing himself to an intellectual world in which a knowledge and special interest in Egyptian myth and ritual was already present.

Since German Romanticism was essentially restricted to what was once the kingdom of Charlemagne — Germany, Austro-Hungary, France, and Italy — what of psychoanalytic biography beyond this psychohistorical context? What of England, where Shakespeare sat on the ground and told sad tales of the death of kings as if he were a member of the Wednesday Night Meetings, out of time and out of place?

Romanticism in England developed from a different psychohistorical premise than did German Romanticism. English Romanticism's self-concerns, for example, were more muted, developing as they did apart from the influence of Eastern mysticism which played so critical a role in the heightened self-consciousness of German Romanticism. Whatever mystical tradition there was in English Romanticism may be said to descend from Neoplatonist sources into the metaphysical poets and William Blake, and from them into the nineteenth century "nature" poets and T. S. Eliot in our own century.

More to the point of the psychobiographic method in England, the Enlightenment's antagonism to the past was carried forward into nineteenth century English evolutionist thinking, which while nominally rationalist in presumption, was really a romantic genre in practice. English evolutionist thinkers—Charles Darwin, Herbert Spencer—enunciated an almost naive faith in the intrinsic goodness of man, believing that man's social nature was a necessarily progressive dialectic driven by the creative force of great men. The comic novels of Jane Austen, William Thackeray, and Anthony Trollope all subscribed to this evolutionist belief in man's dialectic ascension through ontogeny toward goodness. Virginia Woolf saw its presence in the Victorian biographer's faith in the necessarily great goodness of great men, a notion contributing in no small part to what Mack (1971) has described as a significant lack of psychological realism in biography through World War I.

But even before the lights began to go out all over Europe, a world-weariness and a disillusionment with great men and the wars they make for young men to die in already abounded. About 1906, at the same time that the Wednesday Night Meetings were considering the application of the psychoanalytic method to biography in Vienna, an extraordinary complement of sympathetic spirits began to meet in the Bloomsbury home of Sir Leslie Stephens's beautiful and gifted daughters, later to be Virginia Woolf and Vanessa Bell. Called the Bloomsbury Group from where they met, they embodied the brightest and the best of a newly burgeoning spirit in English thought and sensibility: Leonard and Virginia Woolf, Clive and Vanessa Bell, E. M. Forster, Lytton Strachey, John Maynard Keynes, and Roger Fry. The tougher heirs of a pre-Raphaelite spirit that believed art to be the most important thing in the world, they not only gave British painting and sculpture a sense of immediacy and relatedness to the world about it, but gave new life to the novel, biography, and art criticism. No less importantly, they returned the moral imperative of the greatest good for the greatest number to economics and to international affairs. Greek in their spirit and belief that man made his destiny according to the tragic nature of his psychic being, they were immediately sympathetic to the then beginning psychoanalytic idea, subscribing to its commitment to reduce illusion and remove mystery in their own lives and in the lives of the great. Leonard and Virginia Woolf were themselves the founders of the Hogarth Press, the intellectual bridgehead of the psychoanalytic idea in the English speaking world.

Biography would not be the same once their insistence was heeded that the lives and works of great men be parsed for psychological determinacy. With the publication of *Emminent Victorians* (1917) and *Queen Victoria* (1923), Lytton Strachey introduced a principle of psychological realism, masked as an ironic iconoclasm, to biography; his work was compatible in essential premise if not in exact rhetoric with the newer inquiries into psychoanalytic biography then going on in Vienna. Lytton Strachey is Edward Gibbon with a prescient belief in psychic determinism and an amateur's gift for character analysis. The metaphor and premise of his biographic method is that of a topographic analysis, believing that the outer and inner life of his subjects is a continuous if convoluted skein. Strachey insisted that psychological realism replace the Victorian biographer's panegyric tendency to report only the goodness of great men. In one instance, he specifically cited Mrs. Paget Toynbee for omitting a great amount of material which she did not deem fit for publication from her edition of Horace Walpole's letters.

The 1917 biography of Charles Algernon Swinburne, written by his friend Edmund Gosse, is a curious and significant testimonial to the Bloomsbury commitment to psychological realism in biography. While Gosse knew and appreciated the critical role played by Swinburne's masochistic experiences in childhood and their secret continuance as the consuming passion of the poet's adult years, he could not bring himself to write of them in the biography of his friend. Nor can it be said that post-Edwardian England would have suffered them to be told. Keeping faith with both his friend and the intent of the Bloomsbury Group, Gosse, in the same year he published the Swinburne biography, left in the secret archives of the British Museum, as an unpublished appendix to Swinburne's letters to him, a collection of the poet's sadomasochistic writings and memoirs which would not be made public for some fifty years (Gosse 1917b, Lang 1959–1962, Ober 1975).

We are deeply in Gosse's debt for leaving this critical biographic material in trust for a later time more sympathetic to the primacy of psychological realism in biography. For without these critical insights about the many masochistic games the young Swinburne played with his father and the erotized dependency he had on his mother, we would be hard put to fully comprehend those instinctualized beginnings as they resonate within the recurring sea-images that dominate so much of Swinburne's poetry. Lines that ring the many instinctualized changes through the passive aim, singing the sad songs of sweet pain in one held in masochistic thrall to the great mother sea:

> I will go back to the great sweet mother
> Mother and lover of men the sea.
> I will go down to her, I and none other,
> Close with her, kiss her and mix her with me . . .
>
> Fair mother, fed with the lives of men
> Thou art subtle and cruel of heart, men say.
> Thou has taken, and shalt not render again;
> Thou are full of thy dead, as cold as they.
> ["The Triumph of Time"]

Nor could we fully appreciate the poignant, instinctualized apotheosis implicit to such lines as:

> If you were Queen of pleasure,
> and I were the King of pain;
> We would hunt down love together
> and teach its feet a measure.
> ["A Match"]

Having demonstrated that psychobiography is not a psychohistorical artifact of German Romanticism and its environs, we must now return its ultimate consideration as psychoanalytic biography to those environs, specifically to those first Wednesday nights at Bergasse 19. Almost from the first citation of a literary figure—of Goethe by Josef Breuer in *Studies on Hysteria* (Breuer and Freud 1893–1895)—the psychoanalytic approach to great men, their art and their thought, has been predominately by way of the *Kairos* as a psychopathological "decisive moment." A cursory perusal of the minutes of the Vienna Psychoanalytic Society (Nunberg and Federn 1962, 1967), the legendary Wednesday Night Meetings, bears out the truth of the above statement. The watershed years of the psychobiographic method can be taken to fall between 1906 and 1910, hard upon the publishing of the *Three Essays on Sexuality* (Freud 1905a). Prisoner to their time in the psychoanalytic idea, the group dedicated itself to an assiduous search for evidence of libidinal derivatives in the lives of great men and in the art they created. Their methodological vice was a psychosexual reductionism and they practiced it avidly, with Hitschmann, Sadger, and Graf among the most active voices raised on those legendary evenings. On one Wednesday night in 1907, Edward Hitschmann posed the metaphorical question as to why an artist chose a particular artist form over all others, to which Max Graf answered surely and simplistically that "this question is answered by the theory of erotogenic zones" (Nunberg and Federn 1962, p. 265). These were halcyon nights; psychosexual arrest was destiny, and only Freud seemed hesitantly cautious. "Every poet who shows abnormal tendencies can be the object of pathography. But the pathography cannot show anything new. Psychoanalysis on the other hand provides information about the creative process. Psychoanalysis deserves to rank above pathography" (Nunberg and Federn 1962, p. 265).

Yet a little later in the same year Freud (1907a) appears to hedge his bet on the occasion of his analysis of Jensen's *Gradiva,* writing that the "creative writer cannot evade the psychiatrist nor the psychiatrist the creative writer. . . . He has from time immemorial been the precursor of science, and so too of scientific psychology" (Freud 1907a, p. 44). In 1908, he returned once again to a genetic thesis: "Someday one should investigate how infantile impressions influence great achievement, and not only how they influence later illness" (Nunberg and Federn 1962, p. 361). Freud set about reifying this notion in a work on Leonardo da Vinci, its premise more clearly set forth in the newer translation by Alan Tyson than it was in the original by A. A. Brill: *Leonardo da Vinci and a Memory of His Childhood* (Freud 1910). The child is the father to the artist; a position held down to the present day by the preponderance of psychobiographic studies. Unfortunately this has led to a restricting emphasis upon the pre-oedipal and oedipal years, a restriction not imposed by Freud in his original consideration of the crucial screen memory. A measure of this narrow definition by which the genetic premise of the psychobiographic method is restricted to the first five or six years of life is implicit in Bergmann's (1973) reluctance to include Erikson among proper psychoanalytic biographers because Erikson expands that genetic premise to the post-oedipal development stages.

While Freud had already commented to the Vienna Society on December 11, 1907, on the valid aspirations and limits of psychoanalytic biography, only Isidor Sadger acted on the application of that method before the publication of the Leonardo study, writing works on C. F. Meyer in 1908 and on Nicolaus Linaus and Heinrich Kleist in 1909. Of the early psychoanalytic monographs published under the editorship of Sigmund Freud — *Schriften zur angewandten Seelenkunde* — only the same Sadger wrote psychological biographies before 1911. After the publication of the

Leonardo study, between 1911 and 1925, eight of the twelve monographs were psychobiographies (Bry et al. 1953). The psychobiography of Leonardo da Vinci was Freud's first and last comprehensive study of an historical figure, and must be seen as not only the watershed for all subsequent psychobiographic studies but an implicitly less than sanguine commentary on the limitations of the method itself. Its sad fate has been to be badly used as the flawed paradigm for the many methodological problems that beset the method, rather than the brave new start in psychoanalytic biography which Freud meant it to be.

There has been an unfortunate tendency to treat the Leonardo study as though it were holy writ, and any methodological critique an expression of apostasy to psychoanalysis at large. In this, I think we are better served by Alan Tyson's (1957) dispassionate summary of the methodological problems intrinsic to that work than we are by the almost point-by-point defense of Freud's thesis by Kurt Eissler (1961) in his polemical rebuttal of the critique of that study by the art historian Meyer Schapiro (1956). Tyson does not permit the scholarly pettifoggery of the *nibio* controversy to obscure Freud's real psychoanalytic insights. From his first cautionary comment to the Vienna Society in December of 1907, Freud himself was always most aware of the limitations of applying psychoanalytic insights to an historical subject. His famous letter to the painter Herman Struck in 1914 indicates that Freud considered his psychobiographical reconstruction to have been a *Romandichtung* (Gombrich 1965), a hypothetical fiction useful for the enlargement of the several psychoanalytic themes of the work. The most Freud ever claimed for his psychobiographic reconstructions about Leonardo was psychoanalytic validity, not historical truth. This is a critical methodological distinction that too often escapes both critics and defenders alike.

Freud would change this view little down the years, writing in *Moses and Monotheism:*

I am very well aware that in dealing so autocratically and arbitrarily with Biblical tradition — bringing it up to confirm my views when it suits me and unhesitatingly rejecting it when it contradicts me — I am exposing myself to serious methodological criticism and weakening the convincing force of my arguments. But this is the only way in which one can treat material of which one knows definitely that its trustworthiness has been severely impaired by the distorting influence of tendentious purposes. It is to be hoped that I shall find some degree of justification later on, when I come upon the track of these secret motives. Certainly is in any case unattainable and moreover it may be said that every other writer on the subject has adopted the same procedure. [1939, p. 27]

Thus in the less than sanguine spirit of Freud's own awareness of the intrinsic flaws of the method, we can do no less than approach any consideration of the Leonardo study not only as the original model for psychoanalytic biography but also for insight into the methodological problems of that method.

Freud's interest in Leonardo da Vinci was an old passion; when asked in a "questionnaire" about his favorite books, Freud (1907b) named among them Merezhkovsky's biography of Leonardo. As early as October 9, 1898, contingent to his disagreement with Wilhelm Fliess over the latter's belief that a connection existed between bilaterality and bisexuality, Freud remarked parenthetically that "perhaps the most famous left handed individual was Leonardo, who is not known to have had any love affairs" (Freud 1897–1902 [letter 98], pp. 267–268). With that cryptic note, the matter was laid aside until October 17, 1909, when Freud wrote Jung that he had recently seen a patient who was reminiscent of Leonardo save for the absence of his genius, and that he had sent to Italy for a monograph by Scognamiglia on Leonardo's childhood. It was of course the monograph with the fateful memory of the *nibio* that supposedly visited Leonardo in his cradle. The mistranslation of *nibio* by Herzfeld (1906) as *geier* ("vulture") would be central to Freud's reconstruction of the screen memory of the feared orally sadistic mother. *"Questo scriver si distintamente del nibio che sia mia destino"* (Freud 1910, p. 82): and, on occasion, it has almost seemed that the fate of Leonardo as a valid psychobiographic study was as much joined to the insistent presence of that *nibio* as it was for Leonardo the boy.

Freud had no access to original manuscripts and notes, and had to rely heavily on Marie Herzfeld's (1906) apocryphal anthology, whose fateful use of the word *geier* ("vulture") in her account of the famous cradle fantasy, instead of *milan* ("kite"), the word corresponding to the Italian word *nibio,* would flaw the assumptions of Freud's central thesis. The mistranslation *geier* was also used in the cradle fantasy in the well-thumbed German translation of the Merezhkovsky biography of Leonardo, although Merezhkovsky had himself correctly used *korshein,* the Russian word for kite (Tyson 1957, p. 61).

A great weight is given to this mistranslation in all the later critiques of the Leonardo study, particularly by the art historian Meyer Schapiro (1956). For the mistranslation of *nibio* as a vulture and a vulture as perpetrator of Leonardo's memory of a childhood oral trauma is critical to Freud's thesis, permitting him to reify a personal myth according to a more general one. "The child's assumption that his mother has a penis is thus the common source from which are derived the androgynously formed mother goddesses such as the Egyptian *Mut* and the vulture's coda in Leonardo's childhood fantasy" (Freud 1910, p. 97). Noting that the Egyptian hieroglyph for mother — *Mut* — was a vulture, Freud then apposed the vulture-headed goddess of Egypt, *Mut,* to the cruel "sinister smile" now purported to be that of Leonardo's mother, to be "recalled" later in the smiles of the Mona Lisa and St. Anne. "The picture contains the synthesis of his childhood: its details are to be explained by reference to the most personal impressions of Leonardo's life" (Freud 1910, p. 112). More as a tribute to his fealty to Freud than to his scholarly method, Pfister (1913) promptly "discovered" the outlines of a vulture in the folds of one of the woman's clothes in Leonardo's painting in the Louvre of *St. Anne and the Two Women.*

I believe that Freud came to the mistranslation with an anticipating set for an oedipal construction imposed on him by his repeated reading of Merezhkovsky's romanticized novel as biography (Coltrera 1965) — especially the eleventh chapter in which Leonardo visits the places of his childhood, where he recalls in a time-shift, itself reminiscent of a screen memory, his mother's tender and mysterious smile. Leonardo further remembers how he would steal away from his father's house to visit his peasant mother, there to be smothered by her outpourings of affection. Going on in its romantic surmise, the book tells how Leonardo in his nightly visits to his mother would slip into her bed, "pressing his body against hers under the blanket." What was written there illustrated what Freud had seen so often in the oedipal conflicts of his own patients. The sinister smile of the wrong bird and the romanticized reconstruction of purported oedipal satisfactions fused and became subsumed in Freud's faith that this is the way Leonardo's family romance *should* have been realized, in the seemingly serendipitous assumption that *si non é vero, é ben trovato.*

Freud was always much less sanguine in the matter than his more literal defenders have been down through the years, going so far as to write the painter Herman Struck in 1914 that the Leonardo reconstruction was a *Romandichtung,* a romanticized fiction (Gombrich 1965). This is consistent with his earlier statement in "Creative Writers and Day-Dreaming" (Freud 1908), that the application of the psychoanalytic principles to art, literature, and biography should be of an analogical rather than a literal order.

It seems strange that while the criticism of the Leonardo study began almost upon its publication in 1910, its most serious "mistake," the mistranslation of *nibio* as "vulture" and not as the more correct "kite," was not cited till some four decades later. Also no one had noticed that there were kites but no vultures in Italy. The question now poses itself: does the extensive oedipal reconstruction, with its correlate derivation of the feared oral-sadistic mother from Egyptian mythology, also fall of its own weight once the essential image of the vulture is replaced by the correct and more benign one of the kite? While clearly the bird of Leonardo's cradle screen memory cannot be equated with the vulture-goddess of a culturally disparate Egyptian mythology, does this necessarily obviate Freud's discussion of phallic mother-goddesses and their presence in so many of the world's mythologies? Tyson (1957) suggests that all questions of *nibio* aside, we still have to answer why the Egyptian hieroglyph for "mother" is a vulture. Is the Egyptologist's explanation that it is a matter of chance phonetic coincidence that much better an explanation than Freud's about the sinister origin of androgynous mother-goddesses? Even as a kite, Leonardo's screen memory of the bird putting its tail in his mouth still insists on an answer. The point is really that Freud's construction is a psychological explanation meant to facilitate understanding and is not an empirical statement about causality. As such, it is valid in that it is consistent within the conditions of its premises; though one may fairly ask whether it is useful as a biographical construction.

But to continue to the point of critiques such as that of Schapiro (1956), Freud's thesis does not fall like a house of cards once the mistranslation of *nibio* is taken from its purported key position in the construction. And, neither may it be said that we are arguing for an intuitive method according to some random empirical principle of *si non é vero, é ben trovato*. Take away the failed reconstruction keyed to the mistaken sense of *nibio* as the screen for the oral-sadistic, phallic mother, and we are still left with a remarkable constellation of radical insights. Among these radically innovative psychoanalytic approaches is the applied psychoanalytic case history method, already prefigured in the Schreber case (Freud 1911b).

But to return to the valid assumptions of the Leonardo study that survived the *nibio* controversy, certainly the reconstruction of Leonardo's emotional life from his early years, the opposing conflicts between his artistic and scientific needs, and the specific construction placed upon his inferred psychosexual conflicts, all retain their psychoanalytic pertinence. Probably the most acute insight of the work concerns the genetic origins of a particular kind of homosexuality. Freud's construction was organized around certain genetic premises: the erotic relation with the mother, a narcissistic object choice of an object of the same sex, and the sexual theory held by children about the maternal penis. Had Freud written nothing but

but the summation of this developmental progression, the Leonardo study would represent a radically innovative approach:

> I was more strongly impressed by cases in which the father was absent from the beginning or left the scene at an early date, so that the boy found himself left entirely under feminine influence . . . . After this preliminary state a transformation sets in whose mechanism is known to us but whose motive forces we do not yet understand. The child's love for his mother cannot continue to develop consciously any further; it succumbs to repression. The boy represses his love for his mother: he puts himself in her place, identifies himself with her, and her own person as a model in whose likeness he chooses the new objects of his love. In this way he has become a homosexual . . . . He finds the objects of his love along the path of *narcissism* . . . ." [Freud 1910, pp. 99–100]

And where it may be fairly said that the Leonardo study was the first work dealing in any depth with the nature and workings of the creative imagination, it is perhaps more pertinent and consistent with Freud's cognitive style (Coltrera 1965, 1981, Coltrera and Ross 1967) that he was more concerned with the question of creative inhibitions in Leonardo, an artist who had notorious difficulty in finishing a work. "The aim of our work has been to explain the inhibitions in Leonardo's life and in his artistic creativity" (Freud 1910, p. 131). Consequently, the Leonardo study must be viewed as an important beginning in the formulation of the concept of sublimation and its attendant problems, especially those referrent to artistic inhibitions. The question of sublimation would engage Freud's interest to the end of his life. In the Leonardo study, Freud not only critically distinguished sublimation from inhibition and obsession, but in a correlate matter he concluded that the transformation of the instinctual roots of curiosity was an irreducible vicissitude of repression.

Accordingly, psychobiographic studies have often been the chosen vehicle for the sophistication of the concept of sublimation. In his study of Heinrich Schliemann, which must be considered to be in the direct line of descent from the classic case reconstruction model of the Leonardo study, William Niederland (1965: Chapter 5 of this volume) relates how the future discoverer of Troy was named after a dead brother, buried just outside the vicarage where the young Heinrich was raised. Tragedy stressed two most critical developmental times for the young Heinrich Schliemann. When he was four, and presumably at the height of his oedipal conflict, another brother died. His mother died when he was nine, during those critical latency years when sublimation begins to be structuralized. About the same time Schliemann's father also lost his vicarage because of some sexual and financial indiscretions. Niederland concludes that these critical traumas additively induced an identity crisis in Schliemann, one that would bear significantly on his later creative choices. "All through his life Schliemann was never sure whether he was the *dead* brother inside or the *living* one outside the grave" (Niederland 1965, p. 375). When the repression of his aggressive wishes to the now dead rival fails, Schliemann has no defensive recourse but to structuralize sublimatory defenses in their stead: finding a new interest in tombs and cemeteries, but on one occasion going so far as to dig up the grave of his own brother and then examine the skull. Archaeology and the American gold mining ventures in which he would make his fortune all represent a sublimation of these necrophilic interests, serving to deny death by a less instinctualized resurrection of a geological and archaeological past. Niederland believes the sublimation processes in Schliemann to have been incomplete, remaining as they did so close to their infantile libidinized and aggressivized beginnings. Niederland's method and intent is not too far removed from the case method and theory of creative process intrinsic to the Leonardo study wherein creative sublimations were held to represent reparative defenses special to genius. Sublimations in this model show the tenuous palimpsest of their conflictual origins even into their formal elements.

Most psychoanalytic biographies are variants of the case history method bounded in time on the one side by the Schreber case (Freud 1911b) and on the other by the Leonardo study (Freud 1910), but ultimately dependent for their methodological assumptions upon the device of analogical exposition first advanced in "Creative Writers and Day-Dreaming" (Freud 1908). Freud had known from the beginning that applied psychoanalysis was an interpretation *manqué,* removed from the usual clinical anamnestic evidences and occasions of transference resistance that more properly delineate the psychic surface of associations and events to be interpreted. More recently, Greenacre (1963) has described the problems which beset the psychobiographer in his work:

> It is apparent that the psychoanalytic biographer approaches the study of his subject from vantage points precisely the opposite of those of the psychoanalytic therapist. The latter works largely through the medium of his gradually developing and concentrating relationship with the patient who is seeking help and accepts the relationship for this purpose. The personal uninvolvement and neutrality of the therapist [permits the development of the transference situation]. . . . In contrast to this, the

psychoanalytic biographer approaches his subject almost wholly by avenues which are unavailable in therapeutic technique. He has no direct contact with his subject, and there is no therapeutic aim. He amasses as much material from as many different sources as possible. Lacking the opportunity to study the subject's reactions through the transference neurosis, he must scrupulously scrutinize from which the source material is drawn, and assess the personal interactions involved in it. Further, the study is made for the purpose of extending analytic knowledge, and is not sought by the subject. [Greenacre 1963, pp. 10–11]

In full appreciation of the above, Freud once again took up the quest for an interpretive device that would circumvent this methodological impasse, turning his creative interest in 1905 to the problems of the creative writer, finishing but not publishing an essay on "Psychopathic Characters on the Stage" (Freud 1942 [1905]). He returned twice to the problem in 1907, first in the study of *Gradiva,* which represented the initial application of dream-interpretation to the dreams of fiction (which Freud believed had effected a quasi-analytic cure in the hero); second, on December 6, 1907, Freud gave a lecture in the rooms of the Viennese publisher Hugo Heller, himself a member of the Wednesday Night Meetings, on the relation between the work of fantasy and the creative process. A careful summary appeared the next day in the Viennese daily *Die Zeit,* with its completed version, "Creative Writers and Day-Dreaming," being published the next year, not in some parochial journal attached to the Vienna Society but in a new Berlin literary periodical.

In "Creative Writers and Day-Dreaming," Freud suggested that an indirect approach be taken to the creative person and his works by utilizing a series of increasingly close comparisons, advancing the analogical premise that the creative person was *like* a child at play. "He creates a world of fantasy which he takes very seriously — that is which he invests with large amounts of emotion — while separating it sharply from reality" (Freud 1908, p. 144). Freud has now exchanged play and fantasy, not as vaguely metaphorical equivalents, but as a bold intuitive assumption of their necessary connection as way stations in the development of reality testing and the sense of reality. This is an assumption that he will later grant enormous sophistication within the transcendental rhetoric of a notion of inner representability — that the self and its object world are "known" only through that which represents them — in the *Papers on Metapsychology* (Freud 1915–1917). In 1908, however, he stops at the shrewd developmental surmise that a child never gives up a developmental position until he has its successor well in hand.

Freud then states the universal premise of subsequent applied psycho-analytic approaches to the creative genius and his works, saying that there is in "the childhood of the artist" a critical turning away from play toward fantasy—to daydreams—with the implicit and significant assumption that the creative process is a *kind* of daydream, and, as such, it may analogically be interpreted *as if* it were the dream-work done in the waking state. And then by a series of analogous approximations, Freud extrapolates this principle of analogous interpretation, applying it to the novel, art, and poetry. "We may lay it down that a happy person never phantasies, only an unsatisfied one. The motive forces of phantasies are unsatisfied wishes, and every single phantasy is the fulfillment of a wish, a correction of unsatisfying reality . . . . They are either ambitious wishes, which serve to elevate the subject's personality, or they are erotic ones" (Freud 1908, pp. 146–147). Where the dream was the fulfillment of a wish during sleep, the creative work is a species of fantasy, and as such represents a wish-fulfillment of the waking state.

From its first inception in "Creative Writers and Day-Dreaming" (Freud 1908) right through the *Introductory Lectures* (Freud 1916–1917), I believe that this flawed dependence on analogical exposition has effectively seques-tered most applied psychoanalysis from the dialectical progression of the main body of interpretation toward a notion of mental representability which was finally achieved in the *Papers on Metapsychology* (Freud 1915–1917), and the methodological advantages intrinsic to that notion in exam-ining the conjoined questions of narcissism, self, and identity.

Interpretations developed as analogizing expositions may be said to tack closer to the topographic-economic explanations of the Project (Freud 1895) than they do to the true sense of interpretation as a derivation through meaning—as *Deutung*—found in Chapters 6 and 7 of the *Interpretation of Dreams* and in the *Metapsychological Papers*. In terms of the historical cri-tique assumed in this essay, the analogical expositions and the topographic-economic explanations intrinsic to the psychobiographic method from its inception lent themselves to the historical forces that resisted the critical progression from the first to the second instinct theory and the statement of a structural point of view.

Simply put, the topographic-economic explanations intrinsic to so many of the analogizing constructions of such studies, or, more properly, their referents, exist outside of phenomenology and must be exposited analogi-cally (Ricoeur 1970, Coltrera 1981a). In the strict sense of a valid psycho-analytic epistemology, the topographic and economic points of view do not show true behavioral referents as do the other metapsychological points of view. For example, the behavioral referents of the ego can be sought and described according to a phenomenological rhetoric of deferral and delay which represent the defining, operational structural qualities of the ego.

The continuing problem of the paucity of primary psychoanalytic data in most psychobiographic studies has led to a sophisticated use of analogizing exposition, with an increasing tendency to use the subject's letters, notes, diaries, and graffiti as valid analogues of free associations (Coltrera 1965, Mack 1971). In his study of Heinrich Schliemann, for example, Niederland (1965) uses Schliemann's "language exercises" as valid analogues of free association. Schliemann's dreams and unconscious wishes are considered to have been revealed in the random exercise sentences the latter would write down in a new language in his endeavors to gain facility in that language. Eissler (1963) and Greenacre (1963) have elaborated on Bernfeld's (1931) original notion that diaries, as "letters to oneself," may be used as valid associative analogues in psychobiographic constructions. I myself believe we must move cautiously in this matter of accepting such data as the analogical equivalents of associative materials given us by patients in the psychoanalytic situation (Coltrera 1965). For example, Eissler's (1963) use of Goethe's letters as free associative equivalents, with the analogizing insistence that they are as one with the widened states of consciousness intrinsic to the relatively deprived stimulus condition of the psychoanalytic situation, falters once one considers the high order of autonomy implicit to the stylized genre of letter writing in the Enlightenment. As to the matter of Leonardo's own notes and graffiti, the chronological hodgepodge implicit to these notes — on light, on movement, on color, alternating in no special order — defies any method that depends on an implicit order of associative strophing (Gombrich 1965, Coltrera 1965). Gombrich raises the interesting methodological question of whether the notes were really copies in the order they present themselves, or if the left-handed Leonardo started at the end of the book first, or possibly from both sides. Leonardo's well-known dyslexic problems — he was a notorious mirror writer — make suspect any assumption of associative equivalence being imputed of these randomly organized notebooks, no matter how interestingly his scribbled notes, marginal jotting, or graffiti organize themselves within an associative premise.

No amount of methodological circumlocution can avoid the hard operational truth that these analogous "evidences" do not validly exchange with the associative data that most ordinarily provide the conditions for the empirical justification of interpretations in the ongoing psychoanalytic situation. There can be little doubt that the dearth of true transference and resistance data is the one methodological reason for the characteristically unfocussed quality of nearly all psychobiographic and psychohistoric constructions. We have seen an invigorating return in recent times to the spirit of a humanistic dialogue with other cultural and scientific disciplines that was the strength of applied psychoanalysis in its formative years. It becomes increasingly incumbent upon us, therefore, to set to right our several serious methodological problems with evidence, and desist from the cavalier fashion with which most studies have heretofore tended to treat biographic and historical methodologies, and their contained rules of evidence.

One has but to cite the recent embarrassment of the Bullitt–Freud (1967) study of Woodrow Wilson, published as it was by William Bullitt some twenty-eight years after Freud's death. The clumsy, reductionist excesses of the book's savage invectives against Wilson, barely masked by a simplistic psychoanalytic rhetoric, are most certainly that of Bullitt, reflecting little of the elegant psychoanalytic style of Sigmund Freud. While Freud never forgave Wilson's failure to prevent the geographic and intellectual destruction of his beloved *Mitteleurope* world, Freud was too Greek in his anger to stoop to such petty polemic as referring to the president as "little Tommy Wilson." Simply summarized, the book's thesis is that Wilson had a strong and loving father with whom he was very close, and that his entire life became a recurring act of an intensely ambivalent resolution of his oedipal conflict. Bullitt adduces that Wilson was orally fixated from the "evidence" that he sang and debated at college, and later became a gifted orator. And as all men identify in some part with their mother, the argument continues, Wilson used his mother-identification to unconsciously satisfy his passive wishes to his strong father, who then was introjected within his superego as his father-god. Then in a construction curiously reminiscent of the Wolf Man's passive homosexual identification with the crucified Christ (Freud 1918), the "little Tommy Wilson" who never fought as a child and thought of himself as Christ could not later take on the dominating Georges Clemenceau and Lloyd George. After his failure at Versailles, Wilson goes home as the crucified Christ, soon to be joined as in a long *Pietà* with his wife upon the incapacitating stroke suffered in his last year in office. This barely serves as analogy, let alone psychohistory. Little wonder then that while the collaboration had produced a manuscript by 1932, the authors could not agree on each other's draft and, implicitly, on each other's conclusions. Not until six years later, when Bullitt, then U.S. Ambassador to France, helped arrange Freud's release from the Nazis, did a greatful Freud waive his convictions and agree to take out some sections he had written. In deference to Wilson's widow, it was agreed that the book was not to be published until her death. In deference to Freud, someone should have bit the Bullitt and not have published it at all.

In the end, the Bullitt-Freud book may be best remembered for its critiques, raising as it did valid questions about the methodological problems and limits of the psychobiographical method. Erikson (1956), in particular, used the occasion to make a significant statement on the psychohistorical method as well. Perhaps the most lasting importance of the book will be to serve as a negative example of the role countertransference may exert in psychobiographic choice and constructions. While more can be attributed to the personal spite Bullitt bore Wilson, Freud was not entirely blameless in his acquiescence to the many countertransference intrusions which so destroyed the validity, let alone the credibility, of that study. As interpretations, psychobiography and psychohistory are the heirs of the polemical tradition out of which interpretation emerged, a continuance from the Enlightenment's attempt to reduce illusion and remove mystery in the affairs and concerns of men. However, as interpretations *manqué,* they do not contain the empirical checks to countertransference ordinarily provided by an ongoing psychoanalytic situation, so that the motives of the biographer and historian for choosing a particular subject for study must be closely parsed for occasions of countertransference. *Why* a subject is chosen for study should be as much a methodological concern as *how* it is done.

Only with the publication of *Beyond the Pleasure Principle* (Freud 1920) would the tide of analogical interpretation of culture and creativity be stemmed. Constructions would now shift to ones in which the libido is antithetically played off against the death instinct, with a tenuous Manichaean balance being postulated between the forces of Eros and Thanatos. Ricoeur (1970) has pointed out that the shift from the first to a second instinct theory is really a shift from an economics of instincts to a renunciation of libido, so that Freud (1938) in this measure would construe the role of the great man in culture-binding as one in which the great man helps sustain instinctual renunciation in those who follow him. Sadly, too often too many psychobiographic and psychohistoric constructions about specific great men give the unfortunate impression that they could have been made about any person in any time and history. Leonardo was treated as if he were a participating communicant of Egyptian methology, the sinister smiles of the Mona Lisa and St. Anne one with that of the phallic goddess *Mut.*

What is being placed in question is not the universality of a species-specific psychosexual stage epigenesis and its resident conflicts, but rather the unfortunate tendency to treat the history of one man and of all men as the Oedipal conflict writ large. In psychosexual stage epigenesis, the phase sequence is an invariant, with variation being possible in the individual phase both as to duration and in the psychosocial differences in the activity of the phase-specific object. Thus the invariance of psychosexual phase sequence and the variability of the phase in terms of its own structural limits guarantees the universality of certain themes with minor variations as to primacy and in emphasis. Kris (1952) has pointed out that there are but four themes possible to all myth and literature: dependency, aggression, guilt, and incestuous desire. In becoming human we know each theme in its turn but not in the same measure. The problem with most psychobiographic studies is that they more readily explain how great men are similar—through character theory and myth criticism—rather than in the unique ways they differ, in the way they are creative (Coltrera 1965).

To understand why most psychobiographic and psychohistoric studies tend to treat the person as a generalized existent outside of any sociohistorical context save those of family, we must recall the historical arrests to which the method is heir. The first studies, it has been seen, tended to explain in two ways, by topographic-economic constructions and by the analogical examples of dreams. Creativity was a kind of *waking* dream-work, so that the art and literature it created were necessarily vicissitudes of instincts. As such it was a methodology that operated according to the economics of instincts intrinsic to the "first topography," with its balkanization of the psychic apparatus into the discrete energies of the separate systems—conscious, preconscious, and unconscious. The creation and satisfaction taken in art and thought, the statement of and belief in moral and religious systems, all were accounted for as expenditures in a pleasure-unpleasure continuum, with a methodology which essentially defined itself in terms of cathexis, withdrawal of cathexis, hypercathexis, and anticathexis. In the "first topography," the libido was viewed as solipsistic, accountable only to itself in its regressive and progressive passages through the systems unconscious, preconscious, and conscious. This model dominated the psychobiographic method in its halcyon years, from its first statement in "Creative Writers and Day-Dreaming" (Freud 1908) and *Jokes and Their Relation to the Unconscious* (Freud 1905b), through to its last statement in the *Introductory Lectures* (Freud 1916–1917). As late as 1952, Kris, in warning against a tendency to underestimate the capacity of the creative artist to go beyond autobiographic events, found it incumbent to say that "the artist had created a world and not indulged in a daydream" (p. 288).

Consequently there has been a rhetorical clumsiness to the methodological premises of much psychoanalytic biography and history. Their analogical constructions are unequal to the almost cosmological shift imposed on psychoanalytic formulation with the critical passage from the anonymous systems of the "first topography" to the intrinsic role derivatives of the personal pronoun contained in a "second topography" of ego, superego, and id. After 1920, the solipsistic libido of the "first topography" became subject to something other than itself, to a demand for its renunciation by a non-libidinal factor manifesting itself as culture. We must agree with Ricoeur (1970) that the statement of a "second topography"—the structural point of view—critically situates libido within the conditions of culture. In this model, man seeks his need satisfactions within the contextual conditions of a constellation of drive-restraints imposed by the individual himself and his culture. Enlarging the ability of the method to comment more discriminitively on the uniqueness of great men and their works, by an epistemological and operational reworking of the concept of narcissism, the libido was removed from its awkward 1914 placement in the ego and in 1923 finally assigned to the id. Only then would it be possible not only to clearly separate a substantive notion of the ego from its ego processes, but also to separate the ego from the self, both as to substance and process.

With this radical change from an economics of instincts to a renunciation of libido intrinsic to a hegemony of drive-restraints, a critical shift in methodological premise became implicitly incumbent upon applied psychoanalysis, inclusive of psychobiography and psychohistory. Methodological premise could no longer be restricted to topographic-economic consideration alone; no longer could psychic contents be organized solely as to their relation to the state of consciousness, or their mode of organization as to primary or secondary processes, or as to the free or bound states of the psychic energies operative in those psychic contents. Psychobiographic constructions were not only validly possible according to the alternate pertinancies of all the other metapsychological points of view, but they were desirable in accord with the holistic unity of the overdetermined nature of behavior.

But it was not until 1952, with Kris' warning against the tendency to restrict the creative artist to autobiographic events, that a clear methodological break with the analogical model of 1908 finally took place. Kohut (1960) has commented on the paucity of ego psychological constructs in psychobiographic studies up to about 1950. I think the same may be said for the heretofore compromising lack of developmental, aggressive, and normal ego psychology considerations in most studies (Coltrera 1965). A measure of this awareness may also be inferred from the increasing number of psychobiographic and psychohistoric studies since 1950 which have specifically addressed themselves to the problems of development, aggression, narcissism, and structural conflict.

The relatively late appearance of developmental considerations and concern for the problem of aggression—after 1950—in psychoanalytic biography and history can be related in significant part to the long time it took Freud to separate prescient theories of aggression and the superego in his thought, in which questions relating to the one were frequently asked of the other. Curiously enough, the role of early developmental events was present in Freud's thought almost from the beginning. As early as the 1895 Project, he placed the beginnings of the nuclear superego in the early object relationships. Freud would return to the idea in his statement of a structural theory, saying that the superego was formed out of the early object choices of the id (Freud 1923).

Indeed, though they would not be referred meaningfully to each other until a much later time in ego psychology, with its much broader methodological and epistemological interests in the adaptive modes of conflict resolution, the psychobiographic method and the problem of aggression were contiguous, though separate, concerns in Freud's early thought. Hard upon the publication of the Leonardo study in 1910, Freud began a decade—between 1910 and 1920—of concern and inquiry into the critical role of aggression in the affairs and fiats of men, which would end in a statement of the joined theories of aggression and the superego.

This critical conjoining in Freud's thought contributed in great part to the so-called "hostile" model of the superego, the structural representation of the coercive force which could validly account for the high degree of instinctual renunciation which must be effected in the short time allotted by civilized child-rearing (Freud 1932). A "hostile" model of the superego would also help explain the several clinical conundrums posed by negative therapeutic reactions (Freud 1923, 1926, 1937) and the "severe" guilt reactions of obsessional neurosis and melancholia (Freud 1923), and paranoia (Freud 1914, 1923). Too, the ideological schisms with Adler, Rank, and Jung, over the essential primacy of psychosexual epigenesis required the "hostile" model for the greater needs of theoretical justification. All developmental attention was focussed on the triad object relationships of the genital phase and the feared father-rival who dominated it, enforcing the fiats on whose conditions the "hostile" superego is structured contingent on the oedipal resolution which closes that phase.

Only more recently, with Hartmann's (1960) classification of ethical systems according to whether the ideal aims of the superego or the imperatives of the system-superego predominate, and with Schafer's (1960) concept of a "loving" superego, has the metapsychology of the superego been broadened to accommodate libidinal energic modes as well as those that serve aggression. Freud was always conceptually inconvenienced by the libido in the metapsychology of the superego. He had little psychoanalytic patience or understanding for such Christian doctrines as saving grace or the forgiveness of sins, beliefs that clearly refer to earlier contributions made to the superego precursors by the "loving" relationship between the preoedipal mother and the child. It is no psychohistorical coincidence that both Roman Catholics and those who follow the Greek and Russian Byzantine rites pray to the Virgin Mary as the Holy Mother to intercede for them in the forgiveness of their sins, rather than to God the Father.

The wry adaptive commentary contained in Emile Durkheim's (1912) aphorism that societies tend to venerate themselves, is implicitly subscribed to by Freud throughout his writings on the adaptive nature of the superego, citing specifically its critical role in the preservation of object relations (Freud 1923) and in helping to bind men together as culture, through the directive agency it exerts toward values and imperatives within the hierarchical continuities of family, group, and society (Freud 1913, 1930). We have only to enlarge the sense of the above by an inclusion of some later developmental reconsiderations and a modern ego theory of narcissism to arrive at the wider view that moral systems may be regarded as being orders of adaptation, representing modes of confronting the reality context in which consummation is sought.

Committed to the greater needs of theory building and his own moral pique in the matter, Freud (1927, 1928) could not appreciate the adaptive ends served by the doctrine of "holy sinning" in Fyodor Dostoyevsky. "In spite of my admiration for Dostoyevsky's intensity and pre-eminence, I do not really like him. That is because my patience with pathological natures is exhausted in analysis. In art and life I am intolerant of them" (Freud 1928, p. 196). Freud could not appreciate that Raskolnikov and Stavrogin were inverted men of faith whose crimes were ethical acts, wherein the "holy sinning" locked them to a superego community which, as a constant object world, helped to guarantee to cathectic autonomy of their own selves. The sin was an inverted act of faith in the autonomous ordering of things, a cosmological guarantor of self and object constancy in and beyond this world. The crucial role played by ego and superego identifications drived from the shared imperatives of family and society, in determining both the content and form of ethical and moral beliefs, strongly suggests that moral systems devolve in significant part upon the ontogenesis of identifications.

It is interesting to compare Freud's polemical intensity in the matter, and its implicit defense of the "hostile" model of the superego, with the more even-handed approach of Mark Kanzer (1947, 1948, 1951) to Dostoyevsky, not only for Kanzer's more scrupulous regard for an analytic neutrality but also for his ability to make his constructions according to the developmental percepts current in the time he wrote them. In his first consideration of Dostoyevsky, the short novel *Peasant Marey,* Kanzer (1947: Chapter 9 of this volume) tacks quite close to Freud's (1927, 1928) original and classical oedipal construction, stressing the parricidal theme of that short novel. In tracing the critical sublimation of Dostoyevsky's parricidal wishes in this work, Kanzer focuses on the fact that the writer's first epileptic attack followed directly upon hearing that his father had been murdered by his own serfs. I have elsewhere remarked how this epilepsy served as the model for the alienated metaphor intrinsic to "the disease of consciousness" that so plagued his Underground Man and resonated within the many mystical estrangements of the Christ-like Prince Myshkin (Coltrera 1965).

In his subsequent consideration of *Poor Folks,* Kanzer (1948a: Chapter 10 of this volume) widens his original oedipal construction to include the role played in Dostoyevsky's life and work by certain preoedipal vicissitudes of aggression. Kanzer notes that Dostoyevsky's works are replete with the recurrent theme of an intense though frustrated love of a man for a woman, which maddens him to thoughts of murder and suicide. Using the short novel *Poor Folks,* Kanzer sketches the recurring depressive motif found in so much of Dostoyevsky: the desperate and driven search for a lost love-object, a love unrequited in reprise of the child's impossible original love for his mother, and the unconscious hate he bears her for it.

The preoedipal vicisssitudes of aggression resonate throughout the many preoedipal themes used by Dostoyevsky, tragic metaphors derived in the main from the nomenclative symbolism of the Russian Byzantine saints calendar, where all honor accrues equally to Holy Mother Church and Holy Mother Russia. One such device of *The Brothers Karamazov* is the given name of Dimitri Karamazov, which conjures the name of Demeter, honoring both the earth mother and the Virgin Mary, with whom Dostoyevsky especially identifies the Russian people.

Dostoyevsky, with Nietzsche, may be said to have given the modern predicament most of its defining images and metaphors of pervasive existential unease. Most applied psychoanalytic studies decline to comment, and indeed do not possess the broad conceptual devices necessary for valid psychodynamic comment, about these recurring metaphors of the modern predicament. Theirs has been an epistemological choice, declining as they do to comment meaningfully on these contained concerns for identity and reality according to the widened, reciprocal equivalencies of all the metapsychological points of view. These recurring metaphors and images of loss and alienation cannot be ignored as passing intellectual fashions, for where is the fashion in a continuing body of related philosophical, literary, and artistic metaphor and image that persists in time and across a disparity of people? Nor can these contained concerns be reductively fitted to the conceptual iron-maidens indigenous to approaches restricted to a "first topography" and a first instinct theory. There is more to metapsychology, let alone the world, than the topographic and economic points of view.

The problem narcissism presents for the psychobiographic and psychohistoric methods is summated in Flaubert's provocative statement *"Emma Bovary, c'est moi."* The questions accordingly pose themselves: how does the writer empathically split himself among the multiple characters he creates and then grant them psychological verisimilitude? And how do the special developmental events of his life experience contribute to and participate in this process? Psychobiographic studies seem to have come late—after 1950—to a psychodynamic concern for the unique narcissistic vicissitudes found among the creative, and for their special disturbances in the sense of identity and of reality.

Greenacre precisely limns the shape of the problem in such persons:

> There is then an enlargement of the whole field of response, both in its extensiveness and in the subtleties of its complex rhythmic organization. The perception of objects and the relationship to them become endowed with a multiplicity of allied kindred forms; in our technology, the collective alternates to the original objects. This leads to a multiplicity of experience with greater ease in and even necessity for symbolization and a richness in the texture and pile of the fabric of sensation. Expressed in other terms, the child with potential creative ability experiences deeper resonances and more overtones than does the less gifted child. [1953, pp. 14–15]

Interest in the question of narcissism and the psychobiographic method seemed to commingle in the early considerations of the Vienna Society, with one of the first significant statements about narcissism being made in the Leonardo study (Freud 1910, p. 100). On November 10, 1909, Freud told the Wednesday night meeting that he believed narcissism to be a necessary intermediate stage between autoeroticism and object-love (Jones 1955, p. 388). At about the same time, Freud (1905a [1909]) was also preparing the second edition of the *Three Essays on Sexuality,* in which the first mention of the new term was made in a footnote (1905a, p. 145n). At the end of May of 1910, *Leonardo da Vinci and a Memory of His Childhood* appeared with its longer reference to narcissism. It was referred to again in Section III of the Schreber case (Freud 1911b) and in *Totem and Taboo* (Freud 1912–1913, pp. 88–90). The idea for a comprehensive essay on the subject was mentioned in Freud's letters in June of 1913, and a first draft finished in September of that year during his holidy in Rome. In February and March of 1914, Freud completed the final version of "On Narcissism: An Introduction," which was published later in that year. The paper was a closely argued and demanding summation of his views on narcissism up to that time, representing in significant part a polemical tract directed against the recent apostasies of Adler and Jung. Going beyond the developmental role of narcissism in psychosexual development, and as such the valid alternative of Jung's nonsexual "libido" and Adler's "masculine protest," the paper represented a critical turn toward an idealist context, wherein the epistemological paradox foisted on the notion of interpretation in Chapter 7 would find its valid resolution in the transcendentalism of the *Papers on Metapsychology* (Freud 1915–1917). For with the new distinction between "ego-libido" and "object-libido," and the implicit stress it placed on the relations between the ego and external objects, Freud is well into his quest for a theory of inner representability. This quest would end in the central transcendentalist thesis of the *Papers on Metapsychology,* wherein the self and its object world are considered "known" in the unconscious only through that which represents them, namely the self- and object-representations. Additionally, in "On Narcissism" (1914) Freud introduced the critical concepts of the "ego-ideal" and the self-observing function related to it, which would eventually be consolidated within the superego in *The Ego and the Id* (1923).

"On Narcissism" is a difficult and untidy conceptualization, a testament in some part to the operational characteristics of Freud's cognitive style, especially its resistance to synthetic closure. With the heuristic goad of implicit unanswered questions enlarging the concept in several disparate directions in "Mourning and Melancholia" (Freud 1917 [1915], p. 237), and in Chapters VIII and XI of *Group Psychology* (Freud 1921), the question of narcissism took up the greater part of Lecture XXVI of the *Introductory Lectures* (Freud 1916–1917). Freud's unease with the shaping of the concept during this whole time (Jones 1955, Strachey 1957) represented his teleological need to subdue the concept of a process-self within the overriding notion of a substantive ego implicit to his emerging idea of psychic structure. Freud's backing off from the concept of a process-self contingent to any operational notion of narcissism was probably a reflection of his well-known chariness about phenomenological constructions, considering them to be synonymous with surface events belonging to the Syst.-Cs. and, as such, outside the dynamic interests of proper psychoanalytic inquiry (Coltrera 1981a). This reluctance would defer the metapsychological and clinical distinguishing of self from ego until the greater epistemological demands of a later ego psychology (see Hartmann 1950, Jacobson 1964, 1971).

"On Narcissism" must be considered the first running of the tide toward a concept of mental representability, one which would not only end in a validation of an epistemology of interpretation but which would permit the relatedness that ties the self to its object world to be truly *interpreted,* where before it had been only teleologically *described* and *explained.* For where such commonplace constructions as "fusions with the object" and "oceanic feelings" may parse as teleological description, they cannot be accepted as teleological explanations. The psychobiographic method, with its analogical model for interpretation, failed to take this tide at its turning, as did the main body of the theory of interpretation, and in consequence had no valid ability to interpret the question of narcissism as it bore upon the creation of great art and thought, and on certain developmental crises in great lives (Coltrera 1965).

The psychoanalytic notion of interpretation, it should be recalled, grew out of a radical progression of ideas which began in the 1895 Project and progressed through Chapters 6 and 7 of *The Interpretation of Dreams* (1900). This progression turned on a critical shift of emphasis away from the topographic-economic explanations of the Project to one of interpretation — as *Deutung* — at the close of Chapter 6, wherein interpretation was defined as a decoding derivation of one order of meaning through another order of meaning of a manifestly different kind, a definition which was then raised to a metapsychological system in Chapter 7. In this cryptographic model of *Deutung,* interpretation is considered the reciprocal function of the instinctual vicissitudes intrinsic to the dream-work, operating in kind in both the sleeping and waking states.

With the statement that the dream was a *fulfillment* of a *repressed* wish (1900, pp. 122–123), Freud visited upon the derivation of the concept a conceptual embarrassment which would not be resolved until the *Papers on Metapsychology* (1915–1917). The embarrassment turns on the disparate conceptual orders of the definition, in that fulfillment, as *Erfullung,* belongs to an order of meaning, while repression, as *Verdrangung,* belongs to an order of force. In epistemology, explanations about meaning do not reduce to ones about force. By this argument, interpretation as a derivation through meaning cannot parse according to a psychodynamic theory of psychic forces. The thin edge of the argument is being placed against the uneasy accommodation running throughout Chapter 7 between a language of meaning intrinsic to interpretation and the quasi-physical language of topographic-economic explanation implicit to the first topography. The argument ends on the pessimistic judgment that no valid explanation is given in Chapter 7 of how an instinctual drive achieves signification. What cannot be signified is necessarily outside meaning and, implicitly, outside interpretation (Ricoeur 1970, Coltrera 1981).

Freud resolved these joined conceptual embarrassments in the *Papers on Metapsychology*: the unconscious could now be reintegrated within a realm of meaning contingent to a newly stated relationship between instinct and idea (Freud 1915, p. 166). A drive-wish could not be considered the cognate form of the instinctual drive, and, as such, was capable of being "known" through meaning, was capable of being interpreted. Because the analogical orders of interpretation imposed on the psychobiographic method by "Creative Writers and Day-Dreaming" (Freud 1908) were closer to topographic-economic explanations than they were to true interpretation as a derivation through disparate orders of meaning, this kind of interpretation *manqué* remained apart from the empirical pressures that led to the resolution of the epistemological problem for the main body of psychoanalytic interpretation with the statement of a concept of mental representability.

With the positing of a concept of mental representability a valid connection was made "within" the unconscious between an instinctual drive *(Trieb)* and an idea *(Vorstellung)*. The self and its object world could now be considered transcendental in Immanuel Kant's full sense, "known" only through that which represented them, the self- and object-representations. The problematic of the instinctual drive had now become a problematic about the representatives of the instinctual drive (Ricoeur 1970). So while an instinctual drive could not itself be validly interpreted, its cognate form, as a mental representation, could. A psychoanalytic theory of language, and its attendant concerns with symbolic functioning and the derivation of meaning, was now validly possible (Coltrera 1981). Perhaps more important for the applied psychoanalytic method, with the statement of a transcendentalist notion that the symbol mediates between the intending mind and its external object, the method was granted a critical ability to transcend its heretofore restricted interest in an essentially ahistoric man as the maker and user of myths, and could now consider man as the symbol-maker and the user of affective language.

Kant and Freud had carried forward the intent of the Copernican revolution which had originally substituted the question of objectification by the mind's synthetic function for the question of reality itself. The emphasis placed on the synthetic and integrative functions of the ego in modern ego psychology (Nunberg 1930, Hartmann 1939, 1950) must be considered in direct continuance of this idealist tradition, believing with this tradition that how we come to know and test the representations of reality is more pertinent than the reality in itself. Both Kant and Freud had also said that what is conceived or perceived cannot be removed from the motivational orders of that conception or perception; reality from this point forward in modern psychology and psychoanalysis could no longer be validly separated from an attendant notion of psychic reality.

The question of narcissism, subsumed in the transcendental conundrum originally posed by Immanuel Kant, now becomes metapsychologically transposed within an epistemology of interpretation: how is the subjective to be objectified? How the essentially nondiscursive orders of the reflective self are to be granted a discursive rhetorical order of meaning is at the heart not only of the narcissistic conundrum implicit to a psycholinguistics of interpretation, but of the nature of the creative process as well.

All modern psychologies follow Kant in granting primacy to cognition, to a concern for how ideas are generated and how the "appearances" of reality are joined by the mind. Interpretation, as a derived problem of language and meaning, has been a special epistemological interest of present-day ego psychology, an interest whose roots are in that first methodological concern for inner representability in Freud's thought. As such, the idea of interpretation must be considered an integral part of ideas which began with René Descartes, passed through a nineteenth century idealism and into a present-day structuralism, subscribing to the radical notion that it is the transcendental nature of the human mind to impose meaning on its experience.

Here it should be said that any history of ideas must begin in an assumption of some psychohistorical premise; how else can we account for the cultural and historical variance in emphasis on "developmental lines, or sectors of functioning" (A. Freud 1965), that is, fine and gross motor, cognitive, affective, object relation, defensive-adaptive, and verbal speech. Modern Western society, for example, has stressed some kinds of cognitive and intellectual development over affective and motor sectors of development. The quest for a theory of inner representation in modern psychology takes on an added psychohistorical dimension when considered within the developmental context of the work of Inhelder and Piaget (1955) with its focus on the capacity for formal operations, that is, the ability to form hypotheses and deduce their conclusions regardless of whether or not these conclusions are empirically true. This capacity for formal operations is really the capacity for logical-deductive thought upon which Western society — since the Greeks — has placed its greatest stress. The adaptive role language bears in reality—subsumed within the synthetic function—cannot be fully appreciated apart from a psychohistoric consideration of such adaptive cognitive modes.

In Piaget's (1958) middle-class Swiss children, the capacity for formal operations emerges around puberty, but subsequent studies have shown that psychosocial determinants—for example, "cultural deprivation"—can postpone the structuring of this capacity till well after adolescence. Keniston (1974) questions whether this capacity is likely to emerge at all in non-literate societies. Most psychobiographic and psychohistorical studies have been notably deficient in developmental approaches able to appreciate the kinds of narcissistic vicissitudes subsumed in the unique adaptive cognitive modes so often described in the life experiences of great men, and in the radicalizing cognitions contained in their art and thought (Coltrera 1965). I agree with Keniston (1974) that if we compare different cultures and historical periods from a developmental perspective, we must not only compare how life phases are defined and study the extent to which individuals actually pass through these global phases, but we must know how a given cultural and historical context affects each of the many subsectors of human development.

Although it appears that Western society since Ionian times has stressed cognitive over affective sectors of development, it should be noted that the emergence of the Romantic idea in the nineteenth century is integrally associated in time with modern psychology's Kantian concern with a motivational notion of cognition, namely, that the mind imposes meaning on the condition of affect. In modern ego psychology, consciousness ends up being viewed not simply as a unitary phenomenon, but as one with an entire range of varieties, each corresponding to a different cognitive organization. This concept of consciousness as a mode of cognition goes back to at least Democritus (Coltrera 1962, 1965). The Greeks had no single word for feeling as an affective experience; for them one word carried both an affective and cognitive sense. The romantic notion of affect as a nondiscursive mode of cognition was an attempt to join the variance between the cognitive and affective sectors which was imposed by modern Western thought's weighting one developmental sector over another. Romanticism, the affective shadow of modern psychology, represented a critical cosmological reordering of the thought, feelings, and values of Western man, especially in its radical assertion that the self as creative imagination bore a defining office to its experiences, granting them both representation and meaning.

The idea of interpretation, with its transcendentalist notion that the idea is the cognate form of an instinctual drive which may be rhetorically adduced as an order of meaning, must be considered at one with the idealist assumption of Romanticism that all meaning is contingent upon man, who imposes meaning on the affective conditions of his humanity. While I would not go as far as Trilling (1950) to regard psychoanalysis as a romantic genre, it must be once again said that Sigmund Freud lived in a *Mitteleurope* world whose faith and cosmologies were those of German Romanticism, a man of his time whose scientific surmise often seemed to validate romantic premise. The assumption of a narcissistic model implicit to the transcendentalist premise of the *Papers on Metapsychology* (Freud 1915–1917)—that the self and its object world are "known" in the unconscious only through that which represents them—is consensual with the belief in and concern for the shaping force of creative imagination in the Romantic idea.

Since the *trecento* of Nicola di Cusa, the history of ideas has moved away from metaphysics toward forms of epistemology, away from a concern with "things" toward how things are known. The "rise of the transference" may be regarded as an example of the above occurring in the history of the psychoanalytic idea, representing as it does an existential shift away from a concern with psychic contents to one with psychic acts, away from interest in transference identifications toward one for transference ego (self)-states (Coltrera 1981). The shift from the anonymous system of "first topography" of conscious, preconscious, and unconscious, to the derivations of the personal pronoun intrinsic to the "second topography," of ego, superego, and id—with their implicit declension of the verb "to be"—must be considered part of this existential shift away from a substantive toward a process self.

Theories of symbolic form, of which interpretation is most certainly one, tend to become monistic. Since Kant idealism and its component form of psychoanalysis have moved in this monistic direction wherein reality tends to be conceived in a narcissistic model of the self and its object world. The idea of interpretation begins from the narcissistic premise of a Cartesian doubt about the reflective contents of consciousness, an extension into method of the doubt Nietzsche, Marx, and Freud bore toward the apparent truth of consciousness. These reflective concerns of the broad idealist stream that coursed through the nineteenth century, of which interpretation was an integral part, began the century before as a question posed by René Descartes: what is a thinking being? More to the point, Descartes was concerned with a thinking thing as a statement about personal identity. *Cogito, ergo sum* is really a statement about identity as a reflective act in process consciousness. David Hume, on the other hand, believed human consciousness consisted of separate mental states, each detached from the other and from any discernible holistic principle binding them. Here are the bare pre-scient bones of the empty "S-R" model intrinsic to the behaviorist point of view. Hume's essentially behaviorist answer to Descartes' methodological question about the nature of a "thinking thing" was that the respondent self represented the sum of its separate intellectual and affective processes, the behaviorist premise of present-day quanto-historic studies. Leading from Descartes through the consensual line of Kant and Freud, a transcendental-ist notion of inner representability of the self and its object world became the first premise of those psychobiographic and psychohistorical studies which include metapsychological premises of present-day ego psychology and its contained narcissistic theory in their methodological assumptions.

Kant's rebuttal to Hume's answer to the Cartesian question about the nature of a thinking being represents more than the forking of a broad idealist stream into its German and English tributaries, ending as it does in a consensual agreement with Freud about the holistic principle intrinsic to mind, one whose unconscious nature is to impose psychic meaning on its object world and its self-experiences. Implicit to this notion is the beginning radical assumption that a categorical imperative seems to operate within the organizational disposition of the ego as a responding system which imposes an ordering upon psychic determinism.

Beginning with a demonstration that the Cartesian modes of thought con-tained in Hume's essentially behaviorist premise are inadequate to the empirical challenge of Descartes' original question, Kant says that if one conceives the self as a transcendent idea rather than as an object of experi-ence, then it may be taken as a regulative principle for the ordering of all natural knowledge. We would all then make connections between phenom-ena *as if* our mind were a simple substance, existing permanently and with a personal identity. Kant, and implicitly the Freud of the *Metapsychological Papers,* has taken the Copernican revolution, which had substituted the question of objectification by the mind's synthetic function for the question of the reality itself, and brought it forward into the notion of mind as an enduring psychic structure whose categorical imperative is to impose mean-ing on its experience of a unique self and its object world. This would also agree with the later developmental epistemology of Jean Piaget, whose developmental conceptualizing of object constancy can be regarded as a statement about mental representability as a critical developmental event in the cathectic separation of the self from its object world (Coltrera 1981).

All three epistemological positions agree implicitly that language is a dia-lectic of absence and presence, making "things" present through the "empti-ness" of signs, through that which "represents" them in the enduring psychic

structures of mind. A psychoanalytic theory of language and symbolic functioning, of which interpretation is an integral part, must begin from this
developmental premise (Coltrera 1981). Unfortunately, most applied
psychoanalytic studies of creative great men, and of how their art and
thought radicalized their times, are restricted by an uncritical acceptance of
Freud's (1891, 1895, 1900, 1911, 1923, 1939) sketchy theory of language. In
doing so, they accept several suspect topographic and associationist
assumptions, especially the associationist notion that the transition from
the unconscious state is effected by the accruence of verbal-cathexis to the
thing-cathexis (Coltrera 1965, 1981, Wolff 1967). The study of the formal
qualities of language in the creative process, such as the alienating intent
of cliché and language used as derealized "naming" by Flaubert, Joyce, Pinter, Beckett, and Albee, to name but a critical few, becomes infinitely
more sophisticated when considered within a developmental approach to
language.

Beginning with Kant's sense — which Freud surely shares — that an idea of
personal identity is implicitly contained in the notion of a mind whose categorical imperative is to impose meaning on its experience, Johann Fichte
postulated that the self is a truth which posits itself, not able to be verified
or deduced. It is at once the positing of a being and of an act, the positing of
an existence and of an operation of thought. The Cartesian statement about
being is now existentially transposed to *sum, ergo cogito*: I am, therefore I
think. As if to say, that to exist, for me, is to think; I exist inasmuch as I
think. Comment has already been made that the "rise of the transference" in
the psychoanalytic idea (see A. Freud 1968, 1969, Coltrera 1981) is a reflection in another context of this monistic tendency of symbolic forms in idealist constructions to be stated in the model of narcissism. The Cartesian
positing of the self as a *cogito* is now developed by Kant and Fichte as part
of the reflective concerns of the idealist tradition in the nineteenth century
which would reach the existentialist concerns of our own century (Coltrera
1962, 1965, 1981). The intellectual and empirical history of interpretation
is an integral part of the radical progression in the idealist idea, and the ability of an applied psychoanalytic approach to biography or history can be
judged, according to one critical methodological consideration, as to
whether it can validly interpret the special narcissistic vicissitudes which
characterize the creative personality, especially those developmental crises
which are so often determinate in their unique problems with identity and
reality (Coltrera 1965).

The rise of self-awareness was the Icarus-flight of the Romantic idea.
Oneness was raised to a narcissistic ideal, in which each self was taken to be
the "double" of many others. Novalis would say, *Ich bin du;* and Arthur

Rimbaud would hauntingly echo, *Je est un autre.* Earlier, contiguous to a beginning Cartesian concern for the reflective self in the Enlightenment, Denis Diderot introduced in *Rameau's Nephew* the organizing metaphor of the modern predicament, that of man as the eternal "double," as the split self who is both participant and observer. Diderot also presented intimations of a dynamic unconscious then "in the air," picturing man as existing in a persisting condition of intrapsychic conflicts between his rational and irrational natures. The modern philosophical and literary hero is very often a split self, split along the phenomenological cleavage of the experiential and the reflective, with the hero "double" not only to himself but to the writer as well. The "double" is the special literary device of Fyodor Dostoyevsky in modern literature, signalling his deep unease with the evanescent nature of identity and reality. Dostoyevsky, drawing on his own developmental awareness of the evanescent self-states of an epileptic, depicts the several marginal "double" self-states of his characters as being posited by the hypercathectic changes rung in the modality and in the distribution and patterning of attention-cathexis in what he precisely names a "disease of consciousness." Thus the alienated anti-hero of his *Notes from Underground* lectures the young prostitute on the sinfulness of her life in a mounting dialectic of heightening self-awareness, his own life divided among the several erotized and aggressivized self-states of his "disease of consciousness." The Christ-like Prince Myshkin of *The Idiot,* whose "disease of consciousness" as an epileptic becomes a nonlogical, primary process transductive device of cognition, is a closer "double" of Dostoyevsky.

Dostoyevsky's device of the "double," and its implicit assumption of a "disease of consciousness" has had several additional metaphors in modern literature. Several novelists of the first quarter of this century — James Joyce, Marcel Proust, Virginia Woolf — were obsessed with the question of how to recover the moment as an epiphanous immediacy in a discursive language whose formal temporality must necessarily be of a different order in time, thus fragmenting the ambiguous immediacy and affective integrity of the moment described. This is the paradox of parsimony at the center of the "good interpretation." The enduring problem was summarized in Freud's famous and somewhat pessimistic aphorism on the differing discursive ways that analyst and patient understand in the psychoanalytic situation, saying that where "the patient recovers, the analyst reconstructs" (Coltrera 1981). Clearly, the "good interpretation" is the *madeleine* we proffer the patient, closer to the need for an ambiguous immediacy within the transference situation than it is to Proust's metaphor, which once properly bitten into ends in a regressive, epiphanous "recovery" through a simultaneity of transference self-states.

The "double" is an intrinsic device of the modern "theatre of the absurd," with the latter's need to evoke the sense of alienation and estrangement which is held to be the existential existence of modern man, felled, as it were, by his "disease of consciousness" (Coltrera 1966). Among its examples we might cite the use of cross-talk pairs by Samuel Beckett, as with Didi and Pozzo in *Waiting for Godot,* and in Krapp's dialogue with his "double" as tape machine. There are many "doubles" in the plays of Harold Pinter and Edward Albee. Transposing a favored Elizabethan conceit to a commentary on the modern condition, Jean Genet sees man as the eternal "double" lost forever in a hall of mirrors, lost among the myriad reflections of his many self-images, lost among his many shifting reflective awarenesses and identities. Eisnitz's (1961) and Shengold's (1974) comments on the role of the mirror in certain narcissistic characters are quite congruent with Genet's use of them.

In the matter of *Who's Afraid of Virginia Woolf?* Blum (1969: Chapter 8 of this volume) sees the play's central theme of the fantasied adoption as a special variation of the family romance, playing out the many problems the drama's characters have with identity and reality, the many feelings of loneliness and estrangement metaphorically intrinsic to the "games" by which they know life. What has not been seen is Albee's ironic use of fluid identities, in which George and Martha are at once the first adoptive parents of us all as Americans and the "double" of each other. For this is a savage play about a homosexual "marriage" in which all the characters are "doubles" so often chosen as the narcissistic object choices of such "marriages," playing out the cruel sadomasochistic games of wit and invective about loss and betrayal that homosexuals are wont to play among themselves. And, as all homosexual "marriages" must, that of George and Martha ends "childless," when, with all fantasy cruelly failed, the play ends on that last terrible telegram—"Our son is dead."

Consequently, the problem of the "double" as a split self has been a special interest in psychobiographic studies. Eissler (1963), in tacit agreement with Rank's (1914) original thesis, considers Wilhelm Meister to be the *Doppelganger* of Goethe and, through him, of Hamlet, with the "double" representing the projection of Goethe's own feared aggression. I am more in agreement with Greenacre's (1953, 1955, 1958) view on the matter, beginning as she does from a premise of "ego splitting," originally cited by Freud (1927, 1940 [1938]) in the problem of fetishism. Greenacre (1955a, 1958a) postulates the presence of a special developmental narcissistic vicissitude which she observed in certain other disorders, namely fetishism and addiction, wherein an expected body-image closure, which normally occurs about eighteen months attendant upon the structuring of self- and object-constancy, does not occur for inborn or developmental traumatic reasons. In such individuals, a sense of unclosure is retained within the body image contribution to the structuralizations of the self-system. Though originating in the oral phase this sense of body image unclosure becomes elaborated in turn in the conflictual rhetoric specific to each succeeding oral, anal, and genital phase. Greenacre (1953, 1955a) has previously described such narcissistic defect as determinate in the respective quest for body image closure in fetishism and addiction, noting that in certain especially gifted persons the phenomenological correlate of this body image unclosure operates within the structuralized self-system as a sense of "otherness" and "apartness," and which often is resolved as a "family romance" (Greenacre 1958b). This special developmental resolution is often seen in the latency of the creative person, where the sense of being an alienated "loner" becomes subsumed in an attitude of dedicated "apartness" in the artist who creates in exile from his society (Coltrera 1962, 1965), or even as a sense of religious vocation (Coltrera 1965). Greenacre (1958a) believes the creative process to be turned over to the service of this quest for narcissistic closure in such individuals.

In another clinical context, Arlow (1960) has demonstrated how the fantasy system intrinsic to twinship operates according to an implicit principle of the "double," wherein each twin consensually validates the reality testing of the other's self- and object-representations. Operating from a similar premise and citing the creative works of the twin playwrights, Anthony and Peter Shaffer, Glenn (1974a, 1974b, 1974d), has advanced the thesis that the "double" characteristics of twinship are elaborated in the character delineations of these writers. Glenn sees the implicit organizing metaphor of the twin as the "double" operating in the lifelong identification with the other twin and in the prominent rise of identification as a defense in such individuals. Glenn believes that the special developmental difficulty twins have in establishing object constancy has specific resonance in the repetitive themes of the uncertain and fluid nature of identity and reality seen in the plays of these particular twin playwrights.

A variant concern with the role of the "double" in the creative process is seen in those studies which interest themselves with the complementary roles of creative pairs in creativity. In this context, Meyer (1967) has stressed the "secret sharing" central to the relationship of Joseph Conrad and Ford Maddox Ford, pointing out that Conrad's writing block can be dated to his break with Ford. Beres (1951) has also commented on the mutually reinforcing and resonating influence that Samuel Taylor Coleridge and William Wordsworth had on one another's creative work. Certainly the more overtly homosexual relationship between the older Paul Verlaine and the adolescent Arthur Rimbaud represents the reinforcing effect of narcissistic object choice implicit to such "double" relationships upon the creative process of the other. Indeed, can we read *The Waste Land* and know where the lines of T. S. Eliot leave off and the corrective strophes of Ezra Pound take over? Surely, the content of the plays of Anton Chekhov cannot be separated from the director's notes of Constantin Stanislavsky which gave them so much of their form, nor should the writings of Thomas Wolfe and F. Scott Fitzgerald be considered apart from their transmuting relationship with their editor, Maxwell Perkins.

Such relationships are not unknown to clinical practice, representing special problems of split transference in the analysis of creative persons given to such "secret sharing." These most complex problems in narcissistic identifications must be understood, I believe, in the developmental terms of the early beginnings of separation-individuation, animate dialogue and the structuring of reciprocity. In passing, I would warn against excess therapeutic zeal on the part of the analyst in resolving these special transference relationships as though they were ordinary, incapacitating neurotic attachments, for their premature breakup ends often as not in a creative work block on the part of the creative "secret sharer." The "secret sharing" seen in the "double" personality presents some special problems for the training analysis and the supervisory relationship, specifically in the case of those candidates who can do their own analytic work only when in a formal analysis or who can carry on an analysis only when under formal supervision.

For the "double" with his special problems in self- and object-constancy, to be alone is not so much a problem in alienation as it is of an estranged incompleteness. He is dependent on the "secret sharing" with his complementary companion to continually reify his identity and reality. This concern has been raised to poignant metaphor and image in modern literature, in which man is thought of as held prisoner in the eyrie of his own consciousness, each knowing the other only as faint tappings from other closed rooms. It is the organizing metaphor of *The Waste Land,* in which T. S. Eliot comments on this sad reflexive isolation of man locked in the closed rooms of his consciousness:

> I have heard the key
> Turn in the door once and turn once only
> We think of the key, each in his prison
> Thinking of the key, each confirms a prison.

The image is central to the prison metaphors of Franz Kafka and Jean Genet, the closed rooms of Samuel Beckett and Harold Pinter, and in André Malraux's vision of man as a metaphysical loneliness. To Henrik Ibsen "I" is the underground capital where all things happen to us, and in whose closed rooms soul murder is done.

Shengold (1975: Chapter 6 of this volume) has a particular interest in this last crime against identity, especially in the role an early attempt at soul murder played in the early work and thought of Rudyard Kipling. While first used by Anselm von Feuerbach, the concept was brought to modern awareness by Auguste Strindberg, who, in an article on Henrik Ibsen's *Rosmersholm,* noted that while physical murder was declining in the West, psychical (soul) murder was increasing. Ibsen specifically cited this crime against identity in *John Gabriel Bjorkman,* agreeing with Strindberg that soul murder, depriving a person as it did of his basic reason for living, was fast becoming the ultimate identity crisis of the modern condition.

When Ibsen's character Nora slams the door leaving her murderous "doll house," the closed room of her identity, it is to flee and thus save the life still left in her soul. Both Strindberg and Ibsen saw soul murder as not only the destruction of the individuality of another by someone close enough to effect such devastation, but also as the devastation visited on the individual by the dehumanizing intent of an industrialized society. *An Enemy of the People* raises to terrible metaphor the polemic Karl Marx and Heinrich Heine levelled originally against the soul murder of men reduced to objects by the dehumanizing premise of capitalist society. Both Strindberg and Ibsen seem closer to Erikson than to Freud in that they too restrict such soul murder to the identity crises of the post-oedipal years, especially of the adolescent and adult years.

Not coincidentally, the concept first appeared in the psychiatric literature following its citation in the memoirs of Daniel Paul Schreber (1903), thereupon to be investigated by Freud (1911b) and more recently by Niederland (1959a, 1959b: Volume 2 of this series) in their respective psychobiographic studies of that paranoid jurist. The concept has been pertinently widened by such psychohistorical studies of soul murder as those done on the victims of concentration camps (Niederland 1961, 1964) and to the targets of atomic holocaust (Lifton 1968). Certainly Kovel's (1970) study of the roots of anti-black sentiments in a predominately white society should be included as a comparable example of soul murder done to the black identity.

Soul murder appears to be a unique and profound kind of self-esteem pathology which might be best understood within a developmental approach to the problems of narcissism (See Jacobson 1953, 1964, 1971, Mahler 1972, Greenacre 1953, 1957, 1958b). Shengold (1975) has placed his construction within this developmental frame of reference, viewing soul murder as a breaking up of the victim's identity into contradictory fragments that function independently, with the self-images of the parents considered to be vertically split and irreconcilable.

Rudyard Kipling was a loved and secure child until the age of six, when his parents left him behind in England on their return to India. Between the ages of six and twelve Rudyard and his younger sister, Trixie, were like orphans in the care of cruel foster parents. Shengold sees the attempted soul murder devolving upon three critical psychological changes: the loss of the young Kipling's parents, the soul murder itself, with overstimulation and overwhelming rage, threatening as that must have been not only to Kipling's identity but also to the developing autonomies of his self-system; and the castration anxiety readily available to a six-year-old boy at the height of his oedipal conflict. The overwhelming nature of the desertion in this unprepared child is reminiscent of the problems described by Anna Freud (1939–1945) in her studies of the children evacuated during the London Blitz of World War II. Shengold believes this to have been more of a trauma for the younger Trixie, who at three and a half years had not yet fully structuralized need-object constancy. I would also stress that the years of the attempted soul murder in the young Rudyard, six to twelve, spanned those latency years some investigators (Greenacre 1957, 1958a, Coltrera 1962, 1965) have found to be especially critical in creative persons. The reparative uses which fantasy served to explain the abandoned "loner" aspects of the young boy's family romance variant shows up often in the writings of the older Kipling, in the repetitive theme of the different and differing "loner" hero who wins over oppressive and cruel fate and its agents.

In this matter, Shengold believes that Kipling not only defended against his masochistic strivings by an identification with the persecutor, but turned an avenging anger against all displacements of the original oppressors of his years of abandonment and desolation. Kipling never forgot what it was like to be the dehumanized victim of such soul murder, saving some of his most empathic sensibilities and impassioned writings for the dehumanized and disenfranchised poor of Victorian England—the "murdered" Scots, Welsh, and Irish souls—who went off to fight the Queen's colonial wars on a far-off Northwest Frontier or in the Mahdi's Sudan. He saw these soldiers as a motley of "murdered" souls who were granted an architectonic identity as a British square; ironically, they in turn disenfranchised the poor of other lands and visited on them the soul murder intrinsic to a *Pax Brittania*:

> I have eaten your bread and salt
> I have drunk your water and wine
> The deaths ye died I have watched beside
> And the lives ye led were mine.
> ["Departmental Ditties"]

Only John Ford approaches Kipling in this metaphor and sensibility, in his classic films of the post-Civil War West and its cavalry wars with the Indians. His films with their tender and deeply felt imageries portray the Irish poor going out to visit on the Plains Indians, in the name of manifest destiny, the same soul murder which had been done them in the famine years of a nineteenth-century Ireland. The metaphors of both Kipling and Ford honor the old Celtic tradition by which the poet-minstrel sat at the right hand of the king, their exiled soldiery always marching to the fierce skirl of chanting pipes: *Scotland the Brave, The Minstrel Boy,* and all the other tunes-of-glory that aggressively bind men together as brothers and give them identity in death's common cause:

> The minstrel boy to war has gone
> In the ranks of death you will find him.
> His father's sword he has buckled on,
> And a wild harp slung behind him.[1]

Similarly, the blues can be considered the ultimate songs of soul murder. These are Black songs of devastation and loss, of trains that pass north from one soul-murdering country into another:

> I'd rather drink muddy water Lord, sleep in a hollow log,
> I'd rather drink muddy water Lord, sleep in a hollow log,
> Than be up here in New York, treated like a dirty dog.
> [*Muddy Water Blues*]

And of ladies who do what they must as they await the exile's return, from one death to another:

> 219 done took my baby away,
> 219 took my baby away,
> 217 bring him back someday.

---

1. John Huston, in a sensitive reading of Kipling's *The Man Who Would Be King,* binds that terrible failed family romance together as tragic quest, by the sad, thematic repetition through his film of *The Minstrel Boy.*

Stood on the corner, her feet all soaking wet,
Begging each and every man that she met.
If you can't give a dollar, give me a lousy dime,
If you can't give a dollar, give me a lousy dime.
I want to feed that hungry man of mine.
[*Mamie's Blues*]

Several recent inquiries into the reasons for the foreclosure of identity formation that is too often the tragic lot of growing up black in America — the psychohistoric studies of Coles (1967) and Kovel (1970), as well as the more sociocultural one done by Hauser (1971) — have amply demonstrated the many developmental occasions of soul murder that have tragically influenced the black experience in this country, the joined immolations imposed by psychohistorical conditions upon their identity formations and basic commitment to life. The very name *blues* reflects the profound self-esteem pathology that is the mark of such soul murder; sad songs of alienation, denigration, and loss. These are sad songs about the lonely Icarus-flights by which men seek their identity:

Mama may have, Papa may have,
But God bless the child that's got his own,
That's got his own.
[*God Bless the Child,* Holiday-Herzog;
Edward B. Marks Music Corp., BMI]

Almost half of the Union Army in the Civil War and the cavalry wars in the West were the disenfranchised Irish poor, and the war in Vietnam was fought by an almost similar measure of the black poor. We wait for a Kipling of the Black experience, who may draw on his own developmental experience of soul murder and comment meaningfully on his own ironic participation in that tragic Indochina adventure, visiting, as it were, soul murder on another historically disenfranchised people by those who have known more than their own fair share. It seems almost fitting that such consideration comes full circle in its incumbency upon the black heirs of those who first broke a British square, that ultimate metaphor of past cloned soul murders done in the name of manifest destiny, wherein murdered souls were granted identity by the aggressive bonding intrinsic to that architectonic metaphor:

So 'ere's to *you,* Fuzzy Wuzzy, at your 'ome in the Sowdan;
You're a poor benighted 'eathen but a first class fightin' man:

An 'ere's to *you* Fuzzy Wuzzy, with your 'ayrick' 'ead of 'air —
You big black boundin' beggar — for you bruk a British square.
[Rudyard Kipling, "Fuzzy Wuzzy"]

The facts fairly beg for the inclusion of newer developmental approaches in the method, as well as implicitly asking whether psychobiography can be truly separated from psychohistorical considerations in an expanded developmental sense. For example, would not the complementary work of René Spitz and Konrad Lorenz enlarge our understanding of the problems with the preoedipal vicissitudes of aggression so often seen in those who have experienced soul murder? Spitz (1963, 1964) has demonstrated the critical role of the development of animate dialogue, with its implied structuring of reciprocity, in the conjoined epigenesis of aggression and adaptation, as did Lorenz (1963), who, working from ethological evidences, was able to show the critical relation that exists between aggression and object-bonding.

When we examine the concept of soul murder according to such developmental updating of modern narcissistic theory, we are presented with the developmental truth that souls are indeed "murdered" at the alienating behest of a technological society that reduces men to redundant objects. Can a society which systematically and significantly compromises access of the Black poor to an animate dialogue experience, through the early absence of one or both parents because of socioeconomic pressures, not be accused of institutionalized soul murder? Should we not properly invoke the original polemical intent of interpretation to cite the awful developmental consequence of such institutionalized compromising of animate dialogue experience, with its consequently flawed epigenesis of aggression and adaptation? Can we separate the high incidence of violence among the Black poor from this developmental and psychosocial constellation of events? Or, those problems of adaptation, wherein "cool" attitudes are too often characterological expressions of derealization and depersonalization, seriously compromising the "fitting-in" required of a person before he can belong to and use the society for his own ends?

Phyllis Greenacre must be considered the first psychobiographer to apply her special knowledge of early ego development, gained from her own child observations and from reconstructions done with her patients, in her essentially developmental considerations of certain narcissistic vicissitudes in the study of creative persons. Glenn's (1974a, 1974b) use of data from the studies of twins and adopted children in his psychobiographic reconstructions essentially follows Greenacre's emphasis on early childhood apart from any sociohistoric considerations.

The genetic premise of most psychobiographic studies is essentially that of the Leonardo study, their developmental point of view restricted to the dyad and triad relationships and conflicts of the preoedipal and oedipal periods. This has often ended in constructions organized around a "genetic fallacy" (Hartmann and Kris 1945, Erikson 1958, 1974), in which all later events are explained according to earlier ones. And while one cannot accept Erikson's premise that the identity crises of young adulthood are equally as determinant as the classical infantile neurosis, it must be said that the role in creativity of the special developmental events of latency, adolescence, adulthood, and old age are only now being given their due psychodynamic attention. Indeed, the emphasis on the restricted object relationships of the family, the life space of the infant and child, has contributed in significant part to the scanting of a psychosocial and psychohistorical point of view in most psychobiographic studies. For while the infant and child is actually restricted to the dyad and triad situations of the family, the young adult necessarily moves in additional social and historical contexts. Where Greenacre disregards the pertinancy of psychosocial considerations in her constructions, Erikson makes strong argument that psychobiography has no meaning apart from psychohistory. Insisting that "we cannot fit a case history out of history," Erikson (1958, pp. 15–16) focuses upon the great man and his inner conflicts within a specific historical context.

I think that Bergmann (1973) overstates the case in excluding Erikson from the proper psychoanalytic premises of valid psychobiography, for I believe the latter is in valid continuance of late adaptive theory in ego psychology, now applied to the psychobiographic method. While Hartmann's theory of adaptation (1939, Hartmann and Kris 1945, Hartmann, Kris, and Loewenstein 1951) included a generalized theory of reality relations, stressing the special role of social relations, it did not provide a specific and differentiated psychosocial theory (Rappaport 1959). This led Erikson (1950) to particularize Hartmann's theory of reality relations into a psychosocial theory of object relations, postulating a life cycle spanning a sequence of psychosocial phases. Each phase was characterized by a phase specific developmental task it must resolve, with each society cogwheeling with the developmental phases of its members by institutions specific to it. Erikson considers the problems of identity apart from the preoedipal and oedipal conflicts, and in this I find the psychobiographic method better served in the questions of identity and reality—the ultimate questions of narcissism—by the constructions of Jacobson, Greenacre, and Mahler.

Both Erikson and Freud are the familiars of a German Romantic faith in *Kairos,* believing that the lives and thought of great men devolve upon crucial life experiences. While both see the great man as a spiritual hero who redefines and rededicates himself by this critical intrapsychic breakthrough, Erikson is not so much concerned with the psychopathology of his subject as in how he rose above it to greatness. Going beyond Freud's more restricted model of oedipal conflict, Erikson applies the broader developmental theory of cogwheeling like cycles to all the members of a contained psychosocial system, relating those life cycles to the history of their societies. Thus, Luther would overcome his own identity crisis by bringing about a shift in the historical identity of his time.

In this, *Young Man Luther* (Erikson 1958) is closer to *Moses and Monotheism* (Freud 1939) than it is to the Leonardo study, and its title is meant to echo Freud's phrase "the man Moses" (Lifton 1970). As Freud saw Moses taking the Jews to a higher level of spirituality, so does Erikson regard Luther as having led the way to a "new emphasis on man in *inner* conflict and his salvation through introspective perfection" (1958, p. 214). Here is the spiritual hero who changes history on the occasion of a critical intrapsychic breakthrough. Taking a position median between Freud and Kierkegaard, Erikson sees man positing himself according to the moral imperative of a nineteenth-century idealism, man as a *cogito* ever engaged in ontological quests for identity within the existent orders of reflective awareness.

Accepting the defining operational assumption of the psychoanalytic idea that an interpretation is a conjoined dynamic and genetic explanation, Erikson extends the genetic premise to include sociohistorical determinants. Man in this view is an historical animal who not only operates within the contexts of present time and place, but also in a dialectic of psychohistory, operating within a shared continuum of ideas, ideals, values, and directives bound and imposed by the adaptive function of the superego, which grants him a place within the cohesive identity of his social and historical group. Erikson is essentially concerned with the question of how the great man turns over the aggressions intrinsic to his conflicts to the service of leadership, serving as this must the greater ends of culture-building by helping others to deal with their own disruptive oedipal conflicts.

Accordingly, Luther is considered within the psychohistorical conditions of his sixteenth century, an ideological heir to the recent Renaissance emphasis on the singularity of man as an experiential existent, and a temporal ally to lesser German princes in their confrontation with the secular powers of the Church. In resolving a critical personal identity crisis, Luther brought about the historical identity of his own time. Lifting himself above his "individual patienthood" (Erikson 1958, pp. 13–14) to the level of a universal one. Luther solved for all what he could not solve for himself alone.

Luther was born the harbinger and familiar of a newly emerging narcissistic shift in the self-awareness of Western man as a singularly reflective being, a shift that would end in one mode in a nineteenth-century idealist tradition and its contained idea of interpretation. Luther would define the god-experience as being necessarily conditioned by that self-experience of reflective awareness. In this he was preceded by a great revolutionary mystical tradition, that of Theresa of Avila, John of the Cross, and others, all insisting on the instinctualized knowing of a personal God (Coltrera 1965, 1966). Compare the scatological assault on the Godhead by Luther, with the erotized knowing chosen by St. Theresa of Genoa:

> Before my God,
> I am as the sea cleaving open to the fish.

Although we may, with a topographic-economic viewpoint, generally explain these mystical experiences with such teleological descriptive clichés as "fusion" and "oceanic feelings," we still beg the larger psychohistorical question of why did these God-mad mystics, insisting as they did on a most personalized and instinctualized knowing of their God, appear in a certain time and place, contributing as they most certainly did to the breaking up of the last vestiges of the Holy Roman Empire at the sufferance of the several resolutions of their critical identity crises?

While all the other revolutionary mystics cited experienced their God-knowing in essentially erotized terms, Luther is uniquely separate in the aggressivized rhetoric of his mystical experience. Crushed by his father's alternately severe rejecting and caring attitudes, Luther developed a profound fear of him. Buffeted by the severe demands of giving in to his father or experiencing a profound castration anxiety, Luther, in Erikson's view, became of necessity one of the great rebutters and protestants of history. At twenty-one years of age, his adolescence brought to a close by a severe identity crisis, Luther gave in to his father and entered a monastery. He remained a priest until the momentous and apochryphal breaking through of his identity crisis in the choir at Erfut, raving in prescient protest, "It is not me," or "I am not." Whether this was in Latin or German, we do not know; that he was the first Protestant, we do. What is clear was a great mental anguish with his monastic experience of an overwhelming and unremitting Church authority between the ages of twenty-two and thirty, an identity crisis out of which Luther emerged with a new kind of religious and ethical awareness. It was an identity crisis whose resolution forever split the integrity of the Roman Catholic Church and its interposing presence between man and his God.

According to Erikson, the profound neurotic crisis and its serious inhibition was followed by a period of delay and integration out of which came Luther's radical view of the direct relatedness of man to his God, a singular doctrine which caused all others who followed to stand fast before personal and spiritual authorities. His hatred of a personal and religious "father" was mastered, with emancipation winning out over patricidal impulses, and religious teachings prevailing over the more scatological invective to which he was prone. Erikson chooses to emphasize the determinant primacy of the identity crisis of Luther's young adulthood. Luther's celebrated scatological battles with his loved-hated, castrating father, however, indicates the probability of significant preoedipal and oedipal roots to his religious identity crisis as well.

The Luther of this thesis evokes certain narcissistic conflicts seen in some creative patients (Coltrera 1966), in whom the continuance of severe anal phase pressure into the phallic phase not only compromises the ncessary autonomies of that phase upon which will depend the proper structuring of the superego at that phase end, but which will also cause objects to be anally split according to a primitive value system of "all-good" or "all-bad." As was the case with Luther and certainly with Jonathan Swift, these patients are especially given to scatologically reject not only their own creative products but those of others as well, and most especially, those of the analyst himself during the difficult times of negative transference that marks the course of these analyses. Never is analytic tact so critical as in the perilous management of the negative transferences seen during these times of heightened narcissistic fragility, replete with their hurt, angry silences, ending as they so often do in almost paranoid and scatological denunciations of the analyst. Such narcissistic structure formation, with its primitive anal splitting mechanisms, is often coupled with severe self-esteem pathology and a continuance of primitive magical and sadistic preoedipal identifications (Jacobson 1953, 1964, 1971). In these circumstances we may be presented with serious paranoid behavior coupled with experiences of depersonalization, which seem quite reminiscent of the religious identity crisis experienced by Luther.

Jacobson (1964, 1971) has described certain gifted acting-out patients with similar personality structures, individuals who tend to devastating experiences of anxiety, shame, and inferiority because of their aggrandized wished-for self-images. These are unremittingly demanding self-images which remain magical enclaves of primitive preoedipal identifications in the ego and superego of such patients, which lend themselves to grandiose sexual and aggressive narcissistic-exhibitionist strivings. Perhaps most pertinent to the first Protestant, Luther, is that such persons are characterized by an inability to accept and share for any length of time the moral and value imperatives of the society in which they live (Coltrera 1966). With an angry arrogance they walk out of their society, becoming the betrayed "outsider" who now dedicates himself to a life of polemical protest and intellectual insurgency. In truth, they never belonged, and are Pirandellan characters in angry search for an identity that always seems to elude them.

Up to this point stress has been laid on the compromising lack of a developmental point of view in the premises of most studies, but there is an almost equally glaring omission in their constructions of aggression save as analogues of the second instinct theory, in which the death instinct—Thanatos—is made to stand apposed within metaphor to Eros.

Of all psychobiographers and psychohistorians, probably the one most concerned with the vicissitudes of aggression in his subject is Erikson. In *Young Man Luther,* Erikson concerns himself with the question of how the great man turns the aggressions intrinsic to his conflicts over to the service of leadership, binding people together in culture by helping them deal with their disruptive oedipal conflicts. However, Erikson seems to depend more on teleological description than metapsychological premise in accounting for how Luther's great anal-sadistic and narcissistic aggressive conflicts were transmuted from conflicted protest to a culture-transmuting Protestantism. Operating from better methodology in *Gandhi's Truth,* Erikson (1969) pays a somewhat stricter attention to the vicissitudes of aggression in Gandhi's life.

Erikson employed an innovative approach in his study of Gandhi, whose life was contemporary with the biographer's. Erikson travelled to India and stayed in the home of Ambalal Sarabhai, the owner of the textile mill in Ahmedabad against whom Gandhi led the 1918 strike. This was the historic strike in which *Satyagraha*—the non-violent doctrine of passive resistance—was first used.

Erikson advised that the psychoanalytic biographer use himself as an "analyzing instrument" in gathering significant anamnestic materials, not so much in an "attempt to analyse the man [but] rather his participation in the event" (1969, p. 73). Clearly, this is a method whose dependence on projective identification is fraught with opportunity for countertransference excess, and as such must be applied conditionally and in a continuous watchfulness for such possibilities.

The crucial event in Gandhi's life, as with Freud, was the death of his father. In the case of Freud that death initiated a self-analysis, whose autobiography was *The Interpretation of Dreams* and whose radically transmuting idea was interpretation. In the case of Gandhi, that death led to the radical technique of nonviolence, *Satyagraha,* whose transmuted non-violent aggression brought the British Raj to his knees and forced the abandonment of the Indian subcontinent.

Erikson traced the vicissitudes of this aggression throughout Gandhi's life, and the ways which he mastered that aggression by turning his propensity for violence into the nonviolent doctrine of *Satyagraha.* Erikson did this through constructions that remain curiously apart from drive theory and developmental concepts as they are usually employed. While Gandhi directly cited the integrally joined nature of sexuality and aggression for the inherent incompatibility of sexuality and nonviolence and argued for celibacy in those who followed *Satyagraha.* Erikson is curiously hesitant in referring to a dual instinct theory save in metaphysical aside. Erikson vitiates the drive-organized sense of conflicts confronted and mastered by Gandhi as he converted violent oedipal wishes to his father into nonviolent, caring, feminine attitudes to that parent, attitudes that he would transfer to all the other men of the Indian subcontinent. As was the case with Luther and his father, Erikson is able to describe brilliantly the radical shift from active to passive instinctual modes by which Gandhi caused aggression to paradoxically serve the nonviolent needs of *Satyagraha.* But Erikson makes no significant dynamic, let alone genetic, connections to the joined problems of moral masochism and latent homosexuality in Gandhi, especially as they directly bore on the reversal of instinctual modalities upon which *Satyagraha* emerged and developed.

While Erikson is right to stress the neglect heretofore accorded to post-oedipal developmental conflicts in applied psychoanalytic studies, his explanation of nearly everything in terms of post-oedipal identity crises to the virtual neglect of preoedipal and oedipal determinants becomes a psychohistoric fallacy of its own. In this Erikson goes counter to the "rise of the object" (Kris 1952b) in psychoanalysis which has dominated developmental interest since 1926. The statement of a second theory of anxiety (Freud 1926) with its notion of signal anxiety and anxiety as a summating genetic series, shifted interest from the dominant triad object relationship of the oedipal period to the dyadic one — the child to its mother — of the pre-oedipal phase. Interestingly enough, the one psychoanalytic biographer, who did the most to introduce developmental contexts to that method, Phyllis Greenacre, specifically excludes psychosocial contexts from her constructions, refuting, as it were, Erikson's contention that psychobiography subsumes psychohistory.

Probably the great single flaw in Erikson's methodology to my mind is his almost calculated avoidance of drive theory, as it is ordinarily understood, in his constructions. Though the crucial events on which the life and work of both Luther and Gandhi turned are redolent with the most libidinized and aggressivized rhetorics, Erikson's psychohistoric constructions remain strangely removed from any significant reference to the drive-meanings ordinarily ascribed to such situations. Not only is one left with begged psychohistoric questions about how nonviolence as a conjoined doctrine and technique originates in the conditions of a Gandhi as apposed, say, to those of a Leo Tolstoy, but one is also left as before with the special problem aggression presents for both the life and work of creative individuals. The creative person, conditioned as he often is by unique developmental pressures that shape his narcissistic vicissitudes, is heir quite frequently to severe self-esteem pathology (Coltrera 1965), beset by the frequently conjoined problems of creative work block and profound depression that too often end in the tragic and absurd resolution of suicide. The names Virginia Woolf, Ernest Hemingway, John Berryman, Yukio Mishima, Anne Sexton, and Sylvia Plath stand as a sad litany of such resolutions.

Suicide seems to have become the special apocalyptic defiance of the artist toward his alienated lot in a modern society. Suicide, in this sense, has been the failed grace-note of the modern predicament since at least the eighteenth century, granted its elegiac model in the person of Thomas Chatterton, perhaps the most famous of all literary suicides. At sixteen Chatterton had gulled the English literary world by writing an apocryphal body of poetry that he ascribed successfully to a fictive fifteenth-century Irish monk. The deception was successful until, in a fatal miscalculation, Chatterton confessed to Horace Walpole on the mistaken hope that the notoriously parsimonious Walpole would become his patron. Born poor in the eighteenth century, Chatterton was constrained to live ever poor unless he found a patron who could help him rise above his circumstance. Suicides in this age of reason, Alvarez (1971) has pointed out, were more often the result of bankruptcy than of failed love. So it was with Thomas Chatterton, who did not kill himself out of some profound defeat of the spirit or out of any unrequited love, but for the mean and absurd reason that his promised sponsor died unexpectedly and Chatterton could not support himself from his writings.

The age washed out the meanness of the death and Chatterton became the elegiac myth-figure of the romantic agony, transformed by the Romantics into the tragic young god who must die for all the sins of a newly dehumanized society, the doomed poet who chose death over alienation. His presence was so invoked in Shelley's elegy to John Keats:

> Chatterton
> Rose pale, — his solemn agony had not
> Yet faded from him . . . .
>
> ["Adonais"]

Within four years of Chatterton's death, Goethe wrote the *Sorrows of Young Werther,* clearly modeled on and dedicated to the gathering tragic myth of Thomas Chatterton, wherein the youth of a Romantic age were told that suicide was a humanistic and honorable alternative to a degraded and dehumanizing society, Werther and his double, Chatterton, raised suicide to a literary conceit, the suicide note to a high art form. Alfred de Vigney's play, *Chatterton,* was credited with doubling the suicide rate in France between 1830 and 1840. In Goethe's reading and thereafter, Hamlet became young Werther, the doomed poet who chose death to repudiate his dishonored world and fault the conscience of a king. Indeed, Hamlet is closer to the dark romantic spirit of young Werther than he is to the detached suicides of the noble Stoic heroes of Shakespeare's Roman plays.

Albert Camus represents the last throes of the romantic agony brought to its apogee by the tragic examples of Chatterton and Werther. Camus utilized a philosophical consideration of suicide to examine the absurdity of a life that is its own sum, ending as it must in the nothingness of death, arguing insidiously that "what is called a reason for living is also an excellent reason for dying" (1943, p. 4). And while we may not follow Camus in his hyperbole that "there is but one truly serious philosophical problem, and that is suicide" (p. 3), we can say that it is most certainly as serious a clinical choice as it is a philosophical one for the creative person within the modern predicament.

On a November morning in 1970, having finished his masterpiece, *The Sea of Fertility,* and failing to incite the soldiers at Icchigayu Barrack to a rightist revolt, the Japanese writer Yukio Mishima committed ritual *seppuku* as a rebuke to a new industrialized Japan which had forgotten its Samurai past and honor. To his lover and disciple, Morita, he assigned the final decapitation with the Samurai sword upon which traditional *seppuku* ends, a last act which Arlow (1978: Chapter 3 of this volume) sees as the final act of love in Tarachow's (1960: Chapter 2 of this volume) sense in which the disciple, Morita, became the beloved executioner, as Judas was to Jesus.

In Tarachow's construction, Jesus is the willing victim, offering himself in love to be killed and eaten by the Jews to expiate their sins, and especially those of the loving betrayer Judas. In his love for Jesus, Judas became the instrument of a shared aggression, both the lover and ritual executioner. In the same sense that as a participant of the Godhead Jesus stood omnipotently apart from the other-directed determinancies of human choice, He chose ultimately to die and so must be considered the quintessential suicide.[2]

Neither Freud (1928) nor Kanzer (1951: Chapter 11 of this volume) appreciate that the Passion as iconic suffering is central to Dostoyevsky's imagery and organized metaphor. Continuous references are made in Dostoyevsky's journals and other writings of the effect the sufferings depicted in Hans Holbein's *Descent from the Cross* had upon him. Indeed, no understanding of the central position of Father Zossima in *The Brothers Karamazov* is complete without understanding that the sweet smell of decay continually surrounding that holy man was the metaphorical elaboration of the terrible suffering of the Passion out of which all saving grace derived for Dostoyevsky. The full meaning of moral masochism, especially that contained in the notion of "holy sinning" that so offended Freud (1928), has yet to be given a proper psychohistorical understanding. To the epileptic Dostoyevsky, the evanescence at the cathectic center of self-constancy contained dread intimations of mortality, a dying of the light that rang the overdetermined changes of the entire genetic series of anxiety for him. And so Dostoyevsky gambled on the iconic suffering of Christ; for if He was born, suffered, and died, and then defeated the absurdity implicit to death by His resurrection, then Dostoyevsky too would not end his life upon the absurdity of death. But the Dostoyevsky gambler, whose masochistic fate was always to lose, despairs and has Kirillov, the anti-Christ of *The Possessed,* go to his suicide to prove that Christ's death on the Cross was a self-deception.

In this absurd sense, Kirillov's death was to Dostoyevsky a "logical suicide," and to Camus a "metaphysical crime" whose logic is that of the absurd. "The reasoning is classic in its clarity. If God does not exist, Kirillov is God. If God does not exist, Kirillov must kill himself. Kirillov must kill himself to become God . . . . that amounts to clarifying the premise: If God does not exist, I am God" (Camus 1943, pp. 78–79). More than a metaphysical crime the logic of suicide is quintessentially absurd, a metaphorical conceit gone mad. In the end it is a madness we must address ourselves to as analysts both in the applied and clinical sense, for the deaths of such creative persons cannot be borne either in philosophical premise or out of therapeutic compassion.

2. I discussed this last construction with Dr. Tarachow shortly before his untimely death, and he agreed that the Passion was ultimately an expiative suicide, the ultimate declension of moral masochism raised to a Saving Grace.

As Dostoyevsky was critically affected by the terrible sufferings of Holbein's *Descent from the Cross,* so was Yukio Mishima affected by the Crucifixion depicted in Guido Reni's *The Martyrdom of St. Sebastian.* Mishima's first masturbatory orgasm occurred upon seeing that exciting painting. Binding, crucifixion and ritualized cannibalism became the dominant themes of his masturbation in which he cast himself in both the active and passive roles. Arlow (1978: Chapter 3 of this volume) believes these trends to have been adumbrated by his earlier sadomasochistic preoccupation with the ideas of noble and violent death in battle and Samurai tales. The connection Arlow has made between ritual suicide and ritual sacrifice and the recurring themes of arson and primal scenes in Mishima's writing could also be made for Edward Albee's *Tiny Alice.* The name of the tragic hero, Julian, alludes to the last Roman emperor, the Stoic philosopher Julian the Apostate, on whose sacrifice, almost as much as that of Christ's, the Holy Roman Church was founded. The tiny replica of the larger house of the play — of the greater world outside — burns upon the ritual killing of Julian at the play's end.

Indeed, the condensation of the Crucifixion and a flame that joins him to God is a central metaphor of the greatest of the Spanish mystics, St. John of the Cross, who saw himself as a flame mounting to God. This phallic quest for fusion with the Godhead became the organizing visual metaphor of El Greco, whose paintings were organized along the axis of the defining image of St. John of the Cross, as painterly flames mounting to God (Coltrera 1962). Clearly there can be no meaningful psychobiographic interpretation of these several themes outside of psychohistoric considerations focussing on a seeming relation between suicidal tendencies and certain aspects of artistic creativity.

Orgel (1974a, 1974b, 1981: the last, Chapter 4 of this volume) links suicidal behavior, a Christ-like empathy for victims, and poetic sensibilities, demonstrating his thesis by an examination of Sylvia Plath's last six months before her suicide. Orgel (1981) advances the thesis that under the threat of a critical loss of narcissistically cathected objects, a regressive fusion of self and object may impend in these particular individuals in whom the stage of identification with the aggressor concomitantly fails to function as a chosen mode to externalize in part excessive quantities of unneutralized aggression away from self-representations back onto the object world. Suicide is seen in this context by Orgel as a last-ditch attempt to consummate an active identification with the object as an aggressor, but with an inability to use the projection implicit to this defense of identification with the aggressor. Instead, the aggression is turned against the self in a manner reminiscent of primitive ego and superego functioning, so that the suicide kills both the aggressive self and the object which imposes aggressive frustration, making the subject an idealized victim like the original object. This may be defended against by progressive attempts to establish severe sadomasochistic relationships through identification with the aggressor or by paranoid defenses; and regressively in melancholia, by such somatic defenses against fusion as insomnia and anorexia.

For Sylvia Plath death was a vocation, a promise given even when life was good:

> Dying
> Is an art, like everything else.
> I do it exceptionally well.
>
> I do it so it feels like hell.
> I do it so it feels real.
> I guess you could say I've a call.
> ["Lady Lazarus"]

Sylvia Plath represents for Orgel (1981) the quintessential creative person in whom a common reservoir of relatively unneutralized aggressive energies is shared by creative activity and self-destructive tendencies. In such a person, the creation of a poem represents in a displaced form the killing of the hated part of the self in a partially externalized representation that is both self and object. If the creation is experienced as a loss of the narcissistic self and the poem-object is cathected with primitive defused aggression, the creation is felt to be destroyed in the aftermath of the creative activity, and a self-directed rage is thereupon fostered that is experienced as a primitive form of guilt, demanding a life for a life.

Sylvia Plath was a gifted poet, a prodigy published by the time she was nine. When she was eight her father died of a circulatory disease. She celebrated in her poetry an acute awareness of the traumatic strophe this placed upon her development, marking time as the apparition of her father beckoned her just the other side of the poetic image she offered him in her stead:

> I was ten when they buried you.
> At twenty I tried to die
> And get back, back to you.
> I thought even the bones would do.
> ["Daddy"]

The above is an allusion to the suicide attempt central to *The Bell Jar* (Plath 1971). Upon the next strophe of ten years, when she was thirty, Sylvia Plath honored her troth and succeeded in her death.

Swinburne, it would seem, succeeded where Sylvia Plath failed, offering in his stead an erotized quest for death, a quest that would end in a last oedipal joining with the "great sweet mother and lover of men, the sea." Swinburne bound as much primitive aggression as one man might be expected to bear, burning dark, votive romanticisms to exorcise the nothingness he so feared death to be.

> For there is no God found stronger than
> death; and death is a sleep.
> ["Hymn to Prosperine"]

In Orgel's (1974a, 1974b) sense, then, Sylvia Plath offered her poetry in her stead and failed; in the end crying quit to the ghost that waited beyond her imageries.

> Daddy, Daddy, you bastard, I'm through.

Her poetry failed at the end to lay this angry attendant ghost. He not going, she, at the third ten-year's calling, went.

The problem of suicide in the creative is the more tragic aspect of the problem of aggression in such persons. The vicissitudes experienced in drive epigenesis and with the establishing of self- and object-constancy predispose the creative individual to compromising narcissistic personality structure formation (Coltrera 1965, 1966). The question of suicide in the creative, especially as it is related to unremitting work blocks, cannot be understood apart from the developmental history of their intersystemic and intrasystemic superego conflicts. The truth of this statement is stated in different rhetoric and conceptual contexts by both Durkheim (1897) and Wittgenstein (1914–1916), who argue that suicide is the center on which every ethical system turns.

Greenacre (1957, 1958a,b), for example, has emphasized how the creative individual's autonomous gifts and maturational phase pressures may create special developmental problems which determine the special nature of phase pressures in such personalities. As such the coalescence of unneutralized drive pressures in the phallic-oedipal phase would then in turn compromise the ego's autonomous ability to provide the neutralized aggression needed for the structuring of the superego as a system at the close of that phase, ending as that must with an aggressivization of the aims and modalities of subsequent superego functions. As is often the case with such narcissistic personalities there may be an additional inclusion in the structuring of the superego of archaic and magical preoedipal identifications, which will further accentuate the cruel and unforgiving quality of their superego. These will not only almost surely fault the structural coalescence of the superego in latency but would also almost certainly preclude the critical autonomy of the system-superego at the close of adolescence. This last in turn seriously compromises the regulatory agency of the autonomous superego to the self-system and its affect mechanisms, as well as its ability to determine realistic identity formation. Despair and narcissistic depletion are the unfortunate ordinary conditions of the creative person so developmentally compromised, whose only refuge from the unforgiving and unrealistic demands of his superego is too often a creative work block or a suicidal depression.

The alienated and estranged quality of suicide in many creative persons, with its implicit absurdist argument, suggests that a flawed development of animate dialogue in such individuals may be as determinant in them as the compromised structuralization of the superego is for others. The successful development of an animate dialogue experience not only determines the structuring of reciprocity, but the critical epigenesis of aggression and the adaptive act as well. Modern thought, its literature and its art, is a palimpsest of this flawed developmental series contingent to the emergence of animate dialogue, acute in its concern with the effecting of dialogue between animate others. It is at once distraught with the surfeit of alienation and estrangement around us and bemused with the contentions of Camus and Kirillov that if one can not impose meaning on an absurd life, then one can impose meaning through one's death. The dark romanticism of its concerns represents in great measure the failing adaptive intent of the creative act in such individuals, almost Greek in their tragic acquiescence to the fate built into this ultimate developmental flaw.

Suicide then must be considered the last declension of the narcissistic vicissitudes which are too often the tragic lot of the creative in development. As such, these vicissitudes serve to emphasize the special problem aggression continues to pose for the method. The problem has been demonstrated to be one in which methodological and historical arrests are conjoined, and must be considered to begin in the particular absence of developmental contexts in these studies (Coltrera 1965, Mack 1971). This is in itself a failure—after 1926—to parse the genetic point of view to its logical place within the psychoanalytic idea, ending as it has in psychobiographic and psychohistoric constructions that have bowdlerized the tragic intent of the second instinct theory, reducing offsetting instinctual balances to a metaphoric confrontation between Eros and Thanatos.

But the dust of metaphoric encounter settles and analogical exposition leaves us in the operational limbo of "as-if." We are still left to explain not only how man structures and maintains his own psychic systems and his object world at the developmental sufferance of his experience and mastery of aggression, but also the critical role of such mastery in the concerns and beliefs by which men bind themselves in social systems.

Where conflict is the ordinary existential estate of man, how he experiences and masters aggression within and apart from such conflict determines in great part how social and political systems emerge and persevere in that existence. Who better than ourselves, then, to give dynamic meaning to the vicissitudes of power in such political systems and in those to whom power accrues? A measure of this awareness may be inferred from the shift occurring in psychobiographic custom, from studies of artists and writers to political and historical figures. More than a metaphorical question is being posed to method when we ask how political acts can be distinguished from acting-out behavior in political leaders in whom the vicissitudes of power are most ordinarily expressed through public acts and symbolic actions.

Mack (1971) has raised a cogent question as to whether any psychobiographic profile of a political or historical figure can be considered meaningfully apart from developmental considerations. Certainly the adaptive modes of conflict resolution used by that person during specific developmental periods of his life would have great characterological relevance to how he would confront and resolve conflict during the later time of his leadership. Similarly, questions as to how great political leaders use and relate to power would be most germane to how they would respond to the crises which are the ordinary state of great nations in these times.

Lord Acton's warning that power corrupts has passed from an aphorism to a proper psychoanalytic concern. His further admonition that absolute power tends to corrupt absolutely becomes a pressing concern for psychoanalytic investigation. George Stade, in his foreword to Solzhenitzyn's *One Day in the Life of Ivan Denisovich* (1963), tells us of a similar view taken by Nikita Khrushchev before the fateful Twenty-Second Congress of the Communist Party, when in speaking of the many abuses of Josef Stalin, he said: "It is our duty to gain a thorough and comprehensive understanding of the nature of the matters related to the abuses of power" (p. 13).

While not so murderous in its custom and intent as that of Josef Stalin, the paranoid depression which ended in the suicide of James Forrestal while he was Secretary of Defense represented a grave problem not only for ourselves then but for the world at large. Rogow's study (1963) begs the pertinent and rather sinister question of when Forrestal's paranoid process lost its adaptedness and began to compromise his estimates of Russia's intentions toward this country. Rogow considers the more germane and prickly questions implicit in the above: how is a government to judge competently whether an important official's mental illness is no longer adaptive and represents a clear danger to the country? Of course such a question is followed by a corollary: once such a judgment has been made, what shall be done?

A clear case can be made for pertinent and continuing interdisciplinary studies of political leaders and the problems and the uses and abuses of power contingent to such leadership. In consequence, there has been an increasing collaboration between psychoanalysts, psychiatrists, and psychologists with political scientists, sociologists, anthropologists, lawyers, historians, and biographers, with an increasing enrollment of these latter as students in psychoanalytic institutes. There seems to be a harbinger here of a return to a better time in the psychoanalytic idea, to a time where the ideas discussed of a Wednesday night in Vienna had cogency and meaning for Bloomsbury intellectuals in London.

We may be coming to a time when direct anamnestic approaches to important political and cultural figures will be possible. Perhaps these findings might be published sometime after the death of these persons as is now the case with much of their private papers and correspondence. The massive anamnestic and psychological test data from the many important Nazi officials on trial at Nuremberg represents such a critical, though inherently flawed, order of psychobiographic and psychohistoric evidence heretofore not available.

For better and probably for worse, psychoanalysts and psychiatrists have become the familiars of intelligence agencies, taking the measure of the vicissitudes of power and those who exercise it in the world. Thus was Wedge (1968) asked to provide a psychological profile of Nikita Khrushchev for John Kennedy's first meeting with the Russian premier in Vienna in 1960. Khrushchev did indeed sorely test the mettle of the new President as predicted, no doubt according to a psychobiographic profile of the new president supplied by the Soviet intelligence agencies. Two years later, the CIA would use a sophisticated updating of Wedge's original psychological profile in predicting Khrushchev's decision-making tendencies during the Cuban missile crisis. While quite close to an occasion of sin, this may have been psychobiography's finest hour, a surmise that may be drawn from the fact that we are here to make it at all.

References

Alvarez, A. (1971). *The Savage God.* New York: Bantam Books, 1973.

Arlow, J. (1960). Fantasy systems in twins. *Psychoanalytic Quarterly* 29: 175–209.

———(1978). Pyromania and the primal scene: a psychoanalytic comment on the work of Yukio Mishima. *Psychoanalytic Quarterly* 47:24–51. Chapter 3 of this volume.

Bays, G. (1964). *The Orphic Vision.* Lincoln: University of Nebraska Press.

Beres, D. (1951). A dream, a vision, and a poem: a psychoanalytic study of "The Rime of the Ancient Mariner." *International Journal of Psycho-Analysis* 32:97–116.

Bergmann, M. S. (1973). Limitations of method in psychoanalytic biography. *Journal of the American Psychoanalytic Association* 21:833–850.

Bernfeld, S. (1931). Trieb und Tradition in Jugendelter. *Beiheft Z. angew. Psychol.* 54:1–181.

Blum, H. (1969). A psychoanalytic view of "Who's Afraid of Virginia Woolf." *Journal of the American Psychoanalytic Association* 17:888–903. Chapter 8 of this volume.

Breuer, J., and Freud, S. (1893–1895). Studies on hysteria. *Standard Edition* 2:1–335.

Bry, L., Bayne, H., and Myrl, E. (1953). Bibliography of early psychoanalytic monographs. *Journal of the American Psychoanalytic Association* 519–525.

Bullitt, W. C., and Freud, S. (1967). *Thomas Woodrow Wilson, Twenty-eighth President of the United States: A Psychological Study.* Boston: Houghton Mifflin.

Camus, A. (1943). *The Myth of Sisyphus.* New York: Random House, 1959.

Cassirer, E. (1946). *Language and Myth.* New York: Harper.

Coles, R. (1967). *Children of Crisis: A Study of Courage and Fear.* Boston: Little, Brown.

Coltrera, J. T. (1962). Psychoanalysis and existentialism. *Journal of the American Psychoanalytic Association* 10:166–215.

———(1963). The Gifts of Daedalus: An Adaptive Function of the Superego. Presented before the Boston Psychoanalytic Society 24 April 1963.

———(1965). On the creation of beauty and thought: the unique as vicissitude. *Journal of the American Psychoanalytic Association* 13:634–703.

———(1966). The creative imagination, adaptation, and dialogue: metaphor and device in a modern theatre and literature. Presented before the Chicago Psychoanalytic Society 26 April 1966.

————(1981). On the nature of interpretation: epistemology as practice. In *Clinical Psychoanalysis,* ed. S. Orgel and B. Fine (vol. 3 of the Downstate Twenty-fifth Anniversary Series). New York: Jason Aronson.

Coltrera, J. T., and Ross, N. (1967). Freud's psychoanalytic technique— from the beginnings to 1923. In *Psychoanalytic Techniques,* ed. B. Wolman, pp. 13–50. New York: Basic Books.

Croce, B. (1917). *History: Its Theory and Practice.* New York: Russell, 1921.

————(1922). *Aesthetic,* 2nd ed. London: Macmillan.

da Vinci, L. *Treatise on Painting,* ed. A. P. McMahon. 2 Vols. Princeton: Princeton University Press, 1956.

————*Notebooks.* Trans. E. MacCurdy. New York: Braziller, 1954.

Dilthey, W. (1910). *Pattern and Meaning in History.* New York: Harper Torchbooks, 1962.

Dostoyevsky, F. (1864). Notes from underground. In *Notes from Underground and the Grand Inquisitor,* pp. 3–115. New York: Dutton, 1960.

————(1868). *The Idiot.* Trans. D. Magarshack. Harmondsworth: Penguin Classics, 1955.

————(1872). *The Possessed.* Trans. C. Garnett. New York: Macmillan, 1948.

————(1880). *The Brothers Karamazov,* 2 vols. Trans. D. Magarshack. Harmondsworth: Penguin Classics, 1958.

Durkheim, E. (1912). *The Elementary Forms of the Religious Life, A Study in Religious Sociology.* London: Allen and Unwin.

————(1897). *Suicide.* Trans. J. A. Spaulding and G. Simpson. Glencoe: Free Press, 1957.

Eisnitz, A. (1961). Mirror dreams. *Journal of the American Psychoanalytic Association* 9:461–479.

Eissler, K. R. (1961). *Leonardo da Vinci: Psychoanalytic Notes on The Enigma.* New York: International Universities Press.

————(1963). *Goethe: A Psychoanalytic Study* [1775–1786]. 2 vols. Detroit: Wayne State University Press.

Eliot, T. S. (1952). *The Complete Poems and Plays.* New York: Harcourt, Brace.

Erikson, E. H. (1950). *Childhood and Society.* New York: Norton.

————(1958). *Young Man Luther.* New York: Norton, 1962.

————(1959). *Identity and the Life Cycle: Selected Papers* [*Psychological Issues, Monograph 1*]. New York: International Universities Press.

————(1967). Book review: *Thomas Woodrow Wilson* by Sigmund Freud and William Bullitt. *International Journal of Psycho-Analysis* 48:462–467.

————(1969). *Gandhi's Truth.* New York: Norton.

————(1974). On the nature of psychohistorical evidence: in search of Gandhi. In *Explorations in Psychohistory,* ed. R. J. Lifton, pp. 42–77. New York: Simon and Schuster.

Freud, A. (1939–1945). Infants without families: reports on the Hampstead Nurseries. *Writings,* vol. 3. New York: International Universities Press, 1973.

————(1965). Normality and pathology in childhood: assessments of development. *Writings,* vol. 6. New York: International Universities Press.

————(1968). Acting out. *Writings,* vol. 7. New York: International Universities Press, 1971.

————(1969). Difficulties in the path of psychoanalysis: a confrontation of past with present viewpoints. *Writings,* vol. 7. New York: International Universities Press, 1971.

Freud, S. (1891). *On Aphasia.* New York: International Universities Press, 1953.

————(1895). Project for a scientific psychology. In *The Origin of Psychoanalysis: Letters to Wilhelm Fliess, Drafts and Notes* (1897–1902), pp. 355–445. New York: Basic Books, 1954.

————(1897–1902). *The Origin of Psychoanalysis: Letters to Wilhelm Fliess, Drafts and Notes* (1897–1902). New York: Basic Books, 1954.

————(1900). The interpretation of dreams. *Standard Edition* 4/5:1–361.

————(1961). The psychopathology of everyday life. *Standard Edition* 6.

————(1904). Freud's psychoanalytic procedure. *Standard Edition* 7:249–256.

————(1905a). Three essays on the theory of sexuality. *Standard Edition* 7:130–245.

————(1905b). Jokes and their relation to the unconscious. *Standard Edition* 8.

————(1907a). Delusions and dreams in Jensen's *Gradiva. Standard Edition* 9:7–95.

————(1907b). Contributions to a questionnaire on reading. *Standard Edition* 9:245–247.

————(1908). Creative writers and day-dreaming (1908 [1907]). *Standard Edition* 9:142–153.

————(1910). Leonardo da Vinci and a memory of his childhood. *Standard Edition* 11:59–137.

————(1911a). Formulations on the two principles of mental functioning. *Standard Edition* 12:213–226.

————(1911b). Psychoanalytic notes on an autobiographical account of a case of paranoia (dementia paranoides). *Standard Edition* 12:3–84.

————(1912–1913). Totem and taboo. *Standard Edition* 13:1–164.

————(1914). On narcissism: an introduction. *Standard Edition* 14:73–102.

————(1915a). Instincts and their vicissitudes. *Standard Edition* 14:117–140.

————(1915b). Repression. *Standard Edition* 14:145–158.

————(1915c). The unconscious. *Standard Edition* 14:166–215.

————(1915–1917). Papers on metapsychology. *Standard Edition* 14:105–260.

————(1916–1917). Introductory lectures on psychoanalysis. *Standard Edition* 15/16.

————(1917). Mourning and melancholia. *Standard Edition* 14:243–258.

————(1918 [1914]). From the history of an infantile neurosis. *Standard Edition* 17:7–122.

————(1920). Beyond the pleasure principle. *Standard Edition* 18:1–64.

————(1921). Group psychology and the analysis of the ego. *Standard Edition* 18:67–145.

————(1923). The ego and the id. *Standard Edition* 19:12–68.

————(1926). Inhibitions, symptoms and anxiety. *Standard Edition* 20:77–175.

————(1927). The future of an illusion. *Standard Edition* 21:3–56.

————(1928). Dostoyevsky and parricide. *Standard Edition* 21:177–196.

————(1930). Civilization and its discontents. *Standard Edition* 21:59–145.

————(1932). New introductory lectures on psychoanalysis. *Standard Edition* 22:1–182.

————(1937a). Analysis terminable and interminable. *Standard Edition* 23:216–253.

————(1937b). Constructions in analysis. *Standard Edition* 23:257–269.

————(1939). Moses and monotheism. *Standard Edition* 23:3–140.

————(1940 [1938]). Splitting of the ego in the defensive process. *Standard Edition* 23:271–278.

————(1942 [1905 or 1906]). Psychopathic characters on the stage. *Standard Edition* 7:304–310.

Glenn, J. (1974a). Twins in disguise: a psychoanalytic essay on *Sleuth and the Royal Hunt of the Sun*. *Psychoanalytic Quarterly* 43:288–302.

————(1974b). Twins in disguise II: content, style and form in plays by twins. *International Review of Psycho-Analysis* 1:373–381.

————(1974c). The adoption theme in Edward Albee's *Tiny Alice and the American Dream*. *Psychoanalytic Study of the Child* 29:413–429. Chapter 7 of this volume.

————(1974d). Anthony and Peter Shaffer's plays: the influence of twinship on creativity. *American Imago* 31:270–291.

Gombrich, E. H. (1965). The mystery of Leonardo. *New York Review of Books* 4:3–4.

Gosse, E. (1917a). *The Life of Algernon Charles Swinburne.* London: Macmillan.

———(1917b). Swinburne's agitation. In *The Swinburne Letters,* vol. 6, ed. C. Y. Lang, pp. 233–248. New Haven: Yale University Press, 1962.

Greenacre, P. (1950). General problems of acting out. *Psychoanalytic Quarterly* 19:455–467.

———(1953). Certain relations between fetishism and the faulty development of the body image. *Psychoanalytic Study of the Child* 8:79–98.

———(1955a). Further considerations regarding fetishism. *Psychoanalytic Study of the Child* 10:187–194.

———(1955b). *Swift and Carroll: A Psychoanalytic Study of Two Lives.* New York: International Universities Press.

———(1956). Experiences of awe in childhood. *Psychoanalytic Study of the Child* 11:9–30.

———(1957). The childhood of the artist: libidinal phase development and giftedness. *Psychoanalytic Study of the Child* 12:47–72.

———(1958a). The family romance of the artist. *Psychoanalytic Study of the Child* 13:9–43.

———(1958b). The relation of the imposter to the artist. *Psychoanalytic Study of the Child* 13:521–540.

Hartmann, H. (1939). *Ego Psychology and the Problems of Adaptation.* New York: International Universities Press.

———(1950). Comments on the psychoanalytic theory of the ego. *Psychoanalytic Study of the Child* 5:74–96.

———(1960). *Psychoanalysis and Moral Values.* New York: International Universities Press.

Hartmann, H., and Kris, E. (1945). The genetic approach in psychoanalysis. *Psychoanalytic Study of the Child* 1:11–30.

Hartmann, H., and Loewenstein, R. M. (1951). Some psychoanalytic comments on "culture and personality." In *Psychoanalysis and Culture,* ed. G. B. Wilbur and W. Muensterberger, pp. 3–31. New York: International Universities Press.

Hauser, S. T. (1971). *Black and White Identity Formation.* New York: Wiley.

Hughes, H. S. (1958). *Consciousness and Society.* New York: Knopf.

Inhelder, B., and Piaget, J. (1955). *The Growth of Logical Thinking from Childhood to Adolescence.* New York: Basic Books, 1958.

Jacobson, E. (1953). Contribution to the metapsychology of cyclothimic depression. In *Affective Disorders,* ed. P. Greenacre, pp. 49–83. New York: International Universities Press.

——(1964). *The Self and the Object World.* New York: International Universities Press.

——(1971). *Depression.* New York: International Universities Press.

Jones, E. (1949). *Hamlet and Oedipus.* New York: Doubleday Anchor, 1954.

——(1955). *The Life and Work of Sigmund Freud.* Vol. 2. New York: Basic Books.

Kant, I. (1781). *Critique of Pure Reason.* New York: Modern Library, 1958.

Kanzer, M. (1947). Dostoyevsky's "Peasant Marey." *American Imago* 4:78–88. Chapter 9 of this volume.

——(1948a). Dostoyevsky's matricidal impulses. *Psychoanalytic Review* 35:115–125. Chapter 10 of this volume.

——(1948b). The "passing of the oedipus complex" in Greek drama. *International Journal of Psycho-Analysis* 29:1–4.

——(1951). The vision of Father Zossima from *The Brothers Karamazov. American Imago* 8:329–335. Chapter 11 of this volume.

Keniston, K. (1974). Psychological development and historical change. In *Explorations in Psychohistory,* ed. R. J. Lifton, pp. 149–164. New York: Simon and Schuster, 1974.

Kipling, R. (1945). *Rudyard Kipling's Verse. Definitive Edition.* Garden City, New York: Doubleday.

Kohut, H. (1960). Beyond the bounds of the basic rule. *Journal of the American Psychoanalytic Association* 8:567–586.

Kovel, J. (1970). *White Racism: A Psychohistory.* New York: Pantheon Books.

Kris, E. (1935). The image of the artist. In *Psychoanalytic Explorations in Art,* pp. 64–84. New York: International Universities Press, 1952.

——(1952a). *Psychoanalytic Explorations in Art.* New York: International Universities Press.

——(1952b). Notes on the development and on some current problems of psychoanalytic child psychology. *Psychoanalytic Study of the Child* 5:24–46.

Lang, C. Y. (1959). *Swinburne's lost love. Publications of the Modern Language Association* 74:123–130.

——(1959–1962). *The Swinburne Letters.* 6 vols. New Haven: Yale University Press.

Lifton, R. J. (1968). *Death in life: Survivors of Hiroshima.* New York: Simon and Schuster.

————(1970). On psychohistory. In *Explorations in Psychohistory,* ed. R. J. Lifton, pp. 21–41. New York: Simon and Schuster, 1974.

Lorenz, K. (1963). *On Aggression.* New York: Harcourt, 1966.

Mack, J. E. (1971). Psychoanalysis and historical biography. *Journal of the American Psychoanalytic Association* 19:143–179.

Mahler, M. (1972). On the first three subphases of the separation-individuation process. *International Journal of Psycho-Analysis* 53:333–338.

Meyer, B. (1967). *Joseph Conrad: A Psychoanalytic Biography.* Princeton: Princeton University Press.

Niederland, W. (1959a). The "miracled-up" world of Schreber's childhood. *Psychoanalytic Study of the Child* 14:383–413. Reprinted in Vol. 2 of this series.

————(1959b). Schreber, father and son. *Psychoanalytic Quarterly* 8:492–499. Reprinted in Vol. 2 of this series.

————(1961). The problem of the survivor. *Journal of Hillside Hospital* 10:233–247.

————(1964). Psychiatric disorders among persecution victims. *Journal of Nervous and Mental Disorders* 139:458–474.

————(1965). An inquiry into the life and work of Heinrich Schliemann. In *Drives, Affects and Behavior,* vol. 2, ed. M. Schur, pp. 369–396. New York: International Universities Press.

Nietzsche, F. (1891). *Thus Spake Zarathustra.* New York: Macmillan, 1924.

Nunberg, H. (1930). The synthetic function of the ego. In *Practice and Theory of Psychoanalysis.* New York: International Universities Press, 1960.

Nunberg, H., and Federn, E., eds. (1962). *Minutes of the Vienna Psycho-analytic Society.* Vol. I, 1906–1908. New York: International Universities Press.

————(1967). *Minutes of the Vienna Psychoanalytic Society.* Vol. II, 1908–1910. New York: International Universities Press.

Ober, W. B. (1975). Swinburne's masochism: neuropathology and psycho-pathology. *Bulletin of the Menninger Clinic* 39:500–555.

Orgel, S. (1974a). Fusion with the victim and suicide. *International Journal of Psycho-Analysis* 55:531–538.

————(1974b). Sylvia Plath: fusion with the victim and suicide. *Psycho-analytic Quarterly* 43:262–287.

————(1981). Fusion with the victim: a study of Sylvia Plath. Chapter 4 of this volume.

Piaget, J. (1958). *The Growth of Logical Thinking from Childhood to Adolescence.* New York: Basic Books, 1968.

Plath, S. (1966). *Ariel.* New York: Harper and Row.

————(1968). *The Colossus and Other Poems.* New York: Vintage Books.

————(1971). *The Bell Jar.* New York: Harper and Row.

Plato. Republic. *The Dialogues of Plato,* 4 vols., 4th ed., trans B. Jowett. Oxford: University Press, 1935.

————Ion. *The Dialogues of Plato,* 4 vols. 4th ed., trans. B. Jowett. Oxford: University Press, 1935.

Popper, K. (1958 [1934]). *The Logic of Scientific Discovery.* New York: Basic Books, 1959.

Rank, O. (1909). *The Myth of the Birth of a Hero.* New York: Robert Brunner, 1952.

————(1914). *Der Doppelganger.* Leipzig, Vienna, Zurich: Internationaler Psychoanalytischer Verlag, 1925.

Rapaport, D. (1959). *The Structure of Psychoanalytic Theory: A Systematizing Attempt.* Psychological Issues, Monograph 6. New York: International Universities Press.

Ricoeur, P. (1970). *Freud and Philosophy: An Essay in Interpretation.* New Haven: Yale University Press.

Rieff, P. (1963). The meaning of history and religion in Freud's thought. In *Psychoanalysis and History,* ed. B. Mazlish. Englewood Cliffs: Prentice-Hall.

Rogow, A. (1963). *James Forrestal: A Study of Personality, Politics, and Policy.* New York: Macmillan.

Roheim, G. (1950). Oedipus complex: magic and culture. *Psychoanalysis and the Social Sciences* 2:173–228. New York: International Universities Press.

Schafer, R. (1960). The loving and beloved superego in Freud's structural theory. *Psychoanalytic Study of the Child* 15:163–190.

Schapiro, M. (1956). Leonardo and Freud: an art-historical study. *Journal of the History of Ideas* 17:147–178.

Schreber, D. (1903). *Memoirs of My Nervous Illness.* Trans. I. MacAlpine and R. Hunter. London: Dawson, 1955.

Shelley, P. B. (1975). *The Poetical Works of Shelley.* Cambridge edition, ed. N. F. Ford. Boston: Houghton Mifflin.

Shengold, L. (1974). The metaphor of the mirror. *Journal of the American Psychoanalytic Association* 22:97–115.

————(1975). An attempt at soul murder: Rudyard Kipling's early life and work. *Psychoanalytic Study of the Child* 30:683–725. Chapter 6 of this volume.

Solzhenitsyn, A. (1963). Foreword by George Stade. In *One Day in the Life of Ivan Denisovich.* New York: E. P. Dutton.

Spitz, R. A. (1963). Life and the dialogue. In *Counterpoint: Libidinal Object and Subject,* ed. H. S. Gaskill. New York: International Universities Press.

————(1964). The derailment of dialogue: stimulus overload, action cycles, and the completion gradient. *Journal of the American Psychoanalytic Association* 12:752–775.

Spitz, R. A., and Wolf, K. M. (1946). The smiling response: a contribution to the ontogenesis of social relations. *Genetic Psychology Monograph* 34:57–125.

Strachey, J. (1957). Editor's note. On narcissism: an introduction. *Standard Edition* 14:69–71.

Strachey, L. (1917). *Eminent Victorians.* New York: Putnam, 1963.

————(1923). *Queen Victoria.* New York: Harcourt Brace Jovanovich, 1966.

Swinburne, A. C. (1970). *Poems and Ballads. Atalanta in Calydon,* ed. M. Peckham. Indianapolis and New York: Bobbs Merrill.

Tarachow, S. (1960). Judas the beloved executioner. *Psychoanalytic Quarterly* 29:528–554. Chapter 2 of this volume.

Trilling, L. (1950). *The Liberal Imagination.* New York: Viking.

Tyson, A. (1957). Editor's note. Leonardo da Vinci and a memory of his childhood. *Standard Edition* 11:59–62.

Wittgenstein, L. (1914–1916). *Preliminary Studies for the "Philosophical Investigations" (The Blue and Brown Books).* Oxford: Blackwell, 1958.

Wedge, B. (1968). Khrushchev at a distance, a study of public personality. *Transaction* 5:24–28.

Wolff, P. H. (1967). Cognitive considerations for a psychoanalytic theory of language acquisition. In *Motives and Thought: Psychoanalytic Essays in Honor of David Rapaport,* ed. R. R. Holt, *Psychological Issues* 18/19: 299–343. New York: International Universities Press.

PART II

A Walk in a Darker Wood

Chapter 2

JUDAS, THE BELOVED EXECUTIONER

SIDNEY TARACHOW, M.D.

In 1880, in a collection of German and Hungarian folk plays, most with religious themes, the editor, Hartmann, appends the following footnote to a play in which Judas had been portrayed as especially despicable.

The character of Judas, as a malicious and known evildoer, is created in this play with great sharpness. One might reproach the unknown author of this play for his crudeness. However, the intention is only allegorical: the Judas character symbolically portrays before our eyes the ingratitude of all sinful humanity against God.

We may well follow the suggestion of this editor, look beyond the manifest subject matter of the allegory, the hated and despised character of the betrayer Judas, and seek other human truths behind his facade.

To turn briefly to the matter of the historical reality of our two principal characters, Christ and Judas, varying degrees of acceptance of Christ as a historical person exist. Prototypes of such a personality were accepted in some contemporary Jewish literature (Robertson) though the references are contemptuous of Christ because of his failure as a Messiah. With regard to the historicity of Judas, the doubts are serious. Judas is a late, second to third century, development of Christian mythology. Paul, principal proponent of the central idea of Christ as a human sacrifice, nowhere mentions Judas. Robertson (1910, 1911, 1913) goes to great lengths to show that previous historical figures are assimilated into the figure of Judas, thus indicating its late historical origin. He regards the Judas story as derived from early mystery plays, and considers Judas basically an assimilation of the figure of the Jew.

The purpose of the present essay is to call attention to the libidinal aspects of the Judas-Christ relationship, the relationship which is the core of Christian anti-Semitism. Two well-known contributions by Simmel (1946) and Fenichel (1940) discuss current psychoanalytic concepts of anti-Semitism, and both agree that the basic notion is the projection of aggression against Christ onto the Jews. Simmel, particularly, calls attention to the oral, devouring aspects of the aggression projected by the Christian. Loewenstein (1951), in his study of anti-Semitism, mentions another aspect of the psychological problem: the curious need of the Christian for the Jew, the peculiar double bond in the sense that Christians, despite their hostility, were originally Jews. The present paper will discuss the love relationship between Judas and Christ; it will follow the thread of thought beginning with Christ as the willing sacrificial victim for love of the Jews, his love of Judas, and his selection of Judas, his favorite, to be the one to kill and eat him. This essay will also discuss other data, clinical and anthropological, that bear on killing and eating in the service of love or as representing love.

The Willing Victim

Our story begins with the motif of the willing victim. The following conception of Christ's motivation in offering himself as a sacrifice to save the Jews is taken from Graves and Podro (1954). Jesus had failed to persuade the Jews of his mission and as a last resort planned to fulfill the Old Testament prophecy of Zechariah (chapters 11–14). Zechariah, during the Seleucid period of domination, wanted to save his people from the great influence exerted by the Hellenized Jewish priesthood. To this end he offered to go among them and preach true doctrine. The High Priests presented him with only thirty shekels, thus demonstrating their contemptuous evaluation of him. In a rage, Zechariah cast the thirty shekels to a potter, and then prophesied that a worthless shepherd would appear, preach false doctrine, and be killed by his own parents. He foretold that upon the shepherd's death, when the Jews would see his pierced body, their consciences would be pricked, they would repent, the Great Day of the Lord would dawn, and the Jewish nation would be cleansed and purified through severe trials. Zechariah never met with the fate described in this prophecy, so that it became a prophecy postponed for realization at some future time. Jesus decided to fulfill this prophecy; since he had not succeeded by other means he would preach false doctrine, instigating the people to kill him and the sight of his pierced body would move them to repentence and purification.

From this standpoint, the cursing of the fig tree (Mark 11:12-14, 20-23, and Matthew 21:17-22) was the preaching of false doctrine and Jesus' impersonation of the worthless shepherd. His behavior was such that "When his friends heard of it they went out to lay hold on him: for they said, He is beside himself" (Mark 3:21). He was also accused of being possessed by the Devil because he claimed to cast out devils. "And the scribes which came down from Jerusalem said, 'He hath Beelzebub, and by the prince of the devils casteth he out devils'" (Mark 3:22). Moreover, Christian mythology includes a detail that points to Christ as the willing victim. In the ritual sacrifices of some religions the legs of the victim are broken, which, since he does not run away, proves that he is a willing victim (Robertson 1911). In the Christ story, his legs are not broken, but those of the two thieves are. Certain parts of the Passion narrative are taken directly from the prophecy of Zechariah: lowly and riding upon an ass's colt, is from Zechariah 9:9, as well as Matthew 21:5 — from the Old Testament as well as the New. "They shall look on me whom they have pierced" is Zechariah 12:10, as well as John 19:37. The impersonation is carried further by his plying the apostles with drink, a violation of apostolic abstinence, by his command to them to drink blood, a violation of Hebrew prohibitions, and to buy swords. To cap the similarity to the prophecy of Zechariah, at the Last Supper Christ explicitly quotes Zechariah 13:7: "I will smite the shepherd and the sheep shall be scattered." Then he tells his disciples, "All ye shall be offended because of me this night" (Mark 14:27-31). Finally there is the famous prediction that Peter will turn against him.

One might say that from the standpoint of the people, because of the failure of his mission, Jesus had to die for he was in disgrace, a Messiah who had failed. From his own standpoint, Jesus decided to die, but with the ambivalent motivation to be expected in someone contemplating suicide. He wished out of love to save the Jews, but he also wanted to prick their consciences and to punish them for rejecting him. Jesus accepted the glory of dying in ransom for his people, a fate kings have often been prepared to accept. According to Graves and Podro, Judas had planned to save Jesus from the wrath of the people by putting him in the protective custody of the Sanhedrin (1954). That Judas understood Jesus' wish to fulfil the prophecy of Zechariah is attested by the fact that he asked for thirty shekels, the same amount given to Zechariah. In the end Judas was so horrified when he learned Jesus had been turned over to the Romans, he hanged himself.

Judas as the Most Beloved

Once having decided to be the sacrifice, Jesus offered himself to his disciples to be killed and eaten, or less figuratively at the Last Supper he named his favorite Judas, as his ritual slayer. At the Last Supper he said, "Take, eat; this is my body. . . . This is my blood of the new testament, which is shed for many" (Mark 14:22, 24). The specific love relationship to Judas is indicated by the following (John 13:18, 21–28).

> "I speak not of you all: I know whom I have chosen. . . . I say unto you that one of you shall betray me." Then the disciples looked one on another, doubting of whom he spake. Now there was leaning on Jesus' bosom one of his disciples whom Jesus loved. Simon Peter therefore beckoned to him, that he should ask who it should be of whom he spake. He then lying on Jesus' breast saith unto him, "Lord, who is it?" Jesus answered, "He it is to whom I shall give a sop, when I have dipped it." And when he had dipped the sop he gave *it* to Judas Iscariot, *the son* of Simon. And after the sop Satan entered into him. Then said Jesus unto him, "That thou doest, do quickly." Now no man at the table knew for what intent he spake this unto him.[1]

When Judas leaves to carry out the betrayal, Jesus says, "A new commandment I give unto you. That ye love one another; as I have loved you, that ye also love one another" (John 13:34). "Greater love hath no man than this, that a man lay down his life for his friends" (John 15:13).

I am indebted to Peter B. Neubauer for the following suggestion: at this point Jesus became a symbol of love for all humanity, though we shall note that he burdened someone else with the problem of aggression, namely Judas. Christ's remark about no greater love could be paraphrased in Judas's favor: "Greater burden can no man give another than that he ask him to be his executioner." The guilt for the aggression was loaded onto Judas, while the love of man was assumed by Christ. It was Judas's difficult task to use oral aggression in the service of libido and so convert aggression into libido.

---

1. The sop is still a favorite token among Arabs that a host has special affection for a guest.

The homosexual aspects of the love relationship between Jesus and Judas have been noted by Reik (1945), and several novelists have sensed this tie between the two. Moore (1924), van Heurn (1958), Roth (1929), Andreyev (1916), and Graves (1946) portray Judas as loving Christ and as having little interest in women. Beautiful fictional illustrations of the general problem of the love relationship between the killed and the killer appear in stories by Tennessee Williams. In *Suddenly Last Summer* (1958) he describes a man drawn to a group of hungry children who eventually kill and eat him. In "Desire and the Black Masseur" (1954) the central character, attracted to a masseur, persuades the masseur to kill and eat him.

To turn to the other side of the coin Reik notes that at the moment of taking the sop Judas was possessed by—i.e., identified with—the devil. Psychoanalytically we should infer that at the moment of taking the sop Judas became the murderer of God and the devourer of Christ. We emphasize that this is the expression of the love relationship between the two. It is interesting that the first three Gospels describe the kiss of betrayal, while the fourth Gospel of John omits the kiss. The earlier Gospels admit some degree of love relationship; the fourth Gospel suppresses it and replaces it with projection and hostility to Judas. Zeitlin (1942) observes that the first three Gospels were written for Jews, the fourth for Gentile Christians.

To return to Reik, some of his penetrating comments on the Judas problem are found in the first three chapters of *Der eigene und der fremde Gott* (1923), which still awaits translation. He emphasizes: (1) Judas as the God murderer and his identification with the Devil and his sadistic, oral, cannibalistic qualities: Judas as the executioner and Christ as the victim; (2) the Judas-Christ identity, each figure representing contrasting ambivalent aspects of the same god figure and ambivalent aspects of ego fragments of the Christian which undergo projection.

Reik discusses the problem of Christ in terms of the ritual execution of the Son-God, with Judas as ritual executioner. He presents the Old Testament story of Abraham and the sacrifice of Isaac as evidence that the Jews at one time sacrificed to the Son-God, and as reversal of the totemic killing of the father. Reik also deals with the Christ problem in terms of Christ's hatred of the father, the Judas myth being Christ's solution by way of projection. Judas represents the murdered Jahweh who, like Banquo's ghost, returns to wreak vengeance. Judas becomes the carrier of the tendencies unacceptable in Christ. Judas betrayed Christ as Christ betrayed Jahweh, and both die. For the Jews, Jesus sharpened the problem of the son's hostility to father. The Jews had to reject Jesus. In the Toledoth Jeschu (1874), the famous Jewish medieval anti-Christian Gospels, Judas is the hero selected by the Sanhedrin to overcome Jesus and to return him to the Sanhedrin for punishment.

According to Reik, although the Jews carry the guilt of the Christians for murdering their God, Christ nevertheless serves some Jewish purposes as well. Jews project their own rebelliousness onto Christ. Though the Christian sees his own murderous wishes realized when projected onto the Jew, the Jew assumes the guilt for his unconscious deed. The Last Supper is a totem meal in which Jesus is the sacrificial lamb, but one in which he also becomes the Father God. Judas stands for the combined apostles. Jesus as father bids Judas as son to kill and eat him.

In terms of the ambivalent faces of god, Reik believes that when Judas took the sop he became the Devil. In some religions it is difficult to distinguish between true gods and demons. Since Jesus cast out devils, it follows that he too was possessed by Beelzebub. In folk tales Christ and Judas are confused with each other. Thus Judas and Christ together represent the ambivalent picture of God, part good, part evil. Reik points out the similarities between the father-son relationship and the god-devil relationship. Early, superseded gods often take on the characteristics of the devil, and Hell and Heaven are often confused. The Judas problem is one of ego splitting. The Judas fragment accepts punishment from father; the Judas fragment is the murderer of God. In addition, Reik gives clinical examples of betrayal; in one instance a man denounced another for the crime of blasphemy of which he himself was guilty.

Killing as Love and Love of the Dead

Killing as love or in the service of love can be demonstrated clinically without too much difficulty. A male obsessional patient, whose illness began at a moment of unconscious homosexual panic when he was confronted by a reunion with his one-time Naval commander, dreamed of an official execution. The victim was bound upright to a stake and the executioner was killing him with a screw: a brace was being used to screw a bit into his abdomen. Many associations indicated that being "screwed to death" was a homosexual act of love, and that the executioner was his former commander. The same patient, at the time of the executions that followed the recent Cuban revolution, repeatedly dreamed of executions by firing squads. The patient identified himself with both sides, with the victims and with the executioners. In many jokes sexual "screwing" is used as a method of killing. "Screwing" may also mean betrayal of one's interests. Thus screwing may mean betrayal, killing, or loving.

Another example of killing as a friendly act is the well-known Japanese custom, hara-kiri. The Westerner's usual concept of this ceremony is quite incomplete and envisages only the first half of the total action, i.e., the voluntary disembowelment (Hewlett 1946, Joya 1949, Walsh 1914). However, immediately after the disemboweling, a close friend, selected in advance by the victim from the individual's own social and military class, springs from behind and decapitates him with one blow of a sword. Usually, though not always, the practice of hara-kiri is voluntary and is intended to remove offense to the Mikado or to remove a stain on one's own honor. Instances are known where, angry at the Mikado's orders to commit suicide, men have contemptuously thrown their own bowels at the witnesses who report the completion of the deed to the Mikado. In the cases of the willing victim there is a remarkable similarity to the Christ myth. As an analogue of Christ the willing victim, we here have the Japanese samurai. The analogue of God is the Mikado and that of Judas, the friend who decapitates. The abdomen as the choice site of the suicidal act probably comes from the Japanese idea of the stomach as the center of the personality. "Hara" (stomach) stands for courage, power, efficiency, principles, understanding, honesty, etc.; a clean stomach stands for a clear conscience (Joya 19:49).

· Another example of killing as love or in the service of love is illustrated by a medieval Jewish legend about the death of Moses (Bin Gorion 1914). In this story God so loved Moses that He would not permit the Angel of Death to end Moses' life. Instead, at the appointed time, God Himself came down to Earth, kissed Moses on the mouth and thus drew his soul from him—a kiss of death which certainly resembles the kiss of Judas. In another version of the same story, Moses angrily refused to surrender his soul to the Angel of Death, insisting he would surrender it to God alone. God finally agreed to this and again, with a kiss, drew Moses' soul from him. Like Christ, Moses selected his own executioner, one he loved, and in both instances the kiss of love was a kiss of death.

Although the preceding examples are of killing as love and in the service of love they are not sadistic. The libidinal element is dominant.

Let us now consider other related phenomena of killing and death, and the various ways in which the patterns of libido and aggression shape themselves. In all material joining love and death there is a common thread of orality. For example, a fine distinction between love and hatred is illustrated by van Ophuijsen in a case report published in 1929. He describes an incident in the treatment of a girl who hated her sister, and in one session said: "I should like to revile her—spit at her—poison her—beat her—hack her to bits with a hatchet." Van Ophuijsen intervened to say, "And eat the pieces?" The patient paused and said, "No. That would be an act of love." Van Ophuijsen believed the patient's refusal to eat the pieces was "pure sadism" which she refused to adulterate with cannibalism as that would have been an expression of love. Today we would say that van Ophuijsen was contrasting not sadism and love (since sadism is also a form of love), but aggression and libido. In the same paper, van Ophuijsen remarks: "It is notorious that many a lust murderer terminates his violent deed and attains complete satisfaction by tearing up parts of his object with his teeth and hands. Often he goes a step further in equating his love object with nourishment by carrying away such pieces with him, cooking and eating them." Van Ophuijsen emphasizes that the point of sadism is to bite, and not to inflict suffering, this representing possession of the loved object in an oral sadistic fashion.

The Eucharist is an example of a ritualized attempt to overcome the aggressive aspects of the eating of the god and to preserve the purely libidinal aspect. The wafer must be swallowed, but not bitten. Van Ophuijsen's patient wanted to bite but not swallow, thus reversing the eucharistic pattern. Chewing the wafer would be equivalent to biting mother's breast, and swallowing equivalent to sucking. In the lifelong repetition of the religious rite the believer is perpetually at the mother's breast, in love.

Killing the beloved is closely related to lust murder and love of the dead. Bonaparte (1930–1931) draws a distinction between the two latter themes. The lust murderer is aggressive in his oedipal rivalry; but the lover of the dead is timid; he takes his turn only after the father has completed his sadistic sexual act—after someone else has done the killing. Such a theoretical distinction between lust murder and necrophilia—according to aggressiveness in the oedipal role—may well be valid, yet we may note the thread of orality and tie to the mother in all the following data.

To indicate briefly some lust murder material, Wertham (1949) describes a murderer who cooked and ate his victims, and Hirschfeld (1944) reports a similar case. The famous acid-bath murderer, John George Haigh, dreamed of trees dripping with blood, then slowly turning into crosses with the body of Christ, while he was offered a bowlful of blood to drink. He had actually drunk the blood of several victims and after the murders dreamed of doing so (Dunboyne 1953). Ferenczi (1925) interprets lust murder as a defense against castration anxiety and revenge on the woman who robs a man of semen or is otherwise dangerous.

Psychoanalysts are familiar with murderous impulses that arise as a defense against the emergence of genital love and as a substitute gratification, especially in obsessive patients. Dreams of murder and of being murdered are frequent. The forerunners of expressions of love are often those of murder, particularly by way of the mouth. "You are so sweet, I could eat you."

Turning to problems of necrophilia, we note that Bonaparte (1930–1931) tells of a man who sucked the breasts of cadavers in a frenzy. Segal (1953) reports from the analysis of a man with necrophilic fantasies that to him the corpse was an ideal object, never frustrating and never demanding. Hirschfeld (1944) describes similar patients — many of them undertakers or frequenters of morgues — whose conditions for sexual excitement were sleeping or dead women. Pomer (1959) reports a case of a man to whom every cadaver represented the mother, primarily one to be used in a search for a phallus. Necrophilia was his defense against castration anxiety, but he also showed an oral and anal passive trend of fearing to be penetrated. He repeatedly identified himself with Christ.

In another connection, incidental to the psychopathology of a hobby, I reported the case of a male patient whose chief sexual wish was to have intercourse with an unconscious woman (1954). His wife would simulate unconsciousness, he masturbated with fantasies of unconscious women, and he fantasied (again like a Judas) that if he kissed a woman she would die. He wanted to drug his wife "to find out something." At the age of eleven his mother and he played sexual games in which she pretended to be asleep or unconscious and he would roll her inert body about in the bed. His most intense desire was to lift her nightgown and examine her genitals. At the same time he identified himself with women, often imagining he was a woman being wheeling into an operating room. This patient, like Pomer's, certainly used his necrophilic fantasy in an attempt to solve the castration problem. However, for my patient also the castration problem was not the sole issue. His desire for power and control over women was connected with other fears and fascinations. He feared his murderous impulses and he was fascinated by the gruesome, the aboriginal, and the cannibalistic. His play with his mother's inert body exemplifies a comment in Bonaparte's discussion of necrophilia (1930–1931); she suggests that the sadistic desire to possess the disarmed, defenseless, or dead mother finds its prototype in the infantile sight of the mother asleep.

Brill (1941) reported the case of a necrophile in whom genitality was completely suppressed, and among whose pregenital needs orality and skin eroticism were prominent. This patient had fantasies of women's breasts bursting and of his wallowing in milk. He also had a strong desire to drink blood and to eat and drink bodily execretions. The women were to be cadavers so they could not resist his advances. He wanted to bury himself bodily inside a woman's decaying body or in that of a horse or other large animal. He fantasied being inside a living woman, of eating her from the inside and so killing her.

Recently a murderer was apprehended in the Midwest who killed his female victims, skinned them, and then saved both skins and the rest of the corpses separately, the latter being hung neatly in a row on hooks. From time to time he would don the skin of one of his victims. He was much attached to his mother and after her death nailed her room shut, to preserve everything as it had been. This man's behavior, as well as the desires of the necrophilic patient described by Brill, have their lesser counterpart in the actions and fantasies of a transvestite whom I observed. This patient had fantasies of sinking bodily into the bodies of others, both male and female; he regarded his collection of outfits of women's clothing as a stable of willing women who never frustrated him and were ready to offer him any pleasure. It is noteworthy that during the transvestite activities he lost interest in food and had the conscious feeling of hiding in a cave, safe from all danger.

Death itself as an oral regression is described by Lewin (1946, 1955), who cites a case of Gitelson's where resignation to death represented a capacity to accept a profound oral regression in which sleep and death were equated. Lewin also comments on the fear of analysis being equated with fear of death, and he goes on, "Physicians often think of themselves as being dissected when they dream of their analyses, and sometimes they even turn the autopsy into a cannibal procedure." Pomer's patient, a pathologist, regarded all cadavers as his mother and at the same time pictured himself in the analytic situation as a cadaver offered for dissection. The equation of autopsy victim with the object of love is at least partly confirmed by the dream of another obsessive patient of mine. In the dream, while an autopsy was being performed upon a former employer of the patient, the cadaver had an ejaculation. He responded with love to being loved. The former employer had in fact strongly stimulated the patient's latent homosexuality.

Thus we encounter a variety of ways in which libidinal, preponderantly oral, desires find expression in dying, being dead, and in killing. To name them, there are the willing victim, complete surrender, utter compliance and giving, and much orality. These examples point strongly in the direction of the fulfilment of the oral triad, eating, being eaten, and death as sleep. Among oral attributes is the fact that the dead object never refuses and never shows hostility. We find preoccupation with the breasts of the cadaver in sucking, biting, and blood drinking. Coitus is not at all a constant element of necrophilia, although it may be present when the necrophilia has certain normal mourning aspects (1931).

Grotjahn (1969) comes to similar conclusions. He holds that the idea of death is primarily an oral concept of happiness characterized by oral and narcissistic regression and reunion with the mother. According to Grotjahn, death may be acceptable as a final return to the mother. This is regression to a level before ego integration took place and when mental life appeared to follow the primary process. Death fear can be conquered by murdering the ego, the only witness in us to remind us of death. The elimination of the only witness who knows death would make us immortal but also insane. The unconscious may not know death, but it knows sleep and peace; and it longs for the reunion with the primordial mother even if it is the terrible mother who is death herself. The schizophrenic has established such a union. I certainly agree with Grotjahn that the loss of ego identity is closely tied to undoing the sense of reality and reestablishing the tie to the mother. I would put it even more strongly: any ego regression or ego damage automatically reinstates the blissful tie to the mother. This may well be a factor in the etiology of euphoric states in cases of organic brain damage.

Ego regression has another aspect — the aspect of regression to ambiguity and antithesis. Kris and Kaplan (1952) discuss the wide range of ambiguity and antithesis in relation to perception and aesthetics, which for them includes all varieties of connection, even the opposite. Freud before them pointed to the identity of opposites in the sense of the antithetical sense of primal words. We may expand this and say that words, sensations, feelings, and meanings are all relative; they are all really derived from categories, sharing ambiguity and antithesis. Usage alone indicates precise meaning and this only when secondary process and ego functioning are intact. In primitives and in ego regression the categorical range reasserts itself, and opposites are equal. The primitive would have a difficult time grasping our conception of death. And we would have difficulty accepting the primitive correlates which to him are first nature. For the primitive, magic, ambiguity, and antithesis are everyday matters taken for granted. Our own religious feelings share such regressive participation, for example, in the idea that death is simply another life. Many share in the regressive thought that Christ gave his life for us, a belief basically like that of the Punjab father (Frazer 1955) who shares one life with his son. With the aid of entrenched and institutionalized ego splitting, secondary processes and magic have established an at times uneasy coexistence. The above argument can help us to understand killing as love. Ego regression has occurred to a degree where antithesis and ambiguity become valid psychic legal tender. This is not the result of sadism, reaction-formation, or defense against homosexual love, but simply the operation of ambiguity and antithesis in ego regression. The primitive has no difficulty with this concept.

The Magic Renewal of Life

We now return to the theme of ritual-sacrifice and self-sacrifice in the service of other libidinal motives, for example, the magic renewal of life. At the raising of Lazarus, Christ says, "And whosoever liveth and believeth in me shall never die" (John 11:26), an open promise of immortality. Later, as he was waiting to be betrayed and taken, he says, "I am the way, the truth, and the life; no man cometh unto the Father, but by me" (John 14:6).

The sacrificial killing intended to represent the renewal of life is not connected with any specific hostility to the victim. The Aztec captive was quite friendly with his captor and referred to him as "father." The victim, like Christ, was willing. As a soldier he felt it his duty either to take captives or to play the captive role. The role of victim was eagerly embraced, even by the nobility (1953). The renewal of life by sacrifice has two directions; one was the renewal of the life of the tribe by the sacrifice of the king, god, or father. The other was the renewal of the life of the father by the death of the son. While the Aztec captive referred to his captor as father, the captor referred to his prisoner as "himself."

In certain Punjab areas (Frazer 1955c) when a wife is in the fifth month of pregnancy, funeral services are held for the husband. Magical beliefs of this sort lay the groundwork for the killing of the son, or sometimes even all the sons. Even in this problem one still encounters the willing victim. The Punjab funeral service was predicated on the belief that there was only one life available between father and son; only one could possess that life and the other must necessarily die. A Scandinavian tale tells of the king who killed nine sons in turn. The tenth son was rescued by strangers and became king of the country of his adoption. This king, who knew he had been destined for sacrifice, managed to be careless during the slaying of a bull and was killed by the bull (Wellisch 1954). Similar ideas can be encountered in analytic material. Segal (1953) reported a case of a man with necrophilic fantasies who demanded from women immobility in practice and death in fantasy. He had the feeling that he and his analyst possessed one "life" in common; if the analyst was alive he was dead, and vice versa.

As to preserving the life of the tribe, we turn to the killing of the king, for which Frazer (1955c) gives many illustrations. The perfection of the king magically insured the health of the tribe, and any sign of imperfection or weakness led to his killing and replacement by a perfect specimen. If, for example, a wife reported his sexual inadequacy the king was killed. In some groups the king had a fixed tenure, perhaps a year, after which time he was killed or would voluntarily and ritually commit suicide. Even under these circumstances there was no shortage of volunteers for the kingship. One need not go to primitives for examples of renewal of life through the execution of another. In medieval Nuremberg sick townspeople bribed the *Hochrichter* for permission to drink blood streaming from freshly beheaded criminals. The blood was reputed to have high medicinal value (Keller 1928).

Frazer (1955b) recounts many examples of eating beloved relatives, not out of hostility but rather out of love and admiration. After such a relative's death a feast would be held and family members would eat either various parts of the body or would be served portions of what amounted to meat pie or ash pie. After the feast the remains might not be buried, but placed on a platform to decompose, and as the decomposed material dripped down from the platform the relatives would sit underneath and rub the drippings into their skins. This practice resembles several fantasies and actions of necrophiles.

Koestler (1941), in his dramatic novel, *Darkness at Noon,* portrays the character Rubashov, who voluntarily accepts death as a sacrifice for the good of the masses. Rubashov accepts this role only after prolonged interrogation and persuasion, an action reminiscent of the ritual dialogues between executioner and victim which take place in some religious practicing human sacrifice (Robertson 1911). The ritual dialogue is in effect a persuasion of the victim as well as a method of allaying the executioner's own guilt. As in "brainwashing," if one is subjected to sufficient aggression, responsive contact can be made with libido.

This renewal of life by killing may take a further turn. Neumann (1955) describes how in the cult of Xipe, the flayed god, prisoners were shot with arrows to symbolize sexual union with the earth. Killing and mating were psychologically identical; death represented fecundation.

Eating and the Tie to Mother

It is easy to overestimate patriarchal elements in religion, and Róheim (1955) believed that Freud accordingly underestimated the tie to the mother. The Freudian theory of the primal horde and the eating of the father for the purpose of identification and the acquisition of his strength are based on Robertson Smith. In Róheim's opinion, the eating is basically of the mother. The Aztec system, for example, seems to have been a patriarchal one, yet Neumann (1955) notes that on close analysis one finds it dominated by goddesses of fantastic cruelty.

The Christian deity, Christ, seems more and more to resemble a mother figure. There are no direct representations of Christ with breasts, but his representation has become effeminate and a growing tendency to picture him with Mary draws attention to the mother figure. Only recently Mary's position in the hierarchy has again been enhanced. Christianity refers to the Mother Church, but the church is the body of Christ.

Both Jews and Christians had eating myths or practices which guaranteed reunion with mother symbols and immortality. Goodenough (1956) points out that both observed mystic meals for such purposes. In Jewish tradition a monster fish, the leviathan, lives at the bottom of the seas over a spring which feeds the oceans. When the time of the messianic reward arrives, this fish will be captured and will provide food for all deserving Jews who will thereby gain immortality. There are some indications that at one time the monster was ritually killed anew each year. A meal which promises immortality is, of course, supplied in the Christian mythology by Christ, who in some of the symbols even of the early Christians was pictured as a fish. The great messianic fish of the Jews is the Christ of the Christians. The messianic food and immortality keep Christian and Jew at the breast forever. This is Heaven. The legend of the bottomless waters discussed by Bonaparte (1946) resembles the leviathan myth. There is a reunion with mother in both, either at the bottom of the sea or with a creature from the bottom of the sea. A probable reason for the fish's prominence as a mystic and ritual meal is the removal of emphasis from flesh, a partial suppression of the cannibalistic element. Some Christians still limit themselves to fish on certain days of the week and at periods during the year when they celebrate the killing of Christ.

Another symbol frequently used both by Christians and Jews in the early Greco-Roman period was bread and also what Goodenough (1956) terms "round objects." The latter are generally circles with dots or small circles in the center, and they have been incorporated in the Menorah as well as the Cross. The eucharistic wafer has been represented by a round object, and the Jews used round objects to represent the sanctity of bread. In some instances round objects denote the sun. The Egyptians, who regarded light as a fluid, spoke of the sun as suckling the earth. The craving for divine milk is found among the Egyptians, Greeks, Christians, and, at least figuratively, in the writings of Philo, the famous Hellenized Jew. The source of divine milk is often hermaphroditic. In the Dionysiac rituals, one fourth of the priests who carried the insignia of the gods bore golden vases in the form of breasts, from which libations of milk were poured. The symbolism of wine and milk leads to mother. Early Christian symbolism is a confusion of blood, milk, and wine. The early mystics often used the concept of salvation through nursing. A quote from St. Catherine of Siena (Goodenough 1956) is an example.

What I say of the universal body and mystical body of the Holy Church [i.e., the Christian religion] I say also of my ministers, who stand and feed at the breasts of the Holy Church; and not only should they feed themselves, but it is also their duty to feed and hold to those breasts the universal body of Christian people.

He also quotes from St. François de Sales:

Even so our dear Lord offers the breast of his divine love to the devout soul; he draws, gathers it into the lap of his more than motherly tenderness, and then, burning with love, he embraces the soul, presses it to his heart, kisses it with the sacred kisses of his mouth, makes it taste of that love which is better than wine. And so the soul, intoxicated with delight, not merely consents and yields to the divine union, but cooperates with all its might thereto.

The Two Scapegoats

The ambivalent double, the struggle between two opposites and their simultaneous death, is well known to us in fiction; for example, Dr. Jekyll and Mr. Hyde. The subject is most lucidly discussed by Edel (1951) in a study of Walpole's *The Killer and the Slain,* where there is a struggle between a pair representing the evil masculine side and the passive feminine side, and where both die, as did Jesus and Judas. Similarly, in O'Neill's play, *The Great God Brown,* the two members of a pair kill each other. One says to his double, "You are the killer and the killed" (1926).

Jesus and Judas are doubles, perhaps brothers, and in one medieval myth Mary even mistakes Judas for Jesus. In some European countries there are rites of Judas-burning (Taylor 1923, Walsh 1914) which precede the celebration of the Resurrection. The Judas figure is called the *Ostermann.* The excitement and the chasing of a victim before the burning of the effigy is ordinarily called *Judassuchen,* but in some communities *Christussuchen.* It is difficult to escape the impression that the enthusiastic beating and burning of Judas is really meant for Jesus. Fragments of broken and decayed crosses are burned and called Judas.

Killer and victim are close to each other, perhaps as brothers, perhaps through guilt. Their reciprocal love is not far removed from self-love. Certainly object love may be replaced by identification, such as is seen in the ritual sacrificial flaying and wearing of the skins of the victims. As we have noted certain murders and transvestitism seem to have similar motivations.

In the Aztec ceremonies, the priest who wore the skin of the female victim was treated as a living goddess (Frazer 1955a). Priest, murderer, and transvestite show identification of one with the other as love; and murder is only a necessary preliminary.

I am indebted to Sylvan Keiser for an interpretation which underscores the issue of identification between killer and victim. He pointed out an important difference between professional murder and love-murder. In the professional murderer (though not in the sacrificing priest) there is no human relationship, no struggle with the problem of object relationship, and no identification of killer with victim. On the other hand, in the murders we have been considering there may be an exquisite identification. In fact, in ritual and in love-murder the goal is precisely a libidinal union of the two. The killer incorporates the victim or the victim incorporates the killer; it makes little difference. The purpose is to remove the ego boundaries between the two and to experience all affects as love. To a more advanced ego this would be quite impossible. The need is for archaic love, an unclearly defined object and union of the two.

Although Christ is the manifest central figure in Christian mythology, there is the counterpart of Christ, the paired antichrist in its various forms. The antichrist has various shapes (Trachtenberg 1943) — Judas, the Jews, the Devil, and other horrible forms. Some of the antichrists have been romanticized and treated on a grand scale, for example Goethe's Mephistopheles. But Judas has not. The best role that Judas and the Jews have been able to attain has been that of comedian in mystery plays and comic *Zwischenspiele* (Schidvowitz 1925). A review of many early religious plays indicates that the antichrist role is about evenly divided between figures of the Devil, Judas, and the Jew.

In many Latin and German speaking countries (Anonymous 1958, Walsh 1914) there is an annual celebration of the death of Judas, when his effigy is destroyed, but with a curious ambivalence. Sometimes the effigy is filled with silver or food and then exploded, giving the populace a bonanza for which they all scramble. And Judas has been used not only in curses but also in beneficent roles. Mygatt and Witherspoon (1928), as well as Taylor (1920), record old charms invoking Judas against many dangers, especially burns.

Christian mythology solves its ambivalence by having two scapegoats, Christ and Judas. One is for love and the other for aggression, one for killing and the other for being killed, one for eating and the other for being eaten. One figure is pale and ascends to Heaven (although he too made a trip through Hell), the other is dark and assigned to the Devil and the lower regions. One is connected with oral bliss, the other with anality and aggression.

Happiness seems expressible in oral terms but not in anal. Not only in is Heaven depicted in oral terms, with nectar and ambrosia, but is up above. Manna rains down from Heaven. I suspect that this arises from the fact that to the nursing infant the mother's face and breast are always above. A schizophrenic female patient of mine had frequent hallucinations of her mother's face, which was always over her head. On the other hand, the Devil and Hell are below, for Hell is anality. In medieval art Hell often appears as a sea of feces in which the poor, condemned souls swim forever. The stool falls below and behind. The only exception to this allocation is among certain Eskimos who, I have been informed, place Heaven below and Hell above. This may be related to their weather and to the fact that their food supply is below the surface of the sea. Only conjecturally, they may also have infant sleeping and feeding patterns sharply different from ours.

What are the problems which call for scapegoat solution in Christianity? For the Christian, Christ provokes envy because of his passive homosexuality and supreme masochism, and also because he is so close to God. Identification with Christ is attained only at great cost. The acceptance of such masochism comes easily only to schizophrenics and mystics. The problems provoked by the scapegoat for aggression take a different turn. We envy Judas his role as lover and executioner of Christ. Our difficulty in identifying ourselves with either of these attributes leads to hatred and projection. Simmel (1946) and Fenichel (1940) discuss the problem of aggression most thoroughly, though the libidinal side of the problem is neglected. Loewenstein (1951) hints at it. It might be remarked that the aggression has not always been disowned by the Christian. Judas has been pictured not only as a villain but as a savior and hero (Haugg 1930), the latter by heretical, grateful sects who quite logically worshipped Judas for saving the world by providing the necessary human sacrifice.

Allied to attitudes toward Judas are certain public attitudes toward assassins, executioners, and executions. Throughout history public executions and torturings have attracted enormous crowds. There is great envy of the role of public executioners or even murderers. There are many applicants for the position of hangman. The public is fascinated and repelled by him, as if he could kill without guilt. This is, of course, not true. Elliott, the long-time executioner at Sing Sing, did not like to look his victims in the eyes (Elliott and Beatty 1940). The Jewish ritual slaughterer of animals (the *schochet*) utters a prayer at the moment of slaughtering; this prayer puts the onus for the slaughtering on God. I have been informed that in a certain section of Hungary where the Jews were under Chassidic influence, the *schochet* was also required to go through Kol Nidre twice on the Day of Atonement.

The attitudes to the executioner may be delicately ambivalent. If a hangman bungles his job, or through poor technique makes a victim suffer unnecessarily, the crowd may turn on him in fury. Several medieval executioners of Nuremburg were mobbed and killed by an enraged public (Keller 1928). Synge (1911), in *The Playboy of the Western World,* illustrates the ambivalent attitudes to a hero assassin. When the young hero appears in a small town with the story of having killed his father in some distant place, he is idolized, especially by the women. However, when it seems that the killing took place in the town itself, he is shunned.

Some assassins have become great public heroes. The individual assassin is generally of little importance to the community (Feldman 1954). The community creates its own hero according to its needs; the assassin has his own special personal relationship to the victim. The assassin may have no motive such as he may be credited with by the community. Judas was a hero to some sects, a villain to others.

Discussion and Conclusions

In discussing the universal appeal of Christianity, Brierley (1951) notes among other facets that one critical advantage over other religions is "the Christian emphasis on love. . . . The doctrine that 'God is love' is reenforced by the doctrine of the Incarnation and by the greater ease, for many men and women, of themselves feeling love for God Incarnate in Christ Jesus. The Son of Man albeit Son of God offers a personal target for personal affection as well as a suitable object for certain types of identifying relationships." In my opinion, the advantage lies not simply in the opportunity for love, but rather in the opportunity for aggression, partly for its own sake and partly in the service of love and for the purpose of being converted into love. A good share of the aggression is displaced onto Judas. The love is not only passive, but also active in an archaic, antithetical unity. This is the emphasis of this essay.

The Abraham-Isaac story is relevant as a contrast to the Judas-Christ myth. In the Jewish myth the urge to human sacrifice is overcome; in the Christian myth it is carried through and ritually celebrated. Medieval Jewish myths about Abraham and Isaac (Bin Gorion 1914, Wellisch 1954) bear a clear oedipal pattern. For example, one story has Isaac spending his last night before the trip to the mountain with his mother and in another Isaac asks that his ashes be placed in his mother's bedroom. Though aware of his aggression against his father, Isaac, like Jesus, willingly accepts the role of victim. Isaac also resembles Jesus in his gentleness after the ordeal.

The Judaic solution is renunciation of the oedipal object and renunciation of aggression between father and son. The Christian solution is to keep the oedipal object; thus father murder and son murder are perpetually necessary in the ritual. The tie to mother is not surrendered, and this in a preoedipal and pregenital sense too. Fromm (1930) makes the interesting observation that the two great representations of Christ are Christ on the Cross and Christ in the mother's arms. The first dramatizes the oedipal castration theme and the second the oral problem, the tie to and identification with mother. With virgin birth, there is total separation from father.

I think it is easier to support a preoedipal construction than the oedipal one of Christian mythology, even though the oedipal construction is relatively obvious. The Judas theme has also been elaborated in the oedipal direction, both psychoanalytically and historically (Fremantle 1950, Reider 1960).

Summary

This essay has attempted to delineate the libidinal aspects of the Judas-Christ relationship as well as to provide clinically related phenomena. Jesus is pictured as the willing victim offering himself in love to be killed and eaten by the Jews, and by Judas in particular. Judas is pictured as loving Jesus and as being burdened by Jesus with the load of aggression, by the invitation to be the lover and ritual executioner. Various clinical and anthropological data are used to illustrate killing in the service of libido. Surrender in love is equated to being killed and eaten. The intense oral aspects of love of the dead are emphasized. The cadaver is equated with the orally giving mother who never frustrates. Ritual sacrifice or ritual murder may have further libidinal motives such as the magic renewal of life or fecundation. Jesus and Judas are pictured as the pair of scapegoats necessary to solve by projection the ambivalent problems of the Christian: Jesus for passive love, Judas for active. The relationship between the two, however, is one of identification and love, expressed in the theme of the killer and the slain. The equation of love, murder, and death is also viewed as a regression to loss of ego boundaries and reunion with mother, and also as regression to a state of antithesis and ambiguity. Various data suggest that the relationships in love-murder express the oral tie to mother and reunion with her. Our studies may have general theoretical and clinical bearing beyond the limits of this topic. Theoretically, the problems of ambivalence, instinct fusion, and especially the theory of aggression might be further scrutinized. Clinically, the approach to certain dreams and symptoms of an apparently aggressive content might develop libidinal implications of an interesting and useful nature.

References

Andreyev, L. (1916). Judas Iscariot and others. In *The Crushed Flower and Other Stories,* trans. by H. Bernstein, pp. 162-268. New York: Alfred A. Knopf.

Anonymous (1958). Will Judas return? *Mexico This Month,* 4 (April):9-10.

Baring-Gould, S. (1874). *The Lost and Hostile Gospels: An Essay on the Toledoth Jeschu and the Petrine and Pauline Gospels of the First Three Centuries of Which Fragments Remain.* London: William and Norgate.

Bin Gorion, M. J. (1914). *Die Sagen der Juden. Die Erzväter.* Frankfurt a. M.: Rütten u. Loening.

———(1926). *Die Sagen der Juden. Mose.* Frankfurt a. M.: Rütten u. Loening.

Bonaparte, M. (1946). The legend of the unfathomable waters. *American Imago,* IV, pp. 20-31.

———(1930-1931). Dueil, necrophilie et sadisme à propos d'Edgar Poe, Review Français de Psychoanalyse 4:716-734.

Brierley, M. (1951). *Trends in Psychoanalysis.* London: The Hogarth Press.

Brill, A. A. (1941). *Necrophilia. Journal of Criminal Psychopathology,* III, pp. 51-73.

Creizenach, W. M. A. (1875). *Judas Ischarioth in Legende und Sage des Mittelalters.* Halle a. S.: Druck von E. Karras.

Dunboyne, Lord, ed. (1953). *The Trial of John George Haigh (The Acid Bath Murder).* London, Edinburgh, Glasgow: William Hodge.

Edel, L. (1951). Hugh Walpole and Henry James: the fantasy of the "killer and the slain." *American Imago,* VIII, pp. 351-369.

Elliott, R. G., and Beatty, A. R. (1940). *Agent of Death. The Memoirs of an Executioner.* New York: E. P. Dutton.

Feldman, H. (1954). The hero as assassin. *Psychoanalysis,* III, pp. 48-64.

Fenichel, O. (1940). Psychoanalysis of anti-semitism. *American Imago,* I, pp. 24-39.

Ferenczi, S. (1925). Psychoanalysis of sexual habits. *International Journal of Psycho-Analysis,* VI, pp. 372-404.

Frazer, J. (1955). *The Scapegoat.* London: MacMillan.

————(1955). *Spirits of the Corn and Wild.* Two Vols. London: MacMillan.

————(1955). *The Dying God.* London: MacMillan.

Fremantle, A. (1950). The oedipal legend in Christian hagiology. *Psychoanalytic Quarterly* 19:408–409.

Freud: The antithetical sense of primal words. *Collected Papers,* IV.

Fromm, E. (1930). Die entwicklung des Christusdogmas. *Imago,* XVI, pp. 305–373.

Goodenough, E. R. (1956). *Jewish Symbols in the Greco-Roman Period, Vols. V and VI, Fish, Bread, and Wine.* New York: Pantheon Books.

Graves, R. (1946). *King Jesus.* New York: Creative Age Press.

Graves, R., and Podro, J. *The Nazarene Gospel Restored.* Garden City, New York: Doubleday.

Grotjahn, M. (1960). Ego identity and the fear of death and dying. *Journal of the Hillside Hospital* 9:147–155.

Hartmann, A., ed. (1880). *Volksschauspiele in Bayern und Österreich-Ungarn gesammelt.* Leipzig: Breitkopf und Härtel.

Haugg, D. (1930). *Judas Iskarioth in den neutestamentlichen Berichten.* Freiburg im Breisgau: Herder u. Co., CMBH Verlag.

Hewlett, J. (1946). God save Hirohito. Act of suicide in Japan. *Travel,* April, pp. 14–16.

Hirschfeld, M. (1944). *Sexual Pathology.* New York: Emerson Books.

Jones, E. (1931). *Nightmare, Witches, and Devils.* New York: W. W. Norton.

Joya, M. (1949). *Japanese Customs and Manners.* Tokyo: The Sakrai Shoten.

Keller, A., ed. (1928). *A Hangman's Diary. Being the Journal of Master Franz Schmidt, Public Executioner of Nuremberg, 1573–1617,* trans. C. Calvett and A. W. Gruner. London: Philip Alan and Co.

Koestler, A. (1941). *Darkness at Noon.* New York: Macmillan.

Kris, E., and Kaplan, A. (1952). Aesthetic ambiguity. In *Psychoanalytic Explorations in Art,* by Ernst Kris. New York: International Universities Press.

Lewin, B. D. (1946). Countertransference in the technique of medical practice. *Psychosomatic Medicine* 8:195–199.

————(1955). Dream psychology and the analytic situation. *Psychoanalytic Quarterly* 24:169–199.

Loewenstein, R. M. (1951). *Christians and Jews. A Psychoanalytic Study.* New York: International Universities Press.

Moore, T. S. (1929). *Judas.* Chicago: Covici-McGee Co.

Mygatt, T. D., and Witherspoon, E. (1928). *The Glorious Company. Lives and Legends of the Twelve and St. Paul.* New York: Harcourt, Brace & Co.

Neumann, E. (1955). *The Great Mother: An Analysis of the Archetype,* trans. R. Manheim. New York: Pantheon Books.

O'Neill, E. (1926). The Great God Brown. In *The Best Plays of 1925-1926.* New York: Dodd, Mead.

Pomer, S. L. (1959). Necrophilic fantasies and choice of specialty in medicine. *Bulletin of the Philadelphia Association for Psychoanalysis,* IX, pp. 54-55.

Reider, N. (1960). Medieval oedipal legends about Judas. *Psychoanalytic Quarterly* 29:515-527.

Reik, T. (1923). *Der eigene und der fremde Gott. zur psychoanalyse der religiösen entwicklung.* Leipzig, Wien, Zurich: Internationaler Psychoanalytischer Verlag.

Robertson, J. M. (1913). *A Short History of Christianity.* Second edition. London: C. A. Watts.

———(1910). *Christianity and Mythology.* Second edition. London: C. A. Watts.

———(1911). *Pagan Christs. Studies in Comparative Hierology.* Second edition. London: C. A. Watts.

Róheim, G. (1955). Some aspects of semitic monotheism. In *Psychoanalysis and the Social Sciences, Vol. IV,* pp. 169-222. New York: International Universities Press.

Roth, C. (1929). *Iscariot.* London: The Mandrake Press.

Schidrowitz, L., ed. (1925). *Sittengeschichte des Theaters.* Wien, Leipzig: Verlag für Kulturforschung.

Segal, H. (1953). A necrophilic fantasy. *International Journal of Psycho-Analysis,* XXXIV, pp. 98-101.

Simmel, E. (1946). Anti-semitism and mass psychopathology. In *Anti-Semitism, A Social Disease.* New York: International Universities Press, pp. 33-78.

Synge, J. M. (1911). *The Playboy of the Western World.* Boston: John W. Luce.

Tarachow, S. Forepleasure aspects of a hobby as a defense against castration anxiety. *Journal of Hillside Hospital,* III, pp. 67-72.

Taylor, A. (1920). Judas Iscariot in charms and incantations. *Washington University Studies,* VIII, pp. 3-17.

———(1923). The burning of Judas. *Washington University Studies,* XI, pp. 159-186.

Trachtenberg, J. (1943). *The Devil and the Jews.* New Haven: Yale University Press.

Vaillant, G. C. (1953). *Aztecs of Mexico.* Garden City, New York: Doubleday.

van Heurn, A. and E. (1958). *Judas.* Philadelphia: Muhlenberg Press.

van Ophuijsen, J. H. W. (1929). The sexual aim of sadism as manifested in acts of violence. *International Journal of Psycho-Analysis,* X, pp. 139–144.

Wellisch, E. (1954). *Isaac and Oedipus. A Study in Biblical Psychology of the Sacrifice of Isaac, The Akedah.* London: Routledge and Kegan Paul.

Wertham, F. (1949). *The Show of Violence.* Garden City, New York: Doubleday.

Walsh, W. S. (1914). *Curiosities of Popular Customs.* Philadelphia: J. B. Lippincott.

Williams, T. (1954). Desire and the Black Masseur. In *One Arm and Other Stories.* New York: New Directions.

———(1958). *Suddenly Last Summer.* New York: New Directions.

Zeitlin, S. (1942). *Who Crucified Jesus?* New York and London: Harper & Bros.

Chapter 3

PYROMANIA AND THE PRIMAL SCENE:
A PSYCHOANALYTIC COMMENT ON
THE WORK OF YUKIO MISHIMA

JACOB A. ARLOW, M.D.

In the writings of the Japanese novelist, Yukio Mishima, primal scene experiences and derivative expressions of them recur persistently. The element of fire figures prominently in connection with the wish to wreak vengeance on the persons originally observed in the act of intercourse. As a destructive, attention-compelling spectacle, fire is a particularly suitable vehicle for this purpose. In Mishima's works, revenge takes the form of retaliation in kind: parental figures, or their surrogates, are put into the position of having to observe the child, or substitutes for him, in the act of sexual infidelity. These observations as well as clinical reports in the literature suggest some insights into fantasies of pyromania. They also make possible certain speculations concerning Mishima's turbulent life and dramatic suicide.

*   *   *

In 1950 in the ancient capital city of Kyoto, a young Zen priest attached to the Kinkakuji, the Temple of the Golden Pavilion, deliberately set fire to that historic structure and burned it to the ground. Set in a tranquil garden at the edge of a reflecting pool, this masterpiece of Buddhist architecture had been reversed as a national treasure for more than five hundred years and admired by visitors from all over the world.

According to the newspaper account, this young acolyte, son of a Zen Buddhist priest, had been obsessed with envy of the beauty of the Golden Temple — an envy that could be understood in terms of his extreme ugliness and lifelong stutter. The student had intended to die in the fire, but, losing courage, he ran from the burning building to a nearby hill and attempted suicide. Failing, he gave himself up to the authorities and asked to be punished as he deserved. At his trial, however, he said he did not regret having burned the temple. He said that he hated his evil, ugly, stuttering self and that this led him to hate anything beautiful. He was diagnosed as a "psychopath of the schizoid type" (Ross 1959).

This dramatic event intrigued one of Japan's most brilliant writers, Yukio Mishima. Six years after the fire, when Mishima was thirty-one, he presented his artistic apprehension of the character of this priest-turned-arsonist. Using only the essential features of the actual incident, in a novel entitled *The Temple of the Golden Pavilion* (1956), Mishima created a character at once consistent and believable. He intuited the young priest's motivation for arson and self-destruction in terms of a primal scene trauma, the consequence of having observed his mother having sexual intercourse with his uncle.

This article will trace the connection between the primal scene and the act of pyromania in the novel, *The Temple of the Golden Pavilion*. In addition, it will seek to demonstrate how this theme persists and recurs in other works by Mishima. On the basis of this investigation, some speculations about fantasies of pyromania will be offered. Illuminating the nature and role of this persistent fantasy in the life of Mishima, as revealed in his writings, makes possible some tentative hypotheses concerning some of the events in the turbulent life of this most unusual man.

The pathogenic effect on a child of witnessing adult intercourse was described many times in Freud's writings (1900, 1905, 1914, 1925, 1934–1938). Because Freud found that many events in the lives of certain individuals and some of the symptoms and unusual traits of which they complained represented repetitions or derivatives of having witnessed parental intercourse, he referred to this experience as the primal scene. He felt that observing parental intercourse is traumatic because it evokes overwhelming sexual excitement, which is transformed into anxiety. In addition, the child misinterprets the act of love as a sadomasochistic interaction and thinks the father is assaulting the mother. The child tends to identify with both parents during the act and this greatly influences subsequent fantasy life and character formation. Since Freud could not uncover clear evidence that such an event happened in each of his cases, he assumed that through phylogenetic inheritance, children develop such fantasies anyway, i.e., the concept of primal fantasy. There is considerable disagreement on the validity of this latter point.

The concept of the primal scene has been invoked to explain the origin of many different types of behavior. In a thoughtful and comprehensive critique of the literature Esman (1973) was led to say, "One is moved to wonder whether we are here confronted by one of those situations in which a theory, by explaining everything, succeeds in explaining nothing" (p. 65). Fenichel (1945), among many other authors, connects the perversion of voyeurism and voyeuristic activities in general with the primal scene. The compulsive need to witness intercourse represents an actively initiated repetition of the experience to achieve belated mastery over the original trauma. This is accomplished through the mechanism of transforming a painful experience, passively endured, into an actively induced event under the control of the individual.

According to Esman (1973), Freud's views on the etiological role of the primal scene have been repeated in the literature without challenge. He adduces clinical, anthropological, and sociological observations to indicate that these views require modification:

> Primal scene content, derived either from observation or fantasy, seems to be a universal element in the mental life of postoedipal humans. Evidence that observation of parental intercourse is *per se* traumatic to the child is not convincing; certainly, no specific pathological formation can be ascribed to it. The "sadistic conception" of the primal scene . . . appears to be largely, if not entirely, determined by other elements in the parents' behavior—in particular, by the amount of overt violent aggression they exhibit . . . . The child's response to such observations will be determined in a large measure by the cultural setting and emotional set that surrounds him. [p. 76]

The notion that a single event, like the primal scene, could of itself be traumatic seems simplistic and contrary to the dynamic viewpoint of multiply determined etiology in psychoanalysis. This notion probably reflects the lingering influence of an earlier concept of traumatic hysteria (Breuer and Freud 1893–1895), in which one crucial event was taken to constitute the pathogenic core of the entire structure of a symptom. In clinical experience, it is striking how often the patient does not recall the primal scene. The event has to be reconstructed from compelling evidence gathered in the psychoanalytic situation. In a study of fantasy, memory, and reality testing in which the primal scene was used as an example. I suggested that what is recalled as the memory of the specific event in reality represents the fusion of many actual events with fantasies that were operative both before and during the primal scene experience (Arlow 1969). In their recollections, young children are usually not able to distinguish between what they have perceived and what they have fantasied. Later, when a so-called traumatic event is integrated into the organized structure of memory, subsequent events and fantasies, which are thematically related to the original memory, are retrospectively agglomerated and condensed into the memory of the trauma. The primal scene trauma represents a type of memory schema, around which the material related to the individual's crucial oedipal conflict is organized. Edelheit (1967, 1971, 1974) has discussed these and related issues in several studies of the primal scene.

Many things which are well known and widely current in psychoanalysis do not find proportionate representation in the literature. I suspect this is true of many of the so-called sequelae of the primal scene in individuals whose analytic material and lifestyle are organized around primal scene memory schemata. A very common and prominent response in such patients is a sense of deep narcissistic mortification, a wounding of self-esteem. This often leads to the conviction that they are unloved and unlovable. It is incorporated into an all-pervasive feeling of oedipal defeat. The disappointed child feels betrayed and despairs of ever finding true love and happiness. In boys, this may be one determinant for the need to degrade the love object (Freud 1912); in girls, for prostitution fantasies. The little boy often ascribes the fact that he had to play the role of observer rather than participant in the primal scene to his phallic inferiority. He feels he was not as successful as his adult rival because he was not as attractive: he was too weak and small. In reaction to this sense of phallic humiliation, the boy may entertain grandiose, phallic, narcissistic aspirations of an exhibitionistic nature. Related to these wishes are various fantasies of stealing the omnipotent phallus, devouring it, and making it his own.

Perhaps insufficient attention has been drawn to the element of narcissistic rage as a consequence of the primal scene experience. Although most of the hostility may be directed against the parent of the same sex, both parents are held accountable, giving rise in the child to a wish to wreak vengeance on both in destructive fantasies, often of an oral character.

Of the many forms which this wish for vengeance may take, I would like to call attention to one particular kind, because it is very common, often overlooked, and offers an understanding of certain kinds of repetitious behavior growing out of the primal scene. An understanding of this type of vengeance illuminates many of the repetitive patterns of behavior related to the primal scene, without invoking the concept of mastery by active repetition, and makes it possible, instead, to understand these phenomena in terms of motivations observable in the clinical setting. It offers what Waelder (1962) called an explanation at the level of clinical generalization, rather than at the level of metapsychology.

Some years back, I described what I consider a typical dream, that is, a dream of relatively uniform manifest content with a constant latent meaning (Arlow 1961). In this type of dream, the patient is in the act of defecating when suddenly this private activity is transformed into a public spectacle. This may happen in many ways: someone may intrude into the bathroom; the door of the cubicle may disappear; a hitherto unnoticed window may materialize in the bathroom and throngs of people pass by and observe the dreamer in the act of defecating — to the surprise of the dreamer; or the dreamer may find himself in some outrageously public situation being observed by all. Associations to this type of dream lead regularly not only to the primal scene, but to a specific set of unconscious wishes as well. Analysis of the structure of such dreams is particularly instructive. They constitute a regressive representation of the primal scene, in which the act of defecation has replaced intercourse. There is, however, an important transposition of roles. In the original experience, the child was the pained and humiliated observer, while his parents engaged in an act of instinctual gratification. In the typical dream, the dreamer is the center of the stage — engaging in an act of instinctual gratification — while others are cast in the role of the humiliated, defeated observers. The dream fulfills a wish to avenge oneself on the parents by exchanging roles. It inflicts punishment in kind. During the analysis of the transference of such patients, it often happens that they leave the bathroom door unlocked, unconsciously arranging for the analyst or another patient to walk in on them. Frequently, they arrange to be observed in sexual situations, or leave revealing, telltale information sure to humiliate the discoverer for whom it was intended.

Clinical experience shows that the primal scene does not always come as a surprise to children. Often, they seek it out, either to gratify curiosity about sexual activity or to disturb the parents during the act. If children cannot be participants themselves, they can at least prevent their parents from having pleasure. Freud (1914) noted how often the need to defecate appears in connection with the primal scene.

Reference has been made to the intense oral rage aroused in the child against both parents in the primal scene. Lewin (1950, 1968) connected this theme with his concept of the oral triad. In a regressive way, the child interprets the primal scene in oral terms, conceiving the experience as a form of mutual cannibalism or reciprocal sucking. Lewin traced various types of insomnia to the experience of being awakened by parental intercourse. This insomnia, in turn, may be equated with the wakefulness of the unfed baby. The primal scene is often the event which is reproduced in adult depression and elation. It disturbs the child's sleep, leading to a wish to return to sleep, to deepen sleep, and to stay asleep — sometimes forever. Anna Freud (1946) noted that regression from oedipal anxiety to earlier pregenital levels leads to the concept of parental intercourse by mouth.

The relevance of these themes in the writings of Yukio Mishima is clear and unmistakable. *The Temple of the Golden Pavilion* (1956) is written in an autobiographical style, as if the author were the arsonist. The central figure is Mizoguchi, a puny, ugly boy who stutters. Taunted by his peers, he feels unattractive and unlovable. He envies a handsome upper classmate who possesses an excellent athletic physique and a handsome sword. At an opportune time, he seeks out the sword and defaces the scabbard. Immediately afterward, in a spirit of free association, he says, "All of a sudden, my memory alights on a tragic incident in our village."

The incident concerns a beautiful neighbor, Uiko, a girl older than himself, with whom he is enamored. One night, during the war, waking from sleep with lustful thoughts of Uiko. Mizoguchi decides to surprise her as she bicycles home from work. He hides in the dark beneath a tree and springs in front of her as she passes. Frightened and angry, Uiko exclaims, "What an extraordinary thing to do — and you only a stutterer!" Mizoguchi is crushed. He is further enraged when his uncle, having heard of the incident from Uiko, scolds him. "I cursed Uiko and came to wish for her death and, a few months later, my curse was realized."

Once again, Mizoguchi is awakened from sleep; this time by the sounds of commotion in the streets. Uiko has been arrested by the police and charged with concealing her lover, a deserter from the army. Under pressure, she leads the police to a nearby temple where her lover is hiding. Betrayed by Uiko, the soldier — before the horrified eyes of Mizoguchi and the villagers — kills her with his pistol and then commits suicide.

Before his death, Mizoguchi's father entrusts him to the care of Father Dosen at the Golden Temple. The Superior of the temple, Father Dosen, accepts Mizoguchi as an acolyte. Mizoguchi has a premonition that United States air raids will destroy the temple. His secret dream is that all Kyoto will burn. Again, to this thought he associates "an episode that took place in Kyoto toward the end of the war. It was something quite unbelievable." In the company of a friend, he comes upon an astonishingly beautiful young woman, dressed in traditional ceremonial robes. She is preparing tea in a secluded pagoda of the Nansen Temple where she is meeting her soldier-lover to say farewell before he leaves for the front. Hidden from view in this idyllic setting, Mizoguchi observes the lovers' embrace. The young woman then takes her breast from her kimono, squeezes some milk into a cup and offers it to her lover to drink. Watching the woman, Mizoguchi says, "I felt that this woman was no other than Uiko who had been brought back to life."

On the anniversary of his father's death, Mizoguchi is reluctant to return home to say the traditional prayers, because he hates his mother and wants nothing to do with her. "There is a special reason that I have, until now, avoided writing about my mother . . . concerning a certain incident, I never addressed a single word of reproof to mother . . . mother probably did not even realize that I knew about it, but ever since that incident occurred, I could not bring myself to forgive her." The incident is a primal scene trauma. Mizoguchi refers to witnessing his mother having intercourse with a visiting uncle. He awakens from sleep, noticing an abnormal swelling in the mosquito netting about his mother. The netting seems to shake in the wind. The father, dying of tuberculosis, feigns sleep and tries to shield the boy's eyes from his mother's infidelity. In a hyperbole of denial, Mizoguchi comments, "But as far as mother was concerned, apart from the fact that I could not forgive her that memory, I never once thought of avenging myself on her."

Mother soon adds insult to injury. She sells the father's land, and when Mizoguchi mentions that he might be called into the army, his mother, after the fashion of Uiko, says, "If they start taking stutterers like you into the army, then Japan is really finished."

Immediately following this recollection, Mizoguchi feels that if there were no chance of the Golden Pavilion's being destroyed, he would have lost his purpose in living. Clearly, the impulse to punish his mother had become the center of his life and had assumed the form of wishing to destroy the Golden Pavilion. The identification of the woman and her breasts with the temple is explicit in many places in the book and illuminates the difficulties Mizoguchi encounters when he first attempts intercourse. At the moment when he is about to have relations, a vision of the Golden Temple appears before his eyes and he is unable to continue; he loses his erection. Even when the beautiful girl whom he had seen at the Nansen Temple later offers her breasts to him—as earlier she had done to her soldier-lover—Mizoguchi thinks, "Beauty comes too late for me." The

Golden Temple appears before his eyes. It changes back and forth into a vision of the girl's breasts. Mizoguchi leaves her.[1]

While pondering the meaning of the Buddhist *koan* — "When you meet the Buddha, kill the Buddha. When you meet your ancestor, kill him! When you meet your mother and your father, kill them! Only thus will ye attain deliverance." — Mizoguchi's resolve to burn the temple takes definite shape. He attempts intercourse with several other women, but on each occasion a vision of the temple appears and makes it impossible for him to perform sexually. Each woman he associates with the betraying Uiko, a clear substitute for his mother.

The next crisis in the book is a repetition of a derivative of the primal scene. Wandering through the entertainment section of Kyoto, Mizoguchi comes upon the Father Superior of the temple in the company of a notorious geisha. "Unwittingly" he intrudes upon their intimacy and compounds the embarrassment by laughing inappropriately. Some time later, in a provocative, self-destructive gesture, he presents the Father Superior with a newspaper into which he has slipped a large photograph of the geisha. Now Mizoguchi knows that his mother's hope for him to succeed Father Dosen as the Superior of the temple can never be realized. From that point on, his moral decline is precipitous. He neglects his studies and dissipates the tuition money given him by the temple; he runs away, is discovered and returned to the temple where his mother humiliates him once again by slapping him in public.

Once he begins to make definite preparations to set fire to the temple, Mizoguchi feels liberated. Now when he goes to the prostitute, he finds that the vision of the temple no longer plagues him: he is potent and well satisfied. He thinks: "Did he want to lose his virginity so that he could burn the Temple or did he want to burn the Temple so that he could lose his virginity?"

When Mizoguchi finally sets out to burn the temple, he is temporarily delayed by an aged priest who is using the watercloset. Mizoguchi intends to use his luggage and bundles of straw to start the fire, but somehow the *mosquito netting* seems best for the purpose — it is the most inflammable of all the objects. He stretches the mosquito netting over the rest of the luggage; and as he sets fire to it, he is aware of overwhelming hunger.[2] The *koan* of killing one's ancestors comes to his mind. As the flames spring up, they puff out the mosquito netting (just as the wind had puffed it out in the

1. This self-defeating form of vengeance is not an uncommon factor in the etiology of certain types of masochism.
2. For the connection between burning and devouring, see Arlow (1955).

original primal scene experience); everything about him suddenly seems alive. As he runs away from the fire, the burning timbers sound like the cracking of people's joints. At the end of the book, Mizoguchi is watching the fire from atop a nearby hill. He reaches into his pocket and lights a cigarette, feeling like a man who settles down for a smoke after a job well done.

The connection between primal scene derivatives and fire runs through much of Mishima's work. The sense of shock and betrayal from witnessing a loved one having sexual relations becomes the basic motivation of the characters around whom the plots revolve. Vengeance in the form of unconscious, destructive, oral trends predominates. It will not be possible to present in detail the many elaborations of the central theme in the illustrations to follow. However, even these brief summaries will demonstrate how the primal scene dominated Mishima's fantasy life, as expressed in his writings.

Confessions of a Mask (1949) was Mishima's first novel, and is clearly autobiographical in nature. In *Thirst for Love* (1950) the principal character is Etsuko. Approaching the crematorium with the body of her recently deceased husband, she ponders, "I have not come to cremate my husband, but to cremate my jealousy." Some time earlier, she had found evidence of her husband's many sexual infidelities on his desk. Apparently, he had deliberately placed the evidence there for her to find. During his fatal illness, Etsuko had been humiliated by observing a succession of her husband's mistresses come to visit. The rest of the book concerns her obsessive love for a much younger man, by whom she feels betrayed. At its climax, in a midnight assignation scene arranged by Etsuko, she accuses the young man in these words:

> I want to let you know the pain you are all-knowingly causing me, and felt I had to cause you to experience the same degree of unbearable agony. You can't imagine how much I suffered. I wish I could have taken that pain from my heart and placed it alongside the pain you are feeling now. Then we would know which is worse. I even lost control of myself and deliberately *burned my hand in the fire*. Look. I did this because of you. This burn was for you. [p. 165, italics added]

Etsuko has become the mistress of her aged father-in-law. He awakens to find she has left his bed. After checking the young man's bedroom, he arrives in the garden as the young man, goaded by Etsuko's accusations, attempts to rape her. The young man makes no effort to flee, nor does the father-in-law do anything to reproach him. Etsuko seizes a mattock and kills the young man.

The most varied elaboration of primal scene vengeance is found in a novel written in two parts during the years 1951 and 1953, published in English translation under the title, *Forbidden Colors*. Two central figures represent aspects of one character: one is an aging novelist; the other is a young man of ambiguous sexual identity who has been hired by the novelist to serve as his alter ego. The novelist, loathed and betrayed by women, has been rejected by his mother because he is ugly. His writing habits are identical to those of Mishima: he works throughout the night in his upstairs study, sleeping in the early morning. One night, on sudden impulse, he decides to interrupt his writing and surprise his wife in the bedroom. She is not there. In the dim light of the early dawn he finds his way to the kitchen. Unnoticed, he observes his wife and the milkman in conversation; they have clearly been lovers for a long time. As he watches, the milkman performs cunnilingus on his wife.

Yuichi is a young man of surpassing beauty, irresistible to both men and women. The novelist agrees to finance the young man's education, marriage, and subsequent career—if he will be the willing instrument in the novelist's plan for vengeance on women. He says, "First, you are the most beautiful youth in the world. When I was young, I always wanted to be what you are. Secondly, you do not love women. . . . please live my youth again in another way. In short, be my son and avenge me."

With almost infinite variations, the rest of the novel represents the realization and partial miscarriage of this plan. Yuichi succeeds in seducing and injuring all the women who had humiliated the novelist, and more. The pattern of injury is almost always the same. The enthralled woman is made to witness Yuichi's infidelity to her; even Yuichi's mother and wife are not spared. To their pain, they observe his sexual misconduct with men as well as women. Initiated by the novelist into a career of arousing jealousy and betraying his victims, Yuichi becomes increasingly corrupt and dissolute. In the end, he ensnares the novelist himself.

One episode of the vengeance is a patient and naive fulfillment of a typical wish derived from the primal scene. Yuichi seduces a haughty young woman who once spurned the novelist. He takes her to a hotel room and gets her drunk. When she falls asleep, he leaves. According to plan, the novelist takes Yuichi's place in bed with the woman, and has intercourse with her. In the morning, she is surprised and humbled by the deception.

The principal affair of the novel involves Mrs. Kaburagi, who is old enough to be Yuichi's mother. She is explicitly described by Mishima as the mother-prostitute. (Yuichi's identification with the mother-prostitute is also clear.) The affair culminates in several primal scene repetitions, all of them humiliating to Mrs. Kaburagi. The novelist intrudes upon her privacy with Yuichi, and Yuichi arranges for Mrs. Kaburagi to observe him having sexual relations with her husband.

The element of fire recurs throughout the book. Whenever Yuichi feels a surge of sexual excitement, he thinks of fire and sometimes hears the sound of fire sirens. He often dreams of fire sirens. On his honeymoon, Yuichi and his wife used a telescope to watch a young couple embrace. Moving the telescope, they see a large fire in the distance. At turning points in his affairs, Yuichi observes fires. Once, while having intercourse with Mrs. Kaburagi, he is distracted by the sound of fire engines. He leaves her, goes to the fireplace, and idly stirs the coals. To him it sounds as if he were stirring bones. Strolling down the Ginza in the novel's next to last scene, Yuichi is caught up in a crowd watching a fire. The sight of the firemen "gambling against death seems to strike the hearts of the crowd with a pleasure not unlike that lewd one." (Thus fire is equated with sexual intercourse.) The crowd is carried away by excitement. A plateglass window is shattered. Yuichi notices the crowd has trampled some balloons underfoot. A sandal is sloshed about like a bit of flotsam. "The extraordinary energy of the mob scene . . . has stirred in him an inexplicable excitement. Since he had no place to go, Yuichi walked for a time and finally went into a theater that was showing a movie he did not especially want to see." (The relationship between spectacles on screen and stage and the primal scene is well documented in the literature.) Having made Yuichi his heir, the novelist commits suicide.

More chilling in its stark and brutal simplicity is *The Sailor Who Fell from Grace with the Sea* (1963). Several critics have compared this novel with Golding's *Lord of the Flies*. Mishima typically indicates the novel's main theme in the first few pages. Noboru is a young teenager living with his attractive, widowed mother. Because he has been keeping bad company, she puts him to bed early and locks him in his room. As she does so, she thinks: "What would happen if there were a fire—if the door warped in the heat or paint clogged the keyhole, and the door could not be opened?" Left alone, Noboru discovers that by removing the bottom drawer of a built-in dresser, he can look through the ceiling into his mother's bedroom. He begins to spy on her, watching her undress, and masturbate. When his mother takes a sailor as her lover, he watches them have intercourse. "They clutched at each other and collided in frenzied, awkward movements like beasts in the forest lunging at a ring of fire."

Noboru resents the sailor and shares his hostility with the members of his gang who are united in their hatred of fathers. One says that "fathers are filthy, lecherous flies who broadcast to the world that they've screwed with our mothers." Another complains his father won't buy him an air rifle. A third says his father frequently comes home drunk and bullies his mother. "When I stood up for her one time, he got white as a sheet and grinned and said, 'Keep out of this. You want to take away your mother's pleasure?'"

In a scene reminiscent of primitive initiation ceremonies, Noboru kills a cat which the gang proceeds to dissect. The act of killing makes him feel powerful — as if he had achieved true manhood. As he watches the glistening viscera emerge from the belly, he thinks of the nakedness of the sailor and his mother in sexual embrace. (Throughout Mishima's writing, intercourse is associated with death; postcoital partners are described as corpses.)

Shortly after the mother and the sailor decide to marry, they discover that Noboru has been observing their lovemaking. His mother surprises him and humiliates him by beating him for the first time in his life. The sailor, on the other hand, is conciliatory. Noboru's pride is hurt, especially now that the sailor has begun to call him "son."

The gang decides to sacrifice human blood. The sailor is designated the victim. Noboru leads the sailor to the gang's hiding place and serves him tea which had been drugged. The boys begin to tease the sailor in anticipation of what they intend to do. They grab his cap and play with it. The cap has become an "exorbitant firebrand, lighting the way to eternity." As the sailor loses consciousness, the gang members put on rubber gloves and prepare surgical instruments for the ritual murder and dissection.

Similar themes recur in Mishima's (1957) No plays and short stories. In *Sotoba Komachi,* the central figure, the Old Woman, disturbs several couples making love in the park. A young Poet enters. He has a romantic fantasy that he was in love with the Old Woman a generation earlier. He falls dead at her feet after a brief, romantic interlude. The Old Woman tells an arriving policeman that the Poet had been making sexual advances. Suddenly the Policeman calls out to some men, "You there — you're not allowed to make bonfire in the park! Come here! I've got something for you to do." In another No Play, *Cantan,* a young man loves an older woman, his former nurse. He reminds her of the loving care she showed him in a house that burned down. The short story, "The Three Million Yen" (Mishima 1953), concerns a frugal, affectionate, married couple who are saving their money to afford a house and a child. In the end, we learn that they make their living by performing sexual intercourse at private parties. In the same collection of short stories, the theme of betrayal is elaborated in "Thermos Bottle" and "Dojoji." In the former, a man betrayed by his mistress comes home and finds he has been betrayed by his wife. In the latter, the lover — caught *in flagrante* — is killed by the irate husband.

The four-volume *The Sea of Fertility* (1968b, 1969, 1970a, 1970b), is Mishima's literary testament. It is a retrospective summary of his life, beginning in a mood of lyrical romanticism and culminating in disillusion and despair. The unifying thread of the narrative is Honda, a lawyer — as Mishima had been. In the third volume, *The Temple of Dawn,* Honda is an aging man, a voyeur addicted to peeping at couples having intercourse in the park. In the library wall of his summer home, a peephole is made which opens into the guest room. For motives not immediately connected with the theme of this article, Honda is interested in a young Thai princess. He arranges with a young man to seduce the princess in the guest room while he watches. The plan, however, fails. The princess repulses the young man and takes refuge with a friend of Honda's, an aging lesbian. Some time later, Honda observes the princess and the lesbian in the guest room, having sexual relations. A fire breaks out in the summer house that night, and it burns to the ground. During the excitement the princess disappears. For a while one is led to believe that she may have perished in the flames. This turns out to be untrue. Several years later, Honda learns from her twin sister that the princess had died two years after the fire — from a snakebite.

The primal scene and derivative representations constitute a significant and repetitive element in Mishima's writing and, presumably, in his fantasy life. Three responses to the primal scene seem to be prominent: first, the primal scene is experienced as a humiliating defeat leading to a wish to retaliate in kind; second, one observes the evocation of tremendous destructive rage against one or both parents; and third, the primal scene is symbolically represented by the element of fire or is screened off by memories of fire. Fire is also a vehicle for the oral destructive wishes against one or both parents, expressing primitive, unconscious fantasies of devouring, consuming, and incorporating. Because of its great power to destroy, fire lends itself readily as a vehicle to gratify sadistic impulses used to redress grievances from whatever source. The literature on fire-setting is full of case reports of fires set for the purpose of revenge (Karpman 1954, Lewis and Yarnell 1951, Macht and Mack 1968, Podolsky 1953, Stekel 1922).

Fire can create a compelling spectacle of mounting intensity and excitement, one that can get out of control. This aspect is particularly appealing to some individuals bent on destructive revenge originating in a primal scene trauma. Both sexual and aggressive impulses are projected onto the fire, which comes to serve as a symbol and a screen for the original experience or fantasy. In one of the few well-documented case reports of pyromania treated from the psychoanalytic point of view, Karpman (1954) furnished a striking illustration of some of these dynamic elements. Shortly after receiving a letter from his fiancée announcing that she was going to marry someone else, Karpman's patient, a soldier at the front, saw a village go up in flames. In the smoke he saw a vision of his fiancée. Years later, when frustrated or angry over some disappointment, he would set a fire to see once again the image of his fiancée going up in smoke. The report, unfortunately, has no record of the infantile conflicts, except for some references to fears of devouring or being devoured.[3]

In a case reported elsewhere (Arlow 1977), a memory of a fire in which several people were killed served to screen off a primal scene experience that aroused murderous wishes against both parents, particularly the mother. During childhood, the patient had a recurrent dream in which he saw his home burned to the ground. In the dream, he realized with great sadness that his mother had died. As a child, he set fire to a backyard rubbish heap where he had seen a boy making sexual advances to a girl.

Most early psychoanalytic literature emphasizes the element of urethral erotism in relation to fire and fire-setting (Freud 1931, Michaels 1954, Simmel 1949, Stekel 1922). More recent reports are less definite in this regard. Grinstein (1952) noted that fire may symbolize libidinal impulses from all levels of psychosexual development. From my clinical observations, I have noted that the element of fire in dreams, fantasies, and memories often represents oral wishes, erotic and aggressive, active and passive (Arlow 1955).

Almansi (1954) has developed this theme in connection with religious rituals. Because Mishima's imagination was rich in elaborately detailed, exquisitely ritualized fantasies of sacrifice, cannibalism, and drinking blood *(Confessions of a Mask),* I will quote at length a relevant passage from my paper on fire and oral symbolism (1955):

> In a religious ritual, consigning the sacrificial animal to the fire on the altar is suggested as representing a communal re-enactment of the elements of the totem feast. Permission to kill and devour the totem animal is granted to the priest and through symbolic identification with him the members of the group unconsciously gratify their parricidal and cannibalistic wishes. In ancient religions the priests had the prerogative of

3. Axberger (1973), in a paper on arson in literature, called attention to how the themes of fire-setting and incest recur in most of the major works of the American poet, Robinson Jeffers. In almost all the instances he cited, moreover, the fire was set out of vengeance by a humiliated lover who had just witnessed an act of sexual betrayal involving the incestuously loved object. Axberger speculated, as did Lewis and Yarnell (1951), that Jeffers and other authors could have become fire-setters were it not for the sublimation of this trend made possible by creative writing.

eating the flesh of the animals sacrificed as burnt offerings. By the independent but complementary transformation of the aim and the object . . . the fiery sacrifice of the animal evolves into the sacrament of communion. The flesh and blood of the animal are replaced by more remote representatives of the human body, namely, the wafer and the wine, but the element of devouring, heretofore distorted by the act of burning, re-emerges undisguised in the oral incorporation of the host in the sacrament of communion. In funeral rites, the ritual pyre and cremation may be interpreted, as is burial in the earth, as a re-entry into the immortality of the womb; in the former instance, however, the route of oral ingestion is represented by burning. [p. 70]

In three of Mishima's novels *(The Temple of the Golden Pavilion, Forbidden Colors,* and *The Temple of Dawn),* burning is equated with oral destruction. Writing to his mentor, Shimizu, toward the end of World War II, Mishima described his pleasure at watching Tokyo burn: "The air raids on the distant metropolis, which I watched from the shelter of the arsenal, were beautiful. The flames seemed to hue to all colors of the rainbow; it was like watching the light of a distant bonfire at a great *banquet* of extravagant death and destruction" (Nathan 1974, p. 58, italics added).[4]

Edelheit (1967, 1971, 1974) has paid particular attention to the symbolic portrayal of the primal scene in fantasy, literature, art, and mythology. The figure of Christ nailed to the cross represents the parents superimposed and united during intercourse. Edelheit maintains crucifixion fantasies are the most common, though far from the only, symbolic representation of the primal scene in our culture. Several alternative expressions of the primal scene are mentioned, including bullfight fantasies. These are particularly suitable because of the marked ambiguity regarding the roles of victim and aggressor in the classic bullfight. Some additional clinical alternates for crucifixion fantasies include Joan of Arc at the stake, Prometheus, the binding of Isaac by Abraham, and the story of Judith and Holofernes. Mishima's (1953) classic short story, "Patriotism," is especially pertinent. A young bride — and through her, the reader — watches in horror as her husband commits *seppuku.* The act is described in meticulous and gruesome detail, reminiscent of the dissection of the cat in *The Sailor Who Fell from Grace*

---

4. Stekel (1922) described the masturbation fantasies of two patients who had the impulse to set fires. Stekel traced one patient's impotence to his observation of his parents during intercourse. It is not my intention, however, to suggest that primal scene pathology is involved in all cases of fire-setting.

with the Sea. If we use Edelheit's concept, the ritualized *seppuku* in "Patriotism" can be regarded as a disguised representation of the primal scene that the woman is vengefully forced to observe.

Mishima's career was meteoric and dazzling. In approximately twenty-five years, he produced no fewer than twenty-three novels, more than forty plays, almost one hundred short stories, and several volumes of poetry, essays, and travel literature. He was considered for the Nobel Prize in Literature. The committee passed over Mishima, apparently in consideration of his youth, in favor of his countryman and mentor, Kawabata. In addition, Mishima appeared in several stage productions, directed and starred in films, was recognized throughout the world as one of Japan's outstanding writers, and was richly rewarded financially.

Kimitake Hiraoka (Mishima is a pen name) was born in 1925 of mixed lineage. His mother's family were middle-class scholars. His paternal grandfather came from peasant stock, and the grandmother was from a noble family. Mishima's childhood was highly unusual. His irascible, domineering, neurotic grandmother took possession of him when he was only a few weeks old. He was then raised at her sickroom bedside until he was twelve. The baby's mother was summoned by a bell from the upstairs apartment to nurse her child for a carefully measured number of minutes. She was allowed to walk him and was later given permission to escort him to and from school. The regimen imposed by the grandmother was overprotective and emasculating. Mishima was not allowed to play with boys, run about, or make noise. Even the brandishing of a ruler in childish imitation of sword-play was prohibited. To make matters worse, he was a puny, sickly, unattractive child. At the age of four, he almost died of an illness diagnosed as "auto-intoxication." For years after, at monthly intervals, the symptoms recurred in attenuated form. In addition, he suffered from anemia and attacks of respiratory illness (Nathan 1974, Scott-Stokes 1974).

Confession of a Mask (1949), Mishima's first major success, is an astonishingly revealing autobiographical novel. He describes his envy of the beautiful physique of the school's outstanding athlete. His fantasies of attaining his ideal of masculine perfection by murdering and devouring a beautiful youth are described in this book in connection with the struggle against his emerging homosexuality. His fantasy life was indeed bizarre, perverse, and grisly, with detailed descriptions of ritual slaughter, cannibalism, drinking blood, and a wide range of sadomasochistic images.

In these fantasies, Mishima cast himself in both the active and passive roles. These trends had been adumbrated by an earlier preoccupation with the idea of noble, violent death in battle and by fairy tales of sadomasochistic content. As a child he had been enamored of a picture of a beautiful youth in armor. He was shocked to learn from his nurse that the youth was not a boy, but a girl—Joan of Arc.[5] When he was twelve, Mishima found a picture of St. Sebastian bound to a tree, his body pierced by two lone arrows. "The arrows have *eaten* into the tense, fragrant, youthful flesh and are about to consume his body from within the *flames* of supreme agony and ecstasy" (*Confessions of a Mask,* 1949, pp. 39–40, italics added). The image of the bound martyr aroused a surge of sexual passion within the young Mishima that culminated in his first experience of masturbation and ejaculation. For some time thereafter, the image of St. Sebastian or some alternative expression of the same idea played a central role in his erotic fantasies. He also composed a prose poem about St. Sebastian. Until the age of nine, Mishima indulged in transvestite play. In his adult years, he became fanatically dedicated to bodybuilding through weight lifting and Kendo, the classical form of Japanese fencing. The florid psychopathology depicted in this autobiographical novel needs much fuller discussion than is possible here.

After a poor start, Mishima turned into a brilliant student, and graduated first in his class from the ultra-elitist Peers School in 1944. Receiving the prize from the Emperor on that occasion was one of the high points in Mishima's life. At his father's insistence, he took a degree in law at the Imperial University in Tokyo. His father, a staunch admirer of the Nazis, despised writing, and considered it a profession for degenerate, weakling intellectuals. His mother, to whom he was devoted, supported Mishima in his literary ambitions, and he read every page of his writings to her. After one year in government service, Mishima resigned to write full time. Within a few years, he was an acknowledged figure in the rising generation of postwar writers. For all his many interests and talents, he was a disciplined worker. No matter what he might have done earlier in the evening, Mishima returned to his study shortly after midnight and wrote all night, sleeping during the early morning hours. (He had been a poor sleeper as a child. The anticipation of any exciting event made him insomniac.)

To date, two biographies of Mishima have appeared in English. Both begin with his death—and for good reason. As spectacular as the burning of the

5. Bisexual identity, so clear in his own life and in the hero of *Forbidden Colors,* also pervades his final work, *The Sea of Fertility.* In Volume II, *Runaway Horses* (1969), Isao, the leader of an abortive youth rebellion, shortly before he commits *seppuku,* has a dream in which he sees himself as a woman in a sexual situation. It is also noteworthy that in the next volume, Isao is reincarnated as a woman, the Thai princess who has a lesbian relationship which Honda, the hero, observes through a peephole the evening his house burns down.

Golden Temple may have been, it pales in comparison to the awesome way in which Mishima ended his life in November 1970. In the morning, he completed the final page of the manuscript of his masterpiece, *The Sea of Fertility*. Leaving behind detailed instructions for settling his affairs, Mishima drove to the headquarters of the Eastern Army at Ichigaya. He was accompanied by four young students from a private and miniscule *opérabouffe* he had recruited. They gained entrance to the office of the commanding general, and by threatening him with a sword, received permission to address the garrison. Mishima harangued the soldiers to rise up in revolt and to follow him to restore the Imperial prerogative. The soldiers jeered and mocked him. Rebuked and humiliated by the crowd, Mishima left the balcony, and returned to the general's office. With the aid of his accomplices, he carried out his plan. In the traditional *seppuku* ritual, Mishima disembowled himself and was decapitated by his assistants. Like the Golden Temple, his career ended in a spectacle of horror.

Earlier in the paper, I noted that Mishima associated intercourse with ideas of dying and being put to death. Almost without fail, he described lovers after intercourse as corpses. If we add to this observation Edelheit's interpretation of crucifixion and binding fantasies, it becomes possible to illuminate certain aspects of Mishima's life and work. Viewed as an expression of a primal scene fantasy, the story of Judith and Holofernes suggests a deeper understanding of the manner of Mishima's death. He elected to be decapitated by Morita, his favorite disciple and — according to one biographer (Scott-Stokes 1974, pp. 303–305) — his homosexual lover. The act of execution thus became an act of love. In Tarachow's (1960: Chapter 2 of this volume) terms, Morita was assigned the role of the beloved executioner. Accordingly, the dramatic public *seppuku* and decapitation of November 1970 may be interpreted as a spectacular, grandiose acting out of a sadomasochistically conceived, homosexually elaborated, primal scene fantasy.

In this light, it becomes possible to correlate two major trends in the fantasy life of Mishima. The themes of betrayal, revenge, and destruction by fire have already been related to the primal scene. Now Mishima's preoccupation with crucifixion, murder, theater, binding, and ritualized cannibalism can also be included under the same unifying rubric, i.e., the concept of the primal scene.

Mishima's private fantasy and literary imagination ultimately crossed over into real life. He was a man of action, a showman who delighted in and was, perhaps, compelled to create spectacles, a man who acted out his fantasy life. According to Fenichel (1945), this is a feature characteristic of individuals traumatized by the primal scene. A few examples will illustrate how Mishima tended to act out his fantasies. His fascination with the image of St. Sebastian has already been noted. Four years before his death, he posed for a photograph as St. Sebastian, hands bound, his body pierced with arrows, blood dripping from the wounds. In 1968, he completed *Runaway Horses,* a novel about a futile, immature, rightwing revolutionary group of youngsters under the leadership of an older officer. The hero commits suicide at the end of the book by *seppuku.* That same year, Mishima founded a secret, private, rightwing army of young students; he was its leader and the only adult. In the end, he lived out the main elements of the novel. In *Confessions of a Mask,* he related his fantasy of drinking the blood of a ceremonially sacrificed youth. In 1967, when he inaugurated his private army at a blood-oath ceremony, each member of the group dripped his blood into the cup until it was full. After they signed their names in blood, Mishima suggested that they drink it. "He picked up the glass and asked, 'Is anyone here ill? None of you have VD?' He called for a salt cellar and flavored the cup; then he drank from it" (Scott-Stokes 1974, p. 242).

How and why the primal scene came to play so important a role in the works and life of Yukio Mishima is hard to know.[6] However, his literary works are dominated by a primal scene fantasy. Various elaborations of the fundamental fantasy can be inferred. One set of elaborations is the theme of murderous oral revenge against the humiliating parental figures or their surrogates. The aggressive oral wishes associated with this type of elaboration were transformed into fantasies of fire-setting and burning. This theme found sublimated expression in his literary creations. The other principal elaboration went in the direction of sadomasochistic trends. For many years they too were constrained more or less by the sublimation made possible by his literary genius.[7]

In the end, however, the compulsion to act out disemboweling fantasies proved uncontrollable, and Mishima shocked the world in what was probably one of the most bizarre suicides of modern times. In his death, he unconsciously achieved the suicide-murder that Mizoguchi had planned when he set fire to the Golden Pavilion. He brought down upon himself the burning oral rage of the retribution he intended for the principals of the primal scene.

6. Primal scene experiences must be very common in the crowded conditions of Japanese life. This study deals with how the primal scene dominated Mishima's imagination and thought. Discussion of the complex cultural, political, and historical determinants belong to scholars of the realities of Japanese life and tradition. A parallel study from the historical point of view on how traditional factors contributed to the culmination of Mishima's career in the political act of self-destruction was recently presented by Morris (1975).

7. According to one biographer (Scott-Stokes 1974), Mishima was the only major modern Japanese writer to concern himself with *seppuku.*

References

Almansi, R. J. (1954). A further contribution to the psychoanalytic interpretation of the menorah. *Journal of Hillside Hospital* 3:3–18.

Arlow, J. A. (1955). Notes on oral symbolism. *Psychoanalytic Quarterly*
24:63–74.

————(1961). A typical dream. *Journal of Hillside Hospital* 10:154–158.

————(1969). Fantasy, memory, and reality testing. *Psychoanalytic
Quarterly* 38:28–51.

————(1977). Revenge Motif of the Primal Scene. Unpublished.

Axberger, G. (1973). Arson and fiction: a cross-disciplinary study. *Psychiatry,* XXXVI, pp. 244–265.

Breuer, J., and Freud, S. (1893–1895). Studies on hysteria. *Standard
Edition* 2.

Edelheit, H. (1967). Discussion of A. J. Lubin's *The Influence of the Russian Orthodox Church on Freud's Wolf-Man: A Hypothesis. Psychoanalytic Forum* 2:165–166.

————(1971). Mythopoiesis and the primal scene. In *The Psychoanalytic
Study of Society,* vol. V, ed. W. Muensterberger and A. Esman, pp. 212–
233. New York: International Universities Press.

————(1974). Crucifixion fantasies and their relation to the primal scene.
International Journal of Psycho-Analysis 55:193–199.

Esman, A. H. (1973). The primal scene: a review and a reconsideration.
In *Psychoanalytic Study of the Child* 28:49–81.

Fenichel, O. (1945). *The Psychoanalytic Study of Neurosis.* New York:
Norton.

Freud, A. (1946). The psychoanalytic study of infantile feeding disturbances. *Psychoanalytic Study of the Child* 2:119–132.

Freud, S. (1900). The interpretation of dreams. *Standard Edition* 4/5:1–
361.

————(1905). Three essays on the theory of sexuality. *Standard Edition*
7:123–243.

————(1912). The universal tendency to debasement in the sphere of love.
Standard Edition 11:179–190.

————(1914). From the history of an infantile neurosis. *Standard Edition*
17:7–122.

————(1925). Some psychical consequences of the anatomical distinction
between the sexes. *Standard Edition* 19:248–258.

————(1931). The acquisition and control of fire. *Standard Edition* 22:
187–193.

————(1934–1938). Moses and monotheism. *Standard Edition* 23:17–137.

Grinstein, A. (1952). Stages in the development of control over fire. *International Journal of Psycho-Analysis* 33:416–420.

Karpman, B. (1954). A case of fulminating pyromania. *Journal of Nervous and Mental Disease* 119:205–232.

Lewin, B. D. (1950). *The Psychoanalysis of Elation.* New York: The Psychoanalytic Quarterly.

———(1968). *The Image and the Past.* New York: International Universities Press.

Lewin, D. N., and Yarnell, H. (1951). *Pathological Firesetting (Pyromania).* Nervous and Mental Disease Monograph No. 82. New York and Washington, D.C.: Nervous and Mental Diseases Publishing Company.

Macht, L. B., and Mack, J. E. (1968). Firesetter syndrome. *Psychiatry* 31:277–288.

Michaels, J. J. (1954). Disorders of character, persistent enuresis, juvenile delinquency and psychopathic personality. *Journal of Nervous and Mental Disease* 120:408–410.

Mishima, Y. (1949). *Confessions of a Mask.* Trans. M. Weatherby. New York: New Directions, 1958.

———(1950). *Thirst for Love.* Trans. A. H. Marks. New York: Berkley Publishing, 1971.

———(1951–1953). *Forbidden Colors.* Trans. A. H. Marks. New York: Berkley Publishing, 1974.

———(1953). *Death in Midsummer and Other Stories.* Trans. D. Keene, I. Morris, J. Sargent, E. Seidensteiker. New York: New Directions, 1966.

———(1956). *The Temple of the Golden Pavilion.* Trans. I. Morris. Berkley Publishing, 1971.

———(1957). *Five Modern Nō Plays.* Trans. D. Keene. New York: Vintage Books.

———(1963). *The Sailor Who Fell from Grace with the Sea.* Trans. J. Nathan. New York: Berkley Publishing, 1976.

———(1968a). *Sun and Steel.* Trans. J. Bester. New York: Grove Press.

———(1968b). *Spring Snow.* Trans. M. Gallagher. New York: Alfred A. Knopf.

———(1969). *Runaway Horses.* Trans. M. Gallagher. New York: Alfred A. Knopf, 1973.

———(1970a). *The Temple of Dawn.* Trans. E. D. Saunders and C. S. Segile. New York: Alfred A. Knopf, 1973.

———(1970b). *The Decay of the Angel.* Trans. E. Seidensteiker. New York: Alfred A. Knopf, 1974.

Morris, I. (1975). *The Mobility of Failure.* New York: Holt, Rinehart and Winston.

Nathan, J. (1974). *Mishima. A Biography.* Boston and Toronto: Little, Brown.

Podolsky, E. (1953). The mind of the pyromaniac. *Indian Medical Record* 73:240–243.

Ross, N. W. (1959). Introduction to *The Temple of The Golden Pavilion.* New York: Berkley Publishing, 1971.

Scott-Stokes, H. (1974). *The Life and Death of Yukio Mishima.* New York: Farrar, Straus and Giroux.

Simmel, E. (1949). Incendiarism. In *Searchlights on Delinquency,* ed. K. R. Eissler, pp. 90–101. New York: International Universities Press.

Stekel, W. (1922). *Peculiarities of Behavior: Wandering Mania, Dipso-mania, Cleptomania, Pyromania and Allied Impulsive Acts.* New York: Boni and Liveright, 1924.

Tarachow, S. (1960). Judas, the Beloved Executioner. *Psychoanalytic Quarterly* 29:528–554.

Waelder, R. (1962). Review of Psychoanalysis, Scientific Method, and Philosophy, ed. S. Hook. *Journal of the American Psychoanalytic Association* 10:617–637.

Chapter 4

FUSION WITH THE VICTIM:
A STUDY OF SYLVIA PLATH

SHELLEY ORGEL, M.D.

I

Anna Freud describes how a little girl conquered her fear of meeting ghosts in a dark hall. The girl made all sorts of peculiar gestures as she walked, saying, "There is no need to be afraid in the hall, you just have to pretend that you are the ghost who might meet you." This instance of warding off, by externalization as well as by creative magic, the danger of being overwhelmed by the returned dead serves as a beautiful introduction to a paper relating a vicissitude of identification with the aggressor, suicide, and creativity.

Miss Freud describes identification with the aggressor as a "by no means uncommon stage" in the normal development of the superego. The internalized aggression or criticism, not yet immediately transformed into self-criticism, is dissociated from the child's own reprehensible activity (Beres 1958). The dissociation from self-representations places identification with the aggressor in relation to *negation* (Freud 1925) as a necessary intermediate stage in the ego's acceptance of unpleasurable reality. Negation constitutes a partial denial, a transitional stage between the pleasure and reality egos, the first measure of freedom from the consequences of primal repression. In the same sense, identification with the aggressor may be regarded both as a forerunner of the superego and as a stage in the development of the apprehension of reality. This formulation clarifies Freud's speculation (1923) that superego formation, and implicitly, regulation by the internalized superego, constitute the boundary between primary and secondary repression.

In other terms, identification with the aggressor implies a defensive ability to separate self- and object-images by projection of the less neutralized aggressive drives onto external objects at the same time as a sample, as it were, is temporarily taken into the self. Therefore, this kind of identification finds a place analogous to that of signal anxiety in relation to predominantly libidinal or fused drives, and to "negation" as a partial denial of unpleasurable reality in the service of protecting the immature ego (Freud 1925). Externalization of the offense partially spares this ego the destructive effects of insufficiently neutralized aggression. True morality begins when the internalized criticism, now embodied in the standards exacted by the superego (whose contents include aggression of varying degrees of neutralization compatible with the ego's ability to mediate discharge or countercathexis) coincides with the ego's perception of its own fault. The severity of the superego is then turned inward instead of outward, and the subject becomes less intolerant of other people, and more able to make accurate judgments about them.

Identification with the aggressor resembles melancholia in its use of the mechanism of identification, and paranoia in its use of projection. In both melancholic and paranoic reactions, a sensitive, flexible relationship to the "otherness" of objects, and therefore to reality testing is disturbed. True morality, on the other hand, requires a stable retention of self-object differentiation and maintains the object relationship even in the face of threatened aggression by the object or the self. A structured superego is, then, a barrier against suicide, maintaining a balance between identification and projective elements compatible with normal empathy, preventing both object loss and regressive self-object fusion.

In clinical observations and in studying the works and lives of some suicidal literary artists, I believe it is possible to discern the frequent existence of a regressive vicissitude of identification with the aggressor which may be called *fusion with the victim.* In those who suffer the consequence of *fusion with the victim,* one sees evidence of failed attempts to maintain stable aggressive feelings ranging from self-assertiveness, to rational or even paranoid criticism, to sadomasochistic relationships, to hatred toward others who may actually behave as aggressor. It seems impossible to turn passive into active aggression. Ping-nie Pao (1965) notes that even hatred may serve defense and ego stability since it "establishes a sense of continuity, and may be used as an ego-syntonic defense, as a basis of a relationship, and as the core of a person's identity." "Hate" as used in this context is genetically related to the original differentiating relationship to the outside world described by Freud (1915) and to the fifteen months' "No" of Spitz (1965b). Fusion with the victim corresponds to an exact opposite of identification with the aggressor itself and paranoid reactions; decompensation may lead to symptoms resembling melancholia. The idealized object, still largely fused with the primary narcissistic self is seen not as omnipotent but as a victim; the subject, instead of turning passivity into activity and externalizing the aggression or becoming like the aggressor, turns the aggression against himself, becoming one with the victim object.

"Fusion with the victim" is to be differentiated from a masochistic relationship with objects. In the latter, the ego maintains a fused libidinal-aggressive (ambivalent) relationship to objects in the external world. In the masochistic configuration, the sadistic superego — internalized to a greater or lesser degree — seeks as objects of instinctual gratification masochistic self-representations within the ego. The self is felt as deserving this aggression (partly because the superego introjects are loved as well) and submits. Or, the self may reproject the partially reinstinctualized superego components, attach them to substitute objects, and seek suffering and punishment at the hands of a masochistically loved object (Freud 1924).

The fixation on this vicissitude impedes passing into and beyond the stage of identification with the aggressor, and creates conditions that favor regression in the face of instinctual upsurges, as in the height of the oedipal phase, in adolescence, or in the event of the death of a parent in childhood. This paper postulates that when the primary love object fails to provide reliable aggressive resonance with the infant from about six months to fifteen months (more or less the time of Spitz's third organizer of the psyche [1965] and the height of the practicing phase of Mahler [1965]), it impedes the immature ego in its capacity to neutralize its aggressive drives, and to discharge these drives sufficiently in a fused form onto that object to provide a safe focus for projection of aggression away from the ego. Effectively, the object has abandoned the infant in depriving him of gratification of his need to project an omnipotent self capable of absorbing his waves of aggression. Primitive identification involving the fusion of self- and object-images are relatively less able to be overlaid with true object identifications in the ego at a safe distance from the primitive self, and, later, superego identifications at a safe distance from the ego core (Loewald 1962). Loewald states that "There are reasons to assume that internalization per se is only one element of at least certain kinds of identifications, and that projection plays an important part in them." Loewald refers here to the fact that projection (externalization) in this early phase creates differentiated objects that are later internalized in more advanced identifications which may then be projected, as in identification with the aggressor. The inability to externalize primitive aggression is therefore related to the impossibility to use the defense of "identification with the aggressor" effectively in normal development.

I believe that clinical research may lend support to the hypothesis that this situation is the earliest infantile prototype of many presuicidal states in later life, when the revived threat of loss of narcissistically cathected objects leads to their idealization, and to the internalization of aggression in both the ego and the relatively primitive superego. The object is seen as a hopeless victim of the subject's aggression. By attributing to it the subject's own ego overwhelmed by aggressive energies, the subject, unable to externalize the aggression, as could occur in identification with the real or fantasied aggressor, tends toward a regressive revival of incomplete differentiation between the self as uncontrolled aggressor and idealized object representation as fantasied victim. Self-destructive fantasies and behavior may follow. The acting out of these fantasies confirms the blissful illusion that the object fused with the self characterizing the primary symbiotic phase has been recaptured. The external world is hungrily searched for imagos of idealized helpless victims in human, nonhuman objects, and anthropomorphized inanimate forms to consolidate a fragmenting self-image through primitive, global identifications with them.

Internalization of an external object is structure building (Loewald 1962); while internalization of the fused self-object[1] imagos of the primary narcissistic stage means a regression to an undifferentiated state. The ultimate extension of self-victimization, therefore, is to let oneself die, and there is a self-preservative dread of the trend to this type of primitive identification. Restitutional attempts are made to a greater or lesser extent to create counter-aggression in the sought-for objects. (This would be the analogue of Mahler's "mirroring frame of reference" [1961] applied to the *aggressive drive,* with the aim of promoting externalization, self-object boundaries, fusion of drives, neutralization of aggression, and the kind of aggressive dialogue that can become the vehicle of an object tie.) Such a relationship, even with someone who can be safely hated or an aggressor with whom one can safely identify, or to whom one can masochistically submit, provides an

1. Unless otherwise noted, "self-object" is used in this paper to indicate a degree of fusion between self- and object-representations, and not in the sense of Kohut's "self-object."

external object upon whom one may rid oneself of quantities of aggression that threaten ego fragmentation and self-destruction.[2]

The observations of Spitz (1953, 1965b) and others suggest that the first infantile prototype of fusion with the victim may be found in the syndrome of anaclitic depression and recovery from it in the second six months of life, and that this syndrome may be etiologically related to self-destructive impulses and behavior in later life.

The two primal drives, libido and aggression, are functionally differentiated out of the great energy reservoir of the narcissistic stage. At first, they are directed at what Spitz calls the "pre-object," a precursor of the libidinal object which evolves into the object through the circularized interrelation between the integration and structuration of the ego, and the expression of the drives in response to environmental influence (through nonverbal "dialogue").

The reactions of the earliest libidinal object to aggression by the infant begins a distinction between self and nonself, a further distinction between animate and inanimate, and finally a distinction between friend and stranger. The development of the drives, therefore, both libidinal and aggressive, is closely linked to the infant's relation to the (libidinal) object. It is this relationship that gives the infant the opportunity to release his aggressive drives in all the activities provoked in him by the actions of the object.

Solnit's observations (1966) also demonstrate that a need-satisfying object allows the discharge of aggressive energies. Without this discharge these psychic energies remain attached to, and directed against, the self (the bodily self in the first year). The "ability to retain biochemical replacements represents a degree of physiological inhibition that may be the equivalent of the psychological capacity to postpone or wait. The psychological capacity to postpone or wait requires that there be a counter-cathexis against the instinctual drives pressing for immediate discharge." This counter-cathexis is provided by the first object, and helps neutralization of aggression and its alloplastic adaptive discharge in action and socialization (see also Mahler 1961).

In waves of *projection,* used here in the sense of mechanical outward discharge (see Novick and Kelly 1970), the aggression is gradually directed to a

2. See Solnit (1966, 1970) on the necessity for appropriate counter-aggression by adults toward children in cases of severe object loss in order to establish identification with the aggressor and to cure self-destructive, provocative behavior. In fact, Solnit feels that limited object constancy is necessary to establish identification with the aggressor, and certain elements of object constancy can be achieved better in a relationship characterized by aggressive interactions than by libidinal ones.

variably differentiated object who responds to this by an appropriate balance of loving counter-aggression and directive limit setting that aids drive fusion and strengthens the tendency to turn aggression away from being lived out on the body to being turned toward the external world.

This vital step sets limits to self-injury from biting, scratching, etc., although indications of such tendencies can be seen as genuine remnants in children at later ages. (Such remnants should not be confused with the later "turning out of aggression against the self" which is not a defect of maturation, but a defense mechanism initiated at the behest of the superego, and used by the ego under the impact of conflict.) "The normal forward move happens partly due to the setting up of the pain barrier, partly due to the child's answering to the mother's libidinal cathexis of his body with a narcissistic cathexis of his own" (Hoffer 1950, see also Rochlin 1961). Thus, the first object also provides a pathway to the outside by aiding in the development of the reliable cathexis of a pain barrier, a phenomenon which depends on the narcissistic libidinal cathexis of the body. The pain barrier is of clinical importance in later self-destructive activities.

Greenacre (1960) describes the infant's physical resistance to the mother in the second six months of life. The infant jumps up and down with gurgling pleasure while being held by the mother who remains seated. The infant is also in visual contact with the mother. In terms of motivation, Greenacre sees these and other activities not as physical aggression, but rather as "a degree of biologically autonomous againstness, which combines with and may be augmented by the mother's tendencies to respond with reciprocal motion" (p. 217). There develops in these activities an increasing sense of physical power and the inability to initiate it and control it to a degree. There also develops a certain amount of reality testing through rhythmical back-and-forth contact maintained through vision. Later, babies go through these motions without the mother. These processes represent body maturation and awareness linked with ego development, and are mediated through reciprocal activity of the aggressive drives.

Activities of the fifteen to sixteen months walking stage and later phallic phase activities involve both libidinal gratification, a component pleasure in skin, muscle and kinesthetic eroticism, and genital pleasure. They also show an element of integration, organization, and mastery involving a reaction to and on the environment, rather than a primary focus on the control of bodily functions, as is the case in the activities of the special erogenous zones in the libidinal phases of development. Greenacre proposes that pleasure in functioning in the fifteen to sixteen months walking stage and phallic phase activities utilizes the *aggressive instinctual drives* in relation to objects that offer proper opposition and reactions. These observations shed light on the depressive reactions and the presuicidal state in which such pleasure in functioning is impossible, and life loses all its enjoyment.

If the mother does not allow optimal phase-appropriate aggressive stimulation, there is an increment in destructive, cruel, or aggressive drives. Object relations are impeded and turned in a hostile direction; in other words the "object," still poorly differentiated from the self-representations, becomes precociously cathected as a "victim" of the subject's drives.

Hartmann, Kris, and Loewenstein (1949) consider the frustration of aggression analogous to the frustration of libido. If a child is not limited in his aggression, when he needs external controls to maintain the object representation — if his ego and later his superego disapprove of these impulses — if the aggressor (child) is disarmed by indifference, kindness, or love, aggression is frustrated and becomes internalized. The concept of frustration of aggression can also be applied meaningfully to early infantile development. If aggression cannot be discharged on the object (a mother who is depressed, for instance), it creates a victim of the idealized early object whose representations may be, at first, "offending" body parts of infant and mother comprising the early "outside." Thus the first object representations become the first "victims" of aggression, and are incorporated in this form as part of the self-representation.

Similarly, Spitz (1953, 1965) points out that if the infant is deprived of the libidinal object, both drives are deprived of their target. This is what happens to infants affected with anaclitic depression. These infants slowly become self-destructive. Spitz proposes a transitional stage to which those who establish fusions with the victim-object regressively return. The infant has already delimited the self and outer world under routine conditions (see also Jacobson 1964). However, when circumstances of suffering arise in which the infant cannot vent its aggression on the outer world, then the boundaries become fluid again, and the aggressive action is directed against the only object available, its own body. (See also Solnit 1972, on auto-aggressive behavior.) When the mother returns after a limited absence, the infant's manifestations of external aggression are particularly conspicuous, like the reactions after a suicide attempt (Friedman et al. 1972), as if the aggressive drive is the carrier not only for itself, but also for the libidinal drive. This is, of course, an elaboration of Freud's basic description of the process by which primary masochism becomes primary sadism (Freud 1924) with the aid of a libidinal object. This deflection reverses the downhill course of anaclitic depression, the prototype and earliest version of letting oneself die.

In people in whom object-directed aggression threatens not only that guilt or fear of retaliation that implies self-object differentiation, but also the loss of a still-fused self-object, necessary externalization of relatively unneutralized aggression, its partial neutralization and reinternalization is impaired. The parental imago is idealized, and is purified of its aggressiveness in representations that mirror the child's helpless self rather than the omnipotent parent. In contrast with identification with the aggressor, one sees an emphasis on a Christ-like empathy for victims, rather than repudiation of the aggressor. There is clinical evidence to suggest that the negative therapeutic reaction, the need to remain a victim of illness, is based in part on the identification with the original objects as victims. Getting well means losing this loose object tie — in the form of identifications — by the active discharge of aggression outward in the process of recovery.

The overwhelming feeling of being one with all objectless victims, which in the artistic genius or saint may spread to empathic understanding beyond the self to collective alternates, may necessitate the seeking of relief through using animate and inanimate objects to inflict pain in order to set up reciprocity to stabilize the cathexis of ego boundaries. The infant head-banger becomes the accident-prone or counterphobic child and the suicidal, often seemingly heroic adult. The causes of the pain are also narcissistically loved, and surrendered to, in a sense as though they were the love object who relieves distress, or a hypercathected boundary between the self and the outside world.[3] Unlike those who maintain sadomasochistic relationships, these people are often incapable of defending themselves against the aggression they seek. If they wish to fight back, immediately they put themselves in the place of a potential victim, and this paralyzes any attempt at self-defense.

Omnipotent death wishes lead to internalization of the aggression as a defense. Studies by Friedman et al. (1972) reveal that just before an adolescent suicide attempt the mother was often taken ill and seen as helpless and vulnerable. These observations suggest that the suicide attempt may provide, through the shock and pain of self-directed attack, a recathexis with aggression of threatened ego boundaries, and allow a restitutional cathexis of the object as an aggressor, who may now be hated. This hypothesis is supported by Friedman's clinical observations of the adolescents *after* the

---

3. Tarachow (1960) writes of Jesus offering himself to be killed and eaten. He considers Jesus and Judas doubles: Their reciprocal love is not far removed from self-love as killer and victim incorporate each other. The pills collected for suicide attempts are cherished in a similar way. The fusion of killer and victim reflects infant and primary object in perfect unity in the first oral stage.

attempt. Recently I have seen two patients who made suicide attempts. In one case, the patient's mother announced a possible fatal illness just before the attempt; in the other, the mother announced she was seriously depressed.

The suicide attempt is described by Friedman as, first, destroying the body, which the adolescent regards as the instrument through which actual expression can be given the wish to kill the mother, and second, turning the feeling of helplessness in the face of the aggressive and sexual urges into one of omnipotence. I have suggested that the feeling of helplessness preceding a suicide attempt may be understood in terms of primitive identification (fusion) with an insufficiently omnipotent victim object in the face of insufficient libidinal or excessive aggressive cathexis of the bodily self. The suicide attempt arises as a last-ditch action to consummate an active identification with the object as an aggressor. But the developmentally determined inability to use the mechanism of projection (externalization) beyond the self makes the subject the victim of this murderous rage. Suicide is a way of becoming a victim like the abandoning object as well as killing the living representations of this object in the subject's own body. Abandonment here may be defined in relation to the aggressive drive in terms of the impossibility to discharge aggression on the same object who has created narcissistic libidinal frustration.

It has been postulated (Greenacre 1960) that retaining primitive identifications provides the basis of empathy in later life. The ability to become one with objects — animate and inanimate — resembles the state of being in love, surrendering the whole personality in favor of object (erotic) cathexes (Freud 1923). It has often been said that the person in love in this way may "die" for love, or even wish to die as a consummation of love (the comment in Friedman et al. [1972] that the suicidal act resembles orgasm is pertinent). However, the separate role of aggression in these phenomena has been inadequately considered.

Two approaches to the subject include the death instinct theory, and the concept of altruistic surrender. According to the first, the erotic cathexes so empty the ego that the death instinct holds sway. The concept of "altruistic surrender" bypasses the necessity of postulating a death instinct. Critical aggressive strivings are projected onto an idealized object, who was once the object of envy, and who may gratify what the individual's own superego would prohibit. At the same time, through identification, the individual achieves vicarious satisfaction. The relationship here is a narcissistic one, making the gesture both altruistic and egoistic. However, Anna Freud (1936) points out, "anyone who has largely projected his instinctual impulses on to other people knows nothing of the fear of death." Such an individual may "die" of narcissistic love. However, this formulation does not consider the role of aggression as a separate drive. Where does the former aggression go?

I believe the state of being wholly in love, to the point of "dying for it," cannot represent the highest development of libidinal object relationships. Mature love would make life more precious and enforce reasonable self-preservation to preserve the object relationship. Surrendering the wish to live because of motives of "pure love" implies the displacement of an unconverted narcissism onto an object who is fused with the self. This regressive path releases primitive self-directed aggression in the manner described earlier. Fusion with an idealized victim-object threatens life in the interests of so-called love.

Wagner conveys this sequence in his *Tristan and Isolde.* Isolde's poison is turned into a love potion, and in place of her original murder-suicide plot against Tristan, she takes her enemy into herself through the magic potion. Tristan, the intended victim, drinks the potion too, and from then on they are fused as if they are one person. They long for death to release them from the possibility of separation. Isolde dies after Tristan, almost automatically, without self-inflicted violence. His life is the body, hers the soul, released upon the death of the body. Through the shared drink, Isolde became primitively identified with her victim. Both musically and dramatically, the death of Tristan and the Liebestod in Act III parallel the orgasmic climax of the love duet in Act II, and these in turn parallel the climactic moments of the drinking of the love potion in Act I. It is more than oedipal guilt that paralyzes the warrior Tristan and keeps him from defending himself from attack by Isolde's husband's forces. The elderly King Mark may be said to symbolize their father. This representation is seen also in the *Valkyrie,* where Wotan's spear paralyzes the twin Sigmund who is in love with his female other half, Sieglinde. Tristan is in love with a former enemy, Isolde, and the fusion with the female self, his former magical nurse, is equated therefore with the idealized mother imago. This creates the suicidal frenzy. The wounding of Tristan is his own fault, or rather the consequence, of his hypnotic blissful state which allows no self-preservative external aggression. The wounding which in the opera plot leads to a temporary separation from Isolde, also has an unconscious logic. In the kind of infant described earlier, the hypercathexis of painful stimulation (the wound) replaces the neutralizing aggressive dialogue with the early object, releases the painful accumulation of aggressive cathexes, and this pain aids temporarily in reestablishing ego boundaries.

The following clinical vignette illustrates some of the mechanisms described above. A woman patient in analysis reported (concerning her probably psychotic adolescent daughter who is now murderously angry with her) that when the child was between the ages of two and five, she used to hit herself when she was very angry. My patient recently told this to her daughter. Now, at nineteen, the daughter reports as her own memory: "When *you* used to be very angry, I would hit myself." The daughter adds: "I could tell by your eyes that you were going to kill me." This vignette calls to mind Peto's description of frightening eyes as a visual forerunner of the superego (Peto 1969). The girl does to *herself* what she is afraid her mother will do to her. A further significant fact is that a year ago the girl came to her mother and asked to go for professional help because she was afraid she would kill her mother. Perhaps it is relevant that the girl dared to communicate her fears to the mother at the time. The patient had become somewhat firmer and more self-assertive in her behavior to her daughter.

In the latter-day anxiety of the daughter, we may note especially the fear of ego and superego regression, reprojection of the latter, and the fear of attacking the mother now seen partly in a paranoid projected persecutory position. In the daughter's transformed version of the childhood experience we can see the projected precursor of the sadistic superego in the formulation: I am frustrated — I blame you for not helping me control my rage or solve the problem. I am enraged with you. Therefore, I feel you want to kill me. Greenacre (1945) speaks pertinently of the "negative narcissistic relationship to the parents." The mother (paranoid) projects guilt onto the child who introjects it (depression). This pattern repeats what the patient's mother did to *her* as a child, and what the daughter at nineteen is doing to the patient. The patient's image of the daughter as *her* victim, derived in part from her representations of *her own* mother as a multiple victim, have prevented her from dealing firmly with the daughter's aggression to her. She immediately internalizes her daughter's current, furious anger and becomes depressed, immobilized by the thought that she has destroyed the girl.

This child always tried to provoke retaliatory anger in my patient, to find an aggressor to fight with, and to identify with. The mother's inability to help neutralize the aggression, through constant counter-aggressive contact, forced the aggression to become internalized, and the daughter tended to be alternately murderous and suicidal. When the infant daughter was angry or rejecting, even in the first year, the mother would "let go," become frightened, and shrink away. Therefore the child made her own body a victim of the aggression felt toward the mother. Indeed, the mother was depressed during the period of her daughter's infancy, and the murderous eyes were correctly perceived in their rage, but incorrectly interpreted as to their object. In fact, when the daughter was hitting herself, she was identifying with the actual mother as the victim of self-directed aggression.

In the analysis of this patient it was possible to distinguish between "identification with the victim," a regression of identification with the aggressor in the direction of melancholia, and sadomasochism, a progression from identification with the aggressor using projection as a defense mechanism creating paranoid-like trends. For several years, recovery from identification with the victim was followed by hypercritical self-righteousness, suspiciousness, and provocativeness. She treated her husband like a displacement from her parents, who had prematurely disillusioned her. As a child, she had struggled against identification with them. She might catch her husband in a small lie for example, magnify his crime, and then generalize her scorn and distrust to include all men. This change meant she had successfully traversed a developmental path to identification with the aggressor, differentiation of self- and object-representations through projection, and the production of sadomasochistic "relationships." These were often relieved by a confrontation with her husband which he would be allowed to win and which culminated in unusually satisfying sexual intercourse. In this act, his phallus was equated with the breast, and she had fantasies of incorporating him orally once he firmly controlled her, feeling like a newborn baby.[4] She would have an enormous appetite during this period, and her husband became re-idealized. She would begin to feel attractive and capable, would have a sense of solidity, especially if she could gain weight, and would adopt more flexible moral standards.

However, in the more primitive phases, she would identify herself with all of her children in turn, whichever was currently the victim of another. If she saw a movie or read a book in which someone was victimized she would truly "feel" the experience as if it were her own. Her self-representations were projected almost totally onto the object; she talked of herself as though she were describing an object, and of the object as though it were herself. During sessions, incidents had to be recounted in exact chronological order, with utmost accuracy, as though she was an autobiographical novelist. She needed me to feel her state of victimization by her children, and her identification with them when they were victimized exactly as she originally did.

I believe this state of being "in love" (with victims) is akin to that of a mother for her newborn child or in fantasies during pregnancy where one

---

4. In nursing her children, she herself, because of her fusion with them, was unable to cope with their temporary inability or unwillingness to suck peacefully.

waits to give life to the idealized infantile self. The equation of giving birth and rescuing means that those saved (born) are loved for their total helplessness. However, in people like this patient, the infants' demands, and soon, their aggression are like those of a reprojected internalized agency. The infant's crying becomes a self-accusation from which the mother shrinks with guilt; hostility to the child is turned to self-attack and depressive, confused impotence.

Many of the same factors responsible for and descriptive of the psychopathology of this patient apply to certain kinds of poets. While the mechanism of identification with the aggressor makes the individual more differentiated from the object, the projective aspect also creates a distance from the inner nature of objects. The "badness" in objects must be projected away from the self as a part of differentiation, and primitive identifications that allow empathic appreciation of its total essence, its fundamental likeness to oneself, are also lost. The greater retention in some individuals of primary identifications (normally overlaid by secondary identifications after passage through the stage of identification with the aggressor) allows these specially "sensitive" people a heightened empathy for animate human objects (Greenacre 1960), and sometimes an anthropomorphic apprehension of inanimate and non-human objects. Also associated with this greater fluidity of ego structure may be a retention for ego use of significant residues of primary-process equations of the part with the whole, an ability to suspend secondary-process rules of causality, and to retain the liveliness of symbols that may be fused with the thing symbolized. All these may be used in the creative process. The later identifications, especially those which supersede the mixture of internalization and projection of "identification with the aggressor," and form the basic identifications of the superego, heal the breach with the aggressively cathected oedipal objects by internalizing limited amounts and controlled degrees of their aggression at the cost of losing some degree of that earlier precious sensitivity and vulnerability. The fusion of the omnipotent self with the universe in oceanic feelings and feeling of supernatural inspiration maintains, on the other hand, a constant danger to firm psychic structure, conflict-free functioning, and stable counter-cathexes nourished by relatively neutralized aggressive energy.

I believe many of the factors contributing to the sensitivity and creativity of the artist also create psychological conditions in which relatively unneutralized aggressive energies may supply simultaneously, or in alternation, energy for the creative activity and for self-destruction. This is particularly true if the conditions of early object relationships require that the creative work is needed (as an intermediate object) for the partial investment and discharge of these aggressive energies. The work is then like an incompletely introjected enemy created to be destroyed in the completion of the creation. The creator experiences the creation like a "victim" of the pangs of child-birth, like being killed again and again (of course, often accompanied also by a feeling of omnipotence, a phoenix-like feeling), the removal of a malig-nant part of the self like a cancer. During the creative act, what I have called "fusion with the victim" maintains the passive acceptance of these condi-tions that may bring one to the border of self-annihilation, partially for the sake of a demonic and as yet poorly understood need for poetic self-expression.

In the next section of this paper I shall try to demonstrate that until the period of her last poems, Sylvia Plath renounced this acceptance at the very last moment in a cry of rage, or by creating a fantasied self pregnant with living children. It is as though she could willingly go to the border of death and then save herself at the very last minute. Or, in other words, she allowed herself *temporarily* to passively fuse with what was being described. This fusion, in terms of the re-emergence of narcissistic libido, has been widely discussed, and if the created work is cathected with too much narcissistic libido, then finishing it may mean the loss of a narcissistically loved part of the self, like the end of a failed narcissistic love affair.

However, I think it is the relative preponderance of primitive aggression over narcissistic libido that gives the fused self-object of a poet like Plath the predominant dimension of aggressor-victim. In her major poems she metamorphoses into a persona who joins the adult poet and regressed self-object, becomes the victim of her own and the world's aggression, and attempts, though she finally fails, to use her poems and novel as inter-mediate objects to discharge murderous drives that threaten to destroy her.

The completed poem is pathologically mourned like a baby who has died in being separated from the self, rather than brought into life. Artistic cre-ation, therefore, unlike actual childbirth, is depleting of narcissistic ener-gies, rather than replenishing them. In the absence of a "live" object, the consequence of the rage that is now turned against the self, is like a post-partum depression. The guilt and self-destructiveness can be relieved only by more creation. The poet is simultaneously the mother who has lost a part of herself, and the infant who has lost the symbiotic unity without which the outward-directed aggressive discharge is thwarted. Several friends have described Sylvia Plath as happiest during her pregnancies, while her poems "are dead, and their mother near death with distraction,/And they stupidly stare, and do not speak of her" ("Stillborn," *Crossing the Water,*[5] 1971a).

5. Reading the poem aloud may provide a feeling that the poem lives and can talk back.

The artist who "feels" successful has fulfilled his infantile ideal of narcissistic perfection through the work, and, as the creator, has revived a life-giving identification of himself with an idealized omnipotent parent. In creative artists who cathect their works predominantly with primitive aggression, like the poet considered in this paper, the poem or other work is like a dead thing to the artist, and is brought back to dim light by the audience's appreciation.

Perhaps this formulation sheds light on artists who simultaneously killed themselves and tried to destroy their works. Kafka, who requested that his works be destroyed at his death, characterized his works as objects to be mourned, to give pain. In many instances they depict the self as an impotent victim fused with the killing object who is also loved and against whom no resistance is possible because the object will not answer any aggression with a dialogue of counter-aggression (see *In the Penal Colony* for a clear example). Perhaps, too, we may discover in this formulation a further reason why so many poets, despairing of being able to maintain a productive flow, kill themselves as a kind of last creative act. They affirm and consolidate their identities through self-inflicted pain and injury, like anaclitically depressed infants who bang their heads, tear at themselves, and die after sleeplessness and lack of assimilated nourishment. After all, in fantasy and usually in reality as well, the suicidal act does finally force a response from the "loved" ones whose real or fantasied "death-like" indifference impeded aggressive discharge beyond the boundaries of the self, fusion of aggression with libido, and neutralization of the aggression. In killing themselves, they are finally identifying with the aggressor as well as killing him — becoming the haunting ghost in the little girl's dark hall.

II

Sylvia Plath was born in Boston on October 27, 1932.[6] Her father came to the United States at fifteen from a town in the Polish Corridor. He was the author of a well-known treatise on bees, and was further distinguished for his work in ornithology, entomology, and ichthyology. Her mother was born in Boston of Austrian parents and met her husband while studying for a master's degree in German. At Sylvia's birth, Otto Plath announced, "All I want from life from now on is a son born two and a half years to the day." And on April 27, 1935, a son, Warren Joseph, was born. Sylvia and her

---

6. Most of the factual material about Sylvia Plath comes from the excellent collection of essays, *The Art of Sylvia Plath,* edited by Charles Newman (1971).

brother grew up in the seashore town of Winthrop, Massachusetts. Her childhood was filled with sea memories—gathering shells, making toys from objects picked up at the beach, collecting starfish in jars and watching them grow back lost arms,[7] dreaming of Spain on the other side of the Atlantic, believing in mermaids, and observing the ferocity of a hurricane when she was six. She later recalled, "My final memory of the sea is of violence—a still unhealthy day in 1939 [sic] the sea molten, steely thick, heaving at its leash like a broody animal, evil violets in its eye." She seems to have equated the sea with a sadistic oedipal father.

Otto Plath died in 1940, after a long hospitalization for a circulatory disease. Sylvia Plath's fears, expressed in *The Bell Jar* (1971b), of being permanently abandoned by her mother in a hospital, are probably related to a memory of her father's death, as is her panic about going to a hospital to stop a hemorrhage, an episode described in the recollections of her college friend, Nancy Hunter Steiner (1973).

After his death her mother taught shorthand and typing to support the family. The family left the seaside and moved to Wellesley, Massachusetts, where her maternal grandparents lived with them. "My father died, we moved inland" (see Newman 1971). They attended the Unitarian church although Otto Plath had been a Lutheran. During the evening, the family sometimes read aloud, and one evening, Mrs. Plath read Matthew Arnold's poem "The Forsaken Merman." The poem is a lament by a merman who dwells at the bottom of the sea. His wife has left him for the land, for human life, and resists his calls for her return by her steadfast attention to her prayer book, and her devotion to the church. On clear, moonlit midnights the merman's remaining family creeps up to the land to look at the sleeping town where the lost mother lives. The poem ends with the merman singing as he sadly returns after his vigil. "There dwells a lov'd one,/But cruel is she,/She left lonely forever/The kings of the sea."

Sylvia remembered her reaction to hearing the poem: "I saw the goose-flesh on my skin. I didn't know what made it. I was not cold. Had a ghost passed over? No, it was the poetry. A spark flew off Arnold and shook me, like a chill, I wanted to cry; I felt very odd. I had fallen into a new way of being happy" (Newman 1971, p. 157). After this, at about age nine, Plath began to hide short poems in her mother's dinner napkin or beneath her butter plate.

Through Arnold's poetry, her father had reached her. Her mother's reading of the poem had given permission for this reunion, and the sea in which

---

7. Note Plath's later preoccupation with observing fetuses in bell jars.

father dwelled called her back all her life. One of her most chilling poems, "Suicide Off Egg Rock" (1968), concerns a man's feelings as he is about to drown himself. In *The Bell Jar* (1971b) there is a description of her attempt to drown herself as she seeks to reunite with the absent father, an attempt which follows a minor male character's telling her that his father lived overseas. Both the poem and the novel, written several years later, contain the repetition of the words "I am, I am, I am"—evoking the still beating heart after the uncompleted attempt. To thwart the longed-for reunion in the ocean with father as primal parent, as well as the oedipal consummation with the later father, in her poetry Plath turned to the preoedipal mother for aid in repressing these instinctual longings. Like the character in Arnold's poem, Plath remains untouchable as long as she fixes on the Holy Book, worships in the church, and is enclosed in the living family at the dinner table. Sylvia Plath reproached her mother for abandoning her father's religion with its strong, repressive superego cast, and regarded Unitarianism as little better than no religion at all. Moonlight when father as the merman, is close, is a constant symbol in her writings. It represents death in its sterile whiteness, absence of color, and borrowed light that turns everything into stone. (See A. Lavers in Newman 1971.)

In "Lady Lazarus" (Plath 1966) the subject of the poem made a suicide attempt at age ten. "The first time it happened I was ten./It was an accident." It is interesting that, although Sylvia Plath's father died when she was eight, the speaker says in "Daddy" (Plath 1966) "I was ten when they buried you." Possibly the suicidal "accident" at age 10, surely real psychically if not in actuality, marked the first real burial of her father. The heroine reproaches her mother in *The Bell Jar* for not allowing anyone to express clear grief at father's death, and just before her suicide attempt at age twenty (see *The Bell Jar* 1971b), she visits her grave and weeps over him for the first time. In the novel, loving thoughts of an abandoned or victim father are always associated with suicidal impulses. These episodes are interspersed with sequences in which relationships with men are imagined or acted out in violent sadomasochistic terms that enforce differentiation of self and object and "provide the core of a person's identity" (Pao 1965).

Sylvia Plath's adolescence was a time of great academic and extracurricular accomplishments. She produced skillful drawings and was proud when these were approved of by her mother. She remembered herself in these years as a "gawky mess with drab hair and bad skin." She tried to look and act like a typical, all-around student of the 1950s.

At eighteen, after she submitted manuscripts forty-five times to the magazine *Seventeen,* her first story was accepted. In 1950, she entered Smith

College on a scholarship endowed by Olive Higgins Prouty, the author of *Stella Dallas,* whose fictional counterpart is part of two series of idealized mother figures described in *The Bell Jar.* These mothers are sought for their ability to offer a loving, responsive counterpressure when a real mother is unresponsive. For instance, the mother drives the heroine to a hospital against her wishes and in *her* presence the heroine "feels" prevented from making another suicide attempt. In similar terms the novel describes Jay Cee, the editor at the magazine where the heroine works as an apprentice. Although the editor appreciates the heroine's gifts, she warns her against too much self-confidence and advises her to work harder. Dr. Nolan, the woman psychiatrist (Plath's actual psychiatrist at the time was a man) is the only really loved and respected figure in *The Bell Jar.* Dr. Nolan does not promise to spare the heroine the feared shock therapy, but agrees to warn her in advance, and to be present when it is administered.

In college Sylvia Plath used her father's red leather thesaurus to write poetry on a regular schedule whose precision recalls her father's compulsive "perfect" timing. She was brilliantly successful academically, winning every possible prize. At this time her identification with her idealized father was evidently in conflict with her feminine sexual feelings, and took the form of conflicts between "the life-style of a poet-intellectual and that of a wife and mother" (Plath, quoted in Newman 1971, p. 161). At this time she first used the image that became a central theme of her novel ten years later, saying, "It's quite amazing how I've gone around for most of my life as in the rarefied atmosphere under a bell jar" (p. 161). Here Plath was referring to her intellectual isolation, but later the simile became enriched with allusions to a fetus in the womb, to claustrophobic feelings, to seeing the world through distorted eyes, dead babies pickled in jars (preserved specimens presumably derived from father's interests), to her poetry like rows of dead objects being collected. Finally, the bell jar meant rebreathing her own excreted air, cut off by an invisible veil from the outside world where she could not sharply sense the flux of mutually invigorating object relationships in her life.

Plath idealized doers. One is again reminded that the gratification of aggressive drives in promoting self-object differentiation, pleasure in functioning, and the development of both libidinal and aggressive object constancy has been described by Greenacre (1960), Hartmann, Kris, and Loewenstein (1949), and Spitz (1965a). She admired those who could make things run, who were athletes, or who understood the functions of the body and natural phenomena, who could grow vegetables, repair machinery, and "are also trained in the greater areas of philosophy, sociology, literature, and all the rest" (quoted in Newman 1971, p. 161). (These qualities she found in the "family romance" parents of a friend who became the model for Buddy Willard in *The Bell Jar*.) In her brief life Sylvia Plath accomplished most of those things, derogatorily contrasting her idealized mother surrogates who possessed these attributes with those who made up "little fairy worlds like pink cotton wool," a characterization by Plath of her own mother.

After her junior year at Smith she won a *Mademoiselle* scholarship to work and live in New York for a month. This period, which culminated in her suicide attempt (the second) at age twenty is described with painful honesty and art in *The Bell Jar*. However, within six months she returned to college, graduated, and continued her studies in German and poetry. The existence of the oscillating conflict between fused and dual identities—poet and female, aggressor and victim, and her tenuous differentiation between self and object, ego and superego—is suggested by the fact that she began her honors thesis on the "double" in Dostoyevsky's novels. She later turned instead to "the twin" in James Joyce's writings.

The next few years included her early publications and a trip to Europe. In Paris Plath had a splinter removed from her eye while "fully conscious. . . . I was babbling frantically about Oedipus and Gloucester getting new vision by losing their eyes, but me wanting, so to speak, new vision and my eyes too" (quoted in Newman 1971, p. 157). She meant she wanted to keep her inner poetic vision while remaining alive and whole in relation to the outside world. This wish is rendered in poetry in "The Eye Mote," an early poem (1968). In this poem, the poet looks at horses running. The scene is clear, each object held rooted by the sunlighted. As she takes in the scene with her eyes, a splinter "flew in and struck my eye./Needling it dark." As her physical vision is destroyed by the invasion of an innocent splinter and she becomes merged with the now blurred and unanchored scene, her poetic vision flourishes, creating mythical allusions. "Abrading my lid, the small grain burns:/Red cinder around which I myself,/Horses, planets and spires revolve." She becomes one with Oedipus. Yet she yearns to return to her former self, to see as before, but the original moment and scene can never be recaptured in their actuality.

Most of the usual themes of her later poetry are here as well. One may note particularly the self-orienting attention to the experience of localized pain and the representation of the loss of distinction between self and object and among the objects (the horses, trees, and spires suggesting phallic qualities on which it is forbidden to look). It is as though the desire to come closer and closer, to see more and more, creates a blurring of the outer world while it frees and enriches the inner world of the imagination. The cost is one of admitting a miniscule bit of death. (One is reminded of how the world must look to the very young infant or to the child as he brings his face closer and closer to the mother's until landmarks are lost.) The mote gives way to an itch, as it refuses to come out, and she wears "the present itch for flesh." In other words, what was once a foreign body is now a part of her own flesh, a representation of impregnation, and a reversal of the process of birth.

Plath desired a combined inner and outer vision and she achieved it only when in pain or when she was enduring physical challenge in a struggle with other life that would neither kill nor be killed, in particular during pregnancy and childbirth, or in the brief moments of labor on her poems—before the potential became actual. Perhaps these are alluded to in the quotation about Oedipus and Gloucester. An additional level of meaning is suggested by Kanzer (1950) in his paper on the Oedipus Trilogy, where the blind Oedipus "presents an unmistakable representation of re-birth." Sylvia Plath wishes to be reborn in her father's image—as a male—without having to die first, to give birth without having to bleed to death. In one of her last poems, "Kindness," she condenses it all in three brief lines. "The blood jet is poetry,/There is no stopping it./You hand me two children, two roses." (Plath 1966).

In 1956 she met and married Ted Hughes. In 1957–1958 she taught brilliantly for a year at Smith College. In 1958–1959 the couple lived in Boston where they met George Starbuck and Anne Sexton. Plath and Miss Sexton met once a week, drank martinis, and hilariously discussed imaginative ways of committing suicide. (Miss Sexton committed suicide eleven years after her friend, also by asphyxiation.)

In December 1959, the couple moved to England. Sylvia was pregnant with their first child, Frieda Rebecca, who was born on April 1, 1960. Soon after the birth of the child Plath was "seized by fearsome excitement" and began writing *The Bell Jar,* which she thought of as a comic novel. She describes the book as "an autobiographical apprentice work which I had to write in order to free myself from the past." The next year she had a miscarriage, then an appendectomy, and then again became pregnant. In the summer of 1961, she and Hughes moved to the country. Plath loved the "millions of birds" (her father was also an ornithologist). She taught herself to ride bareback and once clinged to her horse's neck after it threw her off its back while it galloped two miles home. This accomplishment demonstrates how thin is the line between self-destruction and heroism. The active attempt to master, to challenge, to keep hold on a dangerous object, is part of an attempt to live, to resist the temptation to surrender herself passively as a victim of a loss of identity, and to avoid returning to the undifferentiated state of "perfection" she described in one of her very last poems, "Edge" (Plath 1966). "The woman is perfected./Her dead/Body wears the smile of accomplishment,/The illusion of a Greek necessity/Flows in the scrolls of her toga,/Her bare/Feet seem to be saying:/We have come so far, it is over."

In her last year she engaged with typical intensity and efficiency in bee-keeping, onion stringing, and potato digging. In June 1962 her son Nicholas was born; she blissfully describes nursing him by candlelight.

That summer Plath suffered repeated attacks of influenza, accompanied by high fevers. A few days before Christmas, 1962, she separated from her husband, returned to London with her children, and felt it was miraculous that she accidentally found and was able to rent an apartment Yeats had once lived in. In this house she achieved her greatest creative output.

In the middle of January 1963 *The Bell Jar* was published in England under the pseudonym Victoria Lucas. In the bitter cold winter of 1962–1963, in the predawn darkness before her children woke, Plath worked feverishly on the *Ariel* poems, sometimes producing two or three poems a day. Perhaps there was a return to the sleeplessness that she described in the presuicidal period in *The Bell Jar* (Plath 1971b). I disagree with Alvarez's contention (1972) that this frenetic creativity was the source of danger to her life. Rather, like the challenging of nature in riding, childbirth, and other activities, it was a way of warding off death by creating objects that could be used to externalize her aggression and serve as a path to object relationships that could be internalized to build ego structure. The poems failed to allow a relatively constant investment of narcissistic libido or aggression; they did not remain as stable transitional objects. This failure is evidence that the poems were not invested with sufficiently neutralized energies; their loss in the process of creation was like a series of deaths. But the aim of Plath's creative impulse was the rescue herself, to make life possible. Alun Jones says pertinently: "The poet exercises his traditional power in using the beneficent passion of poetry to expel the malignant forces of private suffering" (quoted by Dyson in Newman 1971).

In Plath's last days she made plans for the spring, expecting visitors from the States. Although she was under the care of a doctor, she apparently received little more than sedatives. On 11 February 1963, in the early morning, after preparing some food for the children, she put her head in her gas oven and ended her life.

III

Annette Lavers says of Sylvia Plath: "Subject and object, torturer and victim are in her poetry finally indistinguishable, merely lending the depth of their existence to all-powerful entities and symbols." She adds in a footnote: "The theme of adultery, for instance, seems to transcend all possibly biographical sources; if sometimes the writer takes up the position of the victim, at other times she assumes that of the guilty one, guilty of a lover's involvement with her baby or her father, or death itself" (Lavers, in Newman 1971, p. 102). The origins and vicissitudes of the simultaneous identification with the torturer and victim suggested by Lavers can be traced clearly in Plath's writings.

Two interrelated series of identifications require consideration: Identification with the chronically ill, then dead oedipal father, and the more primitive identifications involving fusion of self- and object-representations with the preoedipal mother (parent). For Plath, the later identification with the idealized oedipal father makes death the equivalent for her of the sexual consummation in which both partners die, victims of fatal illnesses. The bee stings in one poem symbolically represent this danger of death equated with castration through oral-sadistic penetration. Both aggressor (the bee who loses its stinger and dies), and the victim (who swells like a pregnant woman, but may be destroyed by the venom) die. The theme is repeated in the many kinds of attacks on the body so prevalent in Plath's poetry. The simultaneous representation of her persona both as the guilty one and the aggressor (rather than as one or the other) also shows that she has only partially internalized self-critical ego and superego components — components segregated by counter-cathectic energies from the self- and object-representations in the ego. For stabilization, these structures require a relationship with the postoedipal father in their vulnerable early stages. The long illness and death of Sylvia Plath's father in her latency period must have been of considerable importance in this failure of internalization (see Loewald 1962). That the oedipal and preoedipal mother were unavailable as aggressor imagoes with whom to identify may be deduced from her writings.

Often, in her poetry and in *The Bell Jar,* Plath expresses the need for a mother to rise up from the position of collapsing victim and avoider of confrontation so that her daughter may find boundaries, limits, and safe "exercise" for her aggression against her mother on oral, anal, and oedipal levels. This creation of fantasied aggressor parents — leading to manifold attempts to confront the most dangerous possible aggression she finds in the natural world — is necessary to shift the balance from Sylvia-as-victim (like the mother- and father-representations) to Sylvia-as-aggressor. The more neutralized aggression may then be internalized to lend enforcing and life-protecting idealizing power to her own superego.

In the poem "Daddy," we find the wish to bring her father back to life temporarily, not as the merman (equivalent to the tempting fatal muses and the Lorelei of other poems), but as the primal scene aggressor who can be hated like the Nazis, or as the devil who can be warded off and killed permanently for the sake of her own survival. To resist the longing for fusion with the dead father, Plath needed to find a way to turn her aggressive wishes outward. One way is by imaginatively creating a "hating" sado-masochistic relationship to father, and to her husband, who, in "Daddy," are given identical, fascist brute images. "I made a model of you,/A man in black with a Meinkampf look/And a love of the rack and the screw./And I said I do, I do" (Plath 1966).

However, establishing such a defensive "hating" relationship, could deprive Plath of enriching identifications (see her use of father's thesaurus in her early writing,[8] the precise Prussian schedule, the conflict between writing and femininity, and especially motherhood) that foster her ambition and desire for independent accomplishment in work that bears some relation to his. She was excited to hear a woman lecturer discuss D. H. Lawrence, and called her "my salvation" because "she seemed to prove that a woman no longer had to sacrifice all claims to femininity and family to be a scholar!" Moreover, keeping her father alive imaginatively provided a vital supply of content and imagery to her poetry. In "Stings" (1966), the keeping of bees is compared to the writing of poetry:

> A third person is watching.
> He has nothing to do with the bee-seller or with me.
> Now he is gone.
>
> In eight great bounds, a great scapegoat.
> Here is his slipper, here is another,
> And here the square of white linen
> He wore instead of a hat.
> He was sweet,
>
> The sweat of his efforts a rain
> Tugging the world to fruit.

The last line makes clear that the passage describes the silent, omnipresent father, the source of life and her poetic "fruit."

---

8. As Plath's poems became "freer" and dealt more openly with suicide, she gave up the use of the thesaurus.

Plath longed for the kind of mother depicted in *The Bell Jar* in the "transference figure" of the psychiatrist Dr. Nolan—a competent, professional woman who can simultaneously be mother and replace father—who controls her firmly, who orders shock therapy, but who stays with her during the fearful procedure. But this relationship works against the creativity: submitting to the "therapy" means surrendering herself in fusion with the symbiotic mother and destroys that part of her mind containing the roots of her talent. Plath is afraid that after shock therapy she will never write again.

If, however, Plath's father is idealized as helpless victim (killed by a circulatory disease, having a leg amputed, castrated in the primal scene by the phallic mother), then identification with him detaches narcissistic libido from self-representations and turns this libido toward him at the expense of the self, bringing a longing for passive reunion and death.

The fragment below suggests more than many biographical essays: "I was seven, I knew nothing./The world occurred./You had one leg, and a Prussian mind!" ("Little Fugue," 1966).

The title of an early poem, "The Colossus" (Plath 1968), appears to refer to herself and her father simultaneously. The persona of the poem attempts to "glue" herself together, to create poetry out of her fragmented self and the clamorous noises in her head. At the same time she attempts to put her father back together, and give him a voice through her poetic self. The reconstruction of fragments of ruins in the hope that they will return to life through her art is to reverse the processes of decay and disintegration in herself in identification with her dead father. (I shall later discuss the appearance of the same theme in the argument with Buddy Willard in *The Bell Jar* over whether poetry is immortal or dust.) At the end of the poem, Plath compares herself, in an allusion to the *Oresteia,* to Electra waiting on the shore for Agamemnon. It is impossible to separate the poet from the poem, or either of them from the absent father. Yet she saves herself at the end. She says she is "married to a shadow." She will no longer wait for "the scrape of a keel/On the blank stones of the landing." Condensed in this is the wish to renounce a life of faithful and endless waiting for her father to return from the dead; when he does, he would only be killed again and ultimately take her with him. This early poem foreshadows the defiant poet of "Daddy." In both poems, the ending affirms the necessity of renouncing the impossible quest to reunite with the father (across the sea). The failure to put together the Colossus is a renunciation of the incestuous consummation which would bring death to both of them; it alludes also to the failure to achieve "perfection" as a poet. In the introduction to Nancy Hunter Steiner's memoir of Sylvia Plath, George Stade (1973) comments that the poem shows no living man could measure up to the Colossus, but that only living men partook of his quality, no matter how far they fell short. And Robert Lowell, in his forward to *Ariel* (Plath 1966) says ". . . her art's immortality is life's disintegration." The perfect Colossus, the perfect merging with the dead father, the creation of the perfect poem out of this merging, are equivalent to her own death.

In many poems, Sylvia Plath depicts a daughter's rage toward the mother-character pounding against an empty, unresisting, unresponsive space. The mixed feelings of longing and frustration may inspire dazzling poetic bursts, but the rage is inevitably turned in a self-destructive direction after the poem is completed. The object, as poem, is once again silent and unresistive. Plath's identity as a woman is disturbed as she struggles against identification with her mother, the hard-working "victim" of life, the plaster saint.

"In Plaster" (Plath 1971a), a transitional poem, deals with this theme, describing the plaster case covering the broken leg of the "I," "squint-eyed old yellow," as another self, a plaster saint. The plaster other-self evokes in poetry the image of the same unresponsive mother who lies asleep next to the sleepless heroine in *The Bell Jar*.

> I hated her, she had no personality —
> She lay in bed with me, like a dead body.
> And I was scared, because she was shaped just the way I was.
> I couldn't sleep for a week, she was so cold.
> I blamed her for everything, but she didn't answer.
> I couldn't understand her stupid behavior!

In the poem, the plaster self begins to develop a personality, "a slave mentality." The poet then describes other attributes of the plaster cast — calmness, patience, "holding my bones in place so they would bend properly." The plaster's firmness is associated with love. As it is absent-minded, lets in drafts, and fits more loosely, thoughts emerge about the plaster's desire to leave her. Roles are reversed, and the poet realizes she cannot live outside the symbiosis. The cast develops a soul, and an itch for adventure. It becomes like the work of art and the child, wanting to soar into light. The poet is now a "half corpse" as the cast (representing the poem and the poetic self) takes on its own life. It drains away the life and strength of the writer who is "quite limp," like a mummy in a case. The writer compares living with the cast to "living with my own coffin." Images of life and death are fused, reversed, and condensed in the images of the relationship between the plaster cast and the poet. The saving note appears at the end: "Now I see it must be one or the other of us." She will throw aside the cast (the mummy case) and it will "perish with emptiness then, and begin to miss me." A threat of suicide is contained in the poem's last line, but defiant hostility too. Differentiation through aggression is predicted. The poem returns to the imagery of mother and child assuming separate identities, and the death-threatening fusion is resolved.

Using this poem as a point of reference, George Stade writes in his introduction to Steiner (1973):

> The persona speaking out of any given poem by Sylvia Plath, then, may be either sulphurous old yellow, or the plaster saint, or a consciousness that sometimes contains these two and sometimes lies stretched between them. In the course of a given poem, especially if it is a later one, any of these personae may dissolve, re-form, take on novel shapes, fuse with whatever it is not, or reverse its charge, so that the plaster saint becomes a queen bee, a comet, God's lioness. The outer shell of consciousness may be completely or dimly aware of the chthonic presence within: it may feel itself a puppet jerked by strings receding into an interior distance where a familiar demon sits in possession, or it may try to locate the menace outside of itself, among shadows, thin people, reflections in water, ghostly presences glimpsed from the corner of the mind, but always with a sense of *déjà vu*. [p. 9]

The process of writing only temporarily externalized the rage that turned against her with the completion of each work. Each poem seemed to fade rapidly into a silent approach against its creator. ". . . worse/Even than your maddening/Song, your silence." These lines are addressed to father's representatives beneath the sea, the "Lorelei" (Plath 1968), who are identical with the three Muses in "The Disquieting Muses" (Plath 1968). The poems may be regarded as attempts to create transitional objects. They evoke the illusion of unity of the self with the absent, unempathic mother and the lost father. But they also serve as vehicles for drive discharge, and, as such "become prime targets of aggression in the process of denigration of self and object" (Kestenberg 1971). With their destruction, rage returns to the self and threatens to make their creator their victim. At the very end of Sylvia Plath's life, a suicide appeared to be the only resolution that would regressively reestablish the "perfect" self through fusion with images of idealized victims. She finally surrendered to the silent seductive "death" so often anthropomorphized in her poems, invitingly waiting side by side with that death so often seized and struggled against, that announced its evil intention and thus promoted heroic struggle and differentiation. Many of her poems appear to be temporary structures for the expression of her instinctual drives. Perhaps this accounts for the uneasy pleasure one feels reading some of them.

Sylvia Plath's ability to feel for, to become one with all men and women, all animate and inanimate objects in the dimensions of both aggressor and victim pervades her writings. It claimed her life in the end. The universality of her empathy is like that of the psychotic patients described by Jacobson (1965) who develop delusional images of the projected object which they never attach to definite, external persons; or who develop delusional self-images through introjection of early infantile object images which hardly resemble any past or present realistic external objects. The difference between Plath and these patients is that Plath had the ego of an artist. Unless she became merged with her poetic personae, she established distance and control over these images, even as she relived them in the process of creating or recreating. them. It is remarkable in how many of her poems, at least until the very last week of her life, her poetic persona is depicted observing herself, fusing or fearing to fuse with a reflected image and ultimately wrenching herself away from drowning in her vision; or giving birth to a new idealized self in pregnancy fantasies that deny the necessity of union with the man in procreation. A. E. Dyson says that "in Sylvia Plath, it is as though the poet finds in personal experience a depth of derangement, but then, in the magnificent sanity of creation, transmutes this into a myth for her age" (in Newman 1971, p. 107).

In most of her poetry, Plath achieves distance from the personal experience by exploration of symbolic and mythical potentialities. This is followed by a more or less tentative return to the individual self from which the poem originated. Many poems seem like a journey to the borders of death which exists as a threat, the body always vulnerable to attack. The mind has the alternative of safe, prosaic lifelessness, or turning to the writing of poetry with the risk of madness in the loss of self. The outside world is let in warily. It threatens to eat away, to incorporate her into itself, and to replace the body and mind it feeds on, like the "dybbuk" image in *The Bell Jar* (Plath 1971b, discussed further in Part IV).

The precarious balance and dialogue between life and death is the major theme of Plath's poems. According to Annette Lavers life is: "color, pulsating rhythm, noise, heat, radiance, expansion, emotion and communication." Death, the other pole, is represented by "darkness, stasis, silence, frost, well-defined edges and the hardness of rocks, jewels, and skulls, dryness, anything self-contained and separate, or which derives its positive attributes from some other source, instead of generating them freely — for death is absence, nothingness."

Reading the poems in chronological sequence, one sees the balance shift until, in the last poems, the struggle against the forces of death weakens and dies. Yet, each disguised death figure, which attracts by its life-like qualities and merges with the persona of the poet, threatens to become the bringer of death. Although very helpful in "decoding" the poems, Lavers' reading of recurrent symbols fails to distinguish between the death which attracts and that which menaces and repels. "Two, of course there are two." To one the poet's persona is "red meat." As for the other, "He wants to be loved." ("Death and Co.," Plath 1966). There is a constant search to recognize the hidden death in all that she wishes to take hungrily into herself without resistance, to make into herself temporarily as a part of the process of creation, and to rid herself of in the completion of the poem before it destroys her from inside.

> The bees found him (father) out,
> Moulding onto his lips like lies,
> Complicating his features.
>
> They thought death was worth it, but I
> Have a self to recover, a queen. . .
> ["Stings," Plath 1966]

The world to be cast off is often expressed in terms of anal expelling imagery (it is bad, black), while Plath struggles to satisfy the wish, usually expressed in terms of fierce oral cravings, regressively to fuse with its whiteness, never to emerge. Her wish to live drew her to those objects and people that clearly bare their fangs, who show their true colors, who offer a counterforce against which she may be inspired to struggle, to neutralize her own aggression and theirs as well. To write poetry, to produce life, Plath impregnated herself with potential death, never knowing if what she produced would be a living child or a voracious monster. She suspended her personal identity to become a voluntary victim to a world waiting to eat her up, to let it disappear inside her in order to create a perfect merging of aggressor object and victim. From this merging ("God's lioness,/How one we grow") ("Ariel," Plath 1966),[9] her identity as a poet was born, but the "imminent

---

9. The title refers to herself and her horse, Ariel. Ariel reminds us of Aurelia, her mother's name.

volcano[10] was always there. The attempt to reexternalize these dangerous materials, at least temporarily, in the form of a poem after letting herself *become* them, by passively accepting the "gift" of her creativity, constituted her Herculean task. In "Who" (Plath 1971a), the poet, fallow after a season of harvest, waits for inspiration:

> This is a dull school,
> I am a root, a stone, an owl pellet,
> Without dreams of any sort.

Then comes the wish:

> Mother, you are the one mouth
> I would be a tongue to. Mother of otherness
> Eat me.

"Kindness" (Plath 1966) fuses all of these themes in a remarkably condensed way. It summarizes the creative life of Sylvia Plath. In it Plath uses elements of a radio play by Ted Hughes about a man who runs over a hare in his car, sells the dead animal for five shillings and buys his girlfriend two roses with the blood money. The poem is written from the point of view of the recipient of the roses; she equates them with her two children. The roses, presumably blood red, like the tulips in an earlier poem, are a sweet gift— and "Sugar can cure everything, so Kindness says." The gift of roses, like sugar crystals, is ironically supposed to silence the crying of children, revive the rabbit, or anaesthetize the pinned butterfly with which it is equated. But the giver enters the room with a cup of tea "wreathed in steam" conjuring up an image of a witch or a devil. The receiver of the gift is simultaneously the crying child, the dying rabbit, and the pinned butterfly. The poem is about being killed by kindness, personified as Dame Kindness, another of those disguised bringers of death. She is to be guarded against because she disarms the victim. However, there is no fighting her off—her seductive ambience offers the sweetness of poetic inspiration at the price of surrender to her.

"Kindness" was written shortly before Sylvia Plath's death. In "Tulips" (Plath 1966), written earlier, the menace of the sweet flower is recognized and warded off as a danger comparable to the salt sea. "The tulips should be

---

10. Ted Hughes (in Newman 1971) has written: "The opposition of a prickly, fastidious defense and an imminent volcano is, one way or another, an element in all her early poems. The earlier the poem, the more powerful the defensive forces."

behind bars like dangerous animals;/They are opening like the mouth of some great African cat." The poet of "Tulips" is made conscious of her heart, her blood. The hypercathexis of the living body as self-object, in Kohut's (1968) sense, mobilizes the wish to live, revives life-saving narcissism.

> And I am aware of my heart; it opens and closes
> Its bowl of red blooms out of sheer love of me.
> The water I taste is warm and salt, like the sea,
> And comes from a country far away as health
> [Tulips, Plath 1966]

The climax of "Kindness is in the last three lines: "The blood jet is poetry,/There is no stopping it./You hand me two children, two roses." The poet equates herself with the murdered animal; out of the wound spurts the life blood which is also the poem itself. The creative urge is as irresistible as the wish for her children, the gift of roses, the pin of the entymologist fixing the butterfly (the reference to her father is unmistakable), the car that bears down on the small animal, the figure of death represented as a female bearing sweets. Death through surrender to the beloved murderer is risked, is foretold in the acceptance of the "gift" of poetry. The poem, written in the last week of her life, ends with a passive acceptance. The two children, the two roses, and the poem are "given" — by Kindness, Dame Kindness, the "Mother of Otherness" — at the price of allowing the poet to "bleed" out her poems to the death.

IV

The nature of Sylvia Plath's attempts, in the service of survival, to ward off the ultimate loss of self-object differentiation in a fusion with an idealized victim-object, is particularly evident in *The Bell Jar*. The last part of this paper will examine these efforts, and the reasons for her ultimate failure, as conveyed in this extraordinary novel.

The Bell Jar is composed of small fragments, each one of which might have become a poem. It travels back in time to constitute an autobiography of its heroine, Esther Greenwood, and it shall be interpreted as a disguised autobiographical account of a period in Sylvia Plath's life. *The Bell Jar* was written as Plath approached the end of the third decade of her life which brought her next major suicide attempt. The writing of the book may be seen as Plath's attempt to return to age twenty in an effort to disrupt the compulsion to repeat the action. She herself described the book as "an autobiographical apprentice work which I had to write to free myself from the past." Harold Bloom has defined the "primordial element" of poetry as "divination, or the desperation of seeking to foretell dangers to the self, whether from nature, the gods, from others, or indeed from the very self" (1973, p. 59). This definition applies to Sylvia Plath's poetry as well as to *The Bell Jar.* Yet the reader is left unconvinced that this self-objectivization will work, and reads her book with an uneasiness only partly the result of her literary skill. Plath takes the reader inside the bell jar, and has him see her surreal world from inside a glass that distorts reality perception, that makes him feel situations without exit. The "outside" is only the glass wall of the entrapped self.

Except for the shock that kills, there is no exit. The heroine-narrator is introduced imagining how the Rosenbergs must have felt being electrocuted, "being burned alive all along your nerves." The book begins with the conflict between excitement and revulsion in contemplating this ultimate, perhaps self-willed, obliteration of the self.

An outline of the plot of *The Bell Jar* will provide some orientation to the aspects of structure and content under consideration. *The Bell Jar* is about Esther Greenwood's descent to a suicide attempt and the beginnings of recovery in her twentieth year. She is a distinguished student at college in the 1950s. After her junior year she wins a prize for creative writing. The award consists of a month in New York with eleven other girls, working as an apprentice at a glossy woman's magazine. Esther is treated to a variety of luncheons, movie previews, fashion shows, and other showcase paraphernalia that should make a small town New England girl happy. However, each externally romantic incident unmasks internal decay. A lunch gobbled up fiercely is poisoned, a street pick-up turns into a sordid seduction of the heroine's friend, while the abandoned Esther falls asleep in the same room, then wakes and makes her way home alone; her glamorous U.N. interpreter date is impotent; another man sadistically tears off her clothes. She returns to her home in New England, and becomes increasingly depressed. Emotionally Esther is out of phase with her mother, and she attempts to run away, to get lost, with a pathetic lack of success. Her repeated, almost comic, attempts at suicide finally culminate in a near-success. Esther crawls into an unused stone cupboard in her house, covers the opening with stones, swallows sleeping pills, and nearly succumbs as her mother searches for her everywhere but at home. The last part of the book deals with her hospitalizations, minimal psychotherapy, and electric shock treatment. She has intercourse for the first time and nearly bleeds to death in its aftermath. After this initiation into "womanhood," as she is about to be discharged from a mental hospital, the book ends.

Every major character in *The Bell Jar* is delineated either as a projection of the heroine—either directly or through an "opposite" representation—or represents key figures in her life, each one playing his assigned role in a series of primal fantasies. There are mothers, brothers, the primal-scene parents, idealized or instinctualized fathers, and so on. The created effect is of an outside world that is a projected inner world from which there is no emergence, and no possibility of expansion beyond the borders of a loathed self. The larger dimensions of space as well—the city, a hillside ski run, the ocean, the big hospital—all reinforce her own tiny finiteness. Her constriction is made concrete by her inability to transcend her own boundaries and penetrate into these larger spaces. The world outside comes at her, imprisons her, impales her, and casts her back into herself. Her attempts to conquer the otherness of the "other" by turning it into herself cause her to personify and anthropomorphize the projected inner world with evil ghosts, cadavers, and dead fetuses; the outer world is distorted by her lack of basic trust and sense of alienation.

With shattering effect, this novel conveys the pain of narcissism and dammed up, self-directed aggression in an outer world that allows no resonance, no echoing balance which permits investment and outflow to "collective alternates." Esther Greenwood literally eats and drinks a bad—sadistic or unresponsive—world of objects. A complete range of libido and aggression is traversed in the course of this journey. She becomes, or is invaded by the gobbling mouth and clutching fingers inbibing poison, the black, fetid excretory product, the primal-scene rape of mother, the bleeding, castrated victim of mutilating vaginal penetration, the flying skier (phallus) who collides with someone in her path and breaks her bones, the unsedated victim of electro-shock. Greenacre (1958b) has commented pertinently on wishes "to restore the lost object not only through one dominant incorporative route, but throughout all of these, which may appear fused or separately" (p. 135). Beginning with the Rosenbergs, each episode confirms her fusion with all objects who are perceived as victims. She fails in one attempt after another to maker herself *willfully* the victim of these objects and their alternative representations, in partnerships that create boundaries through mutual manageable aggression. The word is the state executing the Rosenbergs, and her primitive identification with them creates the art we recognize as Sylvia Plath's. However, in relation to the fragility of the heroine's own boundaries, the quantities and qualities of the world's aggressive energies are greater than her abilities to reproject it. On the first page the electrocutions are contrasted with the heroine's first self-image: "I felt as though I was carrying that cadaver's head around with me on a string, like some black noiseless balloon stinking of vinegar." The balloon is thin, the cadaver-self's skin cannot absorb or discharge traumata; one puncture and the balloon bursts. She attempts to thicken the "skin" of her self in paranoid-like hatred of objects who, in not fighting back appropriately, do not love back either. These include the prosaic mother who loses her and does not know where to look for her; the male psychiatrist (representing the de-idealized father) who is absent and unavailable even when present; the interpreter at the U.N. (the desexualized father) who will penetrate her only with insubstantial words, not physically, who won't seduce her (in part a superego representation); and her boyfriend (equated perhaps with the author's brother) who wants to look and be looked at, but his genitals, which look like a shriveled turkey gizzard and neck, offer no ego or libidinal nourishment (they are the counterpart of the heroine's own balloon head on a string of a neck). Other objects include Esther's father, whose grave has not been visited since his death, so the identifications arising from the mourning process have been unavailable to her; the salesgirl who tells her that no raincoat is water repellent, a reminder that there is no outside barrier to shield her against hostile elements; the other patients in the hospital (her psychopathological self without the redeeming talent) who won't answer her when she attempts a dialogue; the sailor who can't tell her age, who swallows her lies about herself; and the stone cupboard that won't hide her. Her incorporation of each of these elements and her failure to reproject them back into the world creates a loathed, increasingly fragmented, unidealized self.

Perhaps the author said to herself: In writing about them, I can rid myself of them. In one documented instance (Steiner 1973), it is clear that the character Joan Gilling is given the fears and suicidal compulsions that in fact belonged to Sylvia Plath at the time, just as her heroine becomes free of them. Plath's characterizations of people and things are developed, described with the intensity and imagery of a poet, and then cast off, never to return in their original forms. They are like the New York clothes that Esther throws out of her window on her last night in the city. In the novel, almost every experience with objects is untempered by an admixture of object libido with the narcissism and aggression of both heroine and the "others" she encounters. The exceptions are mother-substitutes who are consciously perceived as such by the heroine; Jay Cee, the editor; Philomena Guinea, the novelist; and Dr. Nolan, the second psychiatrist. However, the weight is on the side of those who penetrate beneath her surface to destroy from within, those who inflict mental or physical trauma. Some objects refuse to hold her with loving firmness, feed her the right amounts of assimilable food, or look into her eyes (in all physical descriptions, her mother has her eyes shut, looks past her to others, or turns her back on her). Others fail to dole out proper balances of rewards and restrictions, or shatter her idealization of them. Still others deprive her of the differentiation of her own identity by not allowing developmental crises; they fail to offer intense love or the possibility of hate, and instead show her indifference, slackness of tension, and lack of challenge. Only the wilder aspects of nature satisfy her, and she turns to them — to the sea, the white ski slope, and her horses for challenging, mutually controlling contact. Esther's cure for fears, disappointments in love, and loneliness is a very hot bath — a coffin which turns into a womb. The stimulating pain of its heat reestablishes boundaries, and the water is a possible recipient of dirt and badness which can then be drained away. She steps out feeling "pure and sweet as a new baby."

Many of the characters are alter-egos, who disappear once they have served their purpose in the psychological structure of the novel as identical or opposite doubles of their heroine. Doreen, in a darkened bar, glows in white; Esther, in black, disappears into the darkness. Doreen is her opposite — the first of projected, idealized selves in identification with an idealized mother. In the novel, the mother is serious, hard-working and complains of having passively endured the father's sexual advances. Doreen, in contrast, is a flighty, humorous, unindustrious, sexy blonde with big breasts — the golden girl. Doreen aggressively, yet playfully, participates fully in the sexual act which the sleepy heroine only witnesses. Doreen *is* Esther enjoying fantasies of disguised oedipal triumph, freed of pathological mourning for a dead father. The writer says of Doreen: "Everything she said was like a secret voice speaking straight out of my own bones." Doreen is able to forget everything after sleep; the heroine, sleepless, never forgets anything. For many days before the heroine's major suicide attempt, she is unable to sleep or eat (see Spitz 1965b).

The first chapter closes with: "I liked looking on at other people in crucial situations. If there was a road accident, or a street fight, or a baby pickled in a laboratory jar, I'd stop and look so hard, I never forgot it" (pp. 10–11). The last image is particularly significant. As the person in the bell jar, and as the dead fetus in a permanent womb that she tries to become in her suicide attempt, those eyes do more than just remember. The first two images suggest violent action, and while she may identify with either aggressor or victim, or both, she remains differentiated from what she sees. In the last image, evoking the stillness after the violent encounter, it is clear that she *becomes* the dead infant abandoned in a womb without the nutriment that will make birth into life, and selfhood possible. Her suicidal fate in fusion with victims is predicted throughout the beginning chapter of the novel.

In the course of the novel, many efforts to fight off the final "fusion with the victim object" are described or alluded to. The ultimate failure the author envisions is indicated despite the book's mildly optimistic ending. These defensive attempts at boundary formation are discernible in the form of the novel. The division into brief separated fragments has already been mentioned. Often one can trace the progression of ideas from fragment to fragment with a censoring break between fragments like a break in free association. Later, an example will be given to demonstrate how one can "plot" the broken train of ideas and affects by supplying the missing connections and thus link the fragments as one would in an analytic session.

Another stylistic device that serves and reflects defense while adding immeasurably to the richness of texture and tension of the language, is the use of antithetical, often explicitly bisexual symbolism that creates an affect of conflict and differentiation. (See Roth and Blatt [1972] on the use of polar-opposite imagery in those attempting to establish self-object boundaries.) I noted earlier that for Sylvia Plath, what attracts also contains elements of danger. The moon, in its capacity to draw the tides, is maternal and fusing, while its bald white face, creating sharp outlines, is differentiating, cold, lifeless, to be avoided. The sea draws her; she wishes to drown in it. Father dwells on the other side and beneath it. The maternal, womb-birth-fusion symbolism of the sea is mixed with the opposite, sadistic, positive oedipal image, in Plath's childhood memory I noted earlier. It will not take her yet — neither father nor mother, neither the murderous nor sweet death. The buoyancy of the sea casts Esther up, and as she emerges, she hears her heart beating: "I am, I am, I am."

A third means of establishing boundaries between self- and object-representations is through the creation of thrown-off alter-egos, opposite twins, both of the same and different sexes. Through them she can live vicariously. With their aid she can project opposing sides of internal conflicts and separate identity fragments. For instance, the heroine's boyfriend, Buddy Willard, can be interpreted as representing a male self through whom she can fantasize having a baby all by herself without heterosexual intercourse (see the fig tree allegory of *The Bell Jar* [1971b, p. 45]). These characters offer the possibility of unpunished gratification of her own drives, but their sharp oppositeness also serves to tell her who she is: at least, she is not they. In one fragment, she goes with Hilda, another alter-ego, to see *The Dybbuk,* and "when the Dybbuk spoke from her [the heroine of the play's] mouth, its voice sounded so cavernous and deep, you couldn't tell whether it was a man or a woman. Well, Hilda's voice sounded just like the voice of that Dybbuk" (p. 81). Dissociated from herself, Hilda is presented in feline images, a phallic-sadistic witch-like girl. Opposite to the heroine, Hilda is happy that the Rosenbergs will be executed. She would murder the primal-scene parents who write in their cells of their sexual longings. But the identity of Esther with Hilda is revealed by the use of one of Plath's favorite symbols for herself. Hilda stares at her reflection in the shop windows, "as if to make sure moment by moment that she continued to exist" (p. 82). Hilda, having her picture taken, holds a "bald, faceless head of a hatmaker's dummy," which is equated with Esther's first image for herself, the detached cadaver head like a balloon. Through this double, one sees the struggle between identification with the aggressor who would kill the Rosenbergs, and identification with the victims, the heroine who imagines *being* the Rosenbergs. Hilda, the girl possessed by the dybbuk, is, after all, described as invaded by an alien identity (the dybbuk) against which her ego is able to struggle.

In the following fragment, the heroine weeps as her picture is taken — possibly the experience is associated with a childhood memory involving her father. Later, looking at a snapshot of herself, she equates it with a newspaper photo of a girl who committed suicide. Still later she weeps for a second time at her father's grave. This resonates with the episode concerning having her picture taken. At the picture-taking, she announces she wants to be a poet. In this identity, she feels the loss of her father who will never see her poems that are written for him in his most idealized, immortal form. She imagines being discovered some day, an anonymous, acclaimed author whose true identity is revealed and who is found to be the clumsy adolescent no one appreciated. By reversal, this is an allusion to the reunion with the family-romance father and mother through writing (see Greenacre 1958a). The picture-taking is also a mourning for, and an identification with the Rosenbergs (the dead parents) of the previous fragment. Looking in the mirror, "the face that peered back at me seemed to be peering from the grating of a prison cell."

Another double, Joan, a potential suicide, suddenly appears at the end of the novel. The character of Joan Gilling has recently come to life in the form of a memoir by Nancy Hunter Steiner (1973), the model for the character. Mrs. Steiner seems intuitively to have understood Sylvia Plath's oscillation between fusion and differentiation. Steiner writes that she finally had to leave her friend because Sylvia had turned to Nancy to supply a missing piece in herself. Mrs. Steiner realized that she could not offer herself in this capacity without suffering severe emotional consequences, "so I drew back instinctively, allowing some distance to come between us like an invisible barrier" (p. 75).

At the end of the novel, Esther goes to Joan's house, hemorrhaging after her first intercourse. As usual, the author defines Joan unequivocally. "Joan was the beaming double of my old best self, specially designed to follow and torment me. . . . Sometimes I wondered if I made Joan up. . . . She would pop up at every crisis of my life to remind me of what I have been, and what I have been through, and carry on her own separate but similar crisis under my nose" (p. 179). Here is a perfect ironic description of the projected primitive superego precursor. On one level it represents a defense against homosexual impulses; on another, the narrator indicates that the character will be used to represent her in what is to follow. In a continuation of the same passage, she speaks of how she must resist old women who want to adopt her and turn her into themselves.

Joan takes her bleeding friend to the emergency room of the hospital — none of the doctors she telephoned are available. Then Esther hears that Joan has suddenly killed herself. The suicide is presented almost matter-of-factly, adding to its ominousness. Esther goes to the funeral, "and all during the simple service, I wondered what I thought I was burying" (p. 198). At Joan's funeral, "the coffin loomed in its snow pallor of flowers." The white stands for death here, the death pallor — another instance of the use of antithetical symbolic meanings. Symbolically the whiteness may also be interpreted to represent the blood of the primal scene (the defloration of Esther) and of childbirth killing the victim-mother (represented by Joan). In another passage the "white sweet baby cradles in its mother's belly" (p. 79). In the latter scene, a description of skiing, everything is white with life. Again, what gives life to one self, the active aggressor conquering nature, also brings death to the other self, the passive victim unable to work its way into the outside world.

The character of Joan at the end parallels Doreen at the beginning. But the oppositeness of Doreen is contrasted with the similarities to Joan. Joan's identity is too close to the heroine's to allow Plath to use her for vicarious, instinctual gratification. The similarities to the heroine come through in spite of the author's attempt to deny them. Feelings of dread are evoked in the reader at Plath's failure to successfully project, that is, the author fails to create a Joan-figure who is different enough from her heroine to take on her own life, a figure invested, in a sense, with object-libidinal and differentiating aggressive cathexis.

Joan is obviously a part of the heroine rather than a separate character and is therefore dangerous. In the absence of stable boundaries between them, she must be killed to save Esther from "death" through mutual reincorporation. Steiner has (1973) compared her relationship with Sylvia

Plath to that between Jesus and Judas (see Tarachow 1960: Chapter 2 of this volume). At another time, she notes that Sylvia "referred to me in letters to her mother as her alter-ego and often remarked that we presented a mirror image or represented opposite sides of the same coin." Steiner also describes how Sylvia was visibly shaken when a girl casually remarked that Sylvia had "her" hairdo. (The same hairdo meant a loss of part of the self.) And at another point Steiner describes Sylvia's passionate need to laboriously label two identical bottles of nail polish which were kept on opposite sides of their shared bedroom. These passages give important clues concerning Plath's need to cast off doubles, and her fear of re-fusion. When the projected self appeared to offer the temptation of gratifying her need for incorporation Plath's integrity was threatened. Therefore, the double, Joan, must be presented defensively in unflattering terms. There is a near-paranoid quality given to descriptions of Joan, the repository of those aspects of the author she most criticized in herself.

Like the heroine in the beginning, Joan is forced to witness the primal scene, but when Esther almost bleeds to death afterward, the sexual experience is no longer the casual play of the early episode. At Joan's funeral the heroine comes ominously close to reidentifying with the projected suicidal self. "I wondered what I thought I was burying." Joan's motives for suicide are never explored in the book. We assume that one aspect of Joan's identity represents Esther as female victim. According to Steiner's accounts, Plath courted rape as her first experience in intercourse. The dangerous bleeding was almost consciously sought. Many of the considerations discussed earlier of the study of Friedman et al. (1971) apply pertinently here. The bleeding then represents menstruation, rape, abortion, and childbirth. Joan-Esther is the dying mother giving birth to herself following a sado-masochistic primal scene. Joan-Esther is the child dying in the process of birth. The fusion of the victim's female identities is condensed in Joan's self-destruction by hanging, a method that failed to kill the heroine earlier. It does suggest the strangulation of the unborn fetus in the bell jar.

This manner of killing off of Joan also suggests she may be the victim of the author's death wishes for her brother, who was born when Plath was two and a half (Newman 1971). The day her brother was born, Sylvia Plath walked along the beach and for the first time saw "the *separateness* of everything. I felt the wall of my skin. I am I. That stone is a stone. My beautiful fusion with the things of this world was over." On this day, "the awful birthday of otherness, she [the world] became my rival, somebody else" (Newman 1971, p. 269). In this "memory" the shoreline represents the separation of conflicting selves and the loss of the mother-child unity. It also represents the barrier between life and death, a barrier which Plath repeatedly sought to obliterate. This early memory is condensed with a later one at the death of her father: "My father died, we moved inland."

The ambivalent pull to return to the sea is multiply determined. It signifies rejoining the family-romance father, remerging with mother, and replacing brother in the womb. It also means casting off the "other," the tension between observing and observed selves that maintains the defensive counter-cathexis against the regressive loss of a stable sense of identity. To return to the sea and merge with it represents her ego's denial that brother is born and lives, and that father is dead.[11] To go to the border of the sea, yet not to succumb to its lure, is to face the gulf of separateness dividing the living from the dead, the parent from the child, and the poet from the emergent poem. When, in *The Bell Jar,* the ocean casts her up, and her beating heart proclaims "I am, I am, I am," she receives the message with disappointment. She has not gone far enough. Father has sent her back to the living—inland. Mother has sent her alone into the world—brother is born. The pain of the experience leads to a break between fragments.

After the unsuccessful attempt to drown, the next fragment in the novel begins: "the flowers nodded like bright, knowledgeable children" (Plath 1971b, p. 132). One can interpret the presence of a resistance in this transition which allows resumption of the previous train of ideas and affects when they are disguised by symbolic and allegorical representations. Her wish to distribute only living flowers to new mothers on the maternity ward, to weed out the dead ones (a reaction formation against death wishes toward the baby brother), leads her to mix up mothers and flowers. She gives the wrong flowers (children) to the wrong mothers and is sent away in disgrace from the maternity ward. The birth of her new self is associated with the loss of mother, the absence of father.

A final means of evading fatal fusion with the idealized victim-object fused with self-representations in *The Bell Jar* is afforded through the search for oedipal and postoedipal identifications and relationships with the father, and through heterosexual activities. The instinctualized relationship to the father is represented by the German language, a language which the academically brilliant heroine cannot grasp. She decides to go to bed with a

11. The fantasy that father died to give life to a younger brother who is also thought of as *her* baby, associated with fantasies of father as the victim of a primal scene murder and oral castration by mother is one I have found in a patient. Her father died when she was four, one and a half years after the birth of her brother. This woman has an intense feeling of kinship with Sylvia Plath. She, too, emphasizes fantasies of a sadistic sexual father to ward off regressive oral sadistic wishes that carry suicidal consequences.

simultaneous translator at the United Nations with whom she feels a kinship, but they fall asleep chastely, side by side. The death of her father during her latency and her failure to mourn appropriately have prevented the desexualization of id-derivatives from the oedipal phase. For her first lover she chooses a man who is experienced, described as an impersonal, priestlike official, as in the tales of tribal rites.

To understand somewhat more about Plath's relationship to the father and to males, a brief account of the five main male characters in their relationship to the heroine proves illuminating. These include the chaste interpreter, idealized but sexless, and her steady boyfriend, Buddy Willard, who disappoints her when she discovers he has had a previous sexual experience. She projects her oedipal curiosity onto him in the episode where they both strip—perhaps an echo of childhood sexual exploration with her brother. In one of his roles, Buddy represents the primal-scene father, the de-idealized sexual male. He is anti-poetry. She views poetry as the living child (the dead fetus brought to screaming life), as rendering immortality, the return to primary narcissism—"Godly, as a child's shriek./Spider-like I spin mirrors./Loyal to my image" ("Childless Woman," Plath 1972). This conflicts with Buddy's representation of poetry as the dead thing, symbolized by his dead genitals and sick flesh, which are associated with the cadaver that crumbles into dust and the specimens in jars on the shelf. Buddy, earlier described as a male alter ego, will be discussed further in another context.

A third male is the sadistic, woman-hating Marco, who attempts to rape her at a party in the midst of onlookers, another version of the primal scene. He is made sadistic (like the father in "Daddy") partly to protect against the fusion experience. After the attempted rape, she tosses her clothes "like a loved one's ashes" to the night air. They flutter in the wind, which is inadequate to carry them freely and flowingly. The gesture is self-purification, a casting off of the New York self, the dybbuk, her dress "black as dirt," father's ashes, death itself. The wind which will carry them into the unknown dark heart of New York is her poetic inspiration. The gray scraps, also symbolizing her poems, are (transitional objects) ambiguously poised between life (white) and death (black). But they are only clothes, the outer skin, and, ominously, "the wind made an effort, but failed, and a bat-like shadow sank toward the roof garden of the penthouse opposite."

Dr. Gordon, the fourth important male figure, her first psychiatrist, is narcissistically blind to her. Like the dead father, he is self-satisfied and sufficient like the phallic-exhibitionistic little boy (brother). Finally there is the dead father himself, visited in rain that drenches through to her skin. She takes the place of the mother by wearing a black mourning veil to visit his grave (further antithetical symbolism—the bride wears black, the wedding is a funeral, the sexual flow is tears). The pouring rain under which he lies reminds us of his romance-equivalent, the merman of Arnold's poem. She writes: "I thought it odd that in all the time my father had been buried in this graveyard, none of us had ever visited him. My mother hadn't let us come to his funeral because we were only children then, and he had died in the hospital, so the graveyard and even his death seemed unreal to me." She goes on with ambiguous and ambivalent language: "I had a great yearning lately to pay my father back for all the years of neglect, and start tending his grave. I had always been my father's favorite, and it seemed fitting I should take on a mourning my mother had never bothered with" (p. 135, italics mine).

The coffin is described as a dirty bathtub. This echoes the earlier bath in which Esther washes off the dirty sensuality of her oedipal Doreen self, returns regressively to mother, and is reborn. Here the image takes on the opposite meaning: not mother's womb, but father's grave. Mother's womb is father's grave, and so the mourned for, idealized father was the victim in the primal scene. Esther breaks down, weeps "into the cold salt rain," and in identification with the dead victim father, she creates her own grave—in mother's house, with pills taken from mother's strong box (another coffin-womb), in which she will die and/or be reborn. It should be emphasized that the libidinal wishes for the oedipal father (unless he is made sadistic, repulsive) and the symbiotic mother create the tendency to surrender to regressive fusion in death; while the aggressive impulses toward the abandoning father and emotionally absent, unresisting mother brings death through internalization of unneutralized defused aggression in the absence of a live object. Both erotic and aggressive wishes to either mother or father on all of the levels discussed here lead inevitably to the compulsion to die. The victory of individuality is choosing the time and form of death. Esther takes fifty pills at one time. The poisoning repeats the food poisoning sequence earlier in the book. In the early episode, however, her identification with her opposite, Doreen, who is also poisoned, maintains a stable projected self-representation that allows rejection of the poison.

The heroine's mother occupies relatively little space in the story. She is first mentioned in the chapter where the heroine meets the Russian United Nations interpreter. Esther sees him as father rediscovered, and sitting next to him, she realizes, "that I was only purely happy until I was nine years old" (p. 60). She then describes her mother's joyless scrimping to give her "advantages," and in the next paragraph, speaking of a Russian girl who accompanies this man, Esther wishes she "could crawl into her and spend the rest of my life barking out one idiom after another"—in an unknowable tongue. Perhaps, she is expressing a regressive wish for re-fusion with the early mother before the distancing discrete cognitive verbal communication began. This is combined with the wish to become the dybbuk, a separate self with her own boundaries within the mother's body. Her mother is introduced into the book in this context and she is equated with those who serve men, who cook and write shorthand. Yet the heroine has an empty stomach, and only a man can feed her assimilable food. However, men all require that she submit sexually, and this act, too, must imply joining together of male and female self in a regressive fusion, or in a continuing defensive sadomasochistic struggle of the sort strongly hinted at in Plath's allusions to her marriage (see "Daddy," 1966).

Many of the perceptions of Esther's actual mother in *The Bell Jar* convey the absence of stabilizing constant contact, the failure to provide satisfying libidinal stimulation fused with a differentiating neutralized aggression to promote safe self-object differentiation and secondary identifications against the twin dangers of fusion and object loss. When the mother drives her home from New York, she fails to pursue her curiosity about her daughter's face, cut in an abortive suicide attempt. "My mother climbed behind the wheel and tossed a few letters into my lap, then *turned her back*" (italics mine). "My mother took care never to tell me to do anything. She would only reason with me sweetly, like one intelligent person with another" (p. 99). The enraged child wishes to strangle the mother—either to death or into responsive life. As dawn comes after a sleepless night: "My mother turned from a foggy log into a slumbering middle-aged woman, her mouth slightly open and a snore raveling from her throat. The piggish noise irritated me, and for a while it seemed to me that the only way to stop it would be to take a column of skin and sinew from which it rose and twist it to silence between my hands" (p. 101). When mother leaves for work, Esther crawls under a mattress. It is "like a tombstone. It feels dark and safe under there, but the mattress was not heavy enough. It needed about a ton more weight to make me sleep" (p. 101). It seems obvious enough to interpret the coming suicide attempt as the murder of the mother with the weight of the father upon her turned against the self, and Joan Gilling's suicide lends itself to this interpretation. However, emphasis should also be placed on the stimulus hunger, the absence of pressure against the body, of libidinal nutriment from any animate object that does not disappear and reappear, like a foggy log, silently to take her place beside the daughter.

In the same episode the heroine unsuccessfully tries to split up the hundred letter word on the first page of Joyce's *Finnegan's Wake*. She dimly perceives that the word is somehow associated with the birth of the child and its differentiation from the parents and within its global self-image, but she fails in her attempt at analysis.

The mother's abandonment is also expressed in terms of distortion of self- and object-images. "I watched my mother grow smaller and smaller until she disappeared into the door . . . then I watched her grow larger and larger as she came back . . ." (p. 111). As mother gets bigger, Esther must be getting tinier. The scene evokes the easy regressibility of her own body image reflecting the inconstancy of the mother's affective distance represented by changes in the mother's spatial distance.

Esther's only satisfying identity is as a poet. Poetry is equated with the ideal abstraction of father, supplying sublimated energy to her ego, and idealizing power to her superego. Winning prizes, the only thing she is good at (except for dying—the final prize—see "Lady Lazarus" [1966]) is contrasted with her lack of ability and interest in mundane activities associated with her mother and grandmother. In Esther's extended argument with Buddy, she sees poetry as immortal, the part that survives death; he sees it as dust, equivalent to a cadaver. The figure of Esther, who feels her head is like that of a cadaver (p. 1), conveys the conflict between the two identifications with father (the living soul of the poet, the dead body in the grave) at the very beginning. In this role, Buddy, the son of family-romance parents, is probably partially equated with the author's brother, the intellectual argument originally arising in concrete childhood discussions between brother and sister. For example, one can well imagine the two children discussing "Is father really dead? Will he come back? Is there a soul which survives?" Buddy argues the negative side of all these questions, bringing her back to "the facts of life," as the birth of Sylvia Plath's brother made her aware of otherness. Her brother brought back and represented the degraded sexual father. This endangered her partial identifications with him which nourish her talent, and conjured up the decaying corpse, blotting out the professor, the linguist, and the author of a remembered book. Esther must win the argument to go on living, with her poetic ambitions as her raison d'être. In the novel the arguments end inconclusively. Later, in her fantasies, she imagines winning them.

Esther's visit to her father's grave, however, affirms the reality of father (representing poetry) as dust. It is the final, unbearable loss, and completes the chain that ends with the suicide attempt. In it she creates her own coffin in the ashes, and blocks the opening of the hole with *dustcovered* logs. In killing herself in identification with the father as the victim of the ashes, she revives the sea imagery that expresses the union with the primal parent, and she surrenders to the merman of Arnold's poem. The chapter ends: "the silence drew off, bearing the *pebbles* and *shells* and all the *tatty wreckage* of my life." Then, at the rim of vision, it gathered itself, and in *one sweeping tide* rushed me to sleep" (p. 138, italics mine). She is reborn into a world of women. Her first word spoken by a depersonalized self is: "Mother." The rejection of the symbiotic mother (see Friedman et al. 1972) and the search and discovery of the mother who will supply neutralized aggressive dialogue, who will arrange to have her own mother shut out and kept away, supplies the thematic thread of the rest of the book.

V

Sylvia Plath was one of those individuals described by Anna Freud (1967) in whom

> the survivor's desolation, longing, loneliness are not acknowledged as his own feelings, but displaced onto the dream (poetic) image of the dead, where they are experienced in identification with the dead, ... That identification with the lost object, the deserted person, is derived from specific infantile experiences when the dreamer, as a child, felt unloved, rejected, and neglected. [pp. 17–18]

That some such fantasy must have crystallized is strongly suggested by Plath's description of the visit to the father's grave in *The Bell Jar.* As with Jacobson's patients (1965), the heroine feels that "desertion has not been the fault of the lost parent. It had been caused by the surviving parent's intolerable character traits or moral worthlessness" (p. 194). In the climactic scene of the visit to the grave, Esther experiences a double identification with the idealized, dead father whom she wishes to rejoin; and with the unloving mother whom she will destroy by killing herself.

The failure of Esther Greenwood, the fictional representation of Sylvia Plath, to resist the call from the dead for reunion may be interpreted in many ways and is obviously overdetermined. It shows the failure of the ordinarily temporary regressive identification with the lost object of mourning to become resolved, the failure to reestablish self-object differentiation by externalization of aggression onto the surviving parent, and the inability to displace and retain the idealized object in a structured superego, whose formation has its earliest roots in the vicissitudes of the symbiotic relationship with the mother. The need to retain love from the superego (the psychic structure that is the precipitate of former idealized relations) may arise in part from the wished-for unification between self and object (Jacobson 1964), a residue of the original symbiosis. On the other hand, the structural-ization of the superego in both its restricting and idealizing aspects as a rela-tively autonomous agency, using relatively neutralized aggressive energies to maintain counter-cathectic boundaries, protects the ego against being overwhelmed by the wished-for refusion. Its aggressive energies always keep it set apart from the ego, aiding defense against the urge to be reunited with either the primary mother or, in the case of Esther or her creator, the dead father.

The superego sets up unreachable objectives; that they cannot be realized insures the continuance of life as an individual in the face of loss, and pre-vents the loss of self in the creation of poetry. The unresisting reach toward loss of self is represented most vividly in some of the poems written just before Plath's suicide. One finds this self-abandonment in the form of merging into mirrors, the joining of reflection in water to self, the fusion without conflict with a corpse in "Edge" (Plath 1966), written in the last week of her life. Everything folds inward — nothing turns outward as "The woman is perfected./Her dead/Body wears the smile of accomplishment. . . ." The children are "coiled" and "folded"; "Her breasts, empty, are . . . back into her body as petals/Of a rose close" — at night. In "Words" (Plath 1966), also written during the last week of her life, the external guiding stars are gone. The poet merges with her image in the water. The poem ends: "From the bottom of the pool, fixed stars/Govern a life." A third poem written that week, "Contusion" (Plath 1966), ends: "The heart shuts,/The sea slides back/The mirrors are sheeted."

To the readers of her poems and novel, Sylvia Plath's suicide may be interpreted as the consequence of her attempt to reach the unreachable, and is viewed by many as a kind of tragic heroism of our times. This interpreta-tion, I suspect, accounts for the growing Sylvia Plath legend in recent years as much as anything else.

Summary

Under the threat of the loss of narcissistically cathected objects, regres-sive fusion of self and object may impend in those in whom the stage of identification with the aggressor fails to function as a vehicle to partially externalize excessive quantities of unneutralized aggression away from self-representations back onto the object world. In this context, a suicide attempt is seen as a last-ditch attempt to consummate an active identification with the object as aggressor, but with an inability to use the projection aspect of the mechanism described by Anna Freud (1936). Instead, the aggression is turned against the self, in a manner that suggests a precursor of superego-ego relations on a more primitive level of ego and drive maturation than that postulated for identification with the aggressor. The suicidal act simultaneously kills the aggressive self and the object who imposes aggressive (to be conceived of as separate from libidinal) frustration, and makes the subject an idealized victim like the original object. This tendency is increased in the absence of the other oedipal object during the oedipal and early latency period.

Permanent refusion of subject and idealized victim in death may be sought as a kind of tragic quest unable to be resisted by an overwhelmed ego. Or it may be defended against *progressively* by attempts to establish sadomasochistic or "hate" relationships using the mechanism of identification with the aggressor, or paranoid defenses; and *regressively* in melancholia, or by using such somatic defenses against fusion as insomnia and anorexia. All of these have been demonstrated in the exploration in this paper of the life and works of Sylvia Plath.

This hypothesis has pointed to a relationship between a propensity for suicide and particular aspects of artistic creativity. Greenacre has postulated that the retaining of primitive identifications provides the basis of empathy in later life (1957), and therefore, of the kind of poetic gift found in Sylvia Plath. I feel that the role of the aggressive drive in her often noted ability to become one with both animate and inanimate objects — to conquer the otherness of the other — is inadequately explained by the death instinct theory, and by the process of renouncing self-interest in "altruistic surrender" where life itself may be threatened in the interests of narcissistic love (A. Freud 1936). The hypothesis of a "fusion with the victim" suggests that primitive identification with an idealized victim-object created in Sylvia Plath an inability to project the released unneutralized aggressive cathexes away from self-representations. These aggressive cathexes then were unavailable to energize the enforcing functions of the superego, to promote counter-cathexes, and to build ego and superego structure.

This hypothesis links suicidal behavior, "Christ-like" empathy for victims, and poetic sensibility. While identification with the aggressor makes for greater self-object differentiation in the still-instinctualized relationship to the powerful parents, and prevents premature massive internalization of aggressive forces, the projective aspect of the mechanism also creates a distance from the inner nature of objects. There is a loss of the precious sensitivity and vulnerability of early childhood that only a few gifted people retain. Sylvia Plath is an example of such a creative artist in whom relatively unneutralized aggressive energies may supply simultaneously, or in alternation, energy for creative activity and self-destruction.

This occurs particularly if the created works are used as intermediate objects for the substantial discharge and investment of these aggressive energies. The creation of a poem then represents in a displaced form the killing of a hated part of the self in a partially externalized representation which partakes of both self- and object-qualities. "Suicide is, after all, the opposite of the poem" (Anne Sexton in Newman 1971, p. 175). The more the work can be cathected as a stable object for the creator, the more its creation can serve to discharge aggression outward. The world of the poet's vision then becomes a partial substitute for the real world, and offers a route of escape from the real world itself, and from the self-directed rage that threatens to destroy the ego in the absence of living objects in a trauma-inflicting world. The poetry of Ted Hughes (for example, the poems in *Crow,* 1971) may be an example of the successful externalization of rage through the creation of poetic objects, and Sylvia Plath's selection of him as her husband may one day be profitably explored in this connection. However, if the creation is experienced as a loss of the narcissistic self, and the poem-object is cathected with primitive defused aggression, the creation is felt to be destroyed in the aftermath of the creative activity; self-directed rage is fostered that is experienced as a primitive form of guilt demanding a life for a life. The need to make restitution may energize the kind of treadmill of creative activity ending in self-depletion and self-destruction that marked the last six months of Sylvia Plath's life.

References

Alvarez, A. (1972). *The Savage God.* New York: Random House.

Beres, D. (1958). Vicissitudes of super-ego functions and super-ego precursors in childhood. *Psychoanalytic Study of the Child* 13:324–351.

Bloom, H. (1973). *The Anxiety of Influence.* London: Oxford University Press.

Friedman, M., Glasser, M., Laufer, E., Laufer, M., and Wohl, M. (1972). Attempted suicide and self-mutilation in adolescence. *International Journal of Psycho-Analysis* 53:Part 2, 179–184.

Freud, A. (1936). *The Ego and the Mechanisms of Defense.* New York: International Universities Press.

———(1967). About losing and being lost. *Psychoanalytic Study of the Child* 22:17–18.

———(1972). Comments on aggression. *International Journal of Psycho-Analysis* 3:163–191.

Freud, S. (1915). Instincts and their vicissitudes. *Standard Edition* 14:111–140.

———(1915). On narcissism: an introduction. *Standard Edition* 14:73–102.

———(1923). The ego and the id. *Standard Edition* 19:3–66.

———(1924). The economic problem of masochism. *Standard Edition* 19:157–170.

———(1925). On negation. *Standard Edition* 19:235–242.

Greenacre, P. (1945). The biological economy of birth. *Psychoanalytic Study of the Child* 1:31–53.

———(1957). The childhood of the artist: libidinal phase development and giftedness. In P. Greenacre, *Emotional Growth,* vol. 2, pp. 479–504. New York: International Universities Press, 1971.

———(1958a). The family romance of the artist. In P. Greenacre, *Emotional Growth,* vol. 2, pp. 505–532. New York: International Universities Press, 1971.

———(1958b). Toward an understanding of the physical nucleus of some defense reactions. In P. Greenacre, *Emotional Growth,* vol. 1, pp. 128–144. New York: International Universities Press, 1971.

———(1960). Considerations regarding the parent-infant relationship. In P. Greenacre, *Emotional Growth,* vol. 1, pp. 199–224. New York: International Universities Press, 1971.

Hartmann, H., Kris, E., and Loewenstein, R. (1949). Notes on the theory of aggression. *Psychological Issues,* vol. 4, no. 2, Monograph 14. New York: International Universities Press.

Hoffer, W. (1950). Development of the body ego. *Psychoanalytic Study of the Child* 5:18–23.

Hughes, T. (1971). *Crow.* New York: Harper and Row.

Jacobson, E. (1964). *The Self and the Object World.* New York: International Universities Press.

———(1965). The return of the lost parent. In *Drives, Affects, Behavior,* vol. II, ed. M. Schur, pp. 193–211. New York: International Universities Press.

Kanzer, M. (1950). The Oedipus trilogy. *Psychoanalytic Quarterly* 19:561–572.

Kestenberg, J. (1971). From organ-object imagery to self and object representations. In *Separation-Individuation, Essays in Honor of Margaret S. Mahler,* ed. J. B. McDevitt and C. Settlage, pp. 75–99. New York: International Universities Press.

Kohut, H. (1968). The psychoanalytic treatment of narcissistic personality disorder. *The Psychoanalytic Study of the Child* 23:86–113.

Loewald, H. (1962). Internalization, separation, mourning, and the super-ego. *Psychoanalytic Quarterly* 31:483–504.

Mahler, M. S. (1961). On sadness and grief in infancy and childhood: loss and restoration of the symbiotic love object. *Psychoanalytic Study of the Child* 16:322–351.

———(1965). On the significance of the normal separation-individuation phase. In *Drives, Affects, Behavior,* vol. II, ed. M. Schur, pp. 161–170. New York: International Universities Press.

Newman, C., ed. (1971). *The Art of Sylvia Plath.* Bloomington: Indiana University Press.

Novick, J., and Kelly, K. (1970). Projection and externalization. *Psychoanalytic Study of the Child* 25:69–98.

Pao, Ping-nie (1965). The role of hatred in the ego. *Psychoanalytic Quarterly* 24:257–264.

Peto, A. (1969). Terrifying eyes: a visual super-ego forerunner. *Psychoanalytic Study of the Child* 24:197–212.

Plath, S. (1966). *Ariel.* New York: Harper and Row.

———(1968). *The Colossus, and Other Poems.* New York: Vintage Books.

———(1971a). *Crossing the Water, and Other Poems.* New York: Harper and Row.

———(1971b). *The Bell Jar.* New York: Harper and Row.

———(1972). *Winter Trees.* New York: Harper and Row.

Rochlin, G. (1961). The dread of abandonment. *Psychoanalytic Study of the Child* 16:451–469.

Roth, D., and Blatt, S. (1974). Spatio-temporal parameters and psychopathology. *Journal of the American Psychoanalytic Association,* Vol. 22, No. 4.

Solnit, A. (1966). Some adaptive functions of aggressive behavior. In *Psychoanalysis — A General Psychology,* pp. 169–189. New York: International Universities Press.

———(1970). A study of object loss in infancy. *Psychoanalytic Study of the Child* 25:257–272.

———(1972). Aggression: a view of theory building in psychoanalysis. *Journal of the American Psychoanalytic Association* 20:435–450.

Spitz, R. (1953). Aggression: its role in the establishment of object relationships. In *Drives, Affects, Behavior,* vol. I, ed. R. M. Loewenstein, pp. 126–138. New York: International Universities Press.

———(1965a). The evolution of dialogue. In *Drives, Affects, Behavior,* vol. II, Essays in memory of Marie Bonaparte, ed. M. Schur, pp. 161–170. New York: International Universities Press.

————(1965b). *The First Year of Life, A Psychoanalytic Study of Normal and Deviant Development of Object Relations.* New York: International Universities Press.

Steiner, N. (1973). *A Closer Look at Ariel.* New York: Harper and Row.

Tarachow, S. (1960). *Judas, the Beloved Executioner.* Chapter 2 of this volume.

PART III

The Childhood of the Artist

Chapter 5

AN ANALYTIC INQUIRY INTO THE LIFE
AND WORK OF HEINRICH SCHLIEMANN

WILLIAM G. NIEDERLAND, M.D.

This paper is part of a wider study which deals with psychological and psychodynamic aspects of geographic and archaeological exploration. Inasmuch as this presentation includes findings and observations subject to further study and evaluation, as well as to research on additional material, it is to be understood as a report on work in progress.

Starting from the premise that geography, as the name implies, is the study of *Gaea,* or Mother Earth (the *Urmutter*), and that the great problems of geography — where? wherefrom? the relentless investigation and exploration of the earth — resemble and to an extent repeat some of the basic libidinal questions of every human, thus linking geography and archaeology ultimately to anatomy (which in a sense is the geography of the human body), I presented evidence on certain psychological factors involved in the history of geographic exploration (1956–1957). In an effort to expand these observations further and to correlate them with contemporary analytic-biographical research along more individual lines (Bonaparte 1946, 1949, Sterba and Sterba 1954, Greenacre 1955, 1957, Eissler 1961), I shall attempt in the present report to offer and correlate relevant data pertaining to the life and work of Heinrich Schliemann (1822–1890), the nineteenth-century explorer who discovered and excavated the ancient site of Troy, later explored Mycenae, Tyrins, and other prehistoric places. He thus became what some biographers have called the "father" of modern archaeology, who almost single-handedly opened up a new world for historians and students of the classics and who in the process of proving the veracity of Homer's *Iliad* and actually finding the Homeric site paradoxically destroyed the very city he was looking for. In his passion to reach the Virgin soil (the *Urboden*), "untouched ground rock" to use Schliemann's own wording, he unwittingly dug right through the celebrated city and arrived at a settlement about a thousand years older than Homeric Troy.

Archaeologists, on the whole, are apparently not too happy about their famous pioneer. He has remained a somewhat lonely and controversial figure in the history of science, and it is worth noting that Schliemann himself felt that he did not really belong to the profession. In his later years he spoke of himself as an "explorer of Homeric geography," and this is indeed one of the reasons why, in addition to the special nature of his character and exploits, I included him in an analytic study of this kind.

Before offering a summary of my feelings I wish to express a few thoughts on the current status of applied analytic research within the framework of psychoanalysis in general. As we all know, applied analysis has recently become the target of considerable criticism, emanating mostly from nonanalytic quarters (Schapiro 1956), but not always limited to these quarters only. Students of psychoanalysis have occasionally also felt disinclined toward psychoanalytic studies in pathography, for instance, and have questioned the methodology or validity of such endeavors. Kohut (1960) and more recently K. R. Eissler (1961) have dealt with these problems. There are, of course, numerous difficulties and potential pitfalls inherent in applied psychoanalysis, but they are in my view far from being insurmountable. "A policy of restraint" (Freud 1911), proper documentation, scientific rigor, and the analyst's careful search for prime or well authenticated sources, together with their systematic accumulation and cautious evaluation, can resolve many problems of applied analysis, and the results will more than justify the required effort and necessary reticence. Since one of the essential contributions of psychoanalysis is to trace products of the mind (art, sociology, philosophy, religion) to their roots in infantile mental life, applied analysis should maintain its position in our science, I believe. In the present essay I hope to be able to demonstrate the soundness and reliability of pertinent findings in the field of applied psychoanalysis.

My choice, then, of Schliemann's case history (if I may call it such) for analytic investigation springs from several sources, among which I may first of all point to Freud's notable attention and numerous references to archaeology and archaeological discoveries. In a letter to Stefan Zweig, dated 7 February 1931, Freud says "I have . . . actually read more archaeology than psychology" (1960). In two letters to Fliess he mentions Schliemann by name, each time with admiration and considerable interest. Freud's frequent and poignant comparisons between analytic and archaeological "excavation work" (as early as 1907 in discussing Jensen's *Gradiva,* 1909 in the Rat Man case report, and later elaborated in many subsequent publications) are of course firmly anchored in analytic thinking. Since the question of validation of analytic results in the field of applied psychoanalysis has often been raised, I may add that the present study is based on information extracted from the standard biographies, published works, data provided by members of the Schliemann family[1] through written and personal contact with them, correspondence with the Schliemann experts abroad, especially with Dr. Ernest Meyer of Berlin, the leading European scholar in this field today—and on my own research at the Gennadius Library in Athens where the Schliemann Archives are located. When I learned of the existence of this in a sense unique *source material* consisting, in addition to all of Schliemann's books, of about 60,000 letters, eighteen diaries, many thousands of notes, manuscript pages, and other papers, preserved in Athens and waiting for an analyst to come over and take a look, I decided to do just that. When I found that this abundant material was written in fifteen languages—among them Arabic, Russian, Finnish, Swedish, Polish, Portuguese, Spanish, Italian, and Dutch—and that all this was handwritten on yellowing and partly faded folios of close to one hundred thirty volumes, I had indeed some second thoughts as to the advisability of becoming engaged in a study of such magnitude. But by that time, my preliminary research had revealed a task representing too great a challenge to dismiss, and so I set out to spend "a Greek summer" at the Gennadius Library and to study the firsthand material (literally "firsthand," i.e., handwritten by Schliemann) preserved there."[2]

1. I am greatly indebted to Mrs. Andromache Melas, the ninety-year-old daughter of Heinrich Schliemann, as well as to her son, Mr. Leno Melas, for their kind and most helpful cooperation in making material available to me. Mrs. Melas granted me a personal interview in her home in Athens (in 1961) and I wish to express my gratitude for this and for all the information I obtained from her and her son.

2. I am also indebted to Prof. Francis Walton, Director of the Gennadius Library, and his staff, Athens, as well as to Dr. Ernst Meyer, West Berlin, for their kind cooperation.

I further wish to express my appreciation to the Chapelbrook and New-Land Foundations for their support of this research project; also to Drs. Bertram D. Lewin and Sandor Lorand for their advice and encouragement; last but not least to my brother, Dr. Ernst Niederland, Rehovoth, Israel, for his helpful efforts in extracting and translating much of the original material.

The initially so difficult task of having to deal with and translate fifteen languages turned out to be somewhat less arduous than anticipated, since the biographically and analytically significant letters and diaries were written in the more conventional languages, mainly in German, French, Italian, and English, thus directly accessible to me. I am also glad to report that my inquiry, though far from complete — only about 12,000 out of 60,000 letters and fourteen out of eighteen diaries have been studied so far — have proved rewarding and has brought to light some noteworthy, hitherto unpublished information absent from the available biographies (Ludwig 1947, Payne 1959, Cottrell 1958, Meyer 1961, Schuchhardt 1891) and also from Schliemann's short autobiographical essay which forms the introduction to his book *Ilios* (1881a) and was later published separately in a number of editions (1892, 1961). In fact, during the course of my research I was fortunate to come upon, among other finds, a noteworthy autobiographical fragment, handwritten by Schliemann and concealed among piles of business letters and *"Sprachübungen"* ("Language Exercises"). This fragment, apparently unknown until now, throws new light on certain childhood experiences of its author. I also found several dreams recorded by Schliemann and other material the analytic evaluation of which, I believe, will enable us to get a glimpse of the early life history, conflicts, tribulations, and fantasies of an explorer of near-genius caliber.

Among the tasks I set for myself I should like to mention in very general terms: (1) to clarify and unravel, as far as this is possible, the intricate personality development of a most unusual and important figure in the realm of nineteenth-century science; (2) to understand the unconscious forces involved in the apparent *abrupt change in Schliemann's life* stressed by so many biographers in describing Schliemann's change-over in his forties when he switched from "big business" to archaeology; (3) to explore and demonstrate, if possible, some of "the factors which awaken genius and the sort of subject matter it is fated to choose" (Freud 1933), with specific reference to the particular type of creativity observable in Schliemann.

With this I turn to Schliemann's life history. Instead of presenting the usual developmental history (which can be found in the available biographies) I shall limit myself to highlighting some of the psychodynamically relevant data in his colorful and in various ways strange career, following in the main the autobiographical and standard biographical accounts which I shall supplement, wherever necessary, with documentation from my own research.

Schliemann was born in Neubukow in Mecklenburg (North Germany) on 6 January 1822, the fifth child of the Protestant minister Ernst Schliemann and his wife Sophie, who a year and a half later moved to another parsonage in the village of Ankershagen, also in Mecklenburg.

Schliemann lived in Ankershagen until 1831, the year his mother died. Soon after the mother's death the home was broken up, and the children, now numbering seven, were separated and distributed among distant relatives. The father, having behaved in a manner deemed unbecoming a man of God, lost his position as the parson of Ankershagen and moved to another state. He later married the maid who had been in the household during the mother's long illness. Her name was also Sophie. The autobiographical fragment which I found among the papers in Athens has this to say about his father, mother, the maid (the later stepmother) and his mother's death when the boy was nine years of age:

My father was a minister . . . he had many children and little money. He was a dissolute character and a libertine who did not refrain from having licentious and adulterous affairs with the maids whom he favored over his own wife. He maltreated her and I remember from my earliest childhood that he cursed his wife and spat on her. In order to get rid of her he made her pregnant and mistreated her during her [last] pregnancy more than ever. Thus it came to pass that as soon as she fell ill with a nervefever [possibly postpartum septicemia], the sickness quickly led to her death. My father then feigned great sorrow and grief and arranged a magnificent funeral for her, whom he had killed through his villany, and though it then was wintertime and the earth was frozen, he had a sepulchre of massive bricks constructed, . . . surrounded by a fence, and with the following epitaph: Rest in Peace, sweet wife! Mother! Sleep until the great trumpet sounds and brings you back to us from the darkness of the tomb. We will remember you until the spirit drinks from the cup of Lethe. . . .

Apart from the content of this document with its revealing references to the early family situation, the oedipal implications, death, funeral, sepulchre, tomb and tombstone inscription — elements which we shall encounter again and again in Schliemann's life — I wish to emphasize that *this text is written in Italian as a language exercise,* on a large folio in a study book labeled *Sprachübungen,* that it is conscientiously corrected as to grammar and orthography by Schliemann's Italian language teacher in St. Petersburg, and was probably composed between 1858 and 1862, about thirty years after the mother's death when the father was still alive. Similar feelings about the father were expressed in a letter to his sisters, likewise composed as an Italian language exercise and apparently never mailed. In it he said: "I hate and abhor this man. . . . In fact I am terribly ashamed to be the son of this accursed dog." He then admonished his sisters not to write him further about his father until such times as "the devil should recall unto himself . . . this monster." Nevertheless he continued to send money to his father at regular intervals until the latter's death in 1870.

Since his equally revealing dreams, an example of which I shall discuss below, are also recorded in foreign languages as *Sprachübungen,* it seems permissible to think of these writings as *confessions once removed,* that is, as the precipitates of experiences of such a terrifying character that they could only be expressed intellectually transposed into a foreign language, thus transmuted, alienated, and labeled a linguistic exercise. This can also be seen from the fact that Schliemann's shipwreck at the age of nineteen, a factual experience of the most horrible and traumatizing kind, later also emerges in the pages of the volume *Sprachübungen* in a multitude of languages and versions, as well as in many letters, notes, and other references. Like Leonardo's *Profetie* of which Eissler (1961) writes, the *Sprachübungen* can be likened to a record of free associations which disclose some of Schliemann's personal secrets and which are almost arrived at in a way comparable to a primitive, unsophisticated kind of rudimentary "analysis" with cathartic overtones. In learning a new language Schliemann usually hired a teacher, even in the days of his greatest poverty, and since he often restricted the latter's role to that of a listener who was to correct *impartially and impassively* the grammar and spelling of his written texts, he unwittingly made of him a sort of early "analyst." His father, indeed, had been his first language teacher and had taught him Latin and Homer's poetry before he was seven. In his later life, one of these language teachers, Theocles Vimpos, became an important paternal figure to him and the strong father transference, both positive and negative, can be readily recognized in many of his writings and actions.

To return to Schliemann's childhood years in Ankershagen, I shall forego the detailed chronology and focus instead on the following childhood sequences which merit attention:

He grew up in the vicarage, "the cemetery before our door," as he said in his autobiography (1892). In fact, for all practical purposes he was born in a cemetery or at least in such close proximity to it that the questions of birth, being alive, or being buried and dead apparently never lost their urgent, infantile, puzzling, and presumably exciting character for him. To this has to be added a historical circumstance connected with his birth which gave to the latter a highly significant coloring: he was born a short time before the death of the eldest son of his parents, a boy by the name of Heinrich aged eight; the new arrival, the fifth child in the line, but the second boy in the family, was named Heinrich, presumably after the one just deceased.[3] The dead brother Heinrich was interred in the cemetery of Neubukow in March, 1822; the new Heinrich was born in the vicarage of Neubukow—adjoining this cemetery—early in 1822. In May, 1823 the family moved to Ankershagen, again into a building immediately adjoining a cemetery.

It seems that all through his life Schliemann never was fully sure whether he was the *dead* brother inside or the *living* one outside the grave, and throughout life he apparently had to prove compulsively he was the latter — through overactivity, accumulation of one fortune after another, compulsively engaging in work, travel, sports, moneymaking, and a mass of other activities including the compulsive study[4] of a new language every year or so. In addition to the evidence "acted out" by Schliemann, I found documentary confirmation concerning the identity fusion with the dead brother Heinrich: "After I had visited *little Heinrich's* grave, we continued our trip. . . ." In the very next sentence he says of himself: "what a big, tall man *little Heinrich* has become!" (italics added).

This striking sequence (the reference to "little Heinrich" in the grave, then to himself as the grown and active "little Heinrich" abroad) appears in a letter to his sisters from Amsterdam (20 February 1842) in the context of traveling, sightseeing, visiting people, cities, and cemeteries—activities which he later pursued throughout his life as though to repeat over and over again the early move from Neubukow to Ankershagen (infancy) and subsequent ones from Ankershagen to Kalkhorst-Strelitz-Fürstenberg (puberty). At the age of nine or ten Schliemann inscribes his initials *"H. S. Sailor"* two feet high — as if to document his living presence to everyone—into the bark of a linden tree of the vicarage where the sisters, revising the old building many years later, found the initials of their own famous brother and told him in a letter about it.

The mother, whom the biographers describe as a delicate, music-loving woman thirteen years younger than her husband, the vigorous parson,

3. Only after completion of the manuscript was it possible—with the helpful assistance of Dr. E. Meyer—to establish the exact date of the death of this elder Heinrich Schliemann. He died on 24 March 1822.

4. In several letters Schliemann complains of his "tormenting" compulsion to learn new languages, because "every new language is a new life" (letter of 9 April 1863). His need for the study of many languages can thus be recognized as a vital one, rooted presumably in the unconscious identity conflict with the dead brother as well as in the ambivalent relationship with the father, his first language teacher. A new language gave him the feeling of a "new life" while he was studying it.

seems to have suffered from repeated episodes of depression and to have lived in considerable marital discord with her husband. It is likely that she was in a state of depression at Schliemann's birth — due to the death of her eldest son Heinrich at that time — and that she had another long-lasting episode of depression in connection with the loss of another son, when Schliemann was four years old. I found evidence of a final severe depression of the mother during her last pregnancy when she spoke of her imminent death and wrote to her oldest daughter a letter of accusations against the father which in content, style, and tone sound similar to the *Sprachübung* text already quoted.

I am inclined to believe that the fateful identity conflict concerning his dead brother Heinrich was intensified by the death of another brother, when he was four years old, and by the death of the mother (whose sepulchre he ordered redone into one of his own choosing after he had become rich). His brother Ludwig, one year Schliemann's junior and closest to him in age and fraternal ties, died in California in 1850. His youngest brother Paul committed suicide[5] in 1852, which made Schliemann the sole surviving son. The pervasive and cumulative guilt derived from these events (survivor guilt), enormous castration fear, the identification with the more robust, Homer-loving, psychopathologically tinged preacher-father (who reached the age of ninety), the ceaseless search for his own identity (three citizenships, fifteen languages, compulsive wanderlust), the persistence of an active and at times ominous type of family romance, are recorded in a readily recognizable, albeit by the biographers generally neglected, fashion in Schliemann's writings and actions. To mention only one example of his confusion about his birth: he repeatedly speaks in his letters and notes of Ankershagen as his birthplace, as if admitting that Neubukow was his birthplace would make him the dead Heinrich buried there.

The following table will serve to clarify the intricate family constellation.

Father:	Ernst Schliemann (1780–1870)
Mother:	*Sophie* Schliemann, nee Burger (1793–1831)
Stepmother:	*Sophie* Schliemann, nee Behnke (1814–1890)

5. Unfortunately little is known about this suicide. Neither in the standard biographies nor in the material preserved in Athens have I been able to find any clarification about it. Schliemann's sudden departure from California in 1852, aside from an acute infectious disease which he mentions as the conscious reason for his leaving California, may be connected with the death of Paul, his last surviving brother — just as his journey to California had to do with the death of his brother Ludwig.

Children: *Johann* Joachim *Heinrich* (1814–1822)
Karoline Luise *Elise* Auguste (1816–1890)
Sophie Friederike Anna *Dorothea* (1818–1912)
Friederike Juliana *Wilhelmine* (1819–1883)
JOHANN LUDWIG HEINRICH JULIUS (6 January
  1822–26 December 1890
Karl Friedrich *Ludwig* Heinrich (1823–1850)
Franz Friedrich *Ludwig* Theodor (1825–1826)
Maria *Luise* Helene (1827–1909)
Paul Friederich Ulrich Heinrich (1831–1852)

The above children were born of the first marriage. Two more sons, Karl (1839–1842) and Ernst (1841–1899), were born of the second.

From the age of five to nine he associated closely with Minna[6] Meincke, a girl from the neighborhood and of the same age, who became his "childhood bride" (Schliemann's words!) and with whom he explored the cemetery *"before our door,"* the grave sites, a nearby castle which had the reputation of being haunted and of harboring the treasures of a feudal lord, the robber baron Henning,[7] whose burial place was in the churchyard next to the Schliemann home. The gravedigger swore that a leg grew out of the male-factor's grave every night, that he himself had cut the leg off when he was a boy and had used the bone to knock pears off the trees. He and Minna hunted for Henning's body and treasures, and Heinrich often begged his father to excavate the robber baron's grave, "or to let me open it to see why the leg did not grow out of the earth any more." As Schliemann relates in his *Ilios* (1881a), there was also a small hill in the vicinity, a prehistoric burial place which contained a so-called *Hünengrab,* or giant's grave, wherein, "as the legend ran, a robber knight in times of old had buried his beloved child in a golden cradle."

Vast treasures were also said to be buried close to the ruins of a round tower in the garden *des Gutseigentümers.*[8] My faith in the existence of these treasures was so great that, whenever I heard my father complain of

6. In his letters to his sister Wilhelmine, he usually calls her *Minchen,* a diminutive not only for Wilhelmine, but also Minna.

7. Henning, Henry, Heinrich are virtually identical names.

8. I.e., the feudal landlord. Later in Paris, Havana, Berlin, and Athens, Schliemann became a rich real estate owner himself and derived part of his wealth from the vast properties he owned in many lands.

his poverty, I always expressed my astonishment that he did not dig up . . . the golden cradle, and so become rich.

How closely birth and death remained linked all through his life can be seen in the introduction to his *opus magnum Ilios,* where in the midst of all this cemetery lore he reports a lengthy story about storks migrating from and to Ankershagen.

The two children would play and make sport in those places, and between visits to the churchyard, the giant's grave, and the ancient castle "with its walls six feet thick and an underground road supposed to be five miles long," they would engage in long and exciting talks with the gravedigger who would tell those wondrous stories about corpses, bones, and the violent deaths of people buried in the cemetery. Schliemann (1881a) writes:

> In the winter of 1829–30 we took dancing lessons together [after which] we would either go to the cemetery or sit down in admiration before the church register . . . the oldest records of births, marriages, and deaths inscribed in those registers having a particular charm for us.

Here the close connection between early libidinal pursuits (dancing, love play with Minna with whom he exchanged "marriage vows" described by him in great detail) and visits to the cemetery with inspection of the death registers and other inscriptions is clearly stated. When many years later he visits the catacombs of Rome, the Great Wall of China, the cemeteries and mausoleums of Peträa, Alexandria, Istanbul, New Orleans, or Peking, he repeats precisely this: he does his sightseeing, visits the local burial places and mausoleums, measures the thickness of the walls, estimates the dimensions of the underground passages, studies the tombstones and their inscriptions, admires the durability and imperishable quality of the stones employed, copies the age and contents of the epitaphs (in all languages) and, wherever feasible, inspects the death registers or has long talks with the cemetery personnel — and records everything in his diary. Great parts of his diaries read like church or death registers themselves. The difference between these later visits and the early days with Minna is mainly the fact *that there is no Minna,* that now he is desperately alone, or, at best, in the company of a hired guide.

Two brief diary entries taken at random from his copious volumes will illustrate this with some poignancy. On 23 November 1858, Schliemann finds himself in the catacombs of Rome and records in Italian that:

The catacombs of San Sebastian consist of subterranean passages 6 to 6½ feet high and 2 to 3 feet wide which extend 4½ miles underground . . . there are hundreds of thousands of tombs, it seems to me that all dead Christians were buried here. . . . often one is amazed (one wonders) how the corpses could be placed therein, the opening being so narrow at times that one can hardly place one's arm there. . . . When one opens . . . the tombs, one still sees the corpse fairly well preserved, but as soon as the air hits it, it dissolves into very small pieces and into dust. *I would have taken some of it to send to my wife, had I not feared that she would be horrified* [italics added].

Perusal of the original text in Italian disclosed Schliemann's compulsive attention to detail, including his preoccupation with correct linguistic usage (he made several changes and corrections) even in a foreign language. In my view, these served the purpose of establishing and maintaining an ego distance from the macabre content of the passage.

The emotional element, however, breaks through in the diary notes about his visit to New Orleans in December, 1867. After describing "the splendid mausoleums . . . and the many thousand coffins . . . placed in nine-foot thick hollow walls all around the cemeteries" and noting from "the epitaphs nearly all the inmates of the cemeteries have died in the very bloom of youth," he adds with reference to his incessant roaming through the New Orleans cemeteries during a yellow fever epidemic:

All at once I felt ill and invited the undertaker to a drink with me. I looked over his mortuary records; he had buried on that small cemetery in September abt. 200 white and 3 black people who died of yellow fever and abt. 300 who died of congestion of the brain. . . . He told me of the heart-rending scenes of the relations who had accompanied their friends to their last abode and pointed out the graves (ovens) of 2 brothers, of whom the one in accompanying the corpse of the other was in utter despair and immense grief and a few days later he himself fell a victim to the yellow fever and was buried near his brother. [New Orleans, 4 December 1867.]

The New Orleans diary thus ends with the characteristic theme of *two brothers dying almost simultaneously* and as an afterthought Schliemann adds in a kind of dazed bewilderment: "There are 30 or 36 cemeteries here."

When Schliemann's mother died and his father, in the view of the local parishioners, had disgraced himself, the friendship with Minna came to a sudden. end. The children of the village were strictly *verboten* to associate with the parson's — now an outcast's — children who were sent to various relatives in other villages. The nine-year-old Schliemann went into a severe depression. In a number of letters and autobiographical notes he later recorded the "irreparable misfortune" resulting from the almost simultaneously occurring loss of his mother, his girlfriend, and his home. From that time on, whenever a family member died, he appeared to be disposed to break up his home and to make a new start elsewhere (see footnote 6).

At the age of eight he received from his father, who was interested in poetry, history, and Homer, a Christmas gift: Ludwig Jerrer's *Universal History for Children* (1828) which contained an engraving "representing Troy in flames, with its huge walls and the Scaean Gate, from which Aeneas is escaping, carrying his father Anchises on his back and holding his son Ascanius by the hand . . ." (Schliemann 1881a). The existence and influence of this picture on the young boy's fantasy have repeatedly been questioned, especially when later in life Schliemann attributed his interest in Troy and his conviction that Troy and its walls really existed to the impact of this engraving. Without discounting his need for a personal myth, perhaps in Kris's sense (1956), and for the establishment of a literary-artistic connection between his childhood pursuits and later archaeological interests, suffice it to record that Jerrer's book and picture really exist. With the help of Dr. Meyer to whom I owe thanks in this regard too, I was able to locate both. The rescue and restoration fantasies which attached themselves to this book and picture not only were later recorded by the archaeologist in his autobiographical statements but were actually and creatively lived out in his extraordinary career.

From the age of nine to eleven Schliemann lived in the home of a paternal uncle, the Protestant minister of Kalkhorst, and soon became fond of a cousin approximately his age also named Sophie, who much later (in 1868) played another important, if brief, role in his life — mainly through her death. His formal schooling ended at the age of thirteen, in Strelitz. From the age of fourteen to nineteen he worked as an apprentice in a grocery store in Fürstenberg (Mecklenburg); the conditions were poor, the hours long, and his earnings "too little to live, too much to die."

At nineteen he had a pulmonary hemorrhage of unknown origin; he believed it was caused by his having lifted a heavy barrel. He quit his job, went to Hamburg, and became a cabin boy on a small ship bound for South America. In a severe storm which lasted several days the boat was wrecked, but after nine perilous hours the crew was rescued and he was taken "naked, destitute, and ignorant" first to the Dutch island of Texel, then to Amsterdam, where he was hospitalized. He was given some money that had been collected for him and later secured a job as a messenger boy in a merchant's office.

I am interrupting the chronology at this point again—it is difficult to do justice to such an eventful life in a condensed presentation in which fact finding and analytic interpretation necessarily overlap—to come back to what I said about the shipwreck earlier. As a decription of a traumatic experience it turns up in many languages and versions throughout Schliemann's writings: he had tied himself to an empty barrel, lost consciousness, and was saved from the icy waters of the North Sea half frozen, with deep wounds and broken teeth, and was then hospitalized in a ward for moribund patients. But having survived, so to speak, his own death, this was also an event to which fantasies of birth, rebirth, resurrection, and being destined to greater things in life could readily attach themselves. That this experience occurred during the Christmas season close to his birthday increased its birth-rebirth meaning for him.

Geleerd (1961) has called attention to the impact of traumata which are part real life in adolescence and happen to be a repetition of infantile traumata or fantasies. I also wish to adduce Eissler's observation (1958) that: "adolescence appears to afford the individual a second chance . . . [permitting] the release of forces that were bound in the structure and the ensuing reorganization through new identifications and the cathexis of new objects."

Here is my translation of the dream Schliemann had during the night of the shipwreck as described by him in Italian in one of his language exercises:

For eight days we had a continuous storm—gale—hurricane, which drove us ever more toward the Dutch coast. It was during the, in the night of 11–12 December, 1821.[9] I had gone to bed early and slept deeply; never had I slept so well. I dreamed—I saw in the dream that we arrived in the country of our destination and scarcely had the ship entered—entered into—the port when I dived into the water and amidst sharks, swam ashore and fled—deserted and took myself into the interior of the country where I found employment as a serf on a plantation. I dreamed that the wife of the plantation owner fell in love with me and that we both

9. Among the various slips of the pen I found in studying the Schliemann papers this is the most remarkable: 1821 instead of 1841, when the shipwreck occurred! In 1821 he was not yet born and his namesake brother Heinrich still lived. In the original I found the 2 in 1821 superimposed on a reinforced number, probably 4, so that the original is not fully recognizable.

agreed to poison the owner which we did—carried out—performed very cold-bloodedly and efficiently. After his death we married, copulated, but I dreamed further that besides my wife I also enjoyed—had relations with my black, female slaves. While I was abosrbed in such sweet dreams I was awakened by a tremendous thrust which made me fly—jump in the—on the bed. The boat had run into a cliff and the water penetrated immediately. Dressed only in a cotton shirt I ran on deck where I was thrown down by an enormous wave. . . . I fell, hitting my mouth against the deck and broke all my front teeth. But my terror was such that I didn't feel the pain. I pulled myself up and fastened myself with ropes [to the mast]. . . . I expected to die with every new wave—.

The above version was written between 1858 and 1862 as an Italian language exercise; this same dream reappears in Latin in a somewhat different version. In the latter the description of the oedipal crime is avoided but another detail is added:

. . . the night was black, no sign of the sky could be seen. . . . As if pulled by an invisible hand the ship's bell was tolling up to the very end as though it was sounding for our funeral. [The linguistic changes and corrections found in the original have been omitted.]

One might question whether this was really a dream or an addition of a later date. I am inclined to believe it was indeed a dream, for in a letter written to his sisters two months after the shipwreck he states that on the night of the shipwreck he had the most beautiful dream but gives no details of it.

The amazing career that followed and made him a world-famous figure can perhaps be best understood in the light of the dream, I believe.[10] Within a decade and a half he worked his way up from "serf" to master (as in the dream), became a mixture of "merchant prince" and "robber baron" (Henning!) for whom ships sailed the seas, railroads crisscrossed the earth, slaves toiled in the sugar plantations and tobacco fields he owned. He established agencies and branch offices ("plantations") in many lands, and during the Crimean War became one of the suppliers of war goods to the Russian government. He did so by immersing himself in products gained mostly from earth and soil: gold, silver, minerals, indigo, saltpeter, tea, cotton. By the mid-1860s he had amassed a fortune estimated at many millions of dollars.

10. Lewin (1958) has demonstrated a similar development, though in a very different area, with reference to Descartes' dream at the age of twenty-three.

After the completion of the pregenital phase of the dream he proceeded to the oedipal part. He retired from big business (never fully!) and then set out to dispose of the "fathers," having first made his own father a recipient of his alms, extending this procedure later to former teachers in Anker-shagen and Strelitz to whom he frequently sent small sums of support. Earlier he had proposed marriage to Minna; when he learned that she was already married, he thought of proposing to cousin Sophie in Kalkhorst, was dissuaded by his sister Luise (1852), and married on the rebound a Russian girl, Katarina, with whom he had three children and whom he later divorced, having gone for this purpose to Indianapolis (the Reno of the 1860s) and become an American citizen. Even before his divorce came through, he had proposed, following another oedipal dream about his mother, to a young girl cousin in Mecklenburg, again named Sophie, and when the older cousin Sophie, the one of Kalkhorst, unexpectedly died, in 1868, he became seriously depressed. In many desperate letters from Paris (where he now lived) he expressed undisguised rescue fantasies and said that he could have saved her if the relatives had informed him that she was ill. He demanded that they send him a picture of "Sophie in the coffin," spoke of her as his sister, and had a sepulchre built for her which in all details equaled that of his mother; he even insisted that a fence he erected around cousin Sophie's tomb (as a protection against potential grave diggers and tomb breakers?). A few weeks later, coming out of the depression, he suddenly decided to go to Ithaca and from there to "the battlefield of Troy." In July, 1868, he landed in Corfu, then in Ithaca, in a state of elation; singing and chanting passages from the *Odyssey* in classic Greek, he excavated some ancient urns and vases, declaring the ashes therein to be those of Odysseus and Penelope.[11] Then he sailed to the Bosporus and went to the plain of Troy where after some hesitation and searching in Bournarbashi and its vicinity he decided that the Hill of Hissarlik was the site of Troy—

11. He describes his identification with Odysseus returning to his wife and home in his book *Ithaka, der Peloponnes und Troja* (1869). Before going to Ithaca, he landed in Corfu, according to tradition the ancient Scheria, the island of the Phaeacians and of Nausicaa. There he undressed, waded in the dirty waters of a passing stream until his body was covered with mud and dirt like that of Odysseus when first seen by Nausicaa. Arriving in Ithaca he exultantly recited the twenty-third and twenty-fourth songs of the *Odyssey,* i.e., the return of the hero, the slaying of the rivals (suitors), and his reunion with Penelope, who represents both mother and wife. Identifying with Odysseus made him partake in the hero's suffering, greatness and glory. In a personal communication, Dr. R. Almansi has called my attention to the opening lines of the *Odyssey* which appear applicable to Schliemann's career: "Tell me, Muse, of that man so ready at need, who wandered far and wide, after he had sacked the sacred citadel of Troy. . . ."

against the opinion of nearly all scholars of the time who either regarded Homer's *Iliad* as sheer legend or, if they gave any credence to the existence of Troy, thought of Bournarbashi as its site. As can easily be demonstrated, the Hill of Hissarlik bears a resemblance to the hill of Ankershagen with the *Hühnengrab* of his childhood.

A few months later, from Indianapolis, where he had gone for his divorce (Lilly 1961), he wrote to Theocles Vimpos, his former Greek language teacher in St. Petersburg and then archbishop in Athens. In this famous letter he stated that he wanted to marry a young Greek girl on the condition that she be as interested in Homer as he was and that she go with him (another Minna) for visits to Homeric sites, to wit: castles, cemeteries, and ancient burial grounds. Among the various candidates the archbishop suggested, Schliemann chose the prelate's eighteen-year-old niece, Sophie Engastromenos (here both names are meaningful, *engastromenos* being an old Greek word for pregnant).

Many sources contributed to the genetic link between his most intensive and productive preoccupation with archaeology and his early rescue and restoration ideas, with the main interest focused on tombs and tombstones (and what they contain, i.e., mental representatives of buried family members, the mother, the brothers, and possibly the mysterious Heinrich Schliemann in the grave of Neubukow). Several years before he started his excavations in Troy, he had his first archaeological adventure — if I may call it so — in the cemetery of Sacramento, California, where his brother Ludwig was buried and where Schliemann lived between 1850 and 1852, making then his first big fortune during the California gold rush through trading and exchanging gold. When he learned that his brother Ludwig had died of typhoid fever, he had promptly liquidated his business in Russia and hurried to San Francisco and Sacramento where he arrived at the height of the California gold rush, to reap two million dollars in gold in less than two years. He later accused the California doctors of having poisoned his brother by the administration of mercury. In 1865 Schliemann returned to Sacramento for a few days. An entry in his diary, dated 7 September 1865, reads:

> I started this morning at four and a half. . . . It is impossible to recognize that I am here in Sacramento; not a single house seems to stand of those which were here fourteen years ago. . . . With difficulty I found the small old cemetery in which my poor brother was buried . . . still I found there the monument erected to his memory in 1851, but it was broken and lying horizontally on the ground. At my request Mr. Bennett, the present

undertaker, dug open the grave, because I was anxious *to carry the bones of my beloved brother to Petersburg, but what was my astonishment when I saw that I had not put the monument on the right grave, because the cranium which Mr. Bennett dug out had beautiful teeth, whereas poor Louis had none, thus it could not belong to him.* I therefore abandoned all hope to recover his mortal remains [italics added].

The next day's entry, September 8, reads:

. . . I went again to the large cemetery, which is now fenced in and kept in beautiful order; there are thousands of fine marble monuments. It is *populated* more than the city of the living, but for the most part *the inmates* are children amongst whom the bad climate seems to make a terrible havoc. The only name familiar to me which I found there engraved on a nice marble tombstone was that of Ellen Louisa Gray who died February 1, 1852, aged 17. There is a reservoir on the cemetery from which all grasses are irrigated. . . . I went thence to Mr. Bennett's small farm to bid a last farewell to the old cemetery now converted into a cornfield, in which *the remains of my dearest Louis are entered.* I could not help weeping bitterly when looking on it; unfortunately there are no means to ascertain where he is buried. [These two quotations are taken verbatim from Schliemann's diary in English; italics added.]

Without going into a full discussion of the striking parapraxia about the brother's tomb and identity, or of "entered" instead of "interred," suffice it to say that, acting out his early conflicts centering around identity problems and oedipal conflict, he dramatically repeated them: In 1868 in Ithaca, where he found ashes, he erroneously identified them as those of Odysseus, Penelope, etc.; he even believed he had found Odysseus' "marriage chamber." In 1873 in Troy, where he dug up gold and jewelry, he erroneously attributed them to Homeric Troy and named them the "treasure of Priamus." In 1876 in Mycenae, where he discovered the tombs and skeletons, he erroneously identified them as those of Agamemnon and his kin. "Here is the site where Agamemnon lies," he wrote, "and those who were murdered with him."[12] In 1878 he named his newborn son Agamemnon

---

12. His controversy with the scholars prior to his Mycenaean excavations centered on the scene of the oedipal murders. It was his special triumph when he found the bodies at the site he had indicated and he telegraphed to the King of Greece, not that he had discovered an unknown culture but: "I have found the tomb of Agamemnon and his kin," using similarly exuberant wording also in other communications.

(restitution of the object): Agamemnon is not dead, but alive and restored by him.

Perhaps another parapraxia which I found in his first description of the Trojan excavation throws light on all this. His journal on "Excavations in the Plain of Troia" begins: "Burg Troia 1 August 1872." In the handwritten original the German word *Burg* is crossed out, and the corrected beginning reads: "Pergamus der Troia 1 August 1872."

In other words, in excavating the site of Troy and writing every night detailed reports and diary entries, he is really back in Ankershagen and its *Burg*. The Hill of Hissarlik contains the castle with "its walls six feet deep" and the underground passages where he and Minna played and made sport at the height of their early love play. Indeed, while excavating Troy in the 1870s and constantly quarreling with the Turkish authorities, especially with the Governor of the Troad, he acts out in the field the fantasies and tribulations of his childhood, including the oedipal conflict with the father. Removing the longed-for treasure of Troy from under the nose of the Turkish governor, with the help of his child-bride Sophie, carrying it triumphantly abroad, and literally putting the jewels, diadem, and crown on the head of his young wife, he achieves oedipal victory through his archaeological exploits, acting out at the same time, I believe, his own resurrection fantasy as well as his rescue fantasies with regard to members of his family. His long personal and legal struggle with the governor has all the earmarks of an oedipal fight with the father, even to the point of enlisting the help of others (coworkers, associates, "brothers") in this struggle. As I have shown in a previous paper on geographic exploration and discovery (1956–1957), the explorer ranges widely in a geographical sense. Yet, closer study may reveal that he never really left home.

Discussion

Postponing to a later date the study of such material as his further excavations in Troy; his quarrels with the Turkish and other authorities; his turbulent friendship with Virchow, the pathologist; certain hallucinatory experiences regarding his "seeing" Pallas Athena; even his death not lacking a fantastic note: the world-famous explorer and millionaire stricken in the streets of Naples and destined for a hospital ward as an unknown, shabbily dressed pauper just as in Amsterdam half a century earlier—I shall try to review some of the foregoing data from an analytic point of view.

Obsessive-compulsive traits, depressive episodes often followed by states of excitement and elation, hypomanic features and intense cravings for narcissistic gratification are prominent. In several popular biographies (Ludwig 1947, Payne 1959) the anal aspects of his personality have been stressed, while others have been neglected. It is noteworthy that we find depressive states as well as hypomanic tendencies in Schliemann's father and mother, with a prevalence of depressive features in the latter and elated moods in the former. In addition to being a preacher, the father at one time or other was also a teacher, a farmer, a businessman, and some sort of a poet who translated *God Save the King* into German. The father's strong influence on the son's development is readily recognizable throughout the life and work of the explorer. Even in dreams his interest in Homer, languages, money matters can be traced to the paternal influence.

Of great significance, I think, are the persistence of the family romance,[13] the intensity of sensory experiences, their marked durability (Greenacre 1957, Weissman 1957) the perseverance of his restoration attempts with regard to the lost object (Bychowski 1951) — all characteristics which have been found in many creative personalities. The nonrelinquishment of the incestuous object is as apparent as the oedipal guilt and, in Greenacre's (1957) sense, there is the substitution of cosmic (earth) or prehistoric notions (Troy, Homer, Pallas Athena, Mother Goddess) for parental images. Nevertheless, the sublimation process appears incomplete and the attempted restoration of the object, so prominent among the elements of his creativity, falls repeatedly under the dominance of aggression. Thus, the sublimation of strongly aggressive and probably also necrophilic impulses is only partially successful, as evidenced by the episodes in the catacombs of Rome, the cemeteries of New Orleans, the sleeping in "una tomba anziana" at the foot of the Cheops pyramid (diary entry, Cairo, 5 January 1859), the request for "Sophie in the coffin," the destructive excavations at the sites of Troy and Mycenae, in both places digging through the actual settlements and arriving at sublevels of much earlier periods. We may therefore assume that Schliemann's work remained too close to infantile sexuality and aggression, which were not fully sublimated.

Much of his archaeological work appears to be influenced by the need to prove that Homer was correct and Troy really existed. This seems to stand for the even stronger unconscious need to prove that Heinrich Schliemann, the one born in 1822, was real, and alive, unlike the Heinrich Schliemann who had died about the time of the former's birth and who was buried in a

13. Expressed by the perseverance and intensity of the fantasies connected with rescue and initially attached to the Jerrer picture of burning Troy, which seems to have been a focal point for the child's imaginative processes with regard to the father (Anchises, Aeneas) and also to the mother (Troy, imperishable wall), possibly also to himself as Aeneas's son Ascanius.

cemetery in Mecklenburg. The over-activity, the relentless searching and exploring, the extraordinary exploits in business, science, languages, with their "new life"-giving connotations for him, the compulsive need to record, write, communicate, describe, denote (the very copiousness of the material from which much of the present data are extracted), the tenacity with which all this is assembled and preserved forever, as it were, are suggestive of a constant effort to prove to himself and the environment not only that he is alive and active but also that he will remain so or that at least one aspect of himself will outlast everything. In this connection it may be said that the archaeologist's world and work is *the world of death without death,* the effort to undo the effects of death by bringing the world of death back to life again.

Schliemann's relationship to death and digging[14] appears to have been a complex one. The fear of death producing a feeling that "the self is under constant threat of disorganization" (Eissler 1961) seems closely linked with the libidinal longings for the dead (e.g., "Sophie in the coffin") as well as with the aggressive strivings to gain access to the entombed object,[15] ultimately aimed at joining the beloved one (mother) in the grave. This, of course, carries with it both the desire for and the dreaded fear of being dead oneself. The idea of being dead, i.e., the feeling of losing or having lost one's identity and the preoccupation with the dead—in one of his diary entries Schliemann wonders about his frequent dreams of dead people— would thus indicate the longing for reunion with the dead mother (the regressive return to the mother of which Tarachow [1960] speaks) as well as the attempt to deny the reality of death as such.

In analyzing the life and works of Edgar Allan Poe, M. Bonaparte (1949) demonstrated the poet's "eternal attachment to the dead one," that is, to his young mother who had died when he was a child. In the same way it can be said that Schliemann's unconscious was never to cast off the imago of his dead mother. He searched for her in the Minnas and Sophies he encountered in his life; in the caskets and tombs he opened; in the depth of the earth to which he penetrated; in the "visions" he had about Pallas Athena, his favorite goddess.

---

14. In German, the words *graben* (dig) and *Grab* (grave) are virtually identical.

15. Perhaps nowhere stated more clearly than in a letter written in 1869 to a friend in which he declares "in Greece . . . girls are as beautiful as the pyramids" (Meyer 1958). The direct equation of living feminine beauty with the dead beauty of the entombed past is as emphatic here as in the hero of *Gradiva,* also an archaeologist, who encounters vibrant, libidinally tinged "life" and feminine beauty amidst the very ruins of "dead" Pompeii.

The hypercathexis of the past, more precisely of the *buried* past, and the relentless archaeological pursuits (so relentless that when the Turkish and Greek governments later prevented him from excavating further, he frantically approached the Italian authorities for such permission, stating in effect that to him excavating was tantamount to living) can then be viewed as his unremitting effort to deny the reality of death; to solve the riddles of pregnancy, birth, and his own identity; and to reestablish the libidinal ties with the mother by searching for her deep inside Mother Earth itself. Bibby (1956), a contemporary British archaeologist, puts it this way: "Every archaeologist knows in his heart why he digs. He digs . . . that the dead may live again, that what is past may not be forever lost." In this sense, archaeology can be understood as prehistory brought to life, as the science of "living" prehistory of the buried past and its secrets "unburied."

Of particular interest in Schliemann's turning to archaeology is the sequence of phases observable in his creative development. Thanks to the abundance of biographical data, perhaps also because of the incompleteness of the sublimatory process, one can discern almost step by step his change-over from business to science.

In March, 1860, at the age of thirty-eight, his mother's age when she died, he decided to retire from business.

At this very time he became involved in a court action concerning money matters which occupied him with business affairs for another four years or so, precisely as his father who after the death of Schliemann's mother had become embroiled in a lawsuit regarding the alleged embezzlement of church funds.

From 1864 to 1866 Schliemann journeyed around the world, visited many lands and cities, particularly their walls, cemeteries, mausoleums, tombs, etc.

From 1866 to 1868 he separated himself from his family in Russia, settled in Paris, and began a long series of vague and tentative studies at the Sorbonne (philosophy, philology, geography, literature, history, art). He lived alone in Paris, in a state of brooding preoccupation, punctuated by (business) trips to the United States and Cuba. His fantasies at that time seem to have been focused on the father and the conflict between active and passive tendencies.

Early in March, 1868, he learned of the death of his cousin Sophie and went into a severe depression. It is obvious that her death repeated the early object loss (mother) and caused an acute emotional crisis. Throughout the entire month of March he wrote letter upon letter in which he expressed his despair and repeatedly mentioned that her death had reawakened in him a flood of memories of the past. At the same time he accused himself of having neglected this cousin and believed that he could have rescued her from death if he had but known of her illness (typhoid fever), if he had married her, supported her with money, etc.

In April, 1868, a sudden cathectic shift occurred from the buried object ("Sophie in the coffin") to the buried past — he now turned to imperishable objects (Homer, Ithaca, Troy, Mycenae, marble, rock, earth) and decided to go to Italy, Greece, and Troy. An immediate feeling of relief resulted.

From May through July, 1868, he visited in a state of elation Corfu, Ithaca, Mycenae, and finally the Troad where he made the fateful decision for Hissarlik, triumphantly disregarding the scientific authorities on Troy. After his return to Paris he wrote his book on *Ithaka, der Peloponnes und Troja* in a feverish three-month effort, and announced in a letter to his father that "I overthrow Strabo and all who write about Troy after him." About the same time he wrote (in French) to his son Sergius (thirteen years of age) in Russia:

> I have gloriously refuted the statements of Strabo concerning Ithaca and Troy and I have finished, once and for all, with the absurd dogma of the archaeologists who considered the site . . . of Troy to be on the mountains of Bounarbashi.

Late in 1868, after having thus disposed of the "fathers," he began to make careful preparations for his planned excavations in Hissarlik. But before carrying out these plans, he went early in 1869 to the United States, became an American citizen, obtained his divorce in Indianapolis and his Ph.D., in absentia, at the University of Rostock (Mecklenburg) on the basis of his book on Ithaca. He broke his last ties with his family and business in Russia.

During the summer of 1869 he returned to Europe as an American citizen. As an unattached man without family bonds,[16] he went to Greece where "the girls are as beautiful as the pyramids," married Sophie Engastromenos in

16. This appears to be in conformity with the statement by K. R. Eissler (1961): "it does not seem probable that [the genius] would be capable of his extraordinary creations if his libido were gratified in an adequate object relation. The energy flow into the object relation would be diverted from the artistic process." That Schliemann's object relations remained precarious also after his marriage to Sophie Engastromenos can be readily demonstrated. Shortly after the wedding the young wife fell ill with symptoms strongly suggestive of what would today be called "psychosomatic," and they separated for a certain time. Schliemann's ambivalence concerning his marriages is expressed in many letters and diary entries and though his relationship with his young Greek second wife gradually improved, he complained in many letters — especially to Virchow — about her.

Athens that same autumn, started his excavation in Hissarlik the next spring, and unremittingly continued his archaeological pursuits until his death in 1890. The results of his work soon made his name known throughout the civilized world.

We can discern four creative phases in the development of Schliemann's scientific career:

1. A prolonged *preparatory* phase, intermittently protracted over a num- of years (ca. 1860 through 1867) and initiated by indications of strong bisexual identification.
2. A short and decisive *"inspirational" phase* (Kris 1952) initiated by object loss, depression, and agitation, acute emotional crisis with marked hypercathexis of the past and free availability of memories. It is followed by a state of hypomanic elation, emotional upheaval and further cathectic changes, March to July, 1868. The alterations in cathexis make past personal experiences relevant to the current situation.
3. A *longer elaborative phase* with detailed planning, important internal and external readjustments, environmental changes, and methodically executed efforts leading to a series of significant, if misinterpreted and aggressively arrived-at discoveries, 1869–1876. A high degree of cathexis persists.
4. A *consolidation phase* with continued archaeological explorations, increased communications and associations with experts (Dörpfeld, Virchow), publications of several scientific works, further elaboration and reexamination of previous findings, planning for new excavations, etc.; a period not free, however, of recurrent emotional upheavals and critical episodes culminating toward the end of his life in transient "visionary" and hallucinatory states in which he ecstatically sees and worships the Virgin Goddess Pallas Athena.

The first phase is characterized, among other factors, by intense loneliness[17] and gradual loosening of object relations. With the beginning of the second phase a marked hypercathexis of the past — first of the personal past, then extended and intensified to include the prehistory of mankind and its

17. Bak (1958) has pointed to the "poignant example of desperate loneliness" in the life of Van Gogh and to the latter's "prevading guilt: he was born exactly one year after a still-born child." According to Bak, "the fantasies of dead predecessors stirred up fantasies about birth and creation, facilitated empathy and identification with the inanimate world, perhaps another variation of resurrection fantasies." My inquiry into Schliemann's creativity has disclosed similar unconscious factors.

buried, i.e., imperishable past — becomes observable and this hypercathexis of the obscure part of history and geography (prehistory, subterranean geography) never subsides until the end of his life.

In view of the degree of psychopathology and its connection with the type of creativity — archaeological exploration — which in Schliemann's life history appear to be almost rectilineally related to infantile roots, the question of a close correlation between the two, psychopathology and creativity, poses itself also in this case as in so many others of genius or geniuslike calibre. I am inclined to answer this question in Eissler's sense, who in his recent Leonardo study (1961) suggests that "psychopathology is indispensable to the highest achievements of certain kinds." Although the problem as to the energy sources available to such unusual creative personalities and how such energy can be economically and dynamically accounted for cannot be fully answered at the present stage of our knowledge, I wish to conclude with a brief excerpt from Schliemann's letters which seems to throw some light on the question of libidinal economy involved here, in his letters of 26 and 27 April 1869 to Archbishop Vimpos (Lilly 1961) regarding his divorce and remarriage plans Schliemann writes:

I used to be very sensual. . . . *But my character has completely changed* . . . and I think now of nothing except scholarship. Therefore I want a wife only for companionship. . . . For two reasons I don't know yet whether I am in a position to marry: first, I am not yet sure that I shall get the divorce; second, because of my matrimonial (difficulties) *I have had no relations with a woman for six years* [italics added].

It was during those years of abstinence that Schliemann embarked on his searching studies at the Sorbonne, wrote his first two books, and entered the field of archaeology. This, in my view, tends to support Eissler's findings on Goethe and Leonardo da Vinci in an impressive way. (I shall elaborate on these aspects of Schliemann's creativity in a later study.)

With regard to creativity Kris's (1952) statement "the artist has created a world, and not indulged in a daydream" has often been quoted. I believe this applies to Schliemann as well. By adding a millennium to our knowledge of history, he opened up a new world for historians, geographers, and students of antiquity. Through his preoccupation with the world of Thanatos he added to our knowledge of the living; through his study of the remote past he enriched the history of the present and thus enlarged our understanding of both past and present.

References

Bak, R. C. (1958). Discussion of P. Greenacre's "The family romance of the artist." *Psychoanalytic Study of the Child* 13:42–43.

Bibby, G. (1956). *The Testimony of the Spade.* New York: Knopf.

Bonaparte, M. (1946). The legend of the unfathomable waters. *American Imago* 4:20–31.

———(1949). *The Life and Works of Edgar Allan Poe.* London: Imago.

Braymer, M. (1960). *The Walls of Windy Troy.* New York: Harcourt, Brace.

Bychowski, G. (1951). From catharsis to work of art. In *Psychoanalysis and Culture,* ed. G. B. Wilbur and W. Muensterberger, pp. 390–409. New York: International Universities Press.

Cottrell, L. (1958). *The Bull of Minos.* New York: Rinehart.

Eissler, K. R. (1958). Notes on problems of technique in the psychoanalytic treatment of adolescents. *Psychoanalytic Study of the Child* 13:223–254.

———(1961). *Leonardo da Vinci.* New York: International Universities Press.

———(1963). *Goethe: A Psychoanalytic Study.* Detroit: Wayne State University Press.

Freud, S. (1887–1902). *The Origins of Psychoanalysis: Letters to Wilhelm Fliess, Drafts and Notes.* New York: Basic Books, 1954.

———(1907). Delusions and dreams in Jensen's *Gradiva. Standard Edition* 9:7–95.

———(1909a). Family romances. *Collected Papers* 5:74–78.

———(1909b). Notes upon a case of obsessional neurosis. *Collected Papers* 3:296–383.

———(1911). Psycho-analytic notes upon an autobiographical account of a case of paranoia. *Collected Papers* 3:387–470.

———(1933). Preface to Marie Bonaparte's *The Life and Works of Edgar Allan Poe. Standard Edition* 22:254.

———(1960). *Letters,* ed. E. L. Freud. New York: Basic Books.

Gandert, O. F. (1955). Heinrich Schliemann Briefwechel, ed. E. Meyer (Review). *Germania* 33:429–431.

Geleerd, E. R. (1961). Some aspects of ego vicissitudes in adolescence. *Journal of the American Psychoanalytic Association* 9:394–405.

Greenacre, P. (1955). *Swift and Carroll.* New York: International Universities Press.

———(1957). The childhood of the artist. *Psychoanalytic Study of the Child* 12:47–72.

Grotjahn, M. (1951). About the representation of death in the art of antiquity and in the unconscious of modern men. In *Psychoanalysis and Culture,* ed. G. B. Wilbur and W. Muensterberger, pp. 410–424. New York: International Universities Press.

————(1960). Ego identity and the fear of death and dying. *Journal of the Hillside Hospital* 9:147–155.

Hampe, R. (1961). *Heinrich Schliemann.* Heidelberg: Ruperto-Carola 13: 3–22.

Homer, *The Iliad.* Cambridge: Harvard University Press, 1946.

————*The Odyssey.* Cambridge: Harvard University Press, 1946.

Jerrer, L. (1828). *Universal History for Children.* Nurenberg: F. Campe.

Kohut, H. (1960). Beyond the bounds of the basic rule. *Journal of the American Psychoanalytic Association* 8:567–586.

Kris, E. (1952). *Psychoanalytic Explorations in Art.* New York: International Universities Press.

————(1956). The personal myth. *Journal of the American Psychoanalytic Association* 4:653–681.

Lewin, B. D. (1958). *Dreams and the Uses of Regression.* New York: International Universities Press.

Lilly, E. (1961). *Schliemann in Indianapolis.* Indianapolis: Indiana Historical Society.

Ludwig, E. (1947). *Schliemann de Troie.* Paris: Nouvelles Editions Latines.

Meyer, E. (1936). *Briefe von Heinrich Schliemann.* Berlin: De Gruyter.

————(1953). *Heinrich Schliemann Briefwechel, 1.* Berlin: Mann.

————(1955). Schliemann und Virchow. *Gymnasium* 62:435–454.

————(1956). *Rudolf Virchow.* Wiesbaden: Limes Verlag.

————(1958). *Heinrich Schliemann Briefwechel, 2.* Berlin: Mann.

————ed. (1961). *Heinrich Schliemann Selbstbiographie,* 9th ed. Wiesbaden: Brockhaus.

————(1961). Personal communication.

Milchhöfer, A. (1891). Erinnerungen an Heinrich Schliemann. *Deutsche Rundschau* 17:8–23.

Muller, H. J. (1958). *The Loom of History.* New York: Harper.

Niederland, W. G. (1956–1957). River Symbolism I & II. *Psychoanalytic Quarterly* 25:469–504; 26:50–75.

Nunberg, H. (1961). *Curiosity.* New York: International Universities Press.

Payne, R. (1959). *The Gold of Troy.* New York: Funk and Wagnalls.

Petrie, F. (1931). *Seventy Years of Archaeology.* London: Low-Marston.

Pomer, S. L. (1959). Necrophilic phantasies and choice of specialty in medicine. *Bulletin of the Philadelphia Association for Psychoanalysis* 9:54–55.

Schapiro, M. (1956). Leonardo and Freud. *Journal of the History of Ideas* 17:147–178.

Schliemann, H. (1869). *Ithaka, der Peloponnes und Troja.* Leipzig: Gieske und Derrient.

———(1878). *Mykenae.* Leipzig: Brockhaus.

———(1881a). *Ilios, the City and Country of the Trojans.* New York: Harper.

———(1881b). *Reise in der Troas im Mai 1881.* Leipzig: Brockhaus.

———(1884). *Troja: Results of the Latest Discoveries.* New York: Harper.

———(1886). *Tyrins.* Leipzig: Brockhaus.

———(1892). *Selbstbiographie,* 1st ed., ed. S. Schliemann. Leipzig: Brockhaus.

Schuchhardt, C. (1891). *Schliemanns Ausgrabungen im Lichte der heutigen Wissenschaft,* 2nd ed. Leipzig: Brockhaus.

Sterba, E., and Sterba, R. (1954). *Beethoven and His Nephew.* New York: Pantheon.

Stoll, H. A. (1960). *Abenteuer meines Lebens, Schliemann erzählt.* Leipzig: Brockhaus.

Tarachow, S. (1960). Judas, the beloved executioner. *Psychoanalytic Quarterly* 29:528–554. Chapter 2 of this volume.

Wace, A. J. B. (1949). *Mycenae: An Archaeological and Historical Guide.* Princeton: Princeton University Press.

Waelder, R. (1960). *Basic Theory of Psychoanalysis.* New York: International Universities Press.

Weber, S. H. (1942). *Schliemann's First Visit to America 1850–1851.* Cambridge: Harvard University Press.

Weissman, P. (1957). The childhood and legacy of Stanislavski. *Psychoanalytic Study of the Child* 12:399–417.

Chapter 6

AN ATTEMPT AT SOUL MURDER:

RUDYARD KIPLING'S EARLY LIFE AND WORK

LEONARD SHENGOLD, M.D.

The term *soul murder* appeared in psychiatric literature after its use by the psychotic Daniel Paul Schreber, whose *Memoirs,* written in 1903, were the subject of extensive study, most notably by Freud (1911).

The earliest use of *soul murder,* however, appeared in a popular book of the middle nineteenth century entitled *Kaspar Hauser: An Instance of a Crime Against the Life of the Soul of Man* by Anselm von Feuerbach. Kaspar Hauser, a cause célèbre in his time, had spent the first seventeen years of his life in a dark dungeon, cut off from all human contact except for an occasional glimpse of his jailer (pathetically called by Kaspar "the man who was always there"), and was fed only on bread and water. Feuerbach wrote: "How long soever he may live, he must for ever remain a man without childhood and boyhood, a monstrous being, who, contrary to the usual course of nature, only began to live in the middle of his life. . . . he may be said to have been the subject of a partial soul murder. . . . the life of a human soul was mutilated at its commencement" (1832, pp. 56–57). Feuerbach was a distinguished judge and his work might very well have been read by his fellow jurist Schreber. (I am grateful to Professor Jeff Masson for directing me to Feuerbach's book.)

The term was used by Strindberg in an 1887 article on Ibsen's *Rosmersholm,* entitled "Soul Murder." Strindberg wrote that instances of actual murder were decreasing in the West, but that soul (or psychic) murder was on the increase. He defined soul murder as taking away a person's reason for living. This concept obsessed Strindberg, who was at that time writing *The Father* (see Jacobs 1969). Soul murder was a repetitive theme of Ibsen's and he used the term directly in the 1896 play, *John Gabriel Borkman.*[1] There he spoke of it as a "mysterious" sin mentioned in the Bible "for which there is no forgiveness" (Archer trans. p. 246). He described it (I make use of several translations) as "killing the instinct for love" (Paulson trans. p. 334); "killing the love-life in a human soul' (Archer trans. p. 246); murdering "love in a human being" (Meyer trans. p. 269).

Ibsen and Strindberg wrote mainly about the destruction of the souls of adults, within the arena of the family. In this century, soul murder has spread beyond the home to become public and institutionalized in the brainwashing techniques of political prisons and concentration camps. The confrontation in soul murder is between the all-powerful and the helpless — between hostile, cruel, psychotic or psychopathic parents (or authorities) and the children (prisoners) in their charge.

Soul muder means deliberately destroying the individuality of another. Complementing Ibsen's "mysterious," Schreber presented the concept as inherently vague — he could only furnish "hints" (p. 58) at a definition. He talked of the violation as well as the murder of souls. His literary allusions brought in a pact with the Devil *(Faust, Manfred,* Weber's *Freischütz).* One person absorbs the life of another, and the victim's identity is lost.

And, according to Schreber, so is his sexual identity. The sexual meaning of soul murder first became apparent through the censorship by the original German publishers who first omitted a passage and then the better part of a chapter describing soul murder as being "unfit for publication" (p. 58, p. 61). But specific sexual implications were left in: "All attempts at committing soul murder, at unmanning me for purposes contrary to the Order of the World (that is to say for the sexual satisfaction of a human being), and later at destruction of my reason, have failed" (p. 58). Here intimations of castration and homosexuality were coupled with an assault on Schreber's reason.

For Schreber, the attack on the power of rational thought concurred with the vagueness of the whole topic. We know from Orwell's *1984* (a primer on soul murder) of the confusion and split registration in thinking (Orwell calls it *doublethink*) that are both the effect of brainwashing and the means by

---

1. Ella Renthem says to Borkman: "You are guilty of a double murder — the murder of your own soul, and mine" (Meyer trans. p. 268).

which the torturer keeps his hold. The victim must not be able to reason about—must not be able to know—what has happened to him. Schreber showed *doublethink* about soul murder in a footnote to the passage about "unmanning" quoted above. He set the feeling that the attempt at soul murder made upon him was evil and "contrary to the Order of the World" side-by-side with the probability that his feminization would prove to be "in consonance with the Order of the World" and would unite him with God (p. 58).

Freud explained Schreber was saying his father was God-Devil. Schreber himself identified with the God-Devil soul murderer: "I, myself have been 'represented' as the one who had committed soul murder" (p. 55). Niederland's work on the inhuman, crazy child-rearing ideas and practices of Schreber's father has supplied the environmental genesis for the soul murder (see Niederland 1959a, 1959b, 1960, 1963). As a child, Schreber was manipulated as a "thing"; there was no sign of parental empathy with the boy. He was purposely, systematically, and righteously deprived of his own will, and of his capacity for pleasure and joy.

It is easy to kill the soul of a child. This was something for which Dostoyevsky could not forgive himself, parents, or God. Here is one of his examples:

> This poor child of five was subjected to every possible torture by (her) cultivated parents. They beat her, thrashed her, kicked her for no reason till her body was one bruise. Then, they went to greater refinements of cruelty—shut her up all night in the cold and frost in a privy, and because she didn't ask to be taken up at night . . . they smeared her face with excrement and forced her to eat it, and it was her mother, her mother did this. And that mother could sleep, hearing the groans of the poor child locked up in that vile place at night! A little creature, *who can't understand what's done to her,* in the dark and cold of that vile place, beats her little aching breast with her tiny fist and weeps her bloody meek unresentful tears begging dear, kind God to protect her! [Dostoyevsky 1880, p. 286]

The righteousness, the religiosity of parents like the elder Schreber can undermine the child's ability to register and hate what is done to him. If the victim is in the tormentor's absolute power,[2] the child can only turn for

2. Dostoyevsky, who knew both roles, wrote: "It's just their defenselessness that tempts the tormentor, just the angelic confidence of the child who has no refuge and no appeal, that sets his vile blood on fire" (1880, p. 183).

rescue and relief to the tormentor himself, making the need intense to see
the torturer as good and right.[3] If this is supplemented by a parental claim
to God-like benevolent rightness "consonant with the Order of the World,"
the child must lose his own knowledge of what has happened and his
responsibility for how he has been made to feel and his sense of identity is
compromised.

I will illustrate this with a clinical example of soul murder: A father
entered the dining room. The round table was set for the family meal.
Beside each plate was a fresh banana—the dessert. The man made a complete round of the table, stopping at every chair to reach out and squeeze the
banana to pulp, but spared his own. The older children and the intimidated
mother, used to such happenings, said nothing. But the youngest, a five-
year-old boy, began to cry when he saw the mangled banana at his plate.
The father then turned on him viciously, demanding that he be quiet—how
dare he make such a fuss about a banana (from Shengold 1974b). I want to
emphasize the resultant terrible confusion for the boy. What had happened? Who was to blame? Was he guilty? A child cannot adequate contain, work over, and master a trauma that he is unable to properly register
in his mind. He therefore continues to be subject to the basic psychological
danger of overstimulation. Brainwashing is inherent to soul murder.

For these overstimulated and brainwashed children, the need for "dear,
kind God" is so great that the child must submit to, identify with, and not
only exonerate, but glorify his persecutor. Enough torture, especially in the
terrible absence of anyone who cares, can break down even adults, like
Winston Smith in *1984*. The overwhelming anger and hatred evoked by the
torment must be suppressed and turned against the self in the urgency to
escape annihilation by "loving" and identifying with the "Big Brother" who
brought on the trauma.

I have written several papers about the effects of seduction and brutality
on the part of parents against their children (Shengold 1963, 1967, 1971,
1974a). Soul murder can be overwhelmingly or minimally effected; it can be
partial, or attenuated, or chronic, or subtle. Kipling's case involves desertion by good parents and their replacement by bad, persecutory guardians.

A child can frequently bear much torment if his parents can share his misery, literally or emphatically. To experience trauma alone, with no recourse
to parents, means that in addition to the external insult and the absence of

3. Feuerbach of Kaspar Hauser: "When I expressed my surprise that he should wish to
return to that abominably bad man (his jailer—"the man who was always there"), he replied
with mild indignation, "Man not bad, man me no bad done" (1832, p. 72).

protection and the possibility for rescue, there exists the psychic threat to the identity-sustaining sense of narcissistic promise. The child's feelings of identity and self-esteem depend on his ability to maintain an image of an omnipotent parent who cares about him and who will rescue him. Separation from, and transformation of, this parental imago that originates as part of the image of the self, are necessary for maturation, but to be tolerable the differentiation should be gradual—and the result is always incomplete. No one ever loses the need for "emotional refueling" (Mahler 1972) so obvious in the toddler who finally and triumphantly walks away from the mother, and yet still craves to, and must, periodically return.

A sudden, unprepared-for loss of parental care is one of the greatest human tragedies, even for adults. This is inherent in brainwashing techniques; these involve an alternation of overstimulation and sensory deprivation calculated to increase the need for, yet destroy the hope of, loving concern. Even iron-willed Old Bolsheviks were broken to cringing submission to Big Brother Stalin. It is much easier to destroy the souls of children, especially if they are separated from their parents. Children have little ability to contain overwhelming stimulation and intense feelings of rage. Anna Freud reminds us that for children to tolerate hatred directed against their also-loved parents, those parents' "reassuring presence" (1965, p. 113) is essential.

If, as with Kipling, there has been a period of good parental care prior to the attempt at soul murder, the destruction is less. Still, the fall from bliss to torment is a cruelly traumatic loss. Here is a comment of Kipling's, from an autobiographical story (Kipling 1888b), on parental desertion:

When a matured man discovers that he has been deserted by Providence, deprived of his God, and cast, without help, comfort or sympathy, upon a world which is new and strange to him, his despair, which may find expression in evil-living, *the writing of his experiences,* or the more satisfactory diversion of suicide, is generally supposed to be impressive. A child, under exactly similar conditions *as far as its knowledge goes,* cannot very well curse God and die. It howls till its nose is red, its eyes are sore, and its head aches. [p. 290; italics mine]

Kipling described the child's helplessness, made so terrible by his lack of understanding. He also hinted at a way toward transcendence for himself—the child may grow up and be able to write of his experiences. This means *knowing* what happened to him; and the more he can know (of what happened to soul as well as to body), the freer he can become. The soul—the identity—can be preserved if the adult can say, like Whitman: "I am the man, I suffered, I was there" (1855, p. 76). I shall try to follow Kipling's struggle to use his mind to preserve his soul.

As a child of six Rudyard Kipling experienced the fall from the Eden of an overindulged and privileged childhood to the hell of desertion and a hostile stewardship that made for years of persecution. Born in 1865 in Bombay, to a young and presumably loving British couple, he was a wanted first child whose every wish was indulged by a self-effacing pair of substitute parents: his *ayah* (nurse) and his bearer. He was the only son of an important Sahib, the center of a world full of wonder. His domain consisted of the garden of a bungalow in the compound of an art school presided over by his father. He was treated as a young prince. "His Majesty the King," written when Kipling was in his early twenties, describes the imperiousness of a young Sahib of six, a crucial age for Kipling. "His Majesty's" parents, unlike Rudyard's, are bitterly hostile to one another and indifferent to their child. The boy's partly compensatory narcissistic confidence and his tyranny over his English governess are well delineated (if one can tolerate the baby talk). The story is a kind of family romance—the fulfillment of the wish of an abandoned child (Rudyard himself at six) that the family will be reunited out of love for him. Here is His Majesty going to bed (Chimo is his dog):

> "Yeth! And Chimo to sleep at ve foot of ve bed, and ve pink pikky-book, and ve bwead—'case I will be hungwy in ve night—and vat's all, Miss Biddums. And now give me one kiss and I'll go to sleep. So! Kite quiet. Ow! Ve pink pikky-book has slidded under ve pillow and ve bwead is cwumbling! Miss Biddums! Miss Biddums! I'm *so* uncomfy! Come and tuck me up, Miss Biddums!" [1888c, p. 319]

Apparently Rudyard himself had dogs as a young child—a Chang if not a Chimo. His father wrote about him when the child was two:

> "He gets into imminent peril with chairs and things daily. It's the quaintest thing in life to see him eating his supper, intently watched by three dogs to which he administers occasional blundering blows with a little whip and much shouting. His best playfellow is one 'Chang,' a small Chinese pup." [Green 1965, p. 21]

The letter shows the family atmosphere of laissez-faire, and something of the child's sadism as well as his lordliness.

Rudyard did not have an English governness. His subjects were his Hindu bearer, Meeta and his *ayah,* a Roman Catholic from Goa who sometimes took the child to her church. Rudyard spoke to Meeta in the native tongue that was his predominant speech in his early years and occasionally Meeta took the child with him to the Hindu temple where he worshipped. Rudyard's first memory was of early morning walks to the Bombay fruit market with his *ayah* (Kipling 1937, p. 2). Death and castration were in the background of his idyllic existence. The house in Bombay was near the Towers of Silence, where the Parsee dead were exposed to be devoured by vultures. "I did not understand my mother's distress when she found 'a child's hand' in our garden, and said I was not to ask questions about it. I wanted to see that child's hand. But my *Ayah* told me" (Kipling 1937, p. 2). At bedtime or before the afternoon siesta, the children (a sister was born when Rudyard was two-and-a-half) would be told stories by the servants or their mother. There is an example at the beginning of the autobiographical short story, "Baa, Baa, Black Sheep" (the children here are called Punch and Judy):

> They were putting Punch to bed—the *ayah* and the *hamal* [bearer] and Meeta, the big *Surti* boy, with the red and gold turban. Judy, already tucked inside her mosquito-curtains, was nearly asleep. Punch had been allowed to stay up for dinner. . . . He sat on the edge of his bed and swung his bare legs defiantly.
> "Punch-*baba* going to bye-lo?" said the *ayah* suggestively. "No," said Punch. "Punch-*baba* wants the story about the *Ranee* (princess) that was turned into a tiger. Meeta must tell it and the *hamal* shall hide behind the door and make tiger-noises at the proper time." [Kipling 1888b, p. 283]

Mostly the stories were told by the *ayah* or his mother, and Rudyard may have mixed up the two. At any rate, in Kipling's description of his earliest years, a theme appeared that kept reappearing in his fiction and poems—he is rescued from a bad mother-figure (like the *Ranee*-tiger) by a good father-figure:

> "Meeta unconsciously saved me from any night terrors or dread of the dark.[4] Our *ayah,* with a servant's curious mixture of deep affection and shallow device, had told me that a stuffed leopard's head on the nursery wall was there to see that I went to sleep. But Meeta spoke of it scornfully as 'the head of an animal,' and I took it off my mind as a fetish, good or bad, for it was only some unspecified 'animal'"[5] [Kipling 1937, p. 3]

4. See below for Kipling's lifelong preoccupation with fear of the dark, and the metaphors of light and darkness in his work.

5. Readers of the Mowgli stories might think of the bad tiger Shere Khan and the good panther Bagheera.

Another bad early experience with the feminine (followed by consolation by a man) was an attack by a hen when Rudyard was crossing the garden: "I passed the edge of a huge ravine a foot deep where a winged monster as big as myself attacked me, and I fled and wept." He was comforted by his father who "drew for me a picture of the tragedy with a rhyme beneath:

> There was a small boy in Bombay
> Who once from a hen ran away.
> When they said: 'You're a baby,'
> He replied: 'Well, I may be:
> But I don't like these hens of Bombay.'

This consoled me. I have thought well of hens ever since" (1937, p. 41). Kipling's light humor here expresses a characteristic minimization of fear and hatred, and he ends with a denial. Yet this may be an important memory — later he could identify with his father who set an example for the transcendence of a trauma by "the writing of (one's) experiences" (see above).

The parents, like so many others in the Victorian age, were in the background of the nursery life. After the children's afternoon naps, "we were sent into the dining room after we had been dressed, with the caution 'Speak English now to Papa and Mamma.' So one spoke 'English,' haltingly translated out of the vernacular idiom that one thought and dreamed in. The Mother sang wonderful songs at a black piano and would go out to Big Dinners" (1937, p. 3).

The nursery world was dominated by maternal and maternalizing figures of whom Rudyard was the favorite and lord. He was strengthened against the threats of his own hostility and of the dangerous fascinating world outside the nursery by the grandiosity that comes with maternal favoritism. As Freud (1917) said of Goethe: "If a man has been his mother's undisputable darling, he retains throughout life the triumphant feeling [*Eroberergefühl*: feeling of a conqueror], the confidence in success, which not seldom brings actual success with it" (p. 156). One thinks of the marvelous self-confidence of Kim, or the more cloying aplomb of Wee Willie Winkie.

But the overwhelming promise that is part of being the darling of Mother and of Father is not the best preparation for separation and loss, nor for the change to a rejecting and hateful parental regimen.

When Rudyard was two-and-a-half, there was a sharp break in his life. His mother was pregnant and the family returned to England where she would have the baby. In old age Kipling wrote about this journey: "There was a train across a desert (The Suez Canal was not yet opened) — and a halt in it and a small girl wrapped in a shawl on the seat opposite me, whose face stands out still. There was next a *dark* land, and a *darker* room full of cold, in one wall of which a *white* woman made *naked fire,* and I cried aloud with dread, for I had never before seen a grate" (Kipling 1937, p. 4, italics added). One cannot help wondering if this is a screen memory—the frightening woman again appears. The visual stimulation of the dangerous "naked" fire against the dark background might very well have been, then or later, associated with the child's fantasies of the primal scene, and of his mother's pregnancy. Actually this memory—or at least the Egyptian part of it—came back to him in 1913 when he was making a railroad trip across the isthmus. Again the imagery seems full of scopophilic excitement with light and fire against darkness and desolation:

> On one side our windows looked out on *darkness* of the *waste;* on the other at the *black* canal all spaced with *monstrous headlights* of the night-running steamers. Then came towns, *lighted with electricity.* . . . [this evoked the childhood memory of the trip at age two-and-a-half]. . . . such a town, for instance, as Zagazig, last seen by a very small boy who was lifted out of a railway carriage and set down beneath a *whitewashed* wall under *naked stars in an illimitable emptiness* because they told him the train was *on fire.* Childlike this did not worry him. What stuck in his sleepy mind was the absurd name of the place and his father's prophecy that when he grew up he would "come that way in a big steamer." So all his life the word "Zagazig" carried memories of a brick shed, the *flicker of an oil-lamp's floating wick, a skyful of eyes,* and an engine coughing in *a desert at the world's end.* [1913, p. 247; italics mine]

The unforgettable name "Zagazig" must at some time have become associated with the common Army slang word "zigzig"—meaning copulation—in Kipling's mind. "Zigzig," according to Partridge's *Dictionary of Slang* (1961, p. 1361), was "used throughout the Near and Middle East in the late nineteenth and twentieth century." A linkage of these words would have reinforced the primal scene meaning of the early travel memory. Certainly Kipling had a lifelong intense curiosity—a need to see and know and almost to become those around him, especially the possessors of secrets and inner knowledge. He would quiz comparative strangers ruthlessly in compulsive research about the look, sound, and feel of their lives and occupations. In later life this habit made some of his naive Vermont neighbors think of him as a crazy man.

When the Kiplings arrived in England in 1868 they stayed with Alice Kipling's relatives. The indulged Anglo-Indian child was quite uninhibited and rather aggressive;[6] his behavior was not what was required of an English child of those days. He is remembered as charging down the streets of a country town, yelling: "Out of the way! Out of the way, there's an angry Ruddy coming" (Stewart 1966, p. 1). After the Kiplings left, Rudyard's Aunt Louisa wrote of the visit: "[Alice's] children turned the house into such a bear-garden, and Ruddy's screaming tempers made Papa so ill, we were thankful to see them on their way. The wretched disturbances one ill-ordered child can make is a lesson for all time to me" (Green 1965, p. 23).

The family returned to Bombay after the birth of Rudyard's sister Alice (usually called Trix). The mother's labor had been difficult. A third child was born and died in India when Rudyard was five—shortly before his exile. There is no direct evidence of the effects of these births on Rudyard, but they must have profoundly influenced the child, threatening and perhaps compensatorily increasing his narcissism and adding to his aggressiveness (and his hostility toward the betraying mother). But the boy remembered these first six years of indulgence and magic as overwhelmingly wonderful. The motto to the first chapter of his autobiographical fragment, *Something of Myself,* is a maxim of the Jesuits: "Give me the first six years of a child's life and you can have the rest" (1937, p. 1)—a proper Freudian sentiment. After these six years came the desolation.

Paradise was lost when Rudyard was almost six when his parents again took him to the "dark land." It was customary for the British ruling class in India to send their children to England to be educated. According to Carrington (1955), Kipling's admiring and "definitive" biographer, the timing of the separation in the Kipling family "came early by customary standards" (p. 44). This would appear to be an understatement—Trix was not yet three! Mrs. Kipling had a large, distinguished, and seemingly devoted family in England. One sister, a lifelong favorite of Rudyard's, was married to the successful pre-Raphaelite painter Edward Burne-Jones. Another married a well known painter, Edward Poynter, who was later to become President of the Royal Academy, and a third married a wealthy ironmaster, Alfred Baldwin, and became the mother of the future prime minister, Stanley Baldwin. It is a mystery to Kipling's biographers that the children were not left with

6. A pupil of his father's, the Parsee artist Pestonjee Bomanjee, remembered the boy fondly in his old age and described him as "coming into a room where the students were modeling and proceeding to pelt them with clay. He was a real nuisance to the class until his father came in, took him by the scruff of the neck and pushed him out" (Green 1965, pp. 24–25).

anyone in the family. A friend of Alice Kipling said that "she had never thought of leaving her children with her own family, it led to complications" (Green 1965, p. 29).

The children were put in the charge of complete strangers who had attracted attention through a newspaper advertisement. Rudyard and Trix were abandoned suddenly, without any preparation or explanation—their parents simply disappeared and returned to India. Not knowing why they had lost their parents was an agony to the children. Rudyard's mother told him later that she had been advised it was kindest to spare the children the torment of a goodbye. Whatever her motives, and they cannot really be known, at the least she shared the lack of empathy for the child that seems to have been so prevalent in Victorian times, and that was frequently passed down from one generation to the next as part of a compulsion to repeat the past—sowing misery even in the homes of the wealthy and privileged.

When Kipling was an adult, his mother Alice was a loving and charming person, and very devoted to her son. Yet it is a mystery how, even after she knew of Rudyard's suffering and breakdown under the care of the foster guardians, she could have left her daughter Trix—a sensitive and nervous child—for several more years with them after removing her son. Here is a description of Alice by her younger sister Edith:

> The Irish blood which is pretty certainly in our family seemed to take effect in Alice; she had the ready wit and power of repartee, the sentiment, and I may say, the *unexpectedness* which one associated with that race. *It was impossible to predict how she would act at any given point. There was a certain fascination in this,* and fascinating she certainly was. . . . a cheerful, and loving friend all my life through. [Green 1965, pp. 17–18, italics mine]

The unexpectedness was a quality in her puzzling character that fascinated and tormented her son. Secrecy and unpredictability are evident not only in her failure to say goodbye to the children[7]; when she returned to England six years later it was also without word of warning. Years later she had Rudyard's schoolboy poems privately printed without his knowledge or permission—these included early love poems and involved exposing his

---

7. It is significant that in *Something of Myself* Kipling covers over the failure to say goodbye—talking of "a parting in the dawn with Father and Mother, who said that I must learn quickly to read and write so that they might send me letters and books" (1937, pp. 4–5). This is apparently fiction (and like the account given in his short story "Baa Baa, Black Sheep," written at twenty-one). The old man could not take the truth—the "unexpectedness" still hurt too much.

soul. When Rudyard returned to India and found this out he was furious. Her brother Frederick tells of Alice's verbal aggressiveness: "My sister had the quickest mind and readiest wits I have ever known. She saw things in a moment, and did not so much reason as pounce upon her conclusions. . . . Her wit was for the most part humorous and genial, but on occasion it was a weapon of whose keenness of point there could be no doubt, and foolish or mischievous people were made to feel it" (Stewart 1966, p. 5).

Kipling apparently struggled to keep split mental images of his parents— his real parents remaining "good" and the foster parents taking on the "bad." The intensity of the overt loving and dependent later relationship with his mother is implicit in Kipling's editorial comment in his short story, "The Brushwood Boy." This story, by the way, strongly influenced Strindberg, who was an early significant user of the term *soul murder* [see Burnham 1971]. When the Brushwood Boy returns from India as a man to his home in England, his mother, in some dread, wants to know if he has marriage plans. She comes up to his bedroom to tuck the grown man in: "And she sat down on the bed, and they talked for a long hour, *as mother and son should, if there is to be any future for our Empire*" (1895b, p. 355).[8] Beneath this cosmically significant mother-son harmony lies all the intense antagonism and distrust of women that is so prevalent in Kipling's poetry and prose.[9]

Kipling's father, Lockwood Kipling, was a distinguished artist, artisan, and teacher. His brother-in-law, Frederick, wrote that he was "gentle and kindly in spirit, and companionship with him was a continual refreshing" (Carrington 1955, p. 33). In later years, Rudyard certainly shared that opinion. Frederick Macdonald continues:

> [In comparison with his wife] his mind moved more slowly and cautiously, but covered a wider range. His power of acquiring and retaining knowledge was extraordinary. His memory seemed to let nothing slip from its grasp. On what may be called his own subjects, those connected with the plastic arts, with sculpture, modelling and engraving, with

8. Side-by-side with this mawkish blindness is insight: the tête-a-tête proceeds to an oedipal close. After the mother concludes she has no rival, she "blessed him and kissed him on the mouth, *which is not always a mother's property* . . ." (p. 356; italics added).

9. Two well known examples of this antagonism and distrust arise in "The Betrothed" (1885): "And a woman is only a woman,/but a good Cigar is a Smoke" (Kipling, 1885, p. 99), and "The Vampire" (1897): "A fool there was and he made his prayer/(Even as you and I!)/To a rag and a bone and a hank of hair/(We called her the woman who did not care) (1897, p. 199).

craftsmanship in metals, wood, and clay, with industrial processes where they come into the domain of art, he was a great expert, learned in their history and skilful in their practice. . . . His curiosity was alive and active . . . all things interested him. He seemed to know something about everything as well as everything about some things. [Green 1965, pp. 18–19]

Rudyard's formidable intellectual equipment and memory, as well as his intense curiosity, came from his father through inheritance or identification. The Kiplings left their children in the care of the Holloways — a retired sea captain (a man Rudyard liked and who unfortunately soon died), and his wife, called "Aunty Rosa" by the children. She was a tyrannical, narrow-minded, religiously obsessed woman. "Aunty Rosa" was the boy's prime persecutor and was invariably called the Woman in his writings. The children always referred to the Holloways' house in Sussex, Lorne Lodge, as the "House of Desolation." They stayed there, without seeing their parents, for six years. Trix describes their lodgings:

Down a short flight of stairs was the basement with the kitchen behind and the nursery in front . . . there was a rusty grate there but never a fire, or any means of heat, even in the depths of winter. This perhaps accounted for the severe broken chilblains that crippled me from December to February every year, until Mamma came. "Aunty" had an economical theory that if children played properly they kept beautifully warm, but our mushroom-smelling den, with wall cupboards where even a doll's china dinner-set grew blue mildew in two or three days, was too small for any active games. [Fleming 1937, p. 169]

But it was not the physical discomforts that the children minded most, and they were adequately fed. The atmosphere was full of sadism, disguised as religious righteousness. Kipling says:

It was an establishment run with the full vigour of the Evangelical as revealed to the Woman. I had never heard of Hell, so I was introduced to it in all its terrors — I and whatever luckless little slavery might be in the house, whom severe rationing had led to steal food. Once I saw the Woman beat such a girl who picked up the kitchen poker and threatened retaliation. Myself I was regularly beaten. [1937, p. 6]

As long as the old Captain was alive there was someone to intervene and protect him from the Woman; he occasionally gave Rudyard some kind words and, even more important, rational explanations. (Captain Holloway had served on a whaler and undoubtedly was one of the models for that good substitute father, the whaler Captain Disco Troop in *Captains Courageous*.) He had a fascinating dark deformity. The old man had been entangled in a harpoon line in an accident while whaling and had been dragged down. Almost miraculously he had gotten free. "But the line had scarred his ankle for life—a dry, *black* scar, *which I used to look at with horrified interest*" (Kipling 1937, p. 5, italics added). The Holloways had a son, Henry, who was six years older than Rudyard. "Aunty Rosa" apparently was jealous of the brighter younger boy in relation to her Henry. She appears to have treated Trix well, but Rudyard was rejected as a black sheep (which is what he calls himself in his fictionalized account). Trix wrote:

[Aunty] had long wanted a daughter, therefore she soon made a pet of me, and did her best to weaken the affection between the poor little people marooned on the desert island of her house and heart. From the beginning she took the line that I was always in the right and Ruddy invariably in the wrong; a very alienating position to thrust me into; but he, with his curious insight into human nature, said she was a jealous woman, and of such low caste as not to matter, and he never loved me less for her mischief-making. . . . She never struck me, or threatened me with bodily punishment, and I am still grateful to her for some of her early teaching. But her cruelty to Ruddy poisoned everything. [Fleming 1937, p. 169]

The attempt to separate the children evokes the prison and the concentration camp. Trix writes:

From the first [Aunty Rosa punished] the children whose united aged did not amount to ten years, and who had no relations nearer than London, by forbidding them to speak to each other for twenty-four hours. This penalty, which meant solitary confinement, with Aunty as a very competent jailer, was imposed for such crimes as spilling a drop of gravy at dinner [or] forgetting to put a slate away. . . . [Fleming 1937, p. 168]

Aunty Rosa's divisive attempts ultimately failed. Rudyard could almost always rely on his sister's devotion. The impact of her passionate loyalty in these years must have helped him in later life to fight off his hatred of women.

Harry cooperated with his mother in tyrannizing over and punishing Rudyard: "The Woman had an only son of twelve or thirteen as religious as she. I was a real joy to him, for when his mother had finished with me for the day, he (we slept in the same room) took me on and roasted the other side" (1937, p. 6). Henry was a prototype for a Big Brother figure, hated and loved, evoking murderous, and (the implications are in the words above) homosexual feelings.

Mother and son combined in trying to brainwash the boy:

If you cross examine a child of seven or eight on his day's doings (specially when he wants to go to sleep), he will contradict himself very satisfactorily. If each contradiction be set down as a lie and retailed at breakfast, life is not easy. I have known a certain amount of bullying, but this was calculated torture—religious as well as scientific. [1937, p. 6]

The cross examination was regularly followed by:

. . . punishments and humiliation—above all humiliation. That alternation was quite regular. I can but admire the internal laborious ingenuity of it all. *Exempli gratia.* Coming out of church one day I smiled. The Devil-Boy demanded why. I said I didn't know, which was child's truth. He replied that I *must* know. People don't laugh for nothing. Heaven knows the explanation I put forward; but it was duly reported to the Woman as a "lie". . . . The Son after three or four years went into a Bank and was generally too tired on his return to torture me, unless things had gone wrong with him. I learned to know what was coming from his step into the house. [1937, p. 11]

The driven, consuming, persecutory regimen deprived the children not only of joy, but even of the opportunity for simple, quiet existence—for the timelessness and contemplative relaxation so necessary for the child's soul. The boy was forced into an *adaptive* paranoid attitude:

Nor was my life an unsuitable preparation for my future, in that it demanded constant wariness, the habit of observation, and attendance on moods and tempers; the noting of discrepancies between speech and action; a certain reserve of demeanour; and automatic suspicion of sudden favours. [1937, p. 16]

To ward off the persecution, Kipling had to justify the iterated accusation— he was forced to lie; Kipling describes this as having some creative potential: "[The torment] made me give attention to the lies I soon found it necessary to tell; and this, I presume, is the foundation of literary effort" (1937, p. 6). The inculcated need to deceive by divorcing action from feelings is documented by Trix. After their mother came to rescue the children, she:

> wrote to my father that the children . . . had . . . seemed delighted to see her, but she had been a little disappointed by the way we had both hung round [Aunty Rosa] in the evening. She did not know that well-trained animals watch their tamer's eye, and the familiar danger-signals of "Aunty's" rising temper had set us both fawning upon her. [Fleming 1937, p. 268]

Kipling felt that he had been able to survive because of the month each year he spent with his mother's relatives — especially with his Aunt Georgina (Burne-Jones). There love and affection were not stinted and the boy had an important role in the large family's activities: "It was a jumble of delights and emotions culminating in being allowed to blow the big organ in the studio for the beloved Aunt, while the Uncle worked . . . and if the organ ran out in squeals the beloved Aunt would be sorry. Never, *never* angry!" (1937, pp. 13–14). This follows a passage that links fear of the dark, seeing and being seen, with the need for what was so lacking in the House of Desolation — protection provided by the presence of men:

> At bedtime one hastened along the passages, where unfinished cartoons lay against the walls. The Uncle often painted in their eyes first, leaving the rest in charcoal — a most effective presentation. Hence our speed to our own top landing, where we could hang over the stairs and listen to *the loveliest sound in the world — deep-voiced men laughing together over dinner.* [1937, p. 13; italics mine]

Kipling's work — especially the stories about children *[The Jungle Books, Kim, Captains Courageous)* — are full of the longing for fathers fulfilled by a multitude of good father-figures. The narrative about Aunt Georgina's continues: "But on a certain day — one tried to fend off the thought of it — the delicious dream would end, and one would return to the House of Desolation, and for the next two or three mornings there cry on waking up. Hence more punishments and cross examinations" (1937, p. 15). In some ways "Aunty Rosa's" brainwashing was effective — Rudyard never told on her. Here is his explanation:

> Often and often afterwards, the beloved Aunt would ask me why I had never told any one how I was being treated. Children tell little more than

animals, *for what comes to them they accept as eternally established.* Also, badly treated children have a clear notion of what they are likely to get if they betray the secrets of a prison-house before they are clear of it. [1937, p. 15; italics mine]

Whether children continue to accept what comes to them as eternally established depends largely on parental attitudes — and a parent-figure claiming to speak for God must inhibit the development of the child's own judgment and identity. But Kipling's deepest motivation for keeping silent probably related more to the parents who had betrayed him to the prison-house than to "Aunty Rosa." He had to distance the anger and torment caused by their desertion. The acute need to keep the memory of good parents made silence, minimization, and even denial necessary. How could his parents have done this to him? It was too unbearable to keep that question in mind very long.[10]

Kipling wrote three accounts of his time in the House of Desolation. The first, written in 1888 when he was twenty-two, was the short story, "Baa Baa, Black Sheep," a fairly straightforward narrative[11] of the desertion, torment, and rescue of "Punch" and "Judy" (names which were at least unconsciously associated with the beatings in the family life of that sadomasochistic puppet couple). The second account, altered in many details (including the elimination of Trix by blending her with an older girl who came to live with Mrs. Holloway after Rudyard left), provides the first chapter of *The Light That Failed,* a novel Kipling wrote in 1890 at age twenty-five. It wasn't until the very end of his life, when he was over seventy, that he wrote the autobiographical fragment, *Something of Myself.*

"Baa, Baa, Black Sheep" shows the child attributing to the parent the actions of the cruel parent-substitute. After being beaten for the first time the child thinks: "Aunty Rosa . . . had the power to beat him with many stripes. It was unjust and cruel, and Mamma and Papa would never have allowed it. Unless perhaps, as Aunty Rosa seemed to imply, they had sent secret orders. In which case he was abandoned indeed" (Kipling 1888b, pp. 297–298). In her memoirs, Trix expressed the children's feelings about the desertion:

10. Oedipus, learning that his mother gave him up as an infant, feet shackled, to be abandoned on Mt. Cithaeron, asks: "And dared a *mother* . . ." Dostoyevsky (1880): "and it was her mother, her mother did this."

11. Ironically, an 1890 reviewer found all the tales in *Wee Willie Winkle* commendable "except 'Baa Baa, Black Sheep' which was 'not true to life'" (Carrington 1955, p. 142).

Looking back I think the real tragedy of our early days, apart from Aunty's bad temper and unkindness to my brother, sprang from our inability to understand why our parents had deserted us. We had had no preparation or explanation; it was like a double death, or rather, like an avalanche that had swept away everything happy and familiar. . . . We felt we had been deserted, "almost as much as on a doorstep," and what was the reason? Of course Aunty used to say it was because we were so tiresome, and she had taken us out of pity, but in a desperate moment Ruddy appealed to Uncle Harrison, and he said it was only Aunty's fun and Papa had left us to be taken care of because India was too hot for little people. But we knew better than that because we had been to Nassick [a cool place in the Indian Hills], so what was the real reason? Mama was not ill—Papa had not had to go to a war. They had not even lost their money—there was no excuse; they had gone happily back to our own lovely home, and had not taken us with them. There was no getting out of that, as we often said. Harry, who had all a crow's quickness in finding a wound to pick at, discovered our trouble and teased us unmercifully. He assured us we had been taken in out of charity and must do exactly as he told us—we were just like workhouse brats, and none of our toys really belonged to us. [Fleming 1937, p. 171]

The suddenness, the unexpectedness, of the desertion increased its traumatic effect by depriving the children of any chance to prepare for, to work out in thought and with their parents, what they were to experience. But Rudyard did fight with his mind to keep Trix with him emotionally, and to preserve the memory of the good parents as a refuge from persecutors. Trix says he called "Aunty Rosa" a *Kutch-nay,* a Nothing-at-all, and that secret name was a great comfort to us, and useful too when Harry practised his talent for eavesdropping" (Fleming 1937, p. 169). "Ruddy remembered our lost kingdom vividly" (Fleming 1937, p. 171). The six-year-old provided the vivid details that the younger child had forgotten. Remembering the past was a torment to the children, but it also restored the promise of bliss, and it strengthened them. Rudyard's imagination also helped—in his stories to Trix he conjured up an idealized world and wonderful parents. All this kept the children together so that the desertion didn't mean complete isolation.[12]

12. Compare *1984* where the tormentor is successful in his attempt to break down Winston Smith to the point of dividing him emotionally from his beloved companion, Julia. The soul murder is consummated (that is, the capacity for love is destroyed) when Winston screams: "Do it to Julia! Not me. Julia! I don't care what you do to her. Tear her face off, strip her to the bones. Not me! Julia! Not me!" (Orwell 1949, p. 289). Sibling rivalry is usually tuned up to

Yet, there was so much confusion, an agony of not knowing why, or to whom they belonged, or what their place was in the order of things. No wonder Rudyard was to become an arch-conservative, a pillar of the established order. One can see how the Law of the Jungle in the *Jungle Books* — assigning a place to everyone, making all relationships clear, enforcing "human" decency — represented a wish-fulfillment for Kipling; and so did Mowgli's foster parents — wolves! But these wolves were of outstanding decency and dependability with Mother Wolf ready to fight to the death to keep him.

Another soul-saving factor during this time was the boy's absorption in reading. Rudyard couldn't read or write when left with the Hollidays, and it was "Aunty Rosa" who taught him. At first he resisted learning, but then he discovered that books offered a means of escape into fantasy, by distancing his torment. He called it: "a means to everything that would make me happy. So I read all that came within my reach. As soon as my pleasure in this was known, deprivation from reading was added to my punishments. I then read by stealth and the more earnestly" (Kipling 1937, p. 7). Reading then became a "sin" that involved his eyes, his curiosity, and his fantasies. This is stressed in all the accounts Kipling wrote of this time. The sinning was followed by retribution:

> My eyes went wrong, and I could not well see to read. For which reason I read the more and in bad lights. [Here he shows his masochism.] My work at the terrible little dayschool where I had been sent suffered in consequence, and my monthly reports showed it. The loss of "reading-time" was the worst of my "home" punishments for bad schoolwork. [1937, p. 16]

The eye trouble amounted to near blindness. This was discovered only shortly before Rudyard's deliverance from Lorne Lodge. Before that there was a terrible, humiliating punishment that resembled that given Dickens' alter ego, the fatherless and then orphaned David Copperfield, by the cruel Murdstones.

> [One school report] was so bad that I threw it away and said that I had never received it. But this is a hard world for the amateur liar. My web

---

this cannibalistic pitch under conditions of soul murder. This is effected by the child's intense need to displace rage away from the tormenting parent, and to identify with the tormentor (in relation to the sibling). Fortunately, the attempt to divide the siblings failed with the Kipling children.

of deceit was swiftly exposed — the Son spared time after banking-hours to help in the auto-da-fé — and I was well beaten and sent to school through the streets of Southsea with the placard "Liar" between my shoulders. [1937, p. 16]

What Kipling calls "some sort of nervous breakdown" (1937, p. 17) followed this. The shadows provided by his failing vision were supplemented by shadowy hallucinations — making for a terrible darkness: "I imagined I saw shadows and things that were not there, and they worried me more than the Woman" (1937, p. 17). When a doctor sent by his Aunt Georgina discovered the boy was half blind: "This, too, was supposed to be "showing-off" [according to "Aunty Rosa"], and I was segregated from my sister — another punishment — as a sort of moral leper" (1937, p. 17). His mother returned to England shortly after this; there is more than a hint of direct reproach (so rare for Kipling[13]) in his dry statement: "I do not remember that I had any warning" (1937, p. 17). On the first evening of her visit to the children, his mother afterwards told Rudyard, "when she first came up to my room to kiss me goodnight, I flung up an arm to guard off the cuff that I had been trained to expect" (1937, p. 17). The children were promptly taken away. They had been in the House of Desolation for six years.

For some months Rudyard was tended to by his mother in a small farmhouse near Epping Forest, where he was allowed to run wild; he felt "completely happy . . . except for my spectacles" (1937, p. 17). Although Rudyard was rescued, Trix was subsequently returned to Mrs. Holloway's care. Her experience had been different from her brother's since she had been treated as a favorite and (I quote J. I. M. Stewart):

(had become) a little Evangelical herself. At the same time she was obstinately loyal to a brother who was constantly being exhibited to her not merely as the Black Sheep of his family, but veritably as among the

---

13. Compare Dickens, who was sent out by his parents at age ten to work under terrible conditions at a blacking factory: "It is wonderful to me how I could have been so easily cast away at such an age" (Forster 1873, p. 25). Even when an adult and a famous man Dickens was so affected by his memories that he was unable to pass by the site of the factory. What burned in his memory was that his mother wanted him to stay on even after his father had arranged for his rescue: "I never afterwards forgot, I never shall forget, I never can forget, that my mother was warm for my being sent back" (Forster 1873, p. 35). It is true that Dickens was not able to bear telling anyone about the childhood experiences — he wrote about them to Forster, and his wife and children only learned that Dickens had given David Copperfield his own experiences in the blacking factory when they read of it in Forster's biography. But, unlike Kipling, Dickens knew how he felt.

damned. The strain upon Trix must have been very great, and leaving her with Mrs. Holloway was, upon any possible reading of the total situation, a grave error of judgement. It comes as no surprise when we learn that in later life Trix was subject to recurrent nervous illness. [1966, p. 11]

In her memoir of her early years with her brother, Trix says that her mother, after removing the children from Lorne Lodge, "wanted us to forget Aunty . . . as soon as possible" (p. 168). She doesn't mention being sent back to the House of Desolation after the idyllic summer away from it — perhaps she couldn't bear thinking about it. Trix comes closest to complaint when talking of Ruddy's month away each year at the Burne-Jones's: "that was a very tedious month of the year for me, for I missed him terribly, and for six years I never had one day's holiday from Aunty. I even had to sleep in her room" (Fleming 1937, p. 168).

Kipling makes two somewhat contradictory statements about the effect of the stay at Lorne Lodge on his subsequent life. He ends the 1888 story "Baa Baa, Black Sheep," with Punch telling Judy, three months after they have been taken away from the House of Desolation by their mother:

Told you so. . . . it's all different now, and we are just as much Mother's as if she had never gone. [But the narrator adds]: Not altogether, O Punch, for when your lips have drunk deep of the bitter watters of Hate, Suspicion, and Despair, all the Love in the world will not wholly take away that knowledge; *though it may turn darkened eyes for a while to the light,* and teach Faith where no Faith was. [1888a, p. 315; italics mine]

As an old man, in *Something of Myself,* he says of the torment and humiliation at Lorne Lodge: "In the long run these things, and many more of the like, drained me of any capacity for real, personal hate for the rest of my days. So close must any life-filling passion lie to its opposite. 'Who having known the Diamond will concern himself with glass?'" (1937, p. 16). Both statements show realization of the lifelong effects of Lorne Lodge, but the later one denies that he could subsequently hate in a personal way, as if the hatred had been cathartically discharged once and for all.

Kipling was a most complex man; certainly his creativity was not destroyed by the years in the House of Desolation — it may even have been enhanced. He was not deprived of his ability to love, although it may have been damaged. His capacity for humor and laughter survived, though marked and sometimes marred by sadism. However, Kipling denied an intense and often cruel personal hatred that is obvious to the most casual reader. It is the terrible destructive hatred of the tormented child who "cannot curse God and die" that is perhaps the heaviest burden of soul murder. Where is it to go? After the years in Lorne Lodge the free expression of the "angry Ruddy coming" was no longer possible. Part of the hatred was bound by identifying with the tormentor. But such intense hatred must be disclaimed, not felt, denied — and so it was with Kipling. Yet many, too many, of his poems and stories are about revenge and sadistic practical jokes, revealing naked hatred.[14] Often, but not always, he hates with the oppressor against the oppressed. Jarrell (1963) comments on the hatred towards authority that is hidden in Kipling's celebration and justification of it:

[Kipling's] morality is the one-sided, desperately protective, sometimes *vindictive* morality of someone who has been for some time the occupant of one of God's concentration camps, and has had to spend the rest of his life justifying or explaining out of existence what he cannot forget. [p. 146; italics mine]

His close friend, Mrs. Edmonia Hill, wrote of Kipling when he was working on "Baa Baa, Black Sheep" while staying at her home in 1888:

[Kipling has been writing] a true story of his early life when he was sent with his little sister to England to be educated. . . . It was pitiful to see Kipling living over the experience, pouring out his soul in the story, as the drab life was worse than he could possibly describe it. His eyesight was permanently impaired, and as he had heretofore only known love and tenderness, his faith in people was sorely tried. When he was writing this

---

14. For example, from "The Rhyme of the Three Captains" — about pirates, and written just after Kipling's work had been extensively pirated in America, to his fury. A sea captain who had been robbed speaks of his wishes for revenge on the pirate chief:
Had I had guns (as I had goods) to work my Christian harm,
I had run him up from the quarter deck to trade with his own yard-arm;
I had nailed his ears to my capstan-head, and ripped them off with a saw,
And soused them in the bilgewater, and served them to him raw;
I had flung him blind in a rudderless boat to rot in the rocking dark,
I had towed him aft of his own craft, a bait for his brother shark;
I had lapped him round with cocoa husk, and drenched him with the oil,
And lashed him fast to his own mast to blaze above my spoil;
I had stripped his hide for my hammock-side, and tasseled his beard in the mesh,
And spitted his crew on the live bamboo that grows through the gangrened flesh. . . .
[1890, pp. 256–257]
The reader wants to cry "Enough" as the pathological intensity mounts.

he was a sorry guest, as he was in a towering rage at the recollection of those days. [Green 1965, p. 33]

So much for being deprived of the capacity for personal hatred!

Trix writes a disclaimer about hatred similar to her brother's. (She had probably read *Something of Myself* before she wrote her account of the years at Lorne Lodge.) She says of the "odious Harry": "Perhaps hate is a disease, like measles, that it is well to recover from early, and up to the age of eleven I hated Harry so wholeheartedly that I have only disliked a few people, in a mild tepid way, ever since." But then she adds: "I am ashamed to say that only last year, when I found a scrap of his detested writing on the fly-leaf of an old book, I tore it out and burned it at once, and dark eyes, set near together, and black hair, plastered with pomatum, still make me shudder with dislike" (Fleming 1937, p. 169).

There was a short-lived repetition of the desertion and desolation at Lorne Lodge when the twelve-year-old Kipling was sent to a public school nine months after his removal from "Aunty Rosa's." The school had to be inexpensive, and his parents settled on the United Services Colleges (also called Westward Ho!), a new institution designed mainly to prepare the sons of Army officers for a military career. The headmaster, Cormell Price, was a friend of the Kiplings', a man known and liked by Rudyard (who called him "Uncle Crom" outside of school). The school was made famous by Kipling's glorification of it in his *Stalky* stories. But these stories conceal, and their comic tone belies, that Kipling's first months at school meant a return to hell. During this time his mother was still in England. In *Something of Myself* (1937), Kipling calls the school: "Brutal enough. . . . My first year and a half was not pleasant. The most persistent bullying comes less from the bigger boys, who merely kick and pass on, than from young *devils* of fourteen acting in concert against one boy" (p. 23; italics added). Here were new versions of that "Devil-Boy" Harry.

In *Stalky and Co.* (1899), Beetle (Kipling) rebukes a bully who, he says, is one of those who claim to:

never really bully . . . only knock 'em about a little bit. That's what [you] say. Only kick their *souls* out of 'em, and they go and blub in the box-rooms. Shove their heads into the ulsters and blub. Write home three times a day — yes, you brute, I've done that — askin' to be taken away. . . . [p. 162; italics mine]

And Kipling actually had. His sister writes: "For the first month or so, he wrote to us twice or thrice daily (and my mother cried bitterly over the letters) that he could neither eat nor sleep" (Stewart 1966, p. 22). Despite her tears, Alice Kipling left England before the Easter Holidays when her son could have been with her to tell her firsthand what he had been experiencing. She may have had reassurances from the headmaster. Eventually things did improve for Rudyard — markedly so after the first eighteen months. He was accepted by the others and ceased to be a victim: "After my strength came suddenly to me about my fourteenth year, there was no more bullying; and either my natural sloth or past experience did not tempt me to bully in my turn" (1937, p. 23). He found his special friends Beresford and Dunsterville (M'Turk and Stalky in his stories) and they formed a little group that provided a feeling of active masculine identity. There was a glorious summer holiday when he was thirteen and his father returned from India and took him to Paris for the Exposition of 1878 (this was followed by a lifelong fondness for things French). At school he was under the benevolent eye of the headmaster, "Uncle Crom." In this place the Woman held no sway; he lived with brothers who were mostly good, and the fathers were in power.

But the dark past still threatened. The boy was beaten by the masters — a regular part of English public school education. The prevailing aura of brutality — a continuation of life with Harry, if not with "Aunty Rosa" — is depicted in *Stalky and Co.,* about which Edmund Wilson writes:

> The book itself, of course, presents a hair-raising picture of the sadism of the English public school system. The older boys have fags to wait on them, and they sometimes torment these younger boys till they have reduced them almost to imbecility; the masters are constantly caning the boys in scenes that seem almost as bloody as the floggings in old English sea stories; and the boys revenge themselves on the masters with practical jokes as catastrophic as the Whams and Zows of the comic strip. [1941, p. 21]

Lionel Trilling talks of the book's "callousness, arrogance and brutality" (1943, p. 89). Kipling's mental splits — his being on both sides of the persecutor/victim struggle — are demonstrated. He shows contempt for the school's compulsory games. There is a general acceptance of the cruelty that is presented, and cruelty to animals is a matter of course. In one story a cat is shot by the boys in Kipling's group and its corpse left to stink on the rafters about the dormitory of offending enemies.[15] The sadistic masters are exposed

15. To paraphrase Freud's well-known phrase — a cat is also a cat. But like the Cigar in "The Betrothal" (see above), its symbolic meaning is significant — expressing here the hostility toward the female genital ("pussy") in the predominant anal-sadistic, male homosexual context of these stories.

and get tricked in successful revenge schemes—yet eventually their authority is justified. This is expressed in the poem with which Kipling prefaces the book, "A School Song":

> Western wind and open surge
>   Took us from our mothers;
> Flung us on a naked shore
> (Twelve bleak houses by the shore!
> Seven summers by the shore!)
>   'Mid two hundred brothers.
>
> There we met with famous men
>   Set in office o'er us;
> And they beat on us with rods—
> Faithfully with many rods—
> Daily beat on us with rods,
>   For the love they bore us.

This last ironic line seems to imply criticism. Certainly Kipling does not deny the beatings. In his autobiography he is able to express anger toward the masters, especially toward his first housemaster, the school chaplain, an especially ferocious and sanctimonious man. Kipling saw through him as a schoolboy too. But, characteristically, his poem ends with a glorification of the school system. He first portrays the microcosm of the school as preparing the boys to go out and rule the Empire. Then he praises Big Brother:

> This we learned from famous men,
>   Knowing not we learned it.
> Only, as the years went by—
> Lonely, as the years went by—
> Far from help as years went by,
>   Plainer we discerned it.
>
>   . . . . . .
>
> Bless and praise we famous men—
>   Men of little showing—
> For their work continueth,
> And their work continueth
>   Broad and deep continueth,
> Great beyond their knowing!
>
> > [1899, pp. xv–xvii]

Soul murder results in breaking the victim's identity into contradictory fragments that function independently, without effective synthesis. In psychoanalytic terms, the victim's mental images of the self and parents are vertically and irreconcilably split. After the abandonment by his good parents and the years with the bad, Kipling had contradictory and irresolvable views about authorities. He continually tries to portray them as good, but his rage and need to attack breaks through. And he is not permitted to know it. In telling of his school years, Kipling describes how he started to write—and he connects it with the personal hatred he claimed to be drained of. In the course of his studies at Westward Ho!, he had discovered

> a man called Dante who, living in a small Italian town at general issue with his neighbors, had invented for most of them lively torments in a nine-ringed Hell [It was from Aunty Rosa that he had first learned of Hell], where he exhibited them to after ages. . . . I brought a fat, American-cloth-bound notebook and set to work on an *Inferno,* into which I put, under appropriate tortures, all my friends and *most* of the masters. [Kipling 1937, pp. 33–34; italics mine]

After quoting the last lines, the marvelous Randall Jarrell (whose short essay, "On Preparing to Read Kipling," is so full of psychological insight that reading it made me want to throw away my own almost completed manuscript) adds: "Why only *most*? Two were spared, one for the Father and one for the Mother" (Jarrell 1962, p. 144).

There is a most important part of the young boy's experience about which Kipling wrote nothing and about which nothing is known—his sexual life. Was the memory of the intense wish to see the child's severed hand a screen for masturbation? We know that there was much early indulgence, that the ebullient boy was separated from his parents and from his beloved *ayah* and bearer at the height of his oedipal period. We gather from his writings the importance of primal scene fantasies, and his character and talents show his intense curiosity. From ages six to twelve, the so-called period of sexual latency, he was dominated by a cruel mother figure whose weak husband soon died, and he shared a room with a Big Brother who tormented him. It is not known if anything sexual happened to Kipling during the years of desolation. It is not hard to imagine the Evangelical Woman's attitude toward masturbation. Rudyard and his little sister were drawn together against the persecutors. One infers from his autobiography that puberty came with his spurt of physical growth at fourteen. He developed a precocious mustache and at seventeen, though short, looked like a man.

The conventions of Victorian literature dictated avoiding sexual details; but in contrast to most of his contemporaries, Kipling was aware of the existence and power of sexuality and implicitly described it in his fiction. It is implicit in many of the *Plain Tales From the Hills* (1888a), which are full of predatory women. *The Light That Failed* clearly though discreetly pictures a sexual liaison between Torpenhow and the streetwalker Bessie Broke, and suggests the lesbian potential of "the red-haired girl" with whom the heroine lives.

Kipling's first direct reference to sex in his autobiography concerns his years at school — and it is a disclaimer:

> Naturally, Westward Ho! was brutal enough, but, setting aside the foul speech that a boy ought to learn early and put behind him by his seventeenth year, it was clean with a cleanliness that I have never heard of in any other school. I remember no case of even suspected perversion, and am inclined to the theory that if masters did not suspect them, and show that they suspected, there would not be quite so many elsewhere. [1937, p. 23]

Apparently, it was Cormell Price's policy to exhaust the boys through sports, but the purported absence of sexuality would make Westward Ho! singular indeed. Kipling's denial is different from the ignoring of sex in school life by other Victorian memoir writers. For Kipling, minimization of homosexuality parallels minimization of anger. He says of his being beaten by the Prefect of Games while at school: "One of the most difficult things to explain to some people is that a boy of seventeen or eighteen can thus beat a boy barely a year his junior, and on the heels of the punishment go for a walk with him; neither party bearing malice or pride" (1937, p. 30).

One wants a rejoinder to this partial truth — do the parties know, *can they know* what feelings they are bearing underneath?

In Kipling's early writings women are depicted as sexually attractive, but destructive; or cold and asexual. In his first novel, *The Light That Failed,* the only real affection is between men. At this time of his life, Kipling's ideal girl seems to have been the "regular fellow" type, like Miss Martyn (first name Bill or William) of *William The Conqueror* (1895) who looks like a boy with her cropped hair, is "clever as a man . . . (and who) like men who do things . . . doesn't understand poetry very much — it made her head ache" (p. 172). Kipling gives Miss Martyn his own feelings toward the literary men of London when he returned there in 1889 (age twenty-four) after his years as a journalist in India expressed in:

In Partibus

But I consort with long-haired things
    In velvet collar-rolls,
Who talk about the Aims of Art,
    And "theories" and "goals",
And moo and coo with womenfolk
    About their blessed souls.

It's Oh to meet an Army man,
    Set up, and trimmed and taut,
Who does not spout hashed libraries
    Or think the next man's thought. . . .
And walks as though he owned himself,
    And hogs his bristles short.
                                            [1889, p. 173]

The Light That Failed was published in 1891. At twenty-six Kipling would seem to have shared the belief of Torpenhow, the friend and room-mate of his hero Dick Heldar, who prophesied Dick's finish as an artist and a man if he were to fall in love. (This is expressed in dialogue that would fit in with the preadolescent, unconscious, homosexual myth of the American Western—one can almost hear it in the voice of John Wayne): "She's spoil his hand. She'll waste his time. She'll marry him, and ruin his work for ever. He'll be a respectable married man before we stop him, and—he'll never go on to the long trail again" (p. 76).

One velvet-collar wearer, Max Beerbohm, whose somewhat feminine sensibilities perhaps enabled him to spot (and motivated him to ridicule) Kipling's, appreciated that Kipling was a genius. But he loathed his work. He wickedly pretended to believe that *Rudyard Kipling* was the pseudonym of a female author:

Should the name of Rudyard Kipling be put between inverted commas? Is it the veil of feminine identity? . . . Dick Heldar . . . doted on the military. . . . strange that these heroes with their self-conscious blurting of oaths and slang, their cheap cynicism about the female sex, were not fondly created out of the inner consciousness of a lady novelist. Who else would say, "Oh, to meet an Army man . . . ?" [Green 1965, p. 100]

I have skipped ahead in time, and will now return to the adolescent Kipling. Maisie, the frigid and selfless heroine of *The Light That Failed,* had a direct prototype in Kipling's life—a girl he fell in love with when he was fourteen-and-a-half. She was associated with the House of Desolation.

Rudyard met Florence Garrard when he travelled to Mrs. Holloway's to bring Trix away for a holiday in 1880. Florence was a little older than Rudyard. She was a paying guest at "Aunty Rosa's"; her parents were abroad. Like Maisie, Florence kept a pet goat, and her character too was "self-centered and elusive, lacking in sympathy and affection" (Carrington 1955, p. 76). Rudyard felt himself to be in love with her for five or six years. When he was sixteen and about to go back to India, he begged her to con-sent to become engaged to him and felt she had agreed. He often mentioned her in his letters to his aunts from India but it is still difficult to judge the depth of his feelings. Florence sounds like an official girlfriend mentioned to give himself status as a grown man. But it is clear that he was initially strongly involved,[16] and he was again affected when he met her many years later.

This was just before writing his novel, and no doubt the meeting influ-enced his decision to use her for his heroine, Maisie, who like the Flo of that time was studying to be a painter. Florence made him recall Lorne Lodge, and, substituting her for Trix, he wrote a first chapter about the two chil-dren's stay there. The boy and girl were shown playing with a forbidden loaded pistol—Maisie temporarily blinded Dick by shooting it. Since Maisie is an amalgam of Florence and Trix, the incident (which prefigures the theme of the castrating and blinding woman) might refer to heterosexual (but incestuous) masturbatory play between Trix and Rudyard. If this occurred, ironically enough, it might well have helped save the boy's masculinity.

Rudyard was nearly seventeen when he left England after graduating from Westward Ho! to rejoin his parents in India:

That was a joyous homecoming. For—consider!—I had returned to a Father and Mother of whom I had seen but little since my sixth year. . . . The Mother proved more delightful than all my imaginings or memories. My father was not only a mine of knowledge and help, but a humourous, tolerant and expert fellow-craftsman. . . . I do not remember the small-est friction in any detail of our lives. We delighted more in each other's society than in that of strangers; and when my sister came out, a little later, our cup was filled to the brim. Not only were we happy, but we knew it. [1937, pp. 39–40]

---

16. His Aunt Edith "recalled how impressed she had been by the alarming force of his feel-ings as he gave her an account of his love for Flo Garrard, the girl who took his heart when he was still a schoolboy and did it no good before she tossed it back to him" (Stewart 1966, p. 32).

It was paradise regained. Rudyard's mother began the habit, adopted by them all, of calling the four contented Kiplings "The Family Square."[17]

In his autobiography, Kipling called the period he spent in India (1937) "Seven Years Hard." During this time he worked as a journalist and began to write the poems and stories of India that made him famous as a young man. He learned about Indian life from the inside, getting to know the Indians, but especially the Anglo-Indians. As a reporter he travelled over the entire subcontinent, exploring the levels of the rigid castes of both cultures—from the native underworld of Lahore, and the barracks of Tommy Atkins, to the generals and political leaders of Delhi and Simla. He quizzed and looked and listened, picking up characters for his stories and verses. Kipling's parents became personal friends of the viceroy, Lord Dufferin, providing Rudyard with a view from the top of governmental politics which he made good use of in his newspaper fiction (collected later in *Plain Tales From the Hills* [1888a]). These stories are told in a tone which promises to reveal secret knowledge, that "knowing," "grown-up" tone, so frequent (and sometimes so annoying) in Kipling's writing. It denied the child within who must not know—one expects it in adolescents, but it stayed on with Kipling. Perhaps in part because of this tone, Kipling's stories were eagerly read, and the young man found himself famous in his provincial world. He had the gratification of being asked about the opinions of the enlisted men in the barracks by the Commander-in-Chief himself, General Roberts.

Some of the early stories were about the influential, but fascinating Mrs. Hauksbee, of whom it was said, in *The Education of Otis Yeere,* that a man's scalp was "generally drying at (her) wigwam door" (1888a, p. 6). Green (1965) says, "At the end of 1887, Kipling was so much in thrall to Mrs. F. C. Burton, the 'original' of Mrs. Hauksbee, that he dedicated *Plain Tales From the Hills* to her as 'The Wittiest Woman in India'" (p. 78). She was old enough to be his mother, another great wit. To be in thrall to the Woman continued to be a pattern, as we shall see.

I will mention some of the nonneurotic aspects of Kipling's personality during these years. Kay Robinson, an editor for whom Kipling worked, describes the young man's unprepossessing appearance, and adds:

The charm of his manner, however, made you forget what he looked like in half a minute. . . . Kipling, shaking all over with laughter and wiping

17. It is in a *square* formed defensively by British soldiers that Dick Heldar gets the wound which eventually blinds him in *The Light That Failed.*

his spectacles at the same time with his handkerchief, always comes to mind as most characteristic of him in the old days when even our hardest work on "The Rag"—for fate soon took me to Lahore to be his editor— was as full of jokes as a pomegranate of pips. [Green 1965, p. 81]

Contemporaries also noted Kipling's intense love for children, and his extraordinary ability to communicate with them. And, above all, these years in India brought forth creative work that, despite mixed quality and jejune defects, is marvelous in its variety, quantity, brilliance, and force. Several short stories are masterpieces.

However, his work meant loneliness at times, and even solitude. For years Kipling was left in charge of the newspaper during the sweltering hot season when his family and most of the British community left for the cooler hill country. One year, during this abandonment, Kipling had what he called a "pivot experience." He was twenty, the only Englishman left to do all the editorial and supervisory work—it was too much:

It happened one hot-weather evening, in '86 or thereabouts, when I felt that I had come to the edge of all endurance. As I entered my empty house in the dusk there was no more in me except *the horror of a great darkness,* that I must have been fighting for some days. I came through that darkness alive, but how I do not know. [1937, p. 65]

The desertion and darkness must have meant a return to the House of Desolation, with its threat of the hallucinated "shadows and things that were not there," and the incipient blindness. Being alone at night may have brought with it forbidden masturbatory temptation.

We know from the imagery of his writings that darkness meant for Kipling the desolation of spirit, of "soul murder," the blackness of depression, of hatred and self-hatred mixed with fear of death and castration of the abandoned and tormented child who "cannot very well curse God and die." Kipling's first memories of England were of a dreadful place of darkness— "a dark land, and a darker room full of cold, in one wall of which a white woman made naked fire" (1937, p. 4). His bearer Meeta was credited with saving the child Kipling "from any night terrors or dread of the dark," but we have seen how ineffective this was. Professor Dobree (1967) illustrates the horror of darkness and desolation as a recurrent theme in Kipling's work, usually associated with what Kipling calls "breaking strain," the unbearable overstimulation that is the essence of trauma. This term is applicable both to what he suffered at age twenty in the intolerable heat and with the overwork and to his time with Mrs. Holloway. It appeared in one of his last poems, "Hymn of Breaking Strain":

> But, in our daily dealing
>   With stone and steel, we find
> The Gods have no such feeling
>   Of justice toward mankind.
> To no set gauge they make us, —
>   For no laid course prepare —
> And presently o'ertake us
>   With loads we cannot bear:
> Too merciless to bear [1935, p. 298]

Kipling charged the Gods with responsibility for the "too muchness," with the specific accusation, so relevant to his parents, that they didn't *prepare* human beings for the unbearable strain.[18]

The engineer Hummil in *At the End of the Passage* (1890c) (the title describes the condition of Hummil's soul under the stress of overwork in India such as brought on Kipling's "pivot experience"), died from great fear and shock. He had seen something horrible, and his doctor attempted to photograph the retina of his eyes to see what it was. The reader is not told the result of this dubious scientific attempt. In the nightmare delirium before his death Hummil had seen, "a blind face that cries and can't wipe its eyes, a blind face that chases him down corridors!" (p. 188). Hummil's Indian servant said, "In my poor opinion, this that was my master has descended into the Dark Places, and there has been caught because he was not able to escape with sufficient speed" (p. 192).

In 1907, Kipling addressed a group of students at McGill University:

---

18. But, predictably, the condemnation of the parent-Gods ended in their justification: they were needed:

> Oh veiled and secret Power
>   Whose paths we seek in vain,
> *Be with us in our hour*
>   *Of overthrow and pain;*
> That we — by which sure token
>   We know Thy ways are true —
> In spite of being broken
>   *Because of being broken,*
>   *May rise and build new.*
>   *Stand up and build anew!*
> [1935, p. 299; italics mine]

Some of you here know — *and I remember* — that youth can be a reason of great depression, despondencies, doubts, waverings. The worse because they seem to be peculiar to ourselves and incommunicable to our fellows. There is a *certain darkness into which the soul* of the young man sometimes descends — *a horror of desolation, abandonment and realized worthlessness,* which is one of the most real of hells in which we are compelled to walk. [1907, p. 21; italics mine]

Kipling described experiencing in 1896 "a Spirit of deep deep Despondency" (1937, p. 134) in the first house he and his wife rented in England after their stay in Vermont. (This return, too, meant an enforced exile, as I will describe in another paper.) Kipling called the feeling:

a gathering *blackness* of mind and sorrow of the heart, that each put down to the new, soft climate and, without telling the other, fought against for long weeks. It was the Feng-sui — the Spirit of the house itself — that *darkened the sunshine* and fell upon us every time we entered, checking the very words on our lips. [1937, p. 134; italics mine]

This was worked over in a story about a haunted house, *The House Surgeon,* written years later in 1909, in which the narrator has a terrible experience. It started with something reminiscent of Rudyard's boyhood hallucinations: "And it was just then that I was aware of a *little grey shadow,* as it might have been a snowflake *seen against the light,* floating at an immense distance in the background of my brain" (p. 538). This leads to a climax in which "my amazed and angry soul dropped gulf by gulf into that *horror of great darkness* which is spoken of in the Bible[19]. . . . despair upon despair, misery upon misery, fear after fear" (p. 539, italics added).

---

19. The italicized words are the very ones he used to describe his "pivot experience." It is worth quoting the biblical passage — from the Book of Job:
There are those who rebel against the light, who are not acquainted with its ways, and do not stay in its paths. The murderer rises in the dark, that he may kill the poor and needy; and in the night he is as a thief. The *eye* of the adulterer also waits for the twilight, saying "No eye will see me"; and he disguises his face. In the dark they dig through houses; by day they shut themselves up; they do not know the light. *For deep darkness is morning to all of them; for they are friends with the terror of deep darkness.* [Job 24:13–18; italics mine]
The italicized portion shows the attraction of the darkness which is light to the murderers and thiefs and adulterers and those who "dig through houses." Kipling consciously rejected this identification with the criminals (soul-murderers), yet he was constantly seeking the darkness he fled from. Note that the offending eye in the passage belongs to the adulterer, evoking the oedipal connotations of blindness.

In one of his last stories, a fable called "Unconvenanted Mercies" (written in 1927), Kipling makes Satan, the Prince of Darkness, afraid of the dark: "The glare of the halo he wore in His Own Place fought against the Horror of Great Darkness" (1927, p. 331). For Kipling, Hell was a dark place, blindness a constant threat, and light a promise of salvation, but, in a vicious cycle, a promise that leads, by way of the hellfires of sexuality and anger, back to Hell.

Eighteen months after the seventeen-year-old Kipling returned to India, Florence Garrard wrote him and ended their engagement. He commented on this in his verse. The poem of 1884 anticipated the novel he was to write in 1890 *(The Light That Failed)*—again a fascinating, but frightening woman appears who is linked with darkness, fire, and light. And she extinguishes the light:

Failure

One brought her Fire from a distant place.
And She—what should She know of it?—She took
His offering with the same untroubled look
    Of peace upon her face.

"And I have brought it of my best," quoth he,
"By barren deserts and a frozen land.
What recompense?" She could not understand,
    But let the bright light be.

"A kindly gift," the answer broke at length.
"A kindly gift. We thank you. What is this
That fiercer than all household fire is,
    And gathereth in strength?"

"Strange fires! Take them hence with you, O sir!
Presage of coming woe we dimly feel."
Sudden She crushed the embers 'neath Her Heel,—
    And all light went with Her.

[1884, p. 101]

The capitalized She's and Her's show Kipling is still dealing with the Woman.

There is another connotation of darkness: ignorance, the not knowing that both contributes to, and is the result of, soul murder. Trix uses darkness as a metaphor when writing of her parents not defining the children's situation and exposing them to desolation:

. . . we missed Papa and Mamma far more than these kind parents ever realised. They doubtless wanted to save us, and themselves, suffering by not telling us clearly beforehand that we were to be left behind, but by doing so they left us, as it were, *in the dark,* and with nothing to look forward to. [Fleming 1937, p. 171; italics mine]

Toward the end of his seven years in India, Kipling broke away from the "Family Square" by taking a job on a newspaper in Allahabad. He transferred some of his familial dependence onto the Edgar Hills, a couple with whom he stayed for some time. He was especially devoted to Mrs. Edmonia Hill (nicknamed Ted) who was thirty; Kipling was then twenty-three. The relationship doesn't seem to have been sexual or romantic. As with "Mrs. Hauskbee," Rudyard was "in thrall" to an older managing woman. Significantly, Kipling left India and his family (accompanied by the Hills) shortly after Trix became engaged to an Army Man, one of those doers Kipling so admired. The Hills were going back to "Ted's" family in America ("Ted" was an American). Kipling decided to accompany them for a roundabout journey on his way to London to further his literary career. He spent several months with Mrs. Hill's family, was attracted to her younger sister, Caroline Taylor, and then continued to London with the Hills. His Indian stories and poems had attracted some critical attention in England, but his first year in London, 1890, was a year of marvelous success, very like the success he gave Dick Heldar, the painter-hero of the 1890 novel, *The Light That Failed.* Each took London by storm with his art.

When the Hills returned to India, Kipling was again alone, although his uncles and aunts were in the background as they had been during the years in the House of Desolation. He was working intensely—most of the famous *Barrack-Room Ballads* (published in 1892) were written in London. It must have helped to banish the painful past by again experiencing those feelings of a conqueror of his first years; like Goethe and Freud, he was conquering with his pen.

The Light That Failed begins with a near-autobiographical chapter about two orphan children under the care of an "Aunty Rosa" in the House of Desolation. The first scene (we don't know if this was based on memories) reveals the two pubescent children, Maisie and Dick, playing with a forbidden loaded target pistol—an unconscious allusion to masturbation, perhaps to masturbatory heterosexual play.

Stewart (1966) calls the novel a work of genius but "a very young sick man's book. Its power comes from the irruption, for a time, of something always latent in Kipling: an almost magical fear and hatred of women—of women who are not good chaps, answering to nicknames like William and "Ted" (pp. 93–94), and, one might add, of women who desert one in one's need.

Most ironic, and it surely is unconscious irony, is the dedication poem of the book. On the surface it is a tribute to a loving mother, a mother who would never abandon her son; maternal love can follow the son anywhere:

> If I were hanged on the highest hill,
> *Mother o'mine, O mother o'mine!*
> I know whose love would follow me still,
> *Mother o'mine, O mother o'mine!*
>
> If I were drowned in the deepest sea,
> *Mother o'mine, O mother o'mine!*
> I know whose tears would come down to me,
> *Mother o'mine, O mother o'mine!*
>
> If I were damned of body and soul,
> I know whose prayers would make me whole,
> *Mother o'mine, O mother o'mine!*[20] [1890]

The poem presents the fantasy from childhood that the son will die, and the mother will be sorry, love him, and follow him. Despite this tribute to his mother, Kipling portrayed himself in the book as an orphan. Perhaps he made Dick an orphan to keep from writing a direct attack on his mother. (No doubt Dickens orphaned David Copperfield for the same reason).

Heldar's blindness begins as the child Kipling's had, with the appearance of a grey haze at the periphery of his vision. And blindness was the fate that

20. Unlike Kipling, Eugene O'Neill, fully conscious of the irony makes use of this poem in his autobiographical play, *Long Day's Journey Into Night*. In Act IV Jamie (a portrait of O'Neill's older brother), who frequently quotes Kipling, has just returned, drunk, from a whore house. He extols the comfort a whore can bring; then thinks of his mother, who has resumed her drug-taking. He says:

What's the use of coming home to get the blues over what can't be helped? All over — finished now — not a hope!" (He stops, his head nodding drunkenly, his eyes closing, then suddenly he looks up, his face hard, and quotes jeeringly)
"If I were hanged on the highest hill,
Mother o'mine, O mother o'mine!
I know whose love would follow me still. . . ." [1956, p. 161]
The terrible ambivalence of the first-born son, deserted by the mother, was the same for both Rudyard and Jamie.

the child at Lorne Lodge expected for himself. The theme is introduced in the first chapter, when the child Maisie (the transformed Flo Garrard) almost blinds Dick by accidently shooting a revolver past his face. Heldar's eyes are even more precious than usual, since he needs them for his painting.

Dick Heldar's masterpiece, which he frantically finishes as he begins to go blind is called "Melancolia" — again blackness is involved. It represents the head of a woman who has suffered terribly, but who insolently laughs at fate. Dick obviously fears and admires this Woman defying black depression; the novel covertly shows his identification with her. The portrait's features are taken from cold, selfish Maisie and the model-prostitute Bessie Broke. Bessie destroys the painting to get revenge for the scornful way Dick had treated her (as if she were a "thing" with no feelings) when he broke up her affair with Torpenhow. The female head is apparently malign; Torpenhow says, "Dick, there's a sort of *murderous, viperine* suggestion in the poise of the head that I don't understand" (p. 142; italics added). It is the Dark Woman as Soul Murderer. The novel portrays women as vampires who cannot love and who destroy men and their art. Only masculine love sustains and can be relied on.

The intensity of Kipling's sadism shows in the novel's brutality. Kincaid-Weeks has made a distinction between Kipling's treating a brutal subject or situation objectively, "and a brutal attitude or satisfaction felt toward it" (1964, p. 198). He gives as example the fine description of the brutal attack of three thousand Sudanese on a square of British soldiers, in contrast to an incident at its end that conveyed Kipling's sadism. The gouging out of an eye, the oedipal punishment, first visited on an enemy, is also the hero's fate:

> Torpenhow had gone down under an Arab whom he had tried to "collar low", and was turning over and over with his captive, feeling for the man's eyes. . . . [he] had shaken himself clear of his enemy, and rose, wiping his thumb on his trousers. The Arab, both hands to his forehead, screaming aloud, then snatched up his spear and rushed at Torpenhow, who was panting under the shelter of Dick's revolver. Dick fired twice, and the man dropped limply. His upturned face lacked one eye. [1890a, pp. 27–28]

Later, when blind, Dick asks Torpenhow (presumably the irony is to show his ability to laugh at fate, like his "Melancolia"): "D'you remember that nigger you gouged in the square? Pity you didn't keep the odd eye. It would have been useful" (p. 148).

At the end of the novel, the blind Dick (abandoned by his friends who think Maisie is caring for him) leaves England (and women) to seek out his beloved big brother Torpenhow, the eye-gouger. Earlier, when Dick's blindness becomes manifest, there is a scene between the two men that conveys homosexual contact, although it is obvious that Kipling doesn't know this:

> [Dick] made as if to leap from the bed, but Torpenhow's arms were round him, and Torpenhow's chin was on his shoulder, and his breath was squeezed out of him . . . the grip could draw no closer. Both men were breathing heavily. Dick threw his head from side to side and groaned. [Dick falls asleep after asking to hold Torpenhow's hand, and the scene ends with Torpenhow kissing] him light on the forehead, as men do sometimes kiss a wounded comrade in the hour of death, to ease his departure. [1890, pp. 145–146]

Torpenhow's attentions to Dick (as Meeta's had been to Ruddy) were maternal, protecting from the terror of the dark.

Dick returns to Egypt to die. He has an ecstatic response to arriving in time to take part in, or at least to hear, the battle. Just before finding Torpenhow, Dick again invokes mother: "What luck! What stupendous and imperial luck!" said Dick. "It's just before the battle, *mother*. Oh, God, has been most good to me!" (p. 219; italics added). The blinded child can share in the primal scene. (I have postulated a primal scene meaning for the childhood memory [age two-and-a-half] of the train fire *in Egypt,* see above.) Dick then meets Torpenhow and dies in his arms — a Liebestod.

In contrast to his hero's death in Egypt, Kipling's success in London made him feel a conqueror of Egypt. After *The Light That Failed* was finished, he sent his parents a telegram that read "Genesis 14:9." It must be known that his full name was Joseph Rudyard Kipling. Here is the passage: "Make haste to go to my father and say to him, 'Thus says your son Joseph, God has made me lord of all Egypt; come down to me; do not tarry.'" Here Kipling identifies with his namesake, the biblical prototype of parental favorites; his ambition and confidence have taken him far from the "depression (and) realized worthlessness" that he was to recall to his student audience at McGill in 1907.

In addition to his presumably platonic ties to two older, forceful, married women, "Mrs. Hauksbee" and "Ted" Hill, Kipling had emotional involvements (and these included marriage plans) with two women prior to 1891: Caroline Taylor, the sister of Mrs. Hill, and Florence Garrard, whom he used for the sister-figure Maisie in his novel. He went on to marry another sister, the sister of a man with whom he developed the deepest friendship of his life, Wolcott Balestier. Like Mrs. Hill, Balestier was an American; he came from patrician New England stock. He was a twenty-nine-year-old man of great charm and considerable talent, who made himself very influential in literary London. The middle-aged Henry James was "captivated" by his young compatriot (Edel 1962, p. 283). Balestier was in London as the agent of an American publishing house. He was trying to sign up English writers, recognizing that the impending international copyright agreement would end the literary piracy in America that so infuriated Kipling. Despite Kipling's great distrust of publishers and their agents, he immediately became a close friend of the American, and they soon embarked on the project of a mutual novel, set in America and India, *The Naulahka.* Kipling must have been impressed by Balestier's ability to get what he was after, a quality that always attracted him. (Alice James characterized Balestier after his death as "the effective and the indispensable" [Edel 1962, p. 299].) According to Carrington, "No other man ever exercised so dominating an influence over Rudyard Kipling as did Wolcott Balestier during the eighteen months of their intimacy" (1955, p. 225). Kipling soon met the whole Balestier family. An understanding seems to have been quickly agreed upon between Rudyard and the elder of Wolcott's two sisters, Caroline. Like Flo Garrard, Carrie Balestier was older than Rudyard, three years older. She had taken over a leading role in the Balestier family (the father had died) and was looking after her beloved brother Wolcott and managing his household affairs.

It is said that when Kipling's mother first saw the rather aggressive Carrie Balestier, she declared (with scant enthusiasm): "That woman is going to marry our Ruddy" (Carrington 1955, p. 229). Kipling's father's comment was, "Carrie Balestier (is) a good man spoiled" (Carrington 1955, p. 229). Little is recorded about the progress of the love affair. Partly motivated by poor health, Kipling set off by himself to travel to America, South Africa, Australia, New Zealand, and India. At this time he wrote some of his first imperialist poems, identifying with and becoming the spokesman for the empire. In December 1891, Kipling heard that Wolcott had contracted typhoid fever in Germany. When Wolcott died, Carrie sent Rudyard a cable asking him to come home. Henry James was also summoned (from London), and he arrived to find Carrie in charge of everything. He wrote of her in a letter:

> The three (Balestier) ladies came insistently to the grave . . . by far the most interesting is poor little concentrated Carrie . . . remarkable in her

force, acuteness, capacity, and courage — and in the *intense, almost manly nature* of her emotion. . . . She can do and face . . . for all three of them, anything and everything that they will have to meet now. [Carrington 1955, p. 239; italics mine]

Rudyard married Carrie eight days after he joined the family in London. Henry James gave the bride away, and wrote that Carrie was "a hard devoted capable little person whom I don't in the least understand (Kipling) marrying" (Carrington 1955, p. 241). Carrington comments, "The reason why Rudyard hurried halfway round the world to marry Wolcott's sister is bound up with his devotion to Wolcott. There is little doubt that Wolcott himself fostered the match, that Wolcott on his death bed commended the care of his family to his friend Rudyard, that Wolcott's wishes were accepted by Rudyard as obligations. . ." (p. 241). Wolcott's death was one of the great blows of Kipling's life. The feeling for the beloved brother-figure, shared with Carrie, was part of Rudyard's motivation to marry her.[21] (He was identifying here with his own worshipful sister, Trix.[22]) In addition, the "manly" Carrie would seem to have had some of the significance for Rudyard of both "Aunty Rosa" and Harry (rhymes with Carrie), with the mother and Big Brother qualities transformed from bad to good. Carrie laid down the law in the family, kept his accounts, watched over his every move; she protected him, and kept him from distractions and intruders. She had looked after her brother Wolcott with her "concentrated" intense devotion, and she transferred her management and her feelings to Kipling: "Until Rudyard's death, forty-four years later, the two were inseparable and her services to him were indispensable. . . . (she) gave Rudyard her life's endeavour and grudged him, perhaps, his faculty for withdrawing into a world of the imagination where she could not follow him" (Carrington 1955, pp. 242–243). Here was someone "whose love would follow me still . . . if I were hanged on the highest hill."

After the wedding, the couple travelled to Vermont where they stayed with Carrie's younger brother Beatty (with whom Kipling was to quarrel violently in later years). Their first child, Josephine, was born in Vermont. Kipling had fallen in love with Brattleboro, and they decided to settle there. They built a house, called Naulakha (and so evoking Wolcott). The house, says Stewart:

21. There was a "cryptic reference to his love for Carrie and his friendship for Wolcott in Chapter VII (of *The Naulahka*): 'He was to Tarvin more than a brother; that is to say, the brother of one's beloved'" (Green 1965, p. 105). Carrie was the sister "of one's beloved."

22. "Aunty Rosa" used to say (and seemed to Trix to seriously expect) that Trix would grow up to marry Harry!

had one notable feature, to be reduplicated in essentials wherever the Kiplings subsequently lived. Kipling's study had only one entrance, through a room occupied by his wife. There Carrie would sit at a desk ordering her domestic affairs, and guarding her husband against all possibility of intrusion. He could remain undisturbed for as long as he liked: sometimes perhaps, for rather longer. [1965, p. 104]

Kipling had chosen a female, benevolent big brother who could keep guard over a planned, and intermittent, solitude.

I will break off the narrative of Kipling's life at this point; I intend to continue in another paper. The years as the official poet of imperialism, of political conservatism, of hatred against the Boers and the Boches, of becoming the patron saint of the engineers and builders, of friendship with Cecil Rhodes and King George V all lie ahead. So do many years of intense creative work — his masterpiece, *Kim,* and the wonderful short stories written in his life that bring him closest to being a major artist.

Kipling was scarred by the soul murder. His intense hatred was a burden adversely affecting his art as well as his life. His marvelous talent for seeing and knowing (he was one of the greatest describers in English literature) was often inhibited by the simultaneous need to attack and to justify the established order. He escaped overt homosexuality, but married a domineering, masculine woman. In some ways this was a narcissistic choice since he too had identified with "Aunty Rosa" with a lifelong bent for the Harrys — the doers and bullies of this world. But the relationship with his wife was close and contained much happiness. Kipling was a loving father to his children, and suffered terribly when two of them died. He was subject to moods of depression and irritability, but also could laugh, occasionally even at himself, and make other laugh. He became a great success, a public figure, the most widely read author in English since Shakespeare. Following the first World War, his critical reputation plunged. The intellectual generation that grew up in the twenties was disinterested or hostile to the poet of patriotism and imperialism. Except for his books for children, he had become the "Kipling that nobody read" (Wilson 1941). There was a group of devoted readers he never lost. But the artistry of his later short stories went largely unrecognized until a revival of critical interest in his work occurred in the 1940s.

Summary and Conclusions

The psychoanalyst who is only a reader has no special source of insight. His view of the author's childhood is of necessity superficial. On the surface,

Kipling's childhood is portrayed as six years of bliss followed by six years of hell. The crucial first six years of his life must have provided Kipling with the strength to survive the soul murder in the "House of Desolation;" he says so himself. How much did these early years also provide the seeds of his undoing? The reader can only speculate, reconstructing from what Kipling wrote, and basing his shaky structure on a general knowledge of human development. Seemingly there was an overwhelming acceptance of the boy's importance. He was a wanted child, perhaps too much wanted. There was little curbing of his aggression which was freely displayed in the nursery world. Although his parents may have been distant at times, his *ayah* and bearer were physically close and very indulgent. In his memoirs and stories, Kipling depicts the narcissistic vulnerability that can accompany the grandiosity of the overindulged child. It would be important to know more about the specifics of his relationship with his parents, especially with his mysterious mother. It must be meaningful that Trix wrote of herself in Lorne Lodge as having had "no least recollection of" (1937, p. 168) her mother, while "remember(ing) that dear *ayah* known and loved all my short life in India" (1937, p. 170).

Fears about his anger and sexual feelings must have been evoked in Rudyard by the births of his sister and the stillborn sibling. These births were probably linked to fantasies about parental intercourse and the first trip to the "dark land": England. The lifelong, obsessive metaphors of light and darkness, vision and blindness show the importance of primal scene fantasies for Kipling, fantasies that had exciting and terrifying connotations. Another evidence for his fixation is his lifelong, intense curiosity and need to be "in the know" — mysteriously transmuted into his creative gifts as an observer, describer, and evoker of realistic detail.[23]

During the time of the attempted soul murder (ages six to twelve), Kipling had to face three terrible psychological dangers: the loss of his parents; the soul murder proper (the overstimulation and overwhelming rage which threatened his identity and inner stability, his self- and object-representations); castration anxiety — Rudyard was, at six, at the height of his oedipal development. At Lorne Lodge, there was the situation (perhaps prefigured in his first years in India too) of domination by a cruel, all-powerful woman, with the much-needed, protective father at a distance.

---

23. Randall Jarrell (1963) quotes a wonderful description of a drugstore from Kipling's short story, "Wireless," and adds, "One feels after reading this: well, no one ever again will have to describe a drugstore; many of Kipling's descriptive sentences have this feeling of finality" (p. 269). Elsewhere (1962) he says, "Knowing what the peoples, animals, plants, weathers of the world look like, sound like, smell like, was Kipling's *métier,* and so was knowing the worlds that could make someone else know" (p. 137).

The trauma of the desertion was made more terrible by the boy's being completely unprepared for it.[24] Suddenly, the children were in Hell. Their fate resembles that of children studied and cared for by Anna Freud who were suddenly separated from their parents during the emergency evacuations from London in the Blitz of World War II.

> The child experiences shock when he is suddenly and without preparation exposed to dangers which he cannot cope with emotionally. In the case of evacuation the danger is represented by the sudden disappearance of all the people he knows and loves. Unsatisfied longing produces in him a state of tension which is felt as shock. . . . In reality it is the very quickness of the child's break with the mother which contains all the dangers of abnormal consequences. Long drawn-out separation may bring more visible pain but it is less harmful because it gives the child time to accompany the events with his reactions, to work through his own feelings over and over again, to find outward expressions for his state of mind, i.e., to abreact slowly. Reactions which do not even reach the child's consciousness do incalculable harm to his normality. [A. Freud 1939–1945, vol. 3, pp. 208–209]

Rudyard, at six, was more able than the three-year-old Trix to face the loss, since images of both parents and the predominantly loving servants were firmly established as part of the structure of his mind. He had achieved "object constancy;"[25] as long as he could remember and think, his parents couldn't be completely lost. He could use his mind and his creative imagination to fight against that part of himself that turned toward, gave into,

24. I am grateful to Drs. Charlotte and Joseph Lichtenberg for pointing out to me the instance of soul muder in Kipling's short story "Lisbeth" (from *Plain Tales from the Hills,* 1888a). The story shows the destructive effect of not saying goodbye and lying about a desertion, seemingly with good motive, at the instigation of a bad woman. It reflects Rudyard's childhood experience.

25. About the crucial attainment of object constancy, Anna Freud says, "It is only after object constancy . . . has been reached that the external absence of the object is substituted for, at least in part, by the presence of an internal image which remains stable; on the strength of this achievement temporary separation can be lengthened, commensurate with the advances in object constancy" (1965, p. 65). Speaking of a three-and-a-half year old (that is a child of about Trix's age where object constancy is not firmly established), she states:

> Distress and *desolation* are inevitable [in the young child who needs to separate from the mother on going to nursery school] . . . only if developmental considerations are neglected. . . . if the child has reached object constancy at least . . . separation from the mother is less upsetting. Even then, the change has to be introduced gradually, in small doses, the periods of independence must not be too long, and, in the beginning, return to the mother should be open to choice. [1965, pp. 89–90; italics mine]

and identified with Aunty Rosa and Harry.[26] And his power to know and to remember was specifically attacked by their brainwashing techniques. Reading and writing were crucial skills, and reading (so tied to the forbidden seeing) became the subject of conflict and symptoms. Apparently there were occasional letters from the parents which helped reinforce the children's memories.[27] Rudyard could fight his passive entrapment with an active ordering of, and playing with, the bad reality in fantasies and memories (with Trix as his eager listener-participant). When Rudyard was small, his father had written a nursery rhyme that had consoled him after an attack by a hen. In Lorne Lodge, Rudyard could identify with his protective father's humor and creativity, to try to ward off the attacks by the Woman. There was, after his near-blindness and the breakdown, a flowering of Kipling's creative writing in the predominantly male atmosphere of school. He emerged as a writer and poet, specifically as a master of rhyme. The ambition to become a writer crystallized in adolescence at a time when there must have been a renewal of conflict over masturbation. He was using the writer's hand to keep away (to use the metaphor from his childhood memories) the severed child's hand. In his struggle with his fear of and fascination for castration, he needed to identify with his father to try to conquer the bad Woman—to conquer her in himself, and outside himself.

Since Rudyard was in the midst of his oedipal development he was subject to intense shifting ambivalence toward both parents. The desertion and subsequent sadomasochistic overstimulation made for libidinal regression

26. Trix: "Ruddy at six always understood the realness of things, and his parents knew that his frequent phrase, when three years old, 'Don't disturv me, I'm finking', had a very real meaning" (1937, p. 170).

27. One would like to know more about these letters. They could have meant a lifeline for Rudyard's identity and contributed to his own drive to be a writer. In his memoirs Kipling describes his writing as specifically motivated toward communication with his parents: "I think I can with truth say that those two made for me the only public for whom then I had any regard whatever till their deaths, in my forty-fifth year" (1937, p. 89). How often did the parents write? What did they say? Were the children allowed to read the letters or answer them? In *Something of Myself*, Kipling tells of the (perhaps fictional "parting in the dawn with Father and Mother, who said that I must learn quickly to read and write so that they might send me letters and books" (1937, pp. 4–5). The books sent by his father are mentioned by Kipling; but at six the parents had not yet taught him to read. Indeed he resisted learning from Aunty Rosa and this also could have involved spite against his parents. Trix tells of Aunty Rosa treating as a crime the children's "crying like 'silly babies' when she read us letters from Bombay" (1937, p. 168). But neither Rudyard or Trix has more to say about the existence or the impact of what should have been a vital correspondence.

and a terrifying access of rage. This enhanced his parricidal (especially patricidal) impulses at a time when the boy needed good parents desperately to fight off his own bad inner imagos. Anna Freud is describing children of about Ruddy's age (six) when she says of the desertion involved in school phobias:

> . . . the distress experienced at separation from mother, parents or home is due to an excessive ambivalence towards them. The conflict between love and hate of the parents can be tolerated by the child only in their reassuring presence. In their absence, the hostile side of the ambivalence assumes frightening proportions, and the ambivalently loved figures of the parents are clung to so as to save them from the child's own death wishes, aggressive fantasies, etc. [1965, p. 113]

This need to preserve the internal images of good parents, so intense for the wartime evacuees at the Hampstead nurseries where the parental substitutes were good and understanding, becomes desperate under conditions of soul murder, where hatred is deliberately cultivated. And how devastating if the parental substitutes, with the fanaticism of the religiously righteous and the power of concentration camp commandants, suppress rather than understand the child's thoughts and feelings, and operate to prevent the child from registering what has happened.

The subjection to Aunty Rosa as the Woman—with Harry as her phallic extension—threatened Rudyard's masculiniity. He needed a strong father to take her away. Kipling continued to seek for fathers and older brothers in his work and in his life. The fear of the Woman, the need to submit to the phallic parent, the need to deny his parricidal urges, made homosexuality a continuing danger. The ongoing good external relationship with his father in later life must have helped stave off his strong latent homosexuality. (One can see in his life and work a conflict-ridden range of wishes involving wanting to be, and to have—a man, a phallic woman [the ranee-tiger from childhood], and a woman.)

The presence of his sister at Lorne Lodge helped strengthen Kipling's masculinity and also his identity. Toward her he was able to feel and act like the protective parent that both so needed. Trix was grateful for and craved his care. She was the living link to his home, his parents, and his past. His memory and his gift for storytelling allowed him to become the author of, and Trix his primal audience for, a Family Romance based on real events. He could identify with Mother and Father and the *ayah,* and so both children could hold on to them.[28] Trix's devotion continued the love from and for a female that was not swept away by Rudyard's hatred for the Woman. Together the two children could retreat from the desolation and persecution of their daily life to the sanctuary created by the boy's imagination. To create a wonderful and sometimes a terrible world for abandoned children made Rudyard a god who need not fear abandonment. He could know what was what, reward the deserving and punish the wicked. Throughout his long writing career he was obsessed with the family romance,[29] and what began with Trix continued in his books.

I have speculated that there may have been sexual play between Trix and Rudyard which had some saving effect on his masculinity. He did manage a heterosexual life, despite his aversion for women. There was no real loving sexual woman in his early fiction. Sex was never treated as joyous; at best it was a guilt-ridden pleasure followed by punishment.

The effects of the soul murder on Kipling's subsequent life were intermittently present and complicated by a struggle against them. There was a need to repeat the sadomasochistic experiences in the House of Desolation. Kipling's predominant position as victim had enforced an identification with the persecutors, presumably out of the child's need for "dear kind God." The destructive hatred had to be turned toward others; he required and found enemies: strangers. Boers, Boches, "the lesser breeds outside the law." But he could also remember what it was to have been the victim, and in some of his best work his empathy for and identification with the underdog catches the reader's emotions. He was successful in bringing to sympathetic life the Indians and the Lama in *Kim,* the natives in many of the early stories, the British privates and noncommissioned officers in his prose and verse, and, above all, the abandoned and neglected children.

But persecutor raged against victim within Kipling; making him subject to attacks of depression. Just as he split the images of himself, he needed to split the mental pictures of his parents into good and bad. With intolerable

28. The sharing of the past in the House of Desolation is reflected in Kipling's two collections of historical tales for children: *Puck of Pook's Hill* (1906) and *Rewards and Fairies* (1910). In these stories exciting scenes from the history of England and America are told to two children, Dan and Una, brother and sister. Under the magic guidance of Puck, they meet people from the past who observed and participated in the events. So brother and sister travel through history together, denying their alienation and exile from the great figures and happenings of the past; together they master the primal scene.

29. Randall Jarrell: "To Kipling the world was a dark forest full of families; so that when your father and mother leave you in the forest to die, the wolves that come to eat you are always Father Wolf and Mother Wolf, your real father and mother; and you are—as not even the little wolves ever quite are—their real son. The family romance, the two families of the Hero, have so predominant a place in no other writer" (1962, p. 148).

rage aimed against those he loved and needed, he was forced to deny his hatred. The denial—the need not to know—existed alongside his driving curiosity. The denial made the split registration possible: contradictory images and ideas could exist side by side in his mind without blending, as with Orwell's doublethink. This kind of compartmentalization is a way of dealing with overwhelming feeling, but it is paid for by sacrificing the power of synthesis that is needed for joy, love, and the feeling of identity.[30] The ease with which this splitting was possible is not entirely explainable by the defensive need to ward off hatred and fear from the mental images of his good parents. Even before the assumption of parental roles by the bad Holloways, Kipling had lived through the intense experiences involved in having two sets of parents—white and black, light and dark—as a child in India. It was common in the British colonies for the servants in the family to be closer to the children than the natural parents. The mere existence of the complicated split mental representations of self and parents doesn't involve pathology. That depends on how the splits are used. The crucial question is: can the contradictory mental representations be synthesized, can they be brought together and taken apart again so that they can be worked with in a flow of thought and feeling; or, must they exist for most or all of the time isolated and beyond criticism, as with Kipling (see Shengold 1974a). Beneath the fragile seeming clarity of the bad Aunty Rosa and Harry, and the good Mother and the good Father, was a terrible ambivalent fragmentation and confusion. This is beautifully described by Jarrell: "As it was, his world had been torn in two and he himself torn in two: for under the part of him that extenuated everything, blamed for nothing, there was certainly a part that extenuated nothing, blamed for everything—a part he never admitted, most especially not to himself" (1962, p. 144).

There is a depiction of "being torn in two" in madness, or at least in a dream of madness, in a poem called "The Mother's Son" that Kipling (1928) wrote when he was in his mid-sixties. The speaker is in an asylum and is looking into a mirror, that metaphor for split images.

---

30. Another evidence for splitting can be seen in Kipling's attribution of responsibility for his writing not to himself, but to his Daemon: "My Daemon was with me in the Jungle Books, Kim, and both Puck books, and good care I took to walk delicately lest he should withdraw" (1937, p. 210). Jarrell (1963) describes Kipling as possessed "by both the Daemon he tells you about, who writes some of the stories for him, and the demons he doesn't tell you about, who wrote some others" (p. 140). Kipling talks of having a "contract" with his Daemon (which evokes soul murder á la Schreber) and gives this advice to writers: "*Note here.* When your Daemon is in charge, do not try to think consciously. Drift, wait, and obey" (1937, p. 210). Kipling describes here the creative benefits of passive subjection to his Daemon; he was splitting off what it meant to be in subjection to that "Devil-boy," Harry.

I have a dream — a dreadful dream —
  A dream that is never done.
I watch a man go out of his mind,
  And he is My Mother's Son.

And it was *not* disease or crime
  Which got him landed there,
But because They laid on My Mother's Son
  More than a man could bear.

            .   .   .   .

They broke his body and his mind
  And yet They made him live,
And They asked more of My Mother's Son
  Than any man could give.

            .   .   .   .

And no one knows when he'll get well
  So, there he'll have to be.
And, 'spite of his beard in the looking-glass,
  I know that man is me!
                               [1928, pp. 398–399]

Here the blaming of the mother is not conscious; it appears in the repeated characterization of the self as "My Mother's Son," with Kipling's characteristic accusatory capitalization. The "too-much-ness" is attributed to an impersonal bad They (again capitalized), a projection of the bad self and transference of the bad parents, as in the familiar *They* of the paranoid. For Kipling it means: not me, not the Mother or the Father, but the Holloways. The poem's last line — "spite of his beard in the looking-glass" (vile verse!) — implies that the bearded man is looking for a beardless self in the glass. Kipling developed facial hair very early. The adult victim of unbearable strain is surely expecting to see the image of himself as a boy in the House of Desolation.

   Kipling was most comfortable when the separation of the split mental images operated to suppress hatred. This could happen when he was active and in control, at one with his Daemon so that his creative energy could flow; and when in life he felt he had achieved that perfect ordering of things, that discipline that ruled out sudden desolation: the good could not suddenly become the bad. Here is the image with which he ends *The Jungle Books* — he had begun them with Mowgli abandoned to the mercy of the tiger. Animals and men take part in a magnificent review before the Viceroy, and a native officer responds to a stranger's asking how it was done:

> The animals obey, as the men do. Mule, horse, elephant, or bullock, he obeys his driver, and the driver his sergeant, and the sergeant his lieutenant, and the lieutenant his captain, and the captain his major, and the major his colonel, and the colonel his brigadier commanding three regiments, and the brigadier his general, who obeys the Viceroy, who is the servant of the Empress. Thus it is done. [1894, p. 421]

In such a well-regulated world, the Empress, the Great Mother, watches over all. The Jungle has lost its terror.

I have described an attempt at soul murder directed against Rudyard Kipling as a child. His years in the House of Desolation left effects that continued to inhibit Kipling's ability to feel joy and to love, and that sometimes flawed his art. Yet, the soul murder was far from completely effected: Kipling's identity was preserved, and he became a great artist. The struggle to fight off the soul murder and its effects strengthened him, and gave him motive and subject matter for his writing. I have connected those terrible years of his childhood to his flaws and to his greatness. Kipling's story touches on the mysteries of the origin of mental sickness and of creativity. The explorer must be prepared for contradiction and complexity.

References

Burnham, D. (1971). *August Strindberg's Need-Fear Dilemmas.* Unpublished manuscript.

Carrington, C. (1955). *Rudyard Kipling. His Life and Work.* Middlesex: Penguin Books, 1970.

Dickens, C. (1849–50). *David Copperfield.* New York: Dodd and Mead, 1936.

Dobree, B. (1967). *Rudyard Kipling.* London: Oxford University Press.

Dostoyevsky, F. (1880). *The Brothers Karamazov.* Trans. C. Garnett. New York: Modern Library.

Edel, L. (1962). *Henry James. Vol. 3. The Middle Years. 1882–1895.* New York: Lippincott.

von Feuerbach, A. (1832). *Caspar Hauser.* London: Simpkin and Marchall, 1834.

Fleming, A. (1937). Some childhood memories of Rudyard Kipling. *Chambers Journal,* March, pp. 168–173.

Forster, J. (1873). *The Life of Charles Dickens.* London: Cecil Palmer, 1928.

Freud, A. (1939–45). Infants without families; reports on the Hampstead nurseries. *Collected Works* vol. 3. New York: International Universities Press.

———(1965). *Normality and Pathology in Childhood.* New York: International Universities Press.

Freud, S. (1911). Psychoanalytic notes on an autobiographic account of a case of paranoia (dementia paranoides). *Standard Edition* 12:3–86.

———(1917). A childhood recollection from "Dichtung und Wahrheit." *Standard Edition* 17:145–156.

Green, R. (1965). *Kipling and the Children.* London: Elek Books.

Ibsen, H. (1896). *John Gabriel Borkman.*

———*Ibsen, Collected Works,* vol. 11, trans. W. Archer, pp. 179–353. New York: Scribners, 1926.

———*When We Dead Awaken and Three Other Plays,* trans. M. Meyer, pp. 217–302. Garden City: Anchor Books, 1960.

———*Last Plays of Henrik Ibsen,* trans. A. Paulson, pp. 293–374. New York: Bantam Books, 1962.

Jacobs, B. (1969). "Psychic murder" and characterization in Strindberg's *The Father.* In *Scandinavica,* 1969.

Jarrell, R. (1962). On preparing to read Kipling. In *Kipling and the Critics,* ed. E. Gilbert, pp. 133–149. New York: New York Universities Press, 1965.

———(1963). The English in England. In *The Third Book of Criticism,* pp. 279–294. New York: Farrar, Straus and Giroux, 1969.

Kincaid-Weeks, M. (1964). Vision in Kipling's Novels. In *Kipling's Mind and Art,* ed. A. Rutherford, pp. 197–234. London: Oliver and Boyd, 1964.

Kipling, R. Unless Otherwise Stated, References are to the Volumes in *Complete Works of Rudyard Kipling,* Burwash Edition. New York: Doubleday and Doran, 1941.

———(1884). Failure. *Complete Works,* vol. 28, p. 101.

———(1885). The Betrothed. *Complete Works* vol. 25, pp. 97–99.

———(1888a). Plain Tales From the Hills. *Complete Works* vol. 1.

———(1888b). Baa Baa, Black Sheep. *Complete Works* vol. 3, pp. 281–316.

———(1888c). His Majesty the King. *Complete Works* vol. 3, pp. 317–332.

———(1889). In Partibus. *Complete Works* vol. 28, pp. 171–174.

———(1890a). *The Light That Failed.* Middlesex: Penguin Books, 1970.

———(1890b). The Rhyme of the Three Captains. *Complete Works* vol. 25, pp. 255–260.

————(1890c). The End of the Passage. *Complete Works* vol. 4, pp. 169–196.

————(1892). Barrack-Room Ballads. *Complete Works* vol. 25, pp. 163–214.

————(1894). The Jungle Books. *Complete Works* vol. 11.

————(1895a). William the Conqueror. *Complete Works* vol. 6, pp. 165–206.

————(1895b). The Brushwood Boy. *Complete Works* vol. 6, pp. 329–370.

————(1897a). The Vampire. *Complete Works* vol. 28, pp. 199–200.

————(1897b). Captains Courageous. *Complete Works* vol. 16, pp. 1–175.

————(1899). Stalky and Co. *Complete Works* vol. 14, pp. xi–378.

————(1901). Kim. *Complete Works* vol. 16, pp. 181–525.

————(1907). Values in Life. *Complete Works* vol. 24, pp. 17–22.

————(1909). The House Surgeon. *Complete Works* vol. 8, pp. 533–566.

————(1913). Egypt of the Magicians. *Complete Works* vol. 19, pp. 229–310.

————(1927). Uncovenanted Mercies. *Complete Works* vol. 10, pp. 325–348.

————(1928). The Mother's Son. *Complete Works* vol. 27, pp. 398–399.

————(1935). Hymn of Breaking Strain. *Complete Works* vol. 28, pp. 298–299.

————(1937). *Something of Myself*. London: MacMillan, 1964.

Mahler, M. (1972). On the first three subphases of the separation-individuation process. *International Journal of Psycho-Analysis* 53:333–338.

Niederland, W. (1959a). The "miracled-up" world of Schreber's childhood. *Psychoanalytic Study of the Child* 14:383–413. Reprinted in volume 2 of this series.

————(1959b). Schreber, father and son. *Psychoanalytic Quarterly* 28:151–169. Reprinted in volume 2 of this series.

————(1960). Schreber's father. *Journal of the American Psychoanalytic Association* 8:492–499.

————(1963). Further data and memorabilia pertaining to the Schreber case. *International Journal of Psycho-Analysis* 44:201–207.

Old Testament: Revised Standard Version. (1952). New York: Nelson.

O'Neill, E. (1956). *A Long Day's Journey Into Night*. New Haven: Yale University Press.

Orwell, G. (1949). *1984*. New York: Harcourt, Brace, Jovanovich.

Partridge, E. (1961). *A Dictionary of Slang and Unconventional English*. Vol. 2. London: Routledge and Kegan Paul.

Schreber, D. (1903). *Memoirs of My Nervous Illness*. Trans. MacAlpine and Hunter. London: Dawson, 1955.

Shengold, L. (1963). The parent as sphinx. *Journal of the American Psycho-analytic Association* 11:725–751.

———(1967). The effects of overstimulation: rat people. *International Journal of Psycho-Analysis* 48:403–413.

———(1971). More about rats and rat people. *International Journal of Psycho-Analysis* 52:277–268. Reprinted in volume 2 of this series.

———(1974a). The metaphor of the mirror. *Journal of the American Psychoanalytic Association* 22:97–115.

———(1974b). A Review of "Soul Murder: Persecution in the Family" by Morton Schatzman, M.D. *International Journal of Psychoanalytic Psychotherapy* 3:366–373.

Sophocles. Oedipus Rex. In *Nine Greek Dramas,* trans. E. Plumptre. New York: Collier and Son, 1909.

Stewart, J. I. M. (1966). *Rudyard Kipling.* New York: Dodd and Mead.

Strindberg, A. (1887). Soul murder (apropos "Rosmersholm"). Trans. W. Johnson. *The Drama Review* 13:113–118, 1968.

Trilling, L. (1943). Kipling. In *Kipling's Mind and Art,* ed. A. Rutherford, pp. 85–96. London: Oliver and Boyd, 1964.

Whitman, W. (1855). *Leaves of Grass.* New York: Modern Library, 1921.

Wilson, E. (1941). The Kipling that nobody read. In *Kipling's Mind and Art,* ed. A. Rutherford, pp. 17–69. London: Oliver and Boyd, 1964.

Chapter 7

THE ADOPTION THEME IN EDWARD ALBEE'S
TINY ALICE and *THE AMERICAN DREAM*

JULES GLENN, M.D.

Although adopted children exhibit a variety of personality structures, certain conscious and unconscious preoccupations, strivings, and conflicts appear in them with great frequency. This is not surprising, since the fact of adoption calls forth a limited number of parental responses and consequent reactions from the children. Thus, although the approved style of dealing with adoption has changed from time to time, each method necessarily involves complications. I do not wish to imply that all adopted children encounter the same difficulties, or that the difficulties, when they exist, are crippling. Being adopted, however, does influence personality development, and if the child becomes an artist, the resultant fantasies may reveal themselves in his creative products. Moreover, the adopted child's wishes and defenses may serve as the wellspring of his artistic creativity.

In this paper I intend to show the role which the adoption theme plays in some works by Edward Albee, who was in fact adopted at the age of two weeks. In *Tiny Alice* (1965), this theme appears in disguised form. The play's main character, Julian, acts as if he were an adopted child caught up in the confusions and cravings typical of many such children. Other features of the play also reflect the adopted child's fantasies. I shall also discuss Albee's *The American Dream,* in which adoption is openly portrayed.

I shall draw on the scant analytic literature and some unpublished reports to pull together the few facts that analysts have established about the psychology of adopted children. While there have been no published analyses of adopted children, a sufficient number have been studied in psychotherapy and by observations of families to allow some generalizations about the characteristics of adopted children (Schechter 1960, 1967, Peller 1963, Blum 1969, Blos 1963). I have confirmed or supplemented the descriptions in the literature with my own experience and that of the members of a study group that meets regularly in Great Neck, New York. Two reports on the analyses of adopted children have been very illuminating as well (Daunton 1973, Freeman 1967). The latter's chapter on the "Abandoned Doll" is a report of an analysis conducted by Walter Stewart. Swartz (1973) and Kernberg (1974) also provided unpublished confirmatory data.

Most adopted children, either consciously or unconsciously, know about their adoption. Generally, the new parents tell the child that he is adopted; even if they do not, the child eventually often suspects or overhears the truth. Certainly, the age at which the parent tells the child as well as his method of doing so will influence the child's reaction.

Once the child knows of his adoption, he is faced with the fact that he has two sets of parents. He may well develop mental representations that encompass real and imagined traits of both sets. He may have difficulty differentiating between the "real" and "false" parents, ascertaining which is which. In trying to clarify these confusions the child may have to sacrifice reality testing, may deny or repress the existence of one set of parents. Wieder (1974) has made the additional suggestion that the child's being told of his adoption reinforces fears of abandonment that are already present. Defenses against this anxiety include denial and result in a disturbance of the sense of reality. This may be the case especially if the adoptive parent insists, as he sometimes does, that he is the biological parent, or if the child is commanded to forget or not to mention his biological origins.

The parent may intentionally or inadvertently tell the child falsehoods about his adoption. He may describe, as has been recommended, how the child was chosen by him. He may say that the original parents are not alive or invent exalted motives for the real mother's surrender of her baby. If, as is often the case, the child is aware of the fabrication, he may himself develop a need to lie, with the concomitant superego defect. Here the child identifies with the lying parent and may take revenge by creating falsehoods in ways that hurt the parent. Or the child may react to parent falsifications with hyperbole, imagining the adults to be totally corrupt.

The child may build fantasies on the fact that adoption involves legal machinery and that money is paid to a lawyer, an agency, or to the mother herself, either for her medical care or in frank payment for the baby. He may feel that an illicit exchange has been carried out behind his back and without his control, knowledge, or approval. Hatred for the deserting parents may be fused with fury at the adoptive parents, who, he imagines, have stolen or bought him in a crass and unfeeling way, who consider him a posession rather than a person. He may fear that, having been deserted once, he may be again. More specifically, he may be returned to his original parents. The adopted child's fantasy that he has actually killed his parents (Rosner 1974) may stem not only from his hatred, but also from a defensive need to believe that he has actually gotten rid of them, that he has not been the passive abandoned child (Wieder 1974).

The adopted child often correctly concludes that his situation resulted from his adoptive parents' inability to have children. He then becomes especially preoccupied with the question of how children are born and conceived, with the possible causes of infertility. Illogically, as if he had inherited his adoptive parents' defects, he wonders whether he will be capable of producing a child; he identifies with the sterile parent. The child may attribute the lack of children to parental virginity, impotence, or frigidity.

As is generally true, a family romance fantasy (Freud 1909) occurs, but it often takes an idiosyncratic form in the adopted child. In the usual family romance fantasy, the child imagines that he is adopted and that his real parents were truly exalted personages. He was left with a poor family, but one day will rejoin his wealthy or regal biological parents. Such fantasies serve a number of purposes. They console the child for disappointments in his parents; they relieve his guilt by eliminating the incest barrier; they act defensively against the hostility and incestuous feeling to the parents. The form of the adopted child's family romance, however, is colored by what he has surmised or heard about his biological parents. Thus, he frequently pictures his biological family as low people, poor, and even depraved. His father and mother may not have been married, and hence he is illegitimate. Identification with such parental object representations may lead to self-denigration as well as to wishes to create illegitimate children.

I have mentioned that hatred for the parents who have deserted him may be transferred to the adoptive parents. There may be a concomitant idealization of the biological parents with a strong desire to return to them. Being adopted, he may feel weak, deficient, evil, castrated, or lacking in identity. Hearing that his natural parents have died may lead to identification with the deceased and tendencies to self-injury.

When a child's insatiable curiosity is frustrated by parental and societal reluctance to have him know his real father and mother, he may actively search for them when he is older, or he may attach himself to biological parent substitutes as well as surrogates for his adoptive parents. So intense and frequent is the desire of adopted children to find their original parents, to establish their continuity with the past and their present and future identity, that an organization has been formed by adopted people to overthrow the legal barriers to receiving information about their origins.[1]

Knowing that his adoptive parents are not his natural parents may create special sexual problems because the child—and even the parents—may feel that incest is permissible. Temptations may thus be greater, but despite relaxation of restraint, the superego will probably remain intolerant of real or fantasied breaches of the incest taboo, and the child still feels that he must be punished for his wishes. Indeed he may come to believe that he was adopted as punishment for his incestuous desires.

I wish to emphasize again what I have described are common confusions and concerns of adopted children, not universal configurations. Nor do the conscious and unconscious solutions of the children to these conundrums necessarily lead to pathology. Indeed, in describing the influence of an adopted child's fantasies on his plays, I am emphasizing one individual's highly adaptive utilization of his concerns.

Whether the conflicts and fantasies I have described develop, and how intense they will be, depends upon a number of factors. These include when, how, and how often the child is told that he is adopted. If the fantasies described can serve a defensive function against other, perhaps more pressing, conflicts, they will become more important. Telling the child early and repeatedly that he has been chosen by his parents, as has been recommended in the past, may lead the child to feel that he is special, an exception, and cause him to develop superego defects. Regardless of how he is told, however, his "sense of identity . . . is insecure at best" (A. Freud 1972, p. 624).

Tiny Alice

This strange and beautiful play has been denounced as obscure by many critics. The enigma of the drama diminishes when one recognizes the confusions and conflicts of the adopted child which are hidden within it. Although

---

1. In Scotland the child at seventeen may achieve legal access to his original birth certificate (McWhinnie 1969).

we may elucidate the author's private unconscious symbolism, this is not necessarily the interpretation that Albee intended; he has not disclosed this meaning, contending that it is "quite clear."

The play opens with a scene of vicious confrontation between two former schoolmates, an attorney and a cardinal whom the attorney is visiting. We first encounter the lawyer alone, playfully talking gibberish to his host's caged birds, two cardinals. The ecclesiastic enters, chides his friend, and the two men engage each other in a witty and sarcastic verbal brawl in which despicable traits of each are revealed.

The lawyer has come as an emissary for a Miss Alice, a wealthy woman who wants to donate vast amounts of money, millions of dollars, to the church. The lawyer informs the cardinal that Brother Julian, the private secretary of the cardinal, will be sent for to make arrangements for the delivery of the money.

Brother Julian, a devout lay Catholic brother and apparently an intimate of the cardinal, arrives at Miss Alice's mysterious mansion. A dollhouse, identical with the huge mansion, occupies a prominent place in the library. When a conflagration erupts in the life-sized house, an identical fire burns in the model. When the larger fire is extinguished, the fire in the model disappears. Similarly, lights appear in the smaller house when the larger one is illuminated.

Although the lawyer has requested that Julian be the emissary, the cardinal tells him that he had "chosen" him for this "high honor." Hearing this, the attorney scoffs: "He. Chosen. You." Julian's exact duties are unclear. He is "to take care of odds and ends." Eventually the fact emerges that he is to have an affair with Miss Alice and then marry her; he is to be sacrificed in order that the church may receive the large grant. But Julian is not aware of the plans; he accepts the strange happenings naively and without question.

Julian is courted by the seductive Miss Alice. He reveals to her certain events of the six years of his life that are missing from the dossier that her associates have prepared regarding him. Julian had already revealed to the butler that he had himself placed in a mental home because he could not reconcile himself "to the chasm between the nature of God and the use to which men put . . . God." He contracts God the creator and God created by man. As a result of his doubts, his faith "abandoned" him.

While in the hospital, Julian experienced hallucinations and could not differentiate between the real and the imaginary. Hence, he could not be certain whether he had had sexual relations with a patient who fancied herself to be the Virgin Mary. After their possible intercourse the woman "ascended or descended into an ecstasy, the substance of which was that she was with child . . . that she was pregnant with the Son of God." Actually, she suffered from a uterine malignancy and soon died.

In the second act the lawyer and the butler discuss a conspiracy to take Julian from the cardinal in exchange for $100,000,000 a year for twenty years. Julian is to be married to Alice or to Miss Alice, "one through the other." There are indications that the matter is more mysterious still, when occurrences such as identical fires in the mansion and the model adumbrate strange events to come. That both butler and lawyer have been Miss Alice's lovers and that they direct and supervise her activities further confuse the audience and arouse its expectations. The mystery heightens as Miss Alice succeeds in seducing Julian, saying, "You will be hers [Alice's]; you will sacrifice yourself to her."

In the final act we learn that Julian is to marry, be sacrificed to Alice; not Miss Alice, but an unseen being for whom Miss Alice is merely a surrogate. Miss Alice says, "You have married *her* . . . through me . . . you felt her warmth through me, touched her lips through my lips . . . wrapped yourself in her wings . . . your mouth on her hair, the voice in your ear, hers not mine, all hers; her. You are hers." In fact, the lawyer states, "We are surrogates; *our* task is done now."

But Julian must remain with Alice. The cardinal, the lawyer, the butler, and Miss Alice each call on him to "accept," to make "an act of faith." When Julian rebels against this "mockery" of religion and law, the attorney shoots him. All but Julian leave the building.

Julian lies dying, awaiting Alice. Confusing God with Alice, he at last accepts her, as he is engulfed by the shadow of a great presence, and dies in a crucified state.

Adoption and Tiny Alice

The analytic literature contains a single paper that deals with this uncanny, moving masterpiece (Markson 1966); it does not even mention the possibility that Albee's experiences as an adopted child may have influenced his imagery and imagination. Markson finds a plethora of evidence for oedipal inspirations; and of course these are present in *Tiny Alice* as in most or all creative works. He sees the play as "an intense representation of a chaotic passively resolved oedipal conflict" (p. 20). Blum (1969: Chapter 8 of this volume), on the other hand, has traced the adoption motif in Albee's *Who's Afraid of Virginia Woolf?,* but has chosen to omit the fact that Albee is an adopted child.

We see at once that Julian is in a position similar to that of the adopted child. An arrangement has been made for him to be transferred from one family to another, from the family of the Catholic Church and God the Father to the Alice household. This is being done for money, and it is arranged without his knowledge and approval. The latter, of course, is inevitable in most adoptions, since they take place when the children are infants. In the play the transfer, which uses legal machinery, is arranged by the giver and receiver and carries religious sanction. When Julian realizes what is being done, he objects and calls it a mockery; religion and law are being used illicitly. But he is told that he must accept the new situation, the new parent substitute, who is equated with Mother Mary and God the Father. Miss Alice at one point embraces Julian in a Pietà-like posture. In the end Julian calls the engulfing Alice "God."

The imagery of the mysterious transfer from one family to another is foreshadowed and reinforced by repeated references to surrogates and doubles. The play opens with the lawyer talking to *two* cardinals, birds that in turn symbolize their ecclesiastic counterparts. The huge mansion and its model can be understood as symbols for the two mothers, the original one and the substitute that is confused with the biological parent. Early in the play the millionaire's lawyer contends that he "learned never to confuse the representation of a thing with the thing itself" (p. 39). Nevertheless, he and the others are uncertain about the reality of the mansion and the dollhouse. The miniature is said to be a model, but the larger one is called a replica. Later Julian learns to his dismay that the visible Miss Alice is not the authentic one. Rather the unseen Alice is the real Alice. As the lawyer, referring to those who have arranged the marriage, says, "We are her surrogates" (p. 156).

The double image appears again in Julian's disillusionment with God. He distinguishes between God the creator and the God that men have created, as the adopted child tries to separate the representations of his biological creators and the parents that men have arranged for him. In the end he fails to separate the true God and Alice.

Julian comes to feel uncomfortable in Alice's mansion. His former identity is interfered with as he indulges in pleasures and temptations. He feels that he is being tested. Like the adopted child he must be "good" to be accepted, but is uncertain of his allegiances, unclear as to which identification to adhere to, unable to consolidate the old and the new.

When Julian objects to his new family and wants to return to his established relationship with the cardinal, he is prohibited from doing so. Rather than let him return, his guardians shoot him, as they tell him he must accept and have faith. Certainly, it takes great faith to believe that adoptive parents are true parents and can be trusted. As I have pointed out, the child sometimes sacrifices reality testing as he uses denial to support this belief. Indeed, the uncertainty in separating reality and fantasy is very prominent throughout the play. In addition to the very real element of the audience's confusion, we find that Julian was hospitalized for a psychosis. He had not merely lost his faith; he also lost his capacity for reality testing.

I have noted that the adopted child often ponders over parental inability to have children. He wonders: are they sterile, defective? Do they have intercourse? This preoccupation appears in Julian's relationship with the mental patient who thought she was the Virgin Mary and who bore not a child but a cancer. His uncertainty about their having had sexual relations reflects the adopted child's uncertainties about his parents' sexual activities, internalized and applied to Julian. And the Virgin Mary, like adoptive parents, can have a child without intercourse.

The adopted child may be plagued by lack of clarity as to whether incest is permitted. Who is the forbidden object? Julian showed oedipal desires as he was attracted to a type of mother, the patient who fancied herself Virgin Mary, and later to Miss Alice who posed as Mary. His uncertainty about his sexual activity with the patient is overdetermined: it also suggests the defensive blurring that one may experience in trying to recall prohibited acts or wishes.

Julian's relationship with Miss Alice is interesting for a number of additional reasons. Marriage to her is equated with adoption, that is, being transferred from one family to another as part of a contract. (As such, it is tolerated incest.) There is a sadomasochistic tinge to their relationship, when she invites him to use his crop on her. Possibly, this feature combines the punishment for incest and the regression from oedipal fantasies.

Julian is timid about marrying Miss Alice, but he is terrified about his union with the real Alice. It is as if the latter were the real mother, the unseen mother, with whom he must not unite, as intercourse with her is truly incestuous. Indeed, he is killed before he can consummate this marriage. Quite possibly there is a negative oedipal, a homosexual, implication here, in that Alice represents the father he wished to fuse with. There are hints in the play that the attachment between the cardinal and the lay brother is more than platonic.

Folklore holds that incest breeds monsters. This fantasy appears, I believe, in the production of a cancer following intercourse between Julian and the patient who imagined she was Virgin Mary.

We can find other derivatives of the adopted child's picture of his biological parents as well: they were promiscuous and they abandoned him. The behavior of Miss Alice as the mistress of the lawyer and the butler is relevant here. Of course, Miss Alice and the others do desert Julian at the end of the play. Earlier, Julian describes his faith abandoning him. As is often true, the parent surrogates tell Julian that he was chosen. But he is furious, nonetheless, at the abandoners who have lied to him, tricked him, and traded him. His impotent rage is for naught.

Manifestations of primary process thinking, important in any creative work, carry a special significance in *Tiny Alice*. To mention one outstanding example of condensation, the same characters can stand for biological mother and adoptive mother, for God and father. So it is with many adopted children who project the various superimposed representations of their several families onto those about them. The confusion many viewers felt about the play undoubtedly is the result of the intense reality with which symbols are treated.

The Adoption Theme in Other Plays by Albee

Tiny Alice is not the only play by Albee in which the latent adoption theme appears. It is perhaps significant that three of Albee's thirteen plays — *Malcolm* (1966), *The Ballad of the Sad Cafe* (1963), and *Everything in the Garden* (1968) — are adapted from other authors' works, borrowed and reworked — adopted as it were. Albee lends credence to his hypothesis when he equates a play and a child (Flanagan 1967). Talking of the creative act, he says, "It's a form of pregnancy I suppose, and to carry that idea further, there are very few people who are pregnant who can recall specifically the moment of conception of the child — but they discover that they are pregnant, and it's rather that way with discovering that one is thinking about a play" (p. 344).

Malcolm (1966), based upon Purdy's novel (1959), dramatizes a young man's search for his lost parents. Whereas in *Tiny Alice* Julian dies as he is being enveloped by Alice in a union that has sexual and incestuous connotations, the hero of *Malcolm* dies of excessive sexual intercourse with a young woman he finds and loves as he seeks his parents. Here, too, we find the implication that death is a result of, a punishment for, incest with a mother surrogate.

I have already mentioned Blum's (1969) study of *Who's Afraid of Virginia Woolf?* In contrast to *Tiny Alice,* the protagonists of that drama primarily manifest the traits of adoptive *parents* rather than those of the adopted child. Fantasies about adoption abound in both plays. The four characters of *Virginia Woolf* are potential parents unable to have real children. For the most part the audience identifies with them; the story is told from the point of view of adults who wish to have children but cannot, who thus imagine and invent the offspring they are unable to produce and keep in reality. However, the bitterness of the adopted child reveals itself in the unsympathetic portrayal of the protagonists. At one point, as Blum has noted, Nick, the younger man, changes roles and acquires some of the attributes of the adopted child. He is called a houseboy and a stud; he attains the double "identity of a fantasied adopted son, both sterile and fertile like his father" (p. 895). He also becomes the young adopted child seduced by his mother. By contrast, in *Tiny Alice* the audience identifies primarily with Julian who consistently behaves like an adopted child.

In *The American Dream* (1960), adoption is the *overt* subject matter.

The American Dream

This early play confirms for us Albee's preoccupation with adoption through the appearance of certain themes that we observe in *Tiny Alice* in a more covert form. The teasing out of the adoption motif does not exhaust our understanding of the play, but merely elucidates one facet.

The play opens on a bickering family consisting of Mommy, Daddy, and Mommy's old mother, Grandma. Daddy is a wealthy man whom Mommy, originally a poor girl, was fortunate to marry. The materialistic orientation of the family is clear. Inordinately concerned about possessions, the mother talks about her clothing and complains that the landlord, who had been quick to take their rent and security money, is slow to repair the house. Threats to expel Grandma, to send her to a home, complement the picture of the family.

The story hinges on Mommy's and Daddy's invitation to Mrs. Barker to their home to complain about the loss of their adopted child. Mrs. Barker works for the Bye-Bye Adoption Service; when she arrives, Grandma explains the purpose of the visit to her in a somewhat allegoric way, talking of a man and woman like Mommy and Daddy rather than directly stating who is involved:

The woman, who was very much like Mommy, said that they wanted a bumble of their own; but that the man, who was very much like Daddy, couldn't have a bumble; and that the man who was very much like Daddy, said that yes, they had wanted a bumble of their own, but that the woman, who was very much like Mommy, could't have one, and they wanted to buy something like a bumble (p. 98).

However, the purchased baby was a disappointment. Mutual antagonism characterized the parent-child relationship. When it cried and only had eyes for its father, Mommy gouged out the baby's eyes. Because it masturbated, they cut off its penis and hands. They cut off its tongue when it called Mommy an obscene name. As the child grew older, its most disturbing traits became apparent: ". . . it didn't have a head on its shoulders, it had no guts, it was spineless, its feet were made of clay" (p. 100f.). When the child died the parents were distressed not because they had lost a beloved child, but because the goods they had bought had not been durable. Hence, they telephoned the lady from whom they had purchased the "bumble" and told her to come to their home immediately. They insisted on remuneration for the faulty product.

It is noteworthy that the adopted child is repeatedly referred to as "it"; his gender is never mentioned since he is to his parents a possession to be bought and sold, rather than a human being. His wishes are never considered.

The word "bumble," used to designate the child, is interesting. It is a condensation derived from "bumble," "bundle," and "bungle." "Bundle" is a common term for an infant, derived from the wrapping that the baby is dressed in. The implication is that the baby is a bundle of joy, an ironic comment in this case, in which the child is felt to be merely trouble. "To bungle" means to spoil by clumsy work. This alludes to the adoptive parents' bungling in their attempt to produce a baby. The biological parents, in addition, have bungled by producing a child they did not wish to have and could not care for. "Bungle" also refers to the child who is considered inept and malformed. "Bumble" itself is suggestive of a bumble bee, an insect that frequently stands for a child in dream imagery. Possibly, the word "bum," a loafer, is alluded to as well.

To return to the story of *The American Dream,* the resolution of the difficult and bizarre situation takes place through the appearance of Young Man, who is clearly the twin brother of the adopted child, although this relationship is never explicitly stated. Young Man, who is seeking employment and will do almost anything for money, appears at a crucial moment, apparently by coincidence. Introducing himself, he describes his belief that he is an illegitimate child. "My mother died the night that I was born, and I never knew my father; I doubt my mother did." One of the identical twins, "we felt each other breathe . . . his heartbeat thundered in my temple . . . mine in his . . . our stomachs ached and we cried for feeding at the same time" (p. 114). Albee convinces the audience that the deceased child and Young Man are twins when the latter recalls that he experienced the sensations the dead child did as he was being dismembered. The audience shares the fantasy that twins possess a mystical extrasensory contact.

In the end, through Grandma's manipulations and with Mrs. Barker's collaboration, Young Man, unaware of what is happening, replaces the dead adopted child in the family. Mrs. Barker announces that she will send a bill for her services in arranging the second adoption. Just as Julian is passively bought by Alice in *Tiny Alice,* so the adoptions of *The American Dream* are purchases which are arranged without the child's awareness of the transaction. This was true of the first adoption, as is inevitable, for an infant cannot very well know what is happening. The subterfuge repeats itself, however, when Young Man joins the family. Clearly, adopted children are pictured as possessions which can be bought and disposed of, even castrated if they object to their situation, rather than as persons, as true biological offspring. The grandmother, who is also treated as a thing, can be considered a displaced representation of the adopted child, one who is resourceful and manages to maintain her independence despite family pressures. This is the adopted child's wish come true. Instead of being a defective thing, he wishes to become a whole, independent person.

Parental evasions are prominent both in *Tiny Alice* and in *The American Dream.* In both plays the true situation is often alluded to but never clearly stated. The nature of reality is unclear.

Direct references to the parents' inability to produce a child appear openly in this play, whereas in *Tiny Alice* they are disguised, and appear, as I have suggested, in connection with the psychotic woman who imagines herself to be the pregnant Virgin Mary, but who does not actually conceive. In *The American Dream,* Daddy is impotent, both sexually — he no longer "bumps his uglies" (p. 67) on Mommy — and socially, for he lacks masculinity and decisiveness.

The theme of the double, so prominent in *Tiny Alice,* manifests itself in *The American Dream* as well. The two sets of parents are referred to directly in the latter. In addition, the appearance of twins reflects the adopted child's preoccupations with pairs of parents. So does the fact that a grandmother, similar in many ways to her daughter, is present and that Mrs. Barker manifests many of Mommy's traits. We may surmise that the adopted child can picture himself as a double, since he has two sets of parents. The fantasied twinship also serves the defensive role of preserving himself even when he is, or feels he is, mistreated, dismembered, and diminished.

One adopted child's family romance constellation is stated quite clearly in

The American Dream. Young Man notes the uncertainty of his biological parentage and asserts that his parents were unmarried, did not even know each other well, that his father deserted them and his mother died. Indeed, one of the common fantasies of adopted children, that their original mother is dead, may have a palpable influence on their personality development, leading to self-destructive attempts to reach the lost mother. Perhaps this fantasy throws additional light on Julian's union with his unseen mother surrogate, Alice, as he dies.

Discussion

It is a well-established method to seek to demonstrate how special life circumstances are reflected in the imagery of and the themes chosen by artists. Among the many special circumstances that have been investigated are object loss through the death or illness of a parent or parental desertion (Wolfenstein 1973, Meyer 1967, Greenacre 1955), twinship (Glenn 1973, 1974a, 1974b), and the birth of siblings in rapid succession (Greenacre 1955).

Following this tradition, this study has singled out the theme of adoption in the expectation that the application of psychoanalytic knowledge concerning the psychology of adopted children might throw light on what is generally regarded as a puzzling play. While there is no doubt that other factors also shaped *Tiny Alice,* I believe that viewing it in terms of the adopted child's psychological preoccupations provides a key to unlocking the enigma.

In the past, analysts have frequently turned to literature to test the validity and universality of their hypotheses which were derived from observation of patients (Nunberg and Federn 1962). Others, perplexed by clinical phenomena, have turned to literature in the hope that the poet's intuitive understanding would illuminate their patients' problems (Greenacre 1971), thus viewing applied analysis as a two-way road. Indeed, Eissler (1968) observes that Freud derived considerable insight from his study of Shakespeare's work.

I have earlier referred to the paucity of analytic papers dealing with the special problems of the adopted child. In line with Greenacre's and Eissler's view of applied analysis, our knowledge might therefore also be enhanced by focusing on how a playwright, who was an adopted child, dealt adaptively with this fact in his artistic products. However, such recourse to literature is no substitute for well-documented reports of individual analyses of adopted children.

An additional aim of this paper, therefore, is to draw attention to an area that seems to have been relatively neglected and to underscore the need for work on this problem.

References

Albee, E. (1960). The American Dream. In *Two Plays by Edward Albee.* New York: New American Library.

———(1962). *Who's Afraid of Virginia Woolf?* New York: Pocket Cardinal.

———(1963). *The Ballad of the Sad Cafe.* Boston: Houghton Mifflin.

———(1965). *Tiny Alice.* New York: Pocket Cardinal.

———(1966). *Malcolm.* New York: Atheneum.

———(1968). *Everything in the Garden.* New York: Atheneum.

Blos, P. (1963). The concept of acting out in relation to the adolescent process. In *A Developmental Approach to the Problems of Acting Out,* ed. E. Rexford, pp. 118–136. New York: International Universities Press, 1966.

Blum, H. P. (1969). A psychoanalytic view of *Who's Afraid of Virginia Woolf? Journal of the American Psychoanalytic Association* 17:888–903. Chapter 11 of this volume.

Daunton, E. (1973). The opening phase of treatment in an adopted child with a symptom of encopresis. Presented at the Association for Child Psychoanalysis, Ann Arbor, Michigan.

Eissler, K. R. (1968). The relation of explaining and understanding in psychoanalysis. *Psychoanalytic Study of the Child* 23:141–171.

Flanagan, W. (1967). Edward Albee. In *Writers at Work [The Paris Review Interviews. Third Series]*, pp. 321–346. New York: Viking Press.

Freeman, L., ed. (1967). *The Mind.* New York: Thomas Y. Crowell.

Freud, A. (1972). The child as a person in his own right. *Psychoanalytic Study of the Child* 27:621–625.

Freud, S. (1909). Family romances. *Standard Edition* 9:235–241.

Glenn, J. (1973). Further observations on plays by twins. Presented at the Psychoanalytic Association of New York.

———(1974a). Twins in disguise: a psychoanalytic essay on *Sleuth and the Royal Hunt of the Sun. Psychoanalytic Quarterly* 43:288–302.

———(1974b). Twins in disguise: II. content, form, and style in plays by Anthony and Peter Shaffer. *International Review of Psycho-Analysis* 1: 373–381.

Greenacre, P. (1955). *Swift and Carroll.* New York: International Universities Press.

————(1971). *Emotional Growth*. New York: International Universities Press.

Kernberg, P. (1974). Discussion of this paper at the Psychoanalytic Association of New York.

Markson, J. W. (1966). Albee's *Tiny Alice. American Imago* 23:3–21.

McWhinnie, A. M. (1969). The adopted child in adolescence. In *Adolescence,* eds. G. Caplan and S. Lebovici, pp. 133–142. New York: Basic Books.

Meyer, B. C. (1967). *Joseph Conrad.* Princeton: Princeton University Press.

Nunberg, H., and Federn, E., eds. (1962). *Minutes of the Vienna Psychoanalytic Society,* Vol. 1. New York: International Universities Press.

Peller, L. E. (1963). Further comments on adoption. *Bulletin of the Philadelphia Association for Psychoanalysis* 13:1–14.

Purdy, J. (1959). *Malcolm.* New York: Avon Books.

Rosner, H. (1974). Discussion of this paper at the Psychoanalytic Association of New York.

Schechter, M. D. (1960). Observations on adopted children. *Archives of General Psychiatry* 3:21–32.

————(1967). Panel report: psychoanalytic theory as it relates to adoption. *Journal of the American Psychoanalytic Association* 15:695–708.

Swartz, J. (1973). Discussion of this paper at the American Psychoanalytic Association, New York.

Wieder, H. (1974). Personal communication in discussion at Great Neck Study Group.

Wolfenstein, M. (1973). The image of the lost parent. *Psychoanalytic Study of the Child* 28:433–456.

Chapter 8

A PSYCHOANALYTIC VIEW OF

WHO'S AFRAID OF VIRGINIA WOOLF?

HAROLD P. BLUM, M.D.

Who's Afraid of Virginia Woolf? has been cited as a brilliantly original and powerful contemporary work of art. Demanding attention and stimulating controversy, it has been called "an excoriating theatrical experience, surging with shocks of recognition and dramatic fire." The widespread interest in the play, and the extensive and extended discussion of its meaning, the intensity of audience reaction, invite psychoanalytic investigation.

Dramatic art presents powerful and important fantasies, aesthetically disguised and communicated to evoke relatively universal reactions, and to achieve an immediate intensity by linkage with potent personal and contemporary social concerns. There are many levels of communication and interpretation in a play, including those involving psychological, historical, and cultural issues.

In this examination of Edward Albee's *Who's Afraid of Virginia Woolf?* (1963), I shall not attempt a complete elucidation of all the peripheral ideas and fantasies presented in the play. There is in this coherent work of art a unifying theme which both orders and integrates the various scenes. I shall try to demonstrate that the fantasy of adoption is the fundamental underlying theme, with variations, of this remarkable play. Such fantasies, in aesthetic form, have universal appeal because of the ubiquity of the family romance. The adoption theme is interwoven throughout the play, and lends continuity to its episodes. This theme determines not only the content, but the structure of the play, involving the interaction and games of two couples. The psychoanalytic exploration will supplement rather than supersede the observations of literary critics and the nonanalytic modes of critical evaluation: there is an organic connection between manifest and latent content. I will also consider issues within the play that are related to the sense of reality and identity, as well as issues bearing on creativity.

The plot of *Who's Afraid of Virginia Woolf?* concerns two university couples who meet on a Saturday night and gradually become intimately involved with each other. They drink excessively probe and expose each other's feelings, jest, provoke, and attack. They succeed in wresting secret thoughts from each other. They play remarkable games of "Humiliate the Host," "Hump the Hostess," "Get the Guests," and "Bringing up Baby." The alcoholism, orgastic games, and mordant wit in an atmosphere of seething tension are associated with the constant question of "truth or illusion?" Waves of angry, altercation, invectives, and insults are punctuated by humor and followed by a sense of depression and emptiness, often newly accompanied by protest or grief. The play concludes with a climactic unfolding of bitter truth behind a facade of deception and illusion. At the end of the play the shocking diversions are subordinated to an implacable reality.

The play is set in a "respectable" university environment which is satirized as both arid and crude. Rather than being devoted to the pursuit of truth and higher learning, the professors and their wives are embroiled in infantile disputes, sexual pursuits, and childish drive-dominated interests. There are implications of political corruption, of exploitation and sycophancy for the sake of advancement, and of basic nonacademic predatory values. It is no accident that in this pseudointellectual atmosphere, illusion has become as important as truth and that there is a pervasive sense of intellectual sterility and impotence. George, the history professor, and his wife Martha, the daughter of the college president, are biologically sterile, and George is a failure as both scholar and lover. Nick, the biology professor who studies chromosomes, is also a nonparent, although George states that he will breed a race of chromosomally arranged test-tube babies. Attitudes of doubt and disbelief, of conflict between the physical and social sciences, between biological and historical fact are again interwoven with the problem of reality versus fantasy and history versus myth.

The sterility and emptiness behind the academic facade are also behind the facade of the marriage of George and Martha. The marriage has persisted for twenty-three years, but there is embittered hostility, cold detachment, and humiliating, excoriating vituperation. Human relationships including both heterosexual and homosexual contacts are characterized by a profound ambivalence and mutually degrading and lacerating attacks. In a bloody repartee each partner is disparaged for a lack of virility and fertility, blame is projected, and the shared fantasy of parenthood is an insufficient bulwark against overwhelming feelings of injury (castration) and loss.

The never-to-be mentioned shared secret that finally emerges into the full daylight of verbalized consciousness is that George and Martha have only a mythical son, that he never existed. This truth gradually evolves from the games that are played, like the play within the play in *Hamlet,* to arrive at the truth. The games, which I believe should be compared to children's play, are somewhat divorced from reality and contribute to the blurring of apparent fact and fantasy. However, a closer look at the structure and content of the games will show their connection to the fundamental themes of the play; to the defensive aspect of child play; and to the specific infantile gratifications and attempts at adaptive mastery of disguised traumas that are almost invariably involved in children's games. There is a play on words here, for the writing of a play itself is in some ways genetically comparable to children's play, to play on words, and to the substitution of verbalized fantasy for childhood activities.

There is a histrionic quality to these potentially explosive games which partially denies their serious intent and portent. The mounting tension is partially discharged and relieved by rapier wit and scintillating humor. The capacity for humor in the face of anguish could be indicative of the active attempts to master traumas which are continued in the games. The sources of anxiety may be later objects of humor and play. The sophisticated games are not amorphous, but, like those of the oedipal period, have structure, rules, roles, and titles (Peller 1954). The characters participate, and mutually sanction, the game activities in the playmates' acting out of shared fantasies. The group involvement, the utilization of games, and the excessive drinking reduce guilt and allow the dramatization of forbidden fantasies. The alcoholism invites the emergence of verbalized truth while contributing to immersion in illusion.

In the very titles of the games, "Humiliate the Host," "Hump the Hostess," and "Bringing up Baby" we can readily discern the classical oedipal fantasies of castrating the father, having intercourse with an impregnating mother. Yet both couples are childless. The games attempt to deny the sexual failure, but reaffirm it in the impotence and infertility which become apparent in the play. The disappointment and grief of the characters now appear in literal terms. What becomes evident is the bottomless bitterness of barren (castrated) pseudoparents. One couple, George and Martha, prove to be struggling to maintain a shared fantasy of a mythical baby. The other couple, Nick, the biologist and chromosome scientist, and his "mousey" wife, Honey, are also revealed as pseudoparents, having symbolic impregnations, followed by pseudocyesis. This later appears as pseudopseudocyesis, for Honey has probably secretly been inducing abortions. The biologist's mouse is a symbol of ambivalent pregnancy. Martha plays "Bringing up Baby," while Honey rejects motherhood. Moreover, there are early references to synthetic test-tube babies and to chromosomal heredity; these references foreshadow the later overt manifestations of doubt and unreality of pregnancy and parenthood.

The games are of a striking sexual nature. George, the humiliated host, knows that Nick and Martha, the hostess, are embracing. When Nick cannot sexually perform, there are further barrages of cutting obloquy. The sexual games are replete with voyeurism, exhibitionism, and sadomasochism. The games, dramatizing problems of primal scene and impregnation, develop the marital relationships of the characters and their procreative preoccupation. Premarital pregnancy is the manifest reason for Nick and Honey's marriage. George states of Nick and Honey: "How They Got Married. Well, how they got married is this. . . . The Mouse got all puffed up one day, and she went over to Blondie's house, and she stuck out her puff, and she said . . . look at me . . . and so they were married" (Albee, 1963, p. 146). The premarital baby of Nick and Honey is consciously neither planned nor wanted and finally turns into an illusory pregnancy, a pseudocyesis.

The exchange of sexual partners in the games implies both rearrangement and confusion of origins and of parental identity. The retention and expulsion of the baby, the doing and undoing of pregnancy adds to the doubt of the reality of both parent and child. As George says to Nick, "Truth and illusion, who knows the difference, eh. Toots? Eh? (Albee, p. 201). The mystery of parenthood and birth, origins and identity is heightened by the fact that the play takes place on the eve before the birthday of the child of George and Martha. Like Oedipus unraveling the riddle of the Sphinx, the two couples are engaged in the uncovering of a mythical son from a mysterious birth.

The mythical son and the two couples of four pseudoparents cannot be specifically explained by merely suggesting impotence, homosexual sterility, or marital sadomasochism. (Discussion of these syndromes in relation to the play is outside the scope of this paper.) My specific analytic inference is that the two couples form two sets of parents; one associated with chromosomal biology, the other with known recorded history, both childless, and yet "parents." This is analogous to the two sets of parents of an adopted or foster child. The child, natural and adopted, and the parents, biological or adoptive, could then ambiguously represent illusion or reality. Adopted by childless parents, such a child is not their biological offspring; having been abandoned by his biological parents, he is no longer their child and may no longer regard them as his parents. The references to the mythical baby and pseudocyesis converge in the child who has no visible natural parents; and parents with an imaginary child. This child was not born of his historical (adoptive) parents and was in fantasy "test-tube-bred." He was born and abandoned like the symbolic conception and abortion of pseudocyesis. In the play, when Martha asks Nick why he is terrifying, Honey replies, "It's because of your chromosomes, Dear" (Albee, p. 64). After Martha says she loves chromosomes, George states,

> Martha eats them . . . for breakfast . . . she sprinkles them on her cereal. It's very simple, Martha, this young man is working on a system whereby chromosomes can be altered . . . well not all by himself — he probably has one or two co-conspirators — the genetic makeup of a sperm cell changed, reordered . . . to order, actually . . . for hair and eye color, stature, potency . . . I imagine . . . hairiness, features, health . . . and mind. Most important . . . Mind. All imbalances will be corrected, sifted out . . . propensity for various diseases will be gone. Longevity assured. We will have a race of men . . . test-tube-bred . . . incubator born . . . superb and sublime. [Albee 1963, p. 65]

The references to co-conspirators and the genetic makeup to order of feature, hair, eye color, etc., suggests the disguised selection and matching of the adopted child to adoptive parents. The process of adoption is viewed as a conspiracy to take the child to or from his "parents."

The adoption fantasy is associated with doubt of ego and object identity. The confusion between the chromosomal parents and the historical parents with the "unreal" baby they have raised is elaborated in attitudes of doubt and distance, detachment and estrangement. Who are the real parents, and is an adopted baby a real baby? Who is he? This core confusion is also related to the later problem of identity and sexual identity. There is a constant question of male or female, fact or fantasy, game or grim reality, and creativity or sterility. The uncertainty of origins, parents, and identity is linked to pervasive ambivalence and doubts of the presence or absence of a penis. (Indeed, the illusory baby whose existence is affirmed and denied is in many respects comparable to the treatment accorded to the fetish or "female phallus," and to the disavowal of object loss.)

The finale of the play, "the exorcism," reveals George and Martha's son unmasked as an illusion. In the "exorcism" of the secret mythical child George has mordantly referred to "a son who would not disown his father" and a son who could not tolerate the "splashing braying residue that called itself his MOTHER, MOTHER? HAH!!" Then Martha coldly replies, "All right, you. A son who was so ashamed of his father he asked me once if it — possibly — wasn't true, as he had heard, from some cruel boys, maybe, that he was not our child" (Albee 1963, p. 225). Here are ideas of disowning the parents along with ideas of adoption.

In the searing searching of the parental motives of the two couples are fantasies of an adopted child about his double parents. There are fantasies of discovering the motives for adoption, but also of discovering the natural parents and the motives for abandonment. In this variant of the family romance, is the adopted child bastard or legitimate, and legitimately belonging to whom?

Martha seduces Nick in the middle of the night with George watching. In the primal scene between hosts and guests there is an apparent attempt to cross-breed the biological and the adoptive parents. This could be a wish that the adoptive parents were also the biological parents, that there had been no abandonment, no exceptional childhood. The sterile parent is symbolically fertilized by the biologically fertile parent, which compensates for the hostile dissatisfaction with the sterile partner. In these fantasies of the play, the sexual games fulfill the wishes of the barren adoptive parents for a procreative partner.

In this gathering of the couples, a reunion with all parents, the seemingly degrading games serve the unconscious adaptive purpose of mastering traumatic feelings of abandonment and rejection. Within the fantasies of adoption there are alternating identifications among the parental partners who are themselves very similar. Nick and Honey appear as a younger college couple with strong resemblance to the inner relationship of George and Martha. One marriage is more openly belligerent, the other more apparently affectionate. Both couples are childless, but Martha, twice Honey's age, tries to hold on to a child, while Honey aborts children. At fifty-two Martha is menopausal, while Honey is potentially fertile as the unaging fantasied natural mother. There is a complex of pregnancy-abortion-adoption fantasies including adoption after repeated abortion, adoption equated with unwanted, unwanted or abandoned equated with induced abortion, and adoption as rebirth, abortion as death (murder).

Martha invites Nick, her guest, to "hump the hostess" with the inner hope of impregnation. George questions whether Nick is boy or man. "If you're a houseboy, baby, you can pick up after me; if you're a stud, you can go protect your plow. Either way. Either way. . . . Everything" (Albee 1963, p. 204). Nick the houseboy is now identified with the biological stud just before George announces the final game to be played, entitled "Bringing up Baby." Nick is ambivalently regarded as a potential stud by both George and Martha. As the houseboy and stud he is the double identity of a fantasied adopted son, both sterile and fertile like his father. Nick is also young enough to be Martha's son, and the "houseboy-stud" may be viewed as an oedipal fantasy. The fantasies of incest with both mothers are sanctioned by the refusal to consider either biological or adoptive mother as the "real mother." The adoptive mother is pictured as seductively receptive to her son's incestuous wishes. She (Martha), too, regards him as biologically fertile in contrast to her husband. She berates her husband for not being as creative as her father, who fathered her and symbolically fathered the university. George is only husband, not father, of her or her child. George is sterile and Nick is impotent with this teasing, demanding, and castrating mother.

The sexual games and primal scenes, the mounting excitement and intensity of emotion can be coalesced as dramatized derivatives of oedipal-phase masturbation fantasies. The disguised masturbatory play is associated with the excitement of sadomasochistic primal scenes. The dramatized games resemble derivatives of masturbatory play which have been transmuted through the process of sublimation. The acting out of the masturbation fantasy has been artfully transformed to higher levels of secondary process verbalization and neutralization in play acting; writing and witty dramatization replace masturbation games and fighting (Kanzer 1957).

In this special family romance, if the adopted child were to find his biological "real" parents, would he adopt them? Would they be preferred and idealized in fantasy compared to the adoptive parents? Or the adoptive parents may be idealized and chosen, as they chose the child who becomes "chosen" as well as abandoned. In this play all four "parents" are finally aggressively devalued. The fantasies concern biological parents who have abandoned/aborted their child and sterile parents who are not reconciled to their biological sterility and conceive an illusory child. The sterile parents with the illusory child may be regarded as a representation of adoptive parents who do not consider themselves as true parents with a real child of their own. In terms of the adoption theme, the secret is the adoption, and the illusion is the "unreal" child and parenthood. In a clinical setting such fantasies may coincide with the actual fantasies of adoptive parents. Clinically, the historical actuality of adoption may be interwoven with fantasies in a variety of wishfulfilling, defensive, and adaptive combinations.

The characters in the play present a sense of self-doubt and self-defeat and an untiring expression of anger despite the comic relief. This is related to fantasies of rejection by the adoptive mother and abandonment by the biological mother. Why was the child abandoned? Because he was naughty, unworthy, bad? Is he himself a big bad wolf? Will he be abandoned again? The repetitive provocations of the marital partners may also be viewed as a test of the partners' devotion. When Martha asserts, "If you existed, I'd divorce you" (Albee, p. 16), she threatens reabandonment while reaffirming the relationship to George in addressing him. George tells the story of a boy, now insane, ostensibly because he has unwittingly killed both his mother and father. The boy is therefore a self-created orphan. George wants to publish a book on this boy who, it is intimated, is probably George himself. Martha says, "Imagine such a thing! A book about a boy who murders his mother and kills his father, and pretends it's an accident!" (Albee, p. 136). Moments later she says, using George's voice, "No, Sir, this isn't a novel at all . . . this is the truth . . . this really happened . . . TO ME!" (Albee, p. 137). Here is a derivative of a child's adoption theme: the omnipotent fantasy in which the "deserted" child has actively destroyed his parents rather than having passively been abandoned and rejected. The terror of abandonment is connected with a murderous rage over the desertion. It is a fantasy of active revenge in which the abandoned child says, "If I find my parents, I shall get rid of them as they got rid of me."

The Family Romance and Adoption

Freud (1909) discovered that as a part of normal childhood development the child fantasies that he is not the natural child of his parents and constructs a "family romance" in which he imagines himself to be a stepchild or an adopted child. His real parents do not conform to the omnipotent and eternally benevolent roles he has assigned them. The omnipotent and completely affectionate features are assigned to the imaginary exalted parents who protect the child from the narcissistic injury that he is not receiving the whole of his parental love. In addition, the family romance comes to have new significance during the oedipal phase. The child may then fantasy that he is adopted by foster parents, a guest in the house of his hosts without the incest taboo in their relationship since biological kinship is denied.

Freud observed the motivation of retaliation against the parents for unreciprocated affection and slights, but was also aware "that the most intense impulses of sexual rivalry contribute to the result." The child will attribute to his mother as many fancied infidelities as he himself has competitors. In variants of the family romance the natural mother may be portrayed as a prostitute, the adoptive mother as a virgin with immaculate conceptions (test-tube babies). Freud noted that the development of these fantasies is partially dependent on the child's materials, that is, on reality factors and on his ingenuity. Though seldom remembered, Freud observed that the later stages of the family romance are likely to emerge first in the child's play. Greenacre (1958) reported that well-organized family romances are indicative of marked ambivalence to the parents due to grossly unresolved oedipal problems and phallic-phase masturbation pressures. Child's play and games may show all degrees of disguise and development from crude masturbation fantasies to highly embellished if still erotized family romances.

Such family romance fantasies are universally significant, and can be traced in transference in clinical psychoanalysis (Frosch 1959). They take on an especially profound importance when they are supported by reality. The prolongation of the family romance and its fixation in the adopted child has been noted (Schechter 1960). Such fantasies are bound to be reactivated when the child is actually separated from his parents. Adoption is a special representative of this vicissitude of rearing. The family romance fantasies then have the function of attempting to master the trauma of separation, the reality of having been rejected by the natural parents, and the possible associated unpleasant reality of being ambivalently accepted by the adoptive parents. Clothier (1943) believed that since the adopted child really has two sets of parents, he cannot use the family romance as a game as might occur with the ordinary child whose historical known and biological parents are identical. This view assumes that games are related only to fantasies, and are divorced entirely from real events. Unless the child is so overwhelmed that he cannot play, games have the purpose of gradually mastering trauma and of exploratory solutions to internal and external conflict.

The games in *Who's Afraid of Virginia Woolf?* can also be compared to the adaptive aspects of childhood play on the theme of adoption and the related family romance.

The myth of Oedipus is readily discerned as the classical paradigm of the family romance. Oedipus was himself an adopted child given away at birth by his natural parents to be raised by childless foster parents. In the Greek myth the King of Thebes was warned by an oracle that his son would slay him. He ordered his baby son abandoned, but a pitying Corinthian shepherd rescued the infant. Oedipus was then adopted by the childless king and queen of Corinth. Oedipus as a youth was taunted by a drunk (like the alcoholic taunting in *Who's Afraid of Virginia Woolf?*) and visited the Delphic oracle to learn that he was indeed fated to kill his father and marry his mother. He then resolved never to return home to Corinth, and journeyed toward Thebes. By inference he leaves his adoptive parents to return to his natural parents. His return to his birthplace and reunion with his natural parents is accompanied by parricide and incest.

Resolution in the Play and Applied Analysis

In the reverse of the fantasy of parricide, George enacts a fantasy of infanticide and abortion when he tells Martha the telegram message he has prepared saying, "Our son is dead" (Albee, p. 231). Death here is not only the murder of the rival son, but also the separation of the parent and the child. Death is a final separation and a return to biological nonexistence. In this fantasy, "our son is dead" means we have no "real" son. The dead son is revealed as an illusion at the climax of the play, an illusion which derives from the underlying fantasy of adoption. The adopted child is dead, no longer exists, as the chromosomal offspring of his biologically childless foster parents; a child who is, but is not, their baby. The telegrammed message which George announces, a message of loss, presents a certain historical truth. It could be viewed as a disguised version of the message the adopted child actually receives from his parents, namely, that he is adopted, not conceived from their own reproduction, and by inference has lost his biological parents. The secret that is shared and uncovered in the play is often really shared by adoptive parents and then revealed in a dramatic message to their child. This can be likened to a deadly traumatic telegram unless the revelation is in the context of a lovingly secure parent-child relationship.

The illusion of the son as a secret fantasy is tenuously relinquished in the play on the eve of the "mythical" child's twenty-first birthday. Birth is the first separation and age twenty-one is the cultural-legal time of independence. The parent and child are symbolically independent of each other, and the fantasied child is given up when children actually reach their legal majority. If earlier there has been real or fantasied object loss, the independence may reactivate feelings of desertion and loss.

The mythical child who is annihilated on his birthday of independence represents both the infantile fantasy of abandonment and the realistic renunciation of fantasy as fact. The fantasy of the child is relinquished. The loss (abortion) of George and Martha's mythical baby is balanced in the play by maturing recognition of their conflicts and awareness of anxieties about virility and sterility. In terms of a child's adoption fantasy, the symbolic independence from parents and turning from illusion at twenty-one can also be considered a reversal in the service of mastery of the imagined parental abandonment at birth. At the climax of the play, George says "it will be better" after interpreting the denial and destroying the illusion. Martha is now overtly apprehensive and when George sings "Who's Afraid of Virginia Woolf," Martha then replies, "I . . . Am . . . George" (Albee, p. 241). The song is based on a children's song of reassurance in the face of danger. "Who's Afraid of Virginia Woolf?" here means who is afraid to face reality, who is afraid painfully to renounce a treasured illusion? The eventual acceptance of the loss of an illusory object is closely related to the problem of ego mastery of trauma, and of artistic mastery through sublimation. In the denouement there is a climactic unfolding of the bitter truth behind the deception facade. This resembles analysis with the uncovering of a defensive fantasy and the substitution of truth for illusion in the service of the reality principle.

Like his pseudo-parents, in the disguised theme of this play, the fantasied child can be deciphered as an adoption fantasy. He is an invisible vital character presented as an unreal baby. He is the counterpart of the adopted child's invisible fantasied biological parents. The unreality and feeling of illusion are further derived from the adoption theme in which adoptive parents and child have shared fantasies that they are not truly parents and child.

The childless couples[1] in the play share their fantasies but remain violently ambivalent and potentially belligerent. The characters verbally engage in almost rhythmic mutilating attacks on each other which include powerful elements of blame and recrimination. Problems of fertility and sterility invariably activate conflicts around the castration complex and their attendant affects. The projection of blame for the sterility, the feeling of being deprived of procreation and cheated by the partner, and efforts at magical reassurance and impregnation through extramarital affairs and pseudocyesis are not without everyday parallels.

The degree to which parents have mastered the biopsychological conflicts associated with parenthood will markedly influence the child's fantasies and psychological development. The relationship with the parent is of crucial

1. It is probably not a coincidence that George, the history professor, and his wife, Martha, are the names of the primal parents of American history, George and Martha Washington. George and Martha Washington were themselves a childless couple, and Martha had living and dead children from her prior marriage. George formally adopted two of Martha's grandchildren and signed letters to his adopted grandson as "Your Papa." George Washington was not a biological father, but was adopted as the father of his country.

developmental importance as much for the ordinary child as the child with foster parents.

Identity and Creativity

The achievement of parental identity through successful resolution of developmental conflict and mature maternal and paternal identification is necessary for the mutual maturation of both parents and child. This is intimately related to the development of a mature and cohesive identity (Erikson 1956).

The characters in the play depict serious identity problems, feelings of loneliness and estrangement, of doubt and detachment. These problems and the focus on the conflict of being or nothingness, of existence or illusion can be understood in the light of psychoanalytic insight and do not require metaphysical or existential postulates.

Feelings of deception and alienation are potentials of the human condition amplified by specific developmental experience. Dramatic art relates the unique to the universal. The individual genetic reasons for alienation and estrangement are brought into relation with general problems of society (marriage, the family, education, etc.). The play, in addition to its generally acid commentary on sociocultural sterility, covertly refers to intellectual and artist conflict.

The references to biological and historical research, the writing of a book, and the pregnancy fantasies may all pertain to the creative intellect and art. The work of art may involve unconscious conflicts concerning procreation, fertility, and sterility (Bychowski 1951). Alternating identification between procreative and sterile are probably of profound artistic significance.

It requires extraordinary selection and utilization, discrimination and synthesis to produce a coherent work of art with relatively universal attributes. Virginia Woolf herself was a writer and suicide, a creator who destroyed herself. At one point we are told that the mythical son in *Who's Afraid of Virginia Woolf?* deep in his gut is sorry to have been born (Albee 1963, p. 227). But if this symbolically refers to the play itself, then artistic production survives its own threatened abortion. This drama could be visualized as expressing the conflict of destruction and artistic creation. There is a genetic relationship between ancient fertility rites and modern artistic productions. The psychoanalyst can also appreciate the complex structural and functional changes between primitive rites and aesthetic dramatization, between childhood play and creative sublimation.

Summary

This play, involving two couples and an imaginary child, is viewed from the vantage point of applied psychoanalysis. The adoption fantasy is the hidden underlying theme which gives cohesive unity to the play. The problems of truth or illusion, reality or fantasy, alienation or attachment are disguised derivatives of the central fantasy of adoption. The ambivalent estrangement and identity conflicts of the characters are expressions of this fantasy. The mutual diatribe, the doubt, disillusionment, and disappointment are traced to this core conflict with a universal background in the related family romance. The nature and significance of the games in the play are discussed. Reference is made to the transmutation of childhood play into drama and problems of creativity.

References

Albee, E. (1963). *Who's Afraid of Virginia Woolf?* New York: Pocket Books.

Bychowski, G. (1951). From catharsis to work of art. In *Psychoanalysis and Culture,* ed. G. B. Wilbur and W. Muensterberger, pp. 390–409. New York: International Universities Press.

Clothier, F. (1943). Psychology of adopted children. *Mental Hygiene* 27: 222–230.

Erikson, E. H. (1956). The problem of ego identity. *Journal of the American Psychoanalytic Association* 4:56–121.

Freud, S. (1909). Family romances. *Standard Edition* 9:235–241.

Frosch, J. (1959). Transference derivatives of the family romance. *Journal of the American Psychoanalytic Association* 7:503–522.

Greenacre, P. (1958). The family romance of the artist. *Psychoanalytic Study of the Child* 13:9–36.

Kanzer, M. (1957). Acting out, sublimation, and reality testing. *Journal of the American Psychoanalytic Association* 5:663–684.

Peller, L. (1954). Libidinal phases, ego development, and play. *Psychoanalytic Study of the Child* 9:178–199.

Schechter, M. (1960). Observations on adopted children. *Archives General Psychiatry* 3:21–32.

PART IV

A Holy Sinner

Chapter 9

DOSTOYEVSKY'S "PEASANT MAREY"

MARK KANZER, M.D.

I

Dostoyevsky has been the subject of numerous psychoanalytic studies, including commentaries by Freud (1928). Agreement has been general on his powerful parricidal trends and their root in the oedipus complex. Special interest has been shown in his epilepsy and the role of his illness in his personality make-up. The commonly accepted psychological picture of Dostoyevsky is that of a man with strongly repressed violent drives which erupt spasmodically. He is depicted as a dual personality, a politically conservative and deeply religious family man whose career nevertheless embraced participation in revolutionary activities, imprisonment in Siberia, morbid gambling periods and quixotic impulses of varied description. His reputation, of course, rests fundamentally on his amazing insight into the deepest emotional conflicts, especially in relationship to crime. He delineates characters whose interest for psychologists is rivalled only by Shakespeare's. His works as well as his own character make Dostoyevsky an inevitable "case history."

One of his stories is a brief tale, "The Peasant Marey," which is an avowedly autobiographical sketch. Writing in the first person, Dostoyevsky describes an experience in a Siberian prison camp when he was twenty-nine years old. During Easter week, the convicts had been granted a holiday. "There were numbers of men drunk . . . hideous, disgusting songs and card parties . . . abuse and quarrelling was springing up in every corner." The prison officials kept out of sight "understanding that they must allow even these outcasts to enjoy themselves once a year, and that things would be even worse if they did not." As diversion, several of the convicts had been beaten by their comrades until they were half dead. Dostoyevsky was seized with a sudden fury and words muttered by another prisoner, "I hate these brigands" echoed in his ears. He lay down and pretended to sleep so that he would not be molested. He wished that he could dream or think but was too upset to do so.

Gradually I sank into forgetfulness and by degrees was lost in memories. During the whole course of my four years in prison I was continually recalling all my past, and seemed to live over again the whole of my life in recollection. These memories rose up of themselves, it was not often that I summoned them of my own free will. Each would begin from some point, some little thing, at times unnoticed, and then by degrees there would rise up a complete picture, some vivid and complete impression. I used to analyze these impressions, give new features to what had happened long ago, and best of all, I used to correct it, correct it continually, that was my great amusement. On this occasion, I suddenly for some reason remembered an unnoticed moment in my early childhood when I was only nine years old—a moment which I should have thought I had utterly forgotten; but at that time I was particularly fond of memories of my early childhood.

In these words Dostoyevsky practically describes an experiment in free association, with a streaming into consciousness of forgotten childhood experiences. The memory which recurred to him on this occasion was of an episode when his summer holidays in the country were drawing to an end and he was depressed at the thought of returning to the city and to school. He walked alone into the woods. In the distance, he heard one of his father's peasants plowing in a clearing. The man and his horse were moving with effort as they climbed a steep hill. Young Dostoyevsky began to occupy himself with his favorite diversions. He became interested in small wild life, in beetles and colorful lizards, in snakes (which aroused some fear in him), and in frogs. He broke off switches from trees to whip frogs with and pondered whether birch or nut tree switches were best. Then he began to hunt for mushrooms. A sense of bliss filled him. "There was nothing in the world that I loved so much as the wood with its mushrooms and wild berries, with its beetles and its birds . . . . and its damp smell of dead leaves which I loved so much."

At this moment, "in the midst of the profound stillness I heard a clear and distant shout, 'Wolf!' I shrieked and, beside myself with terror, calling out at the top of my voice, ran out into the clearing and straight to the peasant who was plowing."

The peasant, Marey, quickly discovered that there was no wolf outside of the child's imagination. He gently stroked the boy, reassured him "with an almost motherly smile" until Dostoyevsky grasped the fact that there was no wolf. As he became calmer, he realized that he had had similar imaginary experiences before ("but these hallucinations passed away later as I grew older"). After Marey had made the sign of the cross over the boy and over himself, Dostoyevsky picked up courage to leave, half ashamed of his behavior, half believing in the wolf. Only after meeting his own dog a little later did his anxiety completely vanish.

Arousing himself from his daydreams, the convict Dostoyevsky found himself smiling quietly. He wondered why he had "remembered the meeting with such distinctness to the smallest detail. So it must have lain hidden in my soul, though I knew nothing of it, and rose suddenly to my memory when it was wanted; I remembered the soft motherly smile of the poor serf, the way he signed me with the cross . . . and particularly the earth-stained finger with which he softly and with timid tenderness touched my quivering lips. If I had been his own son, he could not have looked at me with eyes shining with greater love."

Dostoyevsky concludes with the observation that "only God may have seen with what deep and humane civilized feeling, and with what a delicate, almost feminine tenderness, the heart of a coarse, brutally ignorant Russian serf, who had as yet no expectation, no idea even of his freedom, may be filled." With such reflections, he gazed around at his fellow convicts and found that "suddenly by some miracle all hatred and anger had vanished utterly from my heart. I walked about, looking into the faces that I met. That shaven peasant, branded on his face as a criminal, bawling his hoarse, drunken song, may be that very Marey: I can not look into his heart." That night the life of a convict seemed much more tolerable to Dostoyevsky.

II

This brief sketch (occupying only five printed pages) bears the typical Dostoyevsky imprint. Fierce convicts and rough peasants with hidden

Christ-like qualities, complicated emotions, and deep introspection are characteristic of the Dostoyevsky novel, but the very brevity of this tale of "The Peasant Marey" enables us to grasp more readily the essential processes of his thought and fantasy.

The story has as its starting point a mood of frustrated fury. The convict is filled with loathing for his comrades, their turbulence, and released aggression on this Easter holiday arouse feelings of restlessness and a desire to escape from his surroundings. This he is able to do only by daydream which takes him back to childhood, to a forgotten moment of terror when he was soothed by a strange rude peasant. Then, as by a therapeutic process, he emerges from his own turbulent emotions of the moment, sees his surroundings in a new light and experiences a sense of contentment in a situation which only a little while before had seemed completely intolerable. There is obviously an emotional link between the past and the present; as he states, the forgotten incident "rose suddenly to my memory when it was wanted." We learn that in the earlier episode, the child Dostoyevsky had faced a desperate crisis; he was to give up his beloved pastimes in the woods and to return to a school routine and life in the city which were very disagreeable. He seeks solace once again in the woods, shuts out unpleasant thoughts entirely — just as the convict Dostoyevsky was later to attempt — and just at the moment when he appears to have gained complete happiness, is overwhelmed with panic by a hallucinatory experience of a voice crying "Wolf!" The danger of the forest, the menace to little children who play alone in the woods, has suddenly materialized. The shock must have been similar to that which the daydreaming Dostoyevsky must often have felt as he awakened from fantasies of childhood life to the terrible reality of Siberian prison life.

There is a need to avoid and minimize mental shocks; in fact the natural functions of the dream include prolongation of sleep and presentation of fulfilled wishes. The convict Dostoyevsky, in his daydream, was struggling against the awareness that he would reawaken in his prison surroundings and so the "memory that he wanted" involved a danger which had once proved imaginary and a solution which had comforting implications — that the rough powerful Russian peasant would rescue and soothe him. The recovered memory was of the essential material of fairy tales — the woods, the wolf, and the fairy godmother in disguise.

The childhood episode, however, already bears the marks of a serious mental disorder in the nine-year-old Dostoyevsky. It is true that the termination of the summer holiday and the return to school are often the cause of juvenile discontent, but the underlying terror which produced and was released with the hallucination of the wolf is indicative of a severe emotional disturbance which is not accounted for by the explanation. "I would have to go to Moscow to be bored all winter with French lessons, and I was so sorry to leave the country." The state of bliss which the child arrived at in the woods is also suggestive of some habitual refuge from unpleasantness in life.

From the manifest content of the story, we might never delve any further into the psychological forces involved. When we consider some of the incidents, however, we can not fail to be impressed with the resemblance to typical psychoanalytic case material. As the boy plays in the woods, we are impressed with the extraordinary mixture of curiosity, delight, anxiety, guilt, and aggression which he displays. Little animals with their strange colors, forms, and movements attract him and arouse him emotionally. There is fear and aggression toward them. He beats frogs with a switch. He has a longing to gather mushrooms — vegetation with curious suggestive shapes and texture. The odor of the place delights him. In this typical small-boy play, we recognize a characteristic preoccupation with sex problems, phallic symbols, and guilty curiosity. Then suddenly there is an interruption. At the moment of complete bliss, the supposed loneliness of his forbidden delights is shattered by an intrusion of a dangerous destructive figure which has been lurking in the background.

The wolf figure of the hallucination is of course a projection of an internal anxiety derived from an earlier experience. Indeed, Dostoyevsky tells us that he had previously had similar hallucinations. There must have been some traumatic experience earlier in life which reproduced itself in disguised form in this solitary forest play and the intrusion of the imaginary world. It would likewise appear most probable that the unexplained melancholy of the boy on his impending return to the city and his preference for solitude in the woods were associated with the conflicts which had taken such a deep hold of him that his mental life had been reduced to a preference for withdrawal from reality, symbolic play, and hallucinations.

Can we find any clues as to the nature of the traumatic experience? Here the role of the peasant invites consideration. In the sequence of the story, we learn that on entering the woods, young Dostoyevsky "heard a peasant plowing alone on the clearing about thirty paces away. I knew that he was plowing up the steep hill and the horse was moving with effort, and from time to time the peasant's call 'Come up!' floating upward to me. I did not know who it was plowing . . . and I did not care, I was absorbed in my own affairs. I was busy, too; I was breaking off switches from the nut trees to whip the frogs with."

The unseen peasant plowing up the earth and urging on his laboring horse is immediately suggestive of primal scene material. We find Dostoyevsky at once showing signs of a repressive process taking place in his mind. "I did not know who was plowing" and (defiantly) "I did not care." "I was absorbed in my own affairs"; (all this had nothing to do with him). And what "affairs" preoccupied the youngster? "I was busy, too; I was breaking off switches from the nut trees to whip the frogs with." The inference is clear; not only was the indifference of the boy an affectation, but he was impelled by a process of identification to reproduce in disguised form the scene that he was secretly witnessing. In beating and forcing on the reluctant frog, he was acting in imagination like the unseen peasant with his animal, and no doubt like the figures of earlier scenes. As he engaged in his play, the sexual interests become increasingly obvious, the stimulating external scene is completely forgotten, the boy achieves a state of "bliss" when suddenly he is jolted back to reality by a violent intrusion. The intrusion, it is true, emanates from his inner life, but brings about a restitution to reality in the form of impelling him to join the very figure who has given rise to his fantasies, the plowing peasant. No doubt, too, a deeper wish is served; to burst in on the primal scene.

In this woodland episode is a typical reproduction of familiar behavior of children preoccupied with primal scene problems, with secret listening, doubting, masturbating, nightmares and terrors, and bursting at last into the parental bedroom. The parents assume a dual character to the child during this period; the protecting beloved guardian of the daytime and the strange distorted participant in bestial behavior at night. The conflict may assume too severe a form for the emotional resources of the child and the solution found by entering the parental bedroom has many functions; it satisfies curiosity, puts an end to sexual activities of parents and child alike, and restores an earlier stage of infantile security in the close proximity to the parents. The reception awaiting the child who bursts in upon the primal scene is weighted, of course, with the possibility of punishment, primarily from the father. In this light the tender reception of Dostoyevsky by the peasant and the excessive wonder of the boy and even later of the grown man in his reminiscences, may well find their explanation in the contrast between the rather ordinary comforting gestures of Marey and the unconscious anticipations attendant upon the primal scene symbolism.

In light of these interpretations, the catharsis undergone by the convict in prison on that Easter day becomes clearer. He is surrounded by raging violent men who are losing control of their passions. Obscene songs are being sung, men are indulging in sadistic sports. The words "I hate them" ring in his ears. His patricidal impulses are aroused, and he seeks protection in solitude and daydreams, just as in the woods so often during his childhood. Once more an old pattern repeats itself. He is able to conjure up a situation or thought which restores to him an image of an earlier father, gentle and loving, so that "suddenly by some miracle all hatred and anger vanished from my heart." He was able then to face reality — but a precarious reality from which he was to be jolted again and again by confronting the hated aspects of his father.

III

That the patricidal note was the key to Dostoyevsky's personality is indeed perceptible even to the casual reader of his works and has of course been emphasized by Freud and other analysts. The father of Dostoyevsky showed cruelty and indifference to his children in later years, especially after the death of the mother, and was himself murdered during the youth of the writer by peasants whom he had treated oppressively. There is a tradition that Dostoyevsky developed his first attack of epilepsy immediately after receiving news of his father's violent death. It is of special interest, however, that the murder of the older Dostoyevsky took place at his estate near Tchermashnia, the very scene of his son's hallucination of the wolf some years earlier (Neufeld 1923). Moreover, the murderers were never identified; the peasant Marey could well have been one of the very peasants who had turned against their oppressor. Such thoughts may well have been close to the surface in the mind of the daydreaming convict in the Siberian prison.

Moreover, Dostoyevsky's offense which had led to his imprisonment was conspiracy against the Tsar. He had been sentenced to death and had actually mounted the scaffold for his execution when news of his pardon by the Tsar was conveyed to him. After his release from prison, a great change in his character was noted. Whereas previously he had been a revolutionary and agnostic, he emerged intensely loyal to the Tsar and a bitter foe to all enemies of the church. Previous psychoanalytic studies have interpreted this change as symbolic of reconciliation and submission to the father figure against whom he had conspired, but who had spared his life. These interpretations are supported by material from Dostoyevsky's own writings. In *The House of the Dead,* a thinly disguised autobiography of his prison days, the narrator is portrayed as a wife-murderer. In *The Idiot,* an execution is described, again with evident autobiographical coloring. Again, the criminal is a wife-murderer. In *Crime and Punishment,* where the central figure is undoubtedly another disguised representation of Dostoyevsky, his crime consists of murdering a woman. He is sent to Siberia as punishment, but the true drama of this great novel is the internal conflict of the murderer and the story ends on the note that only by exile and punishment can he develop the sense of guilt which will save him from the inner consequences of his crime. The very consistency with which these criminals are presented as murderers indicates the hidden significance of Dostoyevsky's revolutionary activities against the Tsar. That the victims of these fictitious murders are women is doubtless derived from a confluence of motives, among which is a need to disguise an underlying father figure.

In light of evidence that his prison career was regarded unconsciously as a punishment for parricide and served to reconcile him to the father, the day-dream of the peasant Marey acquires further significance. For the occasion is Easter, the arising of the dead and the reunion of Father and Son. The child, in his moment of terror, finds that the crude peasant "could not have looked at me with eyes shining with greater love if I had been his own son." Marey makes the sign of the cross over each in token of kinship (a symbol to be used with great effectiveness in *The Idiot* in a scene between the prince and the man planning to murder him because of rivalry in love). So the figure of Marey is the father, but also the son, the peasant who murdered the father, and reconciliation takes place through identification with the dead father. It is essentially a totemistic ceremony, appropriate to Easter and to the process of mourning through which the guilty convict is passing. The totem animal is the wolf, who is a menace to the child, but who also represents the figure which slew the father in those very woods.

But the problems for Dostoyevsky arising from the crime at Tchermashnia were never to end despite the symbolic solution of that Easter morning in prison. Decades later, toward the end of his life, when he wrote the great novel of parricide, *The Brothers Karamazov,* he allows the son, Ivan, to indirectly accomplish his father's murder by a visit to the very woods of Tchermashnia where he had had the hallucination of the wolf at nine and where the older Dostoyevsky was actually murdered. So enduring and so unique a blend of fantasy and reality has no parallel in the annals of psychopathology.

References

Freud, S. (1928). Dostoyevsky and parricide. *Standard Edition* 21:177–196.
Neufeld, J. (1923). Dostojewski: Skizze zu seiner Psychoanalyse. *Imago-buecher* 4.

Chapter 10

DOSTOYEVSKY'S MATRICIDAL IMPULSES

MARK KANZER, M.D.

Poor Folk

Dostoyevsky's parricidal impulses have been described in Freud's classic work (1928) and have proved indispensable for understanding the character and work of the author. A necessary supplement for insight into Dostoyevsky's psychology, however, is a recognition and evaluation of his equally powerful matricidal impulses.

Dostoyevsky's works are characterized by the recurrent theme of an intense but frustrated love of a man for a woman, which drives him to the point of madness, suicide, or murder. Dostoyevsky's literary career was launched with the short novel, *Poor Folk,* which depicts the yearning of a poor middle-aged clerk for a young girl with whom he is scarcely acquainted, but who has made a powerful impression on him. He feels that his poverty and the "difference in age" make his suit ridiculous and, despite her encouragement, he refuses to visit her, but instead carries on a written correspondence. The girl is unable to continue this shadowy love in the face of realities and is persuaded to marry a wealthy landowner. At the end, the clerk is left to complete a miserable existence whose joys and sorrows will henceforth center about the memory of his frustrated love.

It is quite clear that this story embodies early childhood memories of a boy's love for his mother. The "difference in age," his inability to give her anything, the ridiculousness of his attempts to woo her, and the inevitable defeat in competition with the powerful father, are recognizable reproductions of the earlier situation. Further confirmation of this view is found in a subsidiary theme in *Poor Folk*. The heroine, carrying on her part of the correspondence, tells of a young man living as a boarder in her house, who devotes himself exclusively to his studies. From time to time, he receives visits from his father, whom he treats only with indifference and contempt. The student dies suddenly and there is a pathetic scene of his hearse being borne through the streets followed only by the father, who is half-crazed with grief. In this theme, we may see the supplement to the frustrated desire for the mother; there is the apparently unmotivated dislike of the father and resentment at his undesired "visits" to the house. For some unexplained reason, he is to be punished by the loss of his son — a familiar version of the castration complex. The student, irritable and isolated from life, is doubtless a portrait of Dostoyevsky himself at the time of writing the novel. He was then living in solitude, his childhood home gone forever with the death of his parents, and his future staked on an uncertain literary career. The "elderly clerk" of the story, no doubt, represented a gloomy vision of himself in years to come if there were no improvement in his lot. Dostoyevsky obviously felt that his plight was very pitiful, and managed to inject sufficient pathos into his narrative to win over the public and to establish himself at once as a gifted and popular writer.

Siberian Exile

In the years that followed, the unhappiness of Dostoyevsky, which was essentially neurotic, was to find a basis not only in his fantasy life, but in grim reality. During a period of fame following the publication of *Poor Folk,* he was welcomed into literary circles, which were then stirring with discontent against the Russia of the Czars. Dostoyevsky had no genuine knowledge of or interest in politics, but motivated by a vague utopianism and the influence of friends, found himself drawn into a revolutionary movement. His intentions and activities seem to have been harmless enough, but he was arrested by the police and after being brought to the scaffold for execution, was dramatically spared by the authorities and sentenced to imprisonment in Siberia.

Thrown among hardened criminals and forced to live under bestial conditions, Dostoyevsky at first resorted to characteristic attempts to master the almost intolerable reality situation by repressive mechanisms. He shunned the other convicts as repulsive and degraded beings and sought refuge in daydreams. He was allowed to read the Bible and become engrossed in the scriptures. On an Easter Sunday, when the other convicts were engaged in drunken fights, he settled himself apart from the others and deliberately sought forgetfulness in daydreams. Suddenly a childhood memory came to mind and with it a surge of emotion which had an extraordinary effect. He remembered an outwardly brutal peasant who had been kind and tender when Dostoyevsky had a terrifying experience as a child. As in a vision, he suddenly saw in the riotous convicts about him the same primitive good-heartedness of the Russian peasant. He had been in the wrong to shun them. They were his Russian brothers. All Russia was a prison; all Russians were being punished for their sins and must suffer before they were ready for Christian salvation. A great sense of peace came over him and the formerly solitary intellectual felt that henceforth all Russia was his family.

In an analysis of this episode (in the previous chapter), it was found that the peasant whose memory produced such a revolutionary effect was actually a symbol both of Dostoyevsky's father and of his own aggressive and particularly parricidal impulses. He had nurtured this hatred against his father for years, but now in time of need, he recalled the more tender bonds between them. This was sealed in the vision by the memory of the sign of the cross which the peasant had made over the frightened child. The cross restrained the mutual aggression and relieved the anxiety. With this Easter Sunday vision, the good father was resurrected and the bad father was repressed. A superego could be formed to restrain the criminal impulses. Henceforth, Dostoyevsky was to unite himself with figures of authority and instead of rebelling was to preach the virtues of obedience and suffering. He became a fanatic advocate of church and state institutions and a fierce partisan of Russian nationalism. He prophesied the mission of Russia to redeem the world through her sufferings and faith, and violently opposed efforts to reform his country by rational and materialistic ideas imported from Western Europe. The new Dostoyevsky thus projected his problems on a universal scale with a distinctly paranoid tinge, but the underlying passions were never really brought under control and his fight against their overflow inspired the themes of all his literary works.

Crime and Punishment

The first great literary result of Dostoyevsky's conversion was *Crime and Punishment*. Raskolnikov, the criminal hero, is recognizable at the beginning as the youthful and morbid Dostoyevsky at the time of writing *Poor Folk* and the story is an allegorical account of the events in his life which led to his imprisonment in Siberia. The student Raskolnikov is poor, discontented, and given to brooding. He will not mingle with the other students nor is he willing to alleviate his economic situation as they do by accepting dull, routine jobs such as translating or tutoring for small sums. Instead, he ponders the ways of exceptional men, such as Napoleon. What would Napoleon have done in his place? An idea occurs to him, absurd but possessed of increasing fascination. There is an old woman who acts as pawn-broker for the students. A Napoleon would disregard the conventional views of mediocre people. He would simply step in, kill the old woman, and make off with her money. Why not? Napoleon had seized whatever he wanted. Moral scruples? Just lack of courage and consistency. Of what good to anyone was this usurious old woman, while obviously it is more to the advantage of society to use her money for the assistance of a needy student. The only deterrent a rational man would find to murdering the old woman is fear of detection and a clever man with traces of genius would know how to arrange a crime without a clue. This in a nutshell is the moral problem with which Dostoyevsky presents us.

Raskolnikov, whose neurosis has reduced him to a state of almost complete cessation from any activity except lying on his bed and daydreaming, finds his thoughts about the old woman turning into an obsession. He idly speculates on how a genius would plan the murder and finds to his consternation that his fantasies are turning into schemes. He fights against it, but the idea is stronger than his conscious will. Step by step his dreams become reality and he carries out the murder.

We may again briefly compare Raskolnikov and the clerk of *Poor Folk*. Both men are seclusive, brooding characters. Both are obsessed with thoughts about a woman. The clerk cannot overcome some inhibition which keeps him from approaching her. Raskolnikov has to overcome no less an inhibition than the taboo against murder in order to make the approach. He must alter his goal from love to destruction and the figure of the woman from an attractive girl to a repulsive old crone. There is a clear fusion here of two great drives, the hate against the father and the love for the mother. A compromise is produced according to the mechanisms of symptom formation and an action is carried out which permits a discharge for the two forbidden desires which have tormented him all his life.

Thus, in addition to the taboo against murder which Raskolnikov overcomes, he also finds a perverted outlet in his struggle against the sexual taboo. The entire action of the story prior to the murder shows that the deepest inhibition of Raskolnikov is directed against sex. Even murder is a defense against the greater inner danger. For the theme of *Crime and*

Punishment is its absorption with the female sex. In the welter of compli-cated scenes and situations which succeed each other in the typical Dosto-yevsky style, we encounter women in every aspect of their relationship to sex. There are depraved little girls of five and little girls, still innocent, but destined soon to be sent on the streets. There is a study of young women after their first seduction and curious probings as to their reactions. The conven-tional bourgeois wife, mother, and sister are scrutinized and not only are their incestuous trends brought out, but they are forced into desperate and humiliating situations in which they must sell themselves sexually, in or out of marriage, to help their families. This theme has a special appeal for Dos-toyevsky and the heroine of the book, the prostitute Sonia, illustrates the thesis that a woman may retain her virtue and nobility of character and even enhance them if only her motives in selling her body are unselfish. The truly vile woman is the usurer who hoards her treasures and will not share them.

The relevance of this thesis from Dostoyevsky's viewpoint and uncon-scious needs is obvious. Freud pointed out that the gambling mania to which Dostoyevsky was subject at one time represented an unconscious wish to compel the mother to yield herself to the son in order to spare him from the perils of masturbation. This interpretation is amply confirmed by the analysis of *Crime and Punishment*. His attitude is passive and depen-dent; he is poor and has nothing to give; he can only hope that his pitiable plight will induce women to come to his rescue. But prolonged frustration finally puts an end to his patience and he turns in rage against them. There is here the reproduction of the oral stage of infancy.

Such a state of regression characterizes Raskolnikov at the opening of the story. He has withdrawn from all active participation in the outer world. He has given up his studies and has isolated himself from his few friends. He is surrounded and supported entirely by women. What funds he has come from his mother and sister. The room and food are supplied by a reluctant landlady whom he does not pay. He does not eat or clean himself or leave his bed unless urged to do so by the servant girl. The regression is almost complete. Only his mind is active and concerned with the problem of obtaining sustenance from the woman who hoards her treasures and is indifferent to his needs.

The development of the action which transforms Raskolnikov from his lethargic state to his murderous deed is delineated by Dostoyevsky with his usual psychological subtlety. Roused from his fantasies by a letter that his sister is about to sell herself in a loveless marriage in order to provide for the future, he goes into the streets with the vague intention of "doing something about it." He has not yet put it in words in his own mind, but the something will certainly be murder. Raskolnikov has long passed the stage of distinguishing clearly between dreams and reality and follows his automatic impulses. He walks along absent-mindedly, hardly knowing what he is doing or where he is going. Suddenly he awakens with a start. He sees that a young girl had been made drunk and is wandering in a confused fashion along the street. A man is loitering near her and is obviously waiting for a favorable moment to approach the girl and take her away. In great indignation, Raskolnikov feels impelled to intervene and call a policeman to prevent this. In the midst of this chivalrous impulse, for some unexplained reason, he suddenly smiles ironically, shrugs his shoulders, murmurs, "What is this to me?" and walks off, leaving the girl to her fate.

Shortly thereafter, he finds an isolated spot where he falls asleep and dreams. He is a child again and he and his father are watching a brutal scene in which some drunken ruffians are belaboring a helpless old mare who is unable to draw a heavy load. He beseeches his father to intervene, but the latter refuses and tells him to come away. He can not leave the scene and presently one of the men seizes a bar and bashes in the skull of the animal. In the dream, the child rushes hysterically to the dead horse, kisses it about the bleeding head, kisses it with violent passion, and then throws himself at the murderer. He has to be dragged off by his father. Raskolnikov awakens in horror from the dream and cries, "Can it be that I shall really take an axe, that I shall strike her on the head, split her skull open, tread in the sticky warm blood, break the lock and steal?" Only then do his fantasies of the murder come into full consciousness as deliberate plans.

The psychoanalysis of these episodes offers a subject of intriguing interest. In his almost somnambulistic walk, Raskolnikov is unconsciously preoccupied with the problem of whether to translate his murderous fantasies into reality. That these fantasies are intimately related to and symbolize still deeper sex conflicts is revealed by the episodes through which the unconscious decision is allowed to force itself into Raskolnikov's awareness. Shall he maintain a chivalrous attitude toward women or shall he abandon his inhibitions? Shall he be child or master? Would not Napoleon take what he wants? Raskolnikov abandons the girl and scores a Napoleonic triumph when he allows himself to side with the despoiler of women. The dream takes us to the vital center of the childhood memories from which these conflicts arise. The beating of the horse is typical primal scene material with its emphasis on the child's sadistic concept of sex. The problem before him is the ability to identify himself with the father and behave as ruthlessly as other men do in the sexual act. His unconscious defenses are broken through by the strength of his desires and on awakening he at once perceives the meaning of the dream and the fact that his fantasies demand their satisfaction in reality.

Of great interest is the comparison of this dream with the memory of the childhood experience with the peasant which came to have such significance in the Siberian vision. The father figure of the peasant is encountered ploughing with his horse in an opening in the forest through which Dostoyevsky is fleeing in terror from a hallucinatory wolf. My analysis in the previous chapter shows that this is likewise a representation of the primal scene and that the mother is again represented by the horse, the patient and often brutally treated creature so necessary to the Russian peasant. The terror of the child is really accounted for by the ploughing scene and the fear is displaced to the imaginary wolf. In this instance, the peasant father forgives the intrusion in the sign of the cross, but now Raskolnikov — Dostoyevsky himself — is the wolf and wishes a new ending to the old drama. The cross is no longer his protection from the father, but the protection of all fathers by the sacred taboos which protect them in the possession of the mothers. Raskolnikov, in his Napoleonic scorn for the code of ordinary men, relies on his reason to overthrow these truly childish inhibitions, but is destined to discover the penalty for his transgressions.

Matricide or Parricide?

The question arises as to the reason for the lifelong and devastating conflict through which Dostoyevsky passed. Raskolnikov's murder was, as we know, a figment of the literary imagination, but that Dostoyevsky's mind was not too far removed from similar channels need not be doubted. The witnessing of the primal scene and the sadistic conception of the sex act in childhood are too commonplace to account for Dostoyevsky's particularly morbid reactions. We do know that the disturbance in his personality began in early childhood and that he suffered at that time from a fear of being buried alive. His hallucinatory experience with the imaginary wolf, even if only hysterical, showed further evidence of a serious mental disorder. The question as to the role of epilepsy presents hitherto insoluble problems and we shall probably never know whether the condition was a hysterical discharge phenomenon or a physiological process which helped to keep Dostoyevsky's mind in a state of turmoil. His first attack is linked by untrustworthy evidence either with a frightening experience in childhood, apparently connected with a sexual experience, or with the murder of his father during his student days. The latter event alone could well have had a permanently shattering effect upon Dostoyevsky's unstable balance.

Moreover, there are schizoid and paranoid trends in his mental illness which, in conjunction with the father's psychosis, force us to consider a possible schizophrenia.

That matricidal as well as parricidal tendencies should be present in a mind so dominated by frustration and aggression, is not surprising. The interrelationship may be traced with remarkable clarity in this case. The original hostility of the child is directed against the mother who is the first person associated with his frustrations as well as with his satisfactions. Dostoyevsky's withdrawal from the world and renunciation of women in *Poor Folk* is patterned upon the passive adjustment to oral frustration; the more violent solution of Raskolnikov corresponds to oral sadistic actions in seizing and devouring the body of the negligent mother. He repeatedly and bitterly refers to the usurer as a louse, swollen with the money which he can not have.

In later stages of child development, the hostility to the mother is usually displaced to the father, leaving only the loving attitude dominant in consciousness and simplifying the effective object relationships of the child. An element of hostility toward the mother always remains and plays an important part in normal female development and in the negative oedipus complex. In *Poor Folk,* the blame for frustration is placed entirely upon the father. After Dostoyevsky's punishment for rebellion against the Czar and the reconciliation with the father in the Siberian vision, his identification with the father made him turn his hostility back upon the mother. She now had to be depicted as a frustrating as well as desired object, reviving older memories of oral frustration and at the same time permitting an outlet for disguised erotic drives. The combined figure which could drain these complicated and conflicting emotions was that of the usurer. Beginning with *Crime and Punishment,* the allegorical confession of the inner crime for which Dostoyevsky felt convicted in his exile to Siberia, there are a series of his literary works which monotonously insist on the victim of the murder being a woman. *House of the Dead,* the novel describing his experiences in the Siberian prison, is introduced with the fictitious note that it is the journal of a man who had been imprisoned for killing his wife. A later work, *The Idiot* describes the last sensations of a man on the scaffold who is about to be executed. The description, which is recognizable as an account of Dostoyevsky's own experiences just before his sentence was suddenly commuted, is purportedly that of a man who is being put to death for killing his wife. The insistence on this point is certainly not immaterial. It was necessary for Dostoyevsky at this time to repress the parricidal aspects of his crime.

Nevertheless certain aspects of the figure of the usurer reveal the underlying relationship to the father. In his student days, Dostoyevsky was almost always literally penniless and was constantly involved in futile efforts to obtain a little assistance from his indifferent father. The character of the miserly father reappears in undisguised form in *The Brothers Karamazov* when the parricidal fantasies finally do reemerge. Another significant point is the second murder of Raskolnikov. He had intended to kill only the usurer, but is interrupted by the unexpected arrival of the sister, whom he is forced to slay in order to cover the first crime. This sister is a meek gentle creature, like the good mother, and the utterly wanton slaying is the peak of the horror in the murder scene and the first warning to Raskolnikov that reasoning and plans are folly in the struggle with fate. The contrasting pair of sisters are not only the good mother and the bad, but the representatives of both parents and the double slaying completes the action necessary for complete reenactment of the primal scene. The clinching evidence for the link between the usurer and the father figure is the fact that in real life it was the father that was murdered and we know the lifelong shadow which this event left upon Dostoyevsky.

An interesting confirmation of these interpretations is furnished by Dostoyevsky himself in the plot for *The Idiot,* a novel written between the matricidal *Crime and Punishment* and the *Brothers Karamazov* in which the parricidal theme could at least be openly confronted. Rogozhin is madly in love with Nastasya, a prostitute who, in typical Dostoyevsky style, cares only for Prince Myshkin but receives from him only spiritual understanding. The frustrated Rogozhin feels impelled to stab the prince, but in an effort to restrain himself, swears "brotherhood in the cross" with his rival (the Siberian vision of reconciliation!). Later, when marriage to Nastasya proves to Rogozhin that neither legal nor physical possession will ever win her love, he seizes the same knife with which he had intended to kill the prince and stabs his wife instead. Nastasya is another usurer who will not offer her love. That in one episode, Rogozhin, in spite of the vow on the cross, is about to kill the prince with this knife, but is deterred only when Myshkin suddenly suffers an epileptic seizure, leads into other symbolic variants of Dostoyevsky's problem. The power of the cross has intervened between father and son, and the epileptic seizure is a substitute for death. Epilepsy, the sacred illness, is Dostoyevsky's own affliction, and the ascetic prince as well as the sexual figure of Rogozhin, are both aspects not only of his own personality but also of the father's. Man is made in the image of God. In the pact of reconciliation, the son gives up his parricidal aggression and the father in turn refrains from castration. Freud pointed out that epilepsy signified death for Dostoyevsky and that the epileptic state is an identification with the dead father. The death of the father means the death of the identified son and parricide is inevitably suicide. That this is so emerges in *The Brothers Karamazov.* If Dostoyevsky is to survive at all, his aggression must be turned against the women he loves and hence the insoluble problem which he faced all his life. The cross which unites father and son by restraining their mutual aggression is epilepsy. Only by his illness and general masochism, by turning his aggression against himself, was Dostoyevsky able in real life to avoid the fate of his criminal characters.

The supreme crystallization of his fantasies is found in his last work, *The Brothers Karamazov,* which projects on a universal screen the lifelong problem of Dostoyevsky. Its multitudes of figures and variety of situations are merely a masterly synthesis of the experiences and ideas in which he had worked through his neurosis from early childhood to the end of his days. All action converges upon the murder of the father and spreads out from there to the consequences for the sons. The unconscious wishes and share of the responsibility in the murder are weighed out for each son with the remorselessness and penetration of the Last Judgment and a doom pronounced for each which will follow him through eternity. The son whose hand did the killing first simulates and then really falls victim to an epileptic attack from which he arises only after three days (the traditional interval between the crucifixion and the resurrection.) His inevitable fate is belated remorse and suicide. The son whose hand was deflected from parricide only at the last moment by providential intervention (like Rogozhin's) is sentenced to the living death of Siberia, but may take with him for comfort and hope the prostitute Grushenka for whose sake he had nearly killed his father. Here we may see symbolized the meaning of Dostoyevsky's neurosis. The epileptic portion of the personality bears the burden of parricide and partial death as punishment; the living portion is condemned to a Siberian exile of suffering and imprisonment in the neurosis, but may look forward to some happiness and future forgiveness even under these circumstances.

Reference

Freud, S. (1928). Dostoyevsky and parricide. *Standard Edition* 21:177–196.

Chapter 11

THE VISION OF FATHER ZOSSIMA

FROM THE BROTHERS KARAMAZOV

MARK KANZER, M.D.

Dostoyevsky's *The Brothers Karamazov* was used by Freud himself (1928) as a paradigm of the parricidal drives involved in the oedipus complex. In the present study, an effort will be made to illuminate further this universal tendency as manifested in the Russian novel, particularly with respect to the formation of religious fantasies as defenses against such impulses.

Actually, Dostoyevsky's tale describes two fathers: the sensual and despicable Fyodor Karamazov, the actual parent, and the monk, Zossima, who is the spiritual father of the youth Alyosha. The murder of Fyodor by his presumptive offspring, Smerdyakov, becomes the occasion for the author's thesis that all men harbor parricidal wishes and therefore share, in a measure, the burden of guilt for such a crime. Alyosha alone escapes responsibility since he has already turned to religion and has therefore cleansed himself of such inclinations.

The details of the process by which this is accomplished are indicated in the book, yet will not be apparent in their full significance without the application of psychoanalytic insight. A review of the voluminous literary and psychological commentaries on this famous novel also fails to disclose evidence that the obvious relationship between the deaths of Father Zossima and old Karamazov has been recognized. Actually, these two men meet their ends on successive nights, and the recital of events that occur between the two tragedies contains the key to their inherent psychological relationship and to Alyosha's escape from sharing the responsibility for parricide with his brothers.

The first death, the passing of the monk, unlooses a series of remarkable reactions in the "good son," Alyosha. Father Zossima's repute as a man of God had commanded such awe during his lifetime that his demise was confidently expected by his followers to be the signal for earth-shaking omens and miracles; instead, a prosaic and, under the circumstances, even scandalous turn of events took place — the earthly remains of the venerated saint underwent speedy and offensive decomposition. His recently devoted followers were shocked and dismayed. Even the loyal and deeply intelligent Alyosha seemed to experience an intense revulsion; leaving the monastery without the accustomed permission, he became prey to impulses such as one would scarcely have believed to exist within him.

With obvious symbolism, the passing of Father Zossima is placed on the eve of Lent, and the rebellious spirit that has seized possession of the youthful Karamazov inclines him first toward breaking the fast, then to consumption of intoxicating drinks, and finally, as the repressed tendencies emerge with ever greater dearing, to a visit to Grushenka, the same woman whose charms had already brought his father and his brother into murderous rivalry. It is this encounter between Alyosha and Grushenka which contains the psychological pivot of the novel. In this turning point of the action is concealed the secret of the incestuous aspect of the oedipal problem which the author passes over with symbolism in contrast to the frankness, though not full motivation, with which he treats the parricidal aspect.

Here the master of psychology is forced to resort to artifice in order to prevent the natural consummation of the meeting between this passionate pair; for at this moment a former lover of Grushenka is introduced to the scene and Alyosha is permitted to escape with unscathed virginity. The incest barrier is more than hinted at in the oaths exchanged between Alyosha and Grushenka to care for each other as brother and sister; the almost psychoanalytic procedure with which *The Brothers Karamazov* uncovers the deeper motives of men finds here an impenetrable resistance.

The pendulum whose inner laws have been revealed by the swing from Father Zossima to the mother-sister figure Grushenka has thus reached the limit of its arc. The returning sweep helps us to understanding more clearly the function of the monk in the mental economy of the sexually frustrated young man. Whereas Alyosha's reactions after the death of his esteemed master demonstrated with unmistakable force and clarity the tensions held in check by this veneration, the aftermath of the decisive interview with

Grushenka shows how his piety provides not only a repressive agent but also an outlet for his banished libidinal impulses as well. Retracing literally— and symbolically—his footsteps to the monastery, he arrives once more before the bier of his spiritual father. He has oscillated between love and death, the poles of existence; and as one barrier circumscribed his orbit in the direction of the woman, so another—his own life—interposed itself between him and the man.

The resources of the unconscious now break through this new frustration. In a trance, Alyosha sinks to the ground before the corpse and joins him, in a dream, beyond the gateway of death. He beholds himself in Heaven, and Christ is before him celebrating once more the first of his miracles, the conversion of water into wine for the wedding guests at Cana. In the vision, the Virgin Mary moves among the assembled people, and in a few words Dostoyevsky lets us see that in Alyosha's mind she is identified with Grushenka—that is, she is the mother figure, forever attainable. Jesus sits apart, apparently preoccupied with his own thoughts, but on his mother's insistence takes note of the situation and uses his miraculous powers to provide simple folk with the wine which they require for their happiness.

Then, in the dream, Zossima himself arises from his coffin and in a similar joyful gesture, urges Alyosha to join the festivities. At the touch of his hand and the sound of his voice, the feelings of tension within the young man dissolve and, in a rapturous mood, he awakens. Back in the cell with the corpse of the monk, the impulses of the dream persist. Stepping out into the night, Alyosha throws himself on the earth, weeping, and kisses the ground ecstatically over and over again. Then something from outside himself seems to take possession of him and when he arises, it is with a resolution and certainty about himself that he is to carry with him for the rest of his life. It is also at this hour—perhaps at this very moment, although the author does not make it clear—that Alyosha's real father is being murdered through the joint will of his other sons.

This typical religious conversion scene may now be viewed in its proper psychological perspective. Alyosha, unable to attain the love he craves from Grushenka, finds a substitute in the kindliness of Jesus and Zossima. If they cannot be the chief participants at the wedding feast, they can find joy and a place for themselves by ministering to others. Alyosha, at the bier of the monk, is confronted with the materialization of his death wishes against his own father; the true miracle which occurs on this occasion is the transformation of hatred into love. The passing of Zossima serves as a signal for the eruption of repressed erotic drives which have been held in check by the component of fear present in the awe for his saint. Even his physical departure from the scene, however, could not remove the inhibitions against the breakthrough of the incest barrier, and the reactivated libido could find no other course than to return to the ambivalently regarded religious figure and strengthen the "good father" component in the mixed character which he represented to the youth.

It is not difficult to see here that Dostoyevsky is intuitively presenting us with the same problems that have always constituted the underlying sense of puberty rites for young men; and in particular, his narrative shows an amazing resemblance to and even supplements and gives a deeper meaning to the concepts used by Freud in his delineation of the totem feast. The impulses released in Alyosha by the passing of Zossima are overwhelmingly oral; there is a craving for food, then for drink, and, in the ensuing quest for the mother figure, doubtless a revival of early memories of the breast. Christ and Zossima reexert their claim to libidinal attachments by the dispensal of wine, as though to say that food may be obtained from the body of the father as well as of the mother; the nature of the "water" and the "wine" become apparent in this context.

Within this framework, certain aspects of the odor of the monk's corpse gain a new meaning. The disgust aroused is familiar to analysts as a defense against the desire for oral incorporation. In this light, the unspecified excitement with which the followers were filled must be interpreted in relation to the unconscious cannibalistic fantasies which follow upon the death of the father and play such an important part in shaping the mourning process that ensues.

These oral drives are also used regressively as substitutes for sexual activities of a genital nature. In the culminating drama of Alyosha's conversion— as he lies on the ground, clutching and kissing the earth in ecstasy while an outer force takes possession of him, we find bisexual gratification which is interesting to relate to Lewin's concept of a mania as a reconciliation with the superego at the breast of the mother. It is apparent, too, that in Freud's (1913) outline of the psychological events attendant upon the totem feast, which was put forward at a time before he had recognized the negative oedipus complex, he did not consider the important fact that the father figure in these rites also serves as a screen for components derived from the image of the mother.

Dostoyevsky's unconscious insight into these problems was, of course, derived from personal experience. His own father had been murdered while he was still a youth much like Alyosha and apparently he spent much of the rest of his life attempting to work through the sense of guilt inspired in him by the extent to which this violent act served to fulfill his own wishes. His conflicts over the father-son relationship were particularly intense at the time of writing *The Brothers Karamazov* because of the recent death of his own little son whose name, as might be expected, was Alyosha. The author was apparently acutely possessed at the moment by the sense of identity between father and son, and on the murdered elder Karamazov he bestowed his own name, Fyodor. There is a striking and curious analogy here to the processes which appear to have inspired Shakespeare to compose *Hamlet* after the death both of his father and of his son—who, rather significantly, was named Hamnet. Presumably guilt emanating from the counter-oedipal as well as oedipal tendencies was involved. Father Zossima himself was drawn from the real personality of Father Ambrosius, a monk whose words of comfort to the bereaved writer moved him to the extent of choosing the monastery of this good man for his burial.

Freud (1928) has called attention to the role assigned by the novelist to the epileptic Smerdyakov as the murderer of old Karamazov; the psychological meaning of the writer's own illness both as an expression of uncontrollable forces within himself and as punishment for them becomes fear. There is assuredly some correlation, too, between the writer's creative urges and the convulsive seizures, which increased notably during periods of literary creativity.

Furthermore, we find little difficulty in recognizing, in Alyosha's swoon his falling to the ground, his writhing and his ecstasy—phenomena of epilepsy; his ambivalent religiosity, suppressed criminal impulses, and hallucinatory experiences represent familiar psychic concomitants. Out of such intense travail was born anew the "good son," counterpart to the "good father;" purged in this process were the parricidal impulses which came to fulfillment at the same moment through the hands of the epileptic Smerdyakov. More specifically—since Alyosha's vision was also Dostoyevsky's and conveyed the solution derived by his own unconscious—we may say that the novelist applied to himself the message of Cana and learned to transform the waters of his bitter experiences into the literary wine that was to be set before the multitudes. In the identification with Jesus, he carried to a climax the psychic processes underlying the composition of *The Brothers Karamazov*.

References

Freud, S. (1913). Totem and taboo. *Standard Edition* 13:1–164.

———(1928). Dostoyevsky and parricide. *Standard Edition* 21:177–196.

SOURCES

Tarachow, S. Judas, Beloved Executioner (1960). *Psychoanalytic Quarterly* 29:528–554.

Arlow, J. Pyromania and the Primal Scene: A Psychoanalytic Comment on the Work of Yukio Mishima. *Psychoanalytic Quarterly* 47:24–51.

Orgel, S. Fusion with the Victim and Suicide (1974). *International Journal of Psycho-Analysis* 55:531–538.

Orgel, S. Sylvia Plath: Fusion with the Victim and Suicide (1974). *Psychoanalytic Quarterly* 43(2):262–287.

Niederland, W. G. An Inquiry into the Life and Work of Heinrich Schliemann (1965). In *Drives, Affects, Behavior Vol. 2: Essays in Honor of Marie Bonaparte,* ed. M. Schur, pp. 369–396. New York: International Universities Press.

Shengold, L. An Attempt at Soul Murder: Rudyard Kipling's Early Life and Work (1975).

Glenn, J. The Adoption Theme in Edward Albee's *Tiny Alice* and *The American Dream* (1974). *Psychoanalytic Study of the Child* 30:683–725.

Blum, H. A Psychoanalytic View of "Who's Afraid of Virginia Woolf?" (1969). *Journal of the American Psychoanalytic Association* 17:888–903.

Kanzer, M. Dostoyevski's Matricidal Impulses (1948). *Psychoanalytic Review* 35:115–125.

Kanzer, M. Dostoyevski's "Peasant Marey" (1947). *American Imago* 4:78–88.

Kanzer, M. The vision of Father Zossima from the *Brothers Karamazov* (1951). *American Imago* 8:329–335.

INDEX